WORLDS APART

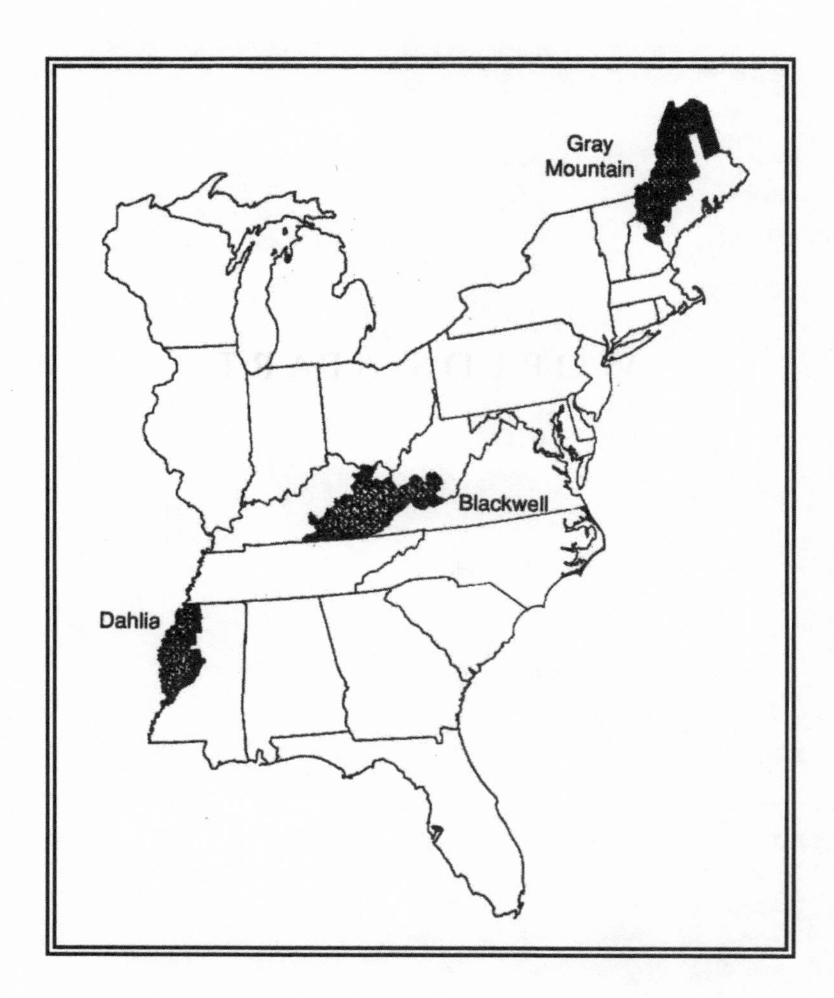
Gray
Mountain
Blackwell
Dahlia

CYNTHIA M. DUNCAN

WORLDS APART

Poverty and Politics in Rural America

Second Edition

Foreword by Angela Glover Blackwell

Yale UNIVERSITY PRESS

New Haven & London

Published with assistance from the foundation established in memory of
Philip Hamilton McMillan of the Class of 1894, Yale College.

First edition published 1999 as *Worlds Apart: Why Poverty Persists in Rural America*. Second edition 2014.

Designed by Jeanette Olender and set in Granjon type by Newgen North America. Printed in the United States of America.

Library of Congress Cataloging-in-Publication Data

Duncan, Cynthia M.
Worlds apart: poverty and politics in rural America / Cynthia M. Duncan—Second edition.
p. cm.
Includes bibliographical references and index.
ISBN 978–0–300–19659–7 (alk. paper)
1. Poverty—United States. 2. Rural poor—United States—Interviews. 3. United States—Rural conditions. 4. United States—Social conditions—1980– I. Title.
HC110.P6D86 2014
305.5′690973—dc23 2014009145

A catalogue record for this book is available from the British Library.

The paper in this book meets the guidelines for permanence and durability of the Committee on Production Guidelines for Book Longevity of the Council on Library Resources.

For Bill Duncan

Contents

Foreword by Angela Glover Blackwell

President Barack Obama has called inequality the defining challenge for America in the twenty-first century. The economic model of recent decades is failing nearly everyone except those at the very top. This is true not only for the very poor but also for lower- and middle-income families. It is especially true in rural communities, where poverty and isolation combine with spatial challenges and a history of disinvestment.

When the first edition of *Worlds Apart* was published, the United States economy seemed to be flying high. The stock market was soaring. The national unemployment rate was only 4 percent, the lowest in nearly a quarter century. Yet poverty persisted. Professor Duncan painted an unforgettable picture of what that looked like in rural America and examined the economic and political forces that left so many remote communities behind.

Things are different now.

The apparent prosperity of the late 1990s and early 2000s turned out to be a bubble that obscured deep structural problems in the U.S. economy. Good jobs are disappearing, the middle class is shrinking, and inequality has reached an all-time high. More than 100 million people—a third of the population—live in or near poverty, and for the first time in modern history, employment does not offer a sure path out. Millions of people work in low-wage jobs that leave them struggling to make ends meet.

In the shadow of worsening economic insecurity, the nation's overall rural population dipped from 2010 to 2012—the first net loss ever recorded. Only 230 rural counties had growth rates higher than the national average of 1.7 percent, while 1,200 rural counties lost population.

America also looks different for another reason: the historic shift in demographics. By midcentury, a majority of the population will be people of color. Already, most babies born in the United States are infants of color. By

2020, more than half of all Americans under the age of nineteen will be of color, and they are more than twice as likely as their white counterparts to grow up poor. In the global economy, diversity can be a tremendous asset for communities, regions, and the nation as a whole. But if racial inequality is allowed to continue, and widen the gaps in education, employment, health, and wealth, the results will be slower economic growth, lower wages for almost everyone, and dimmer hopes for future generations.

To respond to the economic crisis and the shifting demographics, the nation urgently needs to build an equitable economy—one that produces good jobs and full employment, upgrades the skills and education of our increasingly diverse workforce, and creates opportunities for all people, regardless of where they live, to participate, prosper, and reach their full potential. Rural communities, like inner city, urban, and suburban neighborhoods, need these strategies to be tailored to their particular realities.

Rural America, of course, is not a single entity but an array of places and peoples: tribal lands carved from the nation's original sin; communities in the Mississippi Delta that bear the legacy of slavery; the *colonias* along the Mexican border and thousands of similar unincorporated hamlets in California's Central Valley. Many rank among the poorest, most neglected places in our nation, lacking such basics as functioning water and sewer systems.

Rural America includes communities rapidly being absorbed by ever growing suburbs; farmland and an agricultural economy increasingly hampered by a broken immigration system that fails to support a predictable and stable workforce; and small manufacturing and processing towns in Georgia, Tennessee, Kentucky, and Arkansas that have the fastest-growing immigrant populations in the nation. While some of these communities have resisted the newcomers, with anti-immigrant sentiment and restrictive policies, others are reinventing themselves as places of shared prosperity and inclusion for the new generation of Americans.

Every rural community is shaped by its history, geography, and political and economic landscape. Yet each faces challenges playing out all across America. Addressing every community's needs while connecting them to the broad-based struggle for justice and fairness in America will produce equity—just and fair inclusion into a society in which all can participate and prosper. Equity is the antidote to the plight of isolated, disinvested communities across America, including rural communities. The nation must rethink its relationship with its rural areas, which have long provided an outsize share of the food and raw materials on which we all depend, while receiving little in return. (Case in point: of the 19 million Americans not served by broadband, a critical link to participating in the economy, three quarters live in rural areas.) And rural communities must look inward—to grapple with inequities inside their own borders, to embrace the changing faces of their towns and villages, and to reinvent themselves as communities of opportunity for all.

The equity agenda builds on the wisdom, voice, and experience of local residents. It focuses on empowering people while strengthening the places where they live. It reflects the bedrock American value of access to opportunity. It taps into the great strength of rural America, where people often take pride in the small scale of their communities, know their neighbors, and are accustomed to calling on one another to take action.

What action is needed? This book tells us, by revealing why some communities remain stalled, some progress only to slip back, and others manage to change and thrive. Education is key. Without it, rural communities will continue to be left behind. We must set high expectations for rural youth and make the investments necessary for them to succeed. These include high-quality schools, from pre-kindergarten through college; comprehensive education supports such as counseling and enrichment programs; and forward-looking workforce development systems that equip generations of tomorrow—and today—with the skills to participate in an ever changing, globalized, knowledge-based economy.

Federal and state investments in job creation are a must. Not just any jobs, but those that pay family-supporting wages, offer opportunities for advancement, and give young people a reason to stay in rural communities or return to contribute, build businesses, and raise families. Rural areas also need support from the finance and business communities for small business development, which not only spurs local economic growth, but also stands as an inspiring symbol of resurgence.

Rural renewal requires the reversal of the infrastructure deficits that stem from years of underinvestment, policy neglect, and inequitable land use planning. Twenty-first-century infrastructure—roads, bridges, public transportation systems, broadband, state-of-the-art school facilities, to say nothing of functioning water and sewer systems—undergirds strong communities. It connects people to jobs and educational opportunities, and it boosts productivity, business efficiency, and growth. As the stories on these pages remind us, public infrastructure investments must be targeted at rural communities, and they must reach people at all income levels.

These investments reap benefits beyond economic development. Years of research show that where people live determines how healthy they are. Healthy people and robust, opportunity-rich places go together. The converse is true, too, as rural residents know all too well. They grow the nation's food, yet they themselves have the most limited access to fresh, nutritious groceries. They sit amid expanses of land, yet they have the most limited access to parks and other resources for healthy living. As a result, rural communities have some of the highest rates of illness and injury in America. This can change if ailing places are transformed into communities of opportunity in which everyone can participate in every way—economically, socially, culturally, and politically. Yes, political voice and full participation are essential ingredients for healthy lives.

As *Worlds Apart* documents, the path to creating opportunity-rich communities is rarely straightforward and never easy. It takes time, patience, and determined, responsive leadership. The strategies may be unique in rural communities, but the struggle for equity is the same in thousands of communities across America. The burden on all leaders has never been greater. Together we must build a nation in which no one, no group, and no geographic region is left behind.

Let this book serve as our call to action and our guide.

Foreword to the 1999 Edition by Robert Coles

"There are a lot of voices in a novelist's mind while he's writing; and success or failure depends on knowing which voice to hear, when, and why"—so Walker Percy observed in an interview as he was struggling to understand the mysteries of his own writing life. He knew well that each persuasive, compelling novel represents a triumph of a particular person's imaginative life enabled by a mix of psychological energy and talent that, in the end, defies abstract explanatory efforts. So with nonfiction—especially the kind offered in the pages that follow, wherein a dedicated, resourceful sociologist has traveled wide and far, asked dozens of men and women for their stories, and then tried to interpret and relate them in such a way that the rest of us will, in turn, be prompted to pay heed, to keep in mind how it goes for those "others" who live among us in late-twentieth-century America.

Here is a storytelling social science that draws its strength from ordinary people whose lives are brought directly to the reader through remarks made, questions answered, memories shared, experiences told. Here is a social science that connects the theoretical to the particular, that insists upon witnesses as well as formulations, that resists pretentious jargon, that employs clear, compelling narrative writing. Here is a localist social science, intent on immersion in the widest range of individuals, whose words, whose ideas and aspirations and worries and hopes are taken seriously indeed. Here is a social science, finally, that not only aims to describe the bare and sometimes brute facts of class and race in certain parts of the United States but takes a further, exemplary step: a professor asks those she is studying to become colleagues, and their thoughts become a series of lessons respectfully offered to those fellow citizens who become their readers.

The publication of this book has to be considered, in a sense, an occasion of great sadness—that the conditions of daily living described by the people of Appalachia and the Mississippi Delta still persist. I worked in both of those regions during the 1960s and 1970s, and I well remember meeting individuals very much like those we meet here. I also had the privilege of accompanying Senator Robert F. Kennedy during his visits to both regions—and as I read this book I kept remembering him as he sat in the humblest of homes up in the hollows of West Virginia or in one or another Mississippi town. In both places, like Professor Duncan, he was at pains to talk with the widest range of people, the quite well-to-do and the reasonably comfortable as well as the thoroughly vulnerable families who are all too numerous, and whose hard labor, of course, has enabled the cotton and coal economies to thrive over the generations.

I can still hear Robert Kennedy talking with tenant farmers and coal miners, schoolteachers and nurses, professional men and women, plantation owners and those who run coal mines, the same people who figure so prominently in these chapters. At one point, in Greenville, Mississippi, he clearly had become troubled by both what he had observed and what he had figured out—how intractable the social and economic system seemed, how tenacious its resistance to reform efforts on behalf of the majority who live in such dire circumstances. "This situation cannot last forever," he said—his tired, frustrated, yet morally aroused voice indicating an obvious anxiety that, on the contrary, much needed change hardly seemed around any visible corner. Silence greeted his comment—as if everyone in the room knew better than to subscribe to such optimism, knew that the senator was hoping against hope rather than stating an unequivocal conviction. Finally, an African-American minister of great humility and shrewdness, a veteran of the civil rights movement that had recently stirred the Delta no end (while leaving unchanged the distribution of money and power in those heavily agricultural counties), spoke up: "All things do come in time, Senator. Yes sir, maybe by the end of this century, the end of this second millennium, it'll be different here. Maybe the Lord will smile on us, and give us a better life, so you don't have a few with everything and most everybody else with nothing. There are days that I think it'll take the Second Coming for that to come about—but who knows? With the year 2000 the Lord might decide to pay us some attention here, and turn things around."

Lots of nods followed those words, including a vigorous assent by the distinguished senator, whose wry smile helped everyone relax, and whose response prompted another round of bodily affirmation: "I hope you're right, Reverend. I get your point—it may well be beyond all of us, the kind of political and economic change that is needed here. Only the Lord—that's what you're saying—only he can do it. I hope he will. I hope it's not only up to him, though."

More than thirty years later, this book reminds us how long lasting those cries of moral anguish have been, and how right Robert Kennedy was to pick up on a minister's melancholy spiritual fatalism as he fought hard, every day, on behalf of his flock. I believe that he and his important visitor, both, alas, long gone from us, would welcome this book at a time when so many in our country seem all too indifferent to the plight of those millions who are really, rock-bottom poor. What follows is their story, a documentary exposition of great moral energy, informed by impressive intellectual skills: an extraordinary mix of social history, economic and political analysis, and direct observation by a boldly original researcher who has dared call upon those she interviewed to address the men and women who hold this book in their hands—and thereby bring those "worlds apart" a little closer for the rest of us.

Preface to the 1999 Edition

Why do some families stay mired in poverty generation after generation, and why are some regions of the country chronically poor and depressed? This book examines the roots of persistent poverty by taking a journey into two historically impoverished regions—the Appalachian coal fields and the Mississippi Delta—and one more prosperous but remote rural community in northern New England. We meet the men and women who live in these communities, not only the poor but the rich and people in the middle as well. They talk about their families, their work, their hopes for their children and for their communities.

Impoverished communities in the Delta and in Appalachia are divided into *haves* and *have-nots*. The have-nots live worlds apart from the haves, socially isolated and outside the mainstream. Their isolation and poverty are reinforced by the corrupt, undemocratic politics that prevails in this kind of two-class system. The unchallenged, all-encompassing power of the haves keeps the poor personally vulnerable, while the patronage that flourishes in job-scarce communities undermines efforts to bring about political change. The poor are stigmatized, blamed for their poverty, and often deliberately blocked from the opportunities in the world of the haves. They do not develop the habits, skills, and ambitions they need to make it in the mainstream. The schools, churches, and youth groups that might help them bridge those worlds are segregated by class or race, and the schools they attend are chaotic and ineffective. In Appalachia and the Delta we see how inequality erodes a community's social fabric, destroying trust and undermining institutions crucial for helping poor families achieve the American Dream. At the other end of the spectrum, in northern New England, a public-minded middle class maintains a rich civic culture with inclusive institutions that help those who are ready to leave poverty behind, and people of all social classes talk about the trust and lack of differences that make the community a good place to live.

I conducted the interviews for this study over five years in the early 1990s, but I was already familiar with Appalachia and the Delta. During the 1970s and 1980s, my husband and I worked in Central Appalachia with people trying to bring about social change through community-based economic development. Later, while working with the Ford Foundation's Rural Poverty and Resources Program and the Aspen Institute's Rural Economic Policy Program, I met leaders in the Mississippi Delta who work in communities deeply divided by racism. They, too, were struggling to overcome the isolation of the very poor and the corrupt, elite-controlled politics that block community change in these persistently poor regions.

With generous support from the Ford Foundation, and assistance from community development practitioners, I set out to study rural communities in Central Appalachia, the Delta, and for comparative purposes a remote northern New England community that was not plagued by chronic poverty. Between 1990 and 1995 I spent every spring, summer, and winter break from teaching at the University of New Hampshire in the field, working with colleagues and graduate students. We interviewed more than 350 people and analyzed county-level census data from 1890 to 1990. I became so familiar with these communities that I usually knew, and often had interviewed, the people mentioned in the articles, police logs, wedding announcements, and obituaries in the local weeklies.

I wanted to understand poverty and underdevelopment, the families who were persistently poor and the communities that did not change. Who are these poor men and women? What did their parents do? What were their families like when they were children? What were their school experiences? What skills and education do they have? What dreams and plans? How much have they seen of the world outside their home community? How do these communities work? How much do people trust one another and participate in civic life? How do employers, merchants, teachers, politicians, and preachers perceive the poor? What is everyday life like for the people who are not poor but live in places where the poor make up a majority of the population? Why is it so hard to bring about positive community change?

During interviews that typically lasted a couple of hours, I asked people to tell me their life stories and to reflect on the hard times and the best times. I asked them about their community, who has power, how people treat one another, what the future will hold. Although they were often wary at first, convinced that they had "nothing to say," the people I interviewed almost always became caught up in their stories. Many cried as they remembered trying times or loved ones who had encouraged them or made sacrifices for them. One poor young woman whose remarkable story is told here said, *I enjoyed telling things I had almost forgot—some of them things I'll never forget, but I had never talked to no one about it.*

I taped and transcribed the interviews and then analyzed the patterns—patterns among those who are stuck in poverty compared with those who escape, patterns common to communities where opportunities for the poor are more plentiful compared with stagnant communities. Over my five years of work on this project, through analysis of interviews, close reading of local papers, and studying historical and contemporary census data and accounts, I developed a picture of how the communities work. I paint this picture here through a combination of individual profiles and narratives describing the places, their social life and institutions. I quote from the interviews to illustrate the way someone from the community sees things and to allow people to tell their stories in their own words. You will meet about 40 of the 350 men and women interviewed in the three study areas—Blackwell in Appalachia's coal fields, Dahlia in the Yazoo Delta of Mississippi, and Gray Mountain in northern New England. The people I profile are representative of others in each place—their experiences, their advantages and disadvantages, their hopes and disappointments, their bravery or despondency.

I have changed all the names of people and places and many of the circumstances that might identify a particular person. In a few cases, to hide someone's identity, I have created a composite of two people. Sometimes I present rumors and gossip, things I could not verify, because they are part of the social world. My need to disguise and protect those with whom I talked has meant that I am deliberately vague about some details and sources. County-level statistics represent either averages or sums of the study county and a neighboring county to hide the identity of the particular place. But the men and women who speak here present an accurate picture of life in rural America's poor communities in the 1990s, and they tell us much about being poor and building strong communities more generally.

Preface and Acknowledgments for the 2014 Edition

Twenty years after conducting the research for the 1999 edition of *Worlds Apart*, I had the opportunity to return to the three original communities to assess what had changed and what those changes meant for our understanding of persistent poverty in rural America. With generous support from the Annie E. Casey Foundation, the Mary K. Reynolds Babcock Foundation, the Ford Foundation, and the University of New Hampshire's Carsey Institute, graduate student Jessica Ulrich-Schad and I revisited the Appalachian, Delta, and northern New England communities in the winter of 2013. Dr. Gemma Beckley of Rust College worked with us in the Delta and is co-author of the new section on that community.

We conducted about forty interviews in each place in 2013, some with people we had interviewed in the 1990s. A year later I connected with several trusted informants by phone to learn about issues that had been in flux in 2013, and I continued to read the weekly newspapers in each community. Whereas the original research in the 1990s collected hundreds of individual stories over several years to understand the lives of the poor in three communities, the update that follows each original chapter focuses on community changes and how those changes have shaped opportunities to escape poverty.

We have updated the tables in the Appendix. The indicators for the three communities still reflect either the average or the sum of the numbers for the actual county plus a neighboring county. In the text, however, I now use rounded-up numbers for the study county alone because conditions between the neighboring counties have diverged. Identities of people and places are still disguised.

High poverty and inequality persist in America, and those growing up in concentrated poverty are especially vulnerable to being trapped in a life with diminished opportunities. Studies in the past two decades continue to show that place matters, and that community institutions like good, challenging schools and quality early childhood education can improve the life chances of those growing up poor in poor places. However, we fail to invest enough in the institutions and policies that could alleviate poverty, and today nearly 18 percent are poor in rural America, 15 percent overall. There are still rural communities where more than half of black and Hispanic children are growing up in poverty. This edition of *Worlds Apart* explores the circumstances of poor rural Americans in chronically disadvantaged places, examining the social and political factors that shape their communities and their opportunities, based on research conducted in the 1990s and 2013.

Times are hard in much of rural America, as economic change and job loss disrupt longtime patterns and institutions. Outmigration is the rule in many places. Young people who have the resources continue to leave for urban places where there are more opportunities for a better life. Those who stay are often deeply committed to small-town life, the familiarity, the looking out for one another, especially extended family members, the quieter pace, and the natural beauty. They find ways to stay. But some also stay because they are trapped by poor education and limited work skills. Poverty and dependency persist in many remote places.

In the end, rural children face obstacles to escaping poverty that are not fundamentally different from those of their urban peers. Poor children need good quality early childhood education and effective schools that expect a lot from them. Their parents need the stability that comes with family-supporting wages so they can parent effectively. Most other developed countries do much better than the United States in ensuring that children can flourish. Rural and urban America have way too many "lost children," as Judge Bobby Lee King said so many years ago. We can do better.

Jess Carson, Jessica Ulrich-Schad, and Gemma Beckley provided excellent research assistance and, with Melanie Higgins-Dostie, were wonderful colleagues. Michele Dillon, Sally Ward, Margaret Walsh, Leslie Hamilton, Chris Colocousis, Dee Davis, and Cathy McDowell helped me improve the updates. We "ground truthed" the accounts of the changes with local informants, to whom we are very grateful. Bill Duncan is my anchor, and our sons Graham and Ian and their beautiful families fill us both with joy and pride.

People Profiled

Appalachia

Creed Parker	Coal operator, early sixties
Joey Scott	Grocery store and business owner, late fifties
Willy Granger	Construction company and truck dealership owner, political operative, mid-fifties
Gwen Boggs	Waitress, early thirties
Wanda Turner	Welfare recipient, mid-twenties
Randy Perkins	Junkyard trader, mid-thirties
Virgil Bratcher	Odd-jobs man, mid-thirties
Donna Campton	Welfare administrator, late fifties
Jim Campton	Coal executive, early forties
Joanne Martin	Health care administrator, early fifties
John Martin	Education counselor, early sixties
Bobby Lee King	County judge administrator, late forties
Marlene Combs	Welfare caseworker, mid-forties
Greg Benton	Welfare caseworker, mid-thirties
Sara Hensley	Waitress, late teens in 2013
Benny Corbett	Public works employee, early twenties in 2013
Bobbie Jean Corbett	Homemaker, early twenties in 2013
Leonard Burns	County judge administrator, early sixties in 2013
Sue Wells	Magistrate, early forties in 2013
Johnny Bledsoe	Community college teacher, early sixties in 2013

Mississippi Delta

Caroline Gage	Factory worker, mid-thirties
James Hill	Plantation store worker, mid-twenties
John Cooper	Field worker, mid-thirties
Jack Peabody	Former school superintendent, auctioneer, early sixties
Edward Carter	Furniture store and real estate owner, mid-thirties
Sharon Carter	Teacher, mid-thirties
Clare Green	Funeral director and politician, early seventies
Shirley Jones	Retired teacher, late sixties
Michael Long	Disabled veteran and organizer, early forties
Harold Jackson	Former plant worker, handyman, early fifties
Charles Smith	Politician and real estate agent, late thirties
Diana Smith	Education administrator, mid-thirties
Sarah Early	Nurse practitioner, early thirties
Robert Wilson	School principal and coach, late thirties
John Brown	School superintendent, late twenties in 2013
John Turner	Community organizer, mid-fifties in 2013

Northern New England

Sean McCay	Sawmill owner, mid-forties
Peter Luntz	Plumbing contractor, late fifties
Cassidy Morse	Community college administrator, late forties
Jennifer Casey	Hospital administrator, mid-forties
Sister Anne	Catholic sister, late fifties
Katy Chambers	Day care director, late thirties
Beth Sharpe	Health clinic director, mid-forties
Dan Tourneau	High school teacher, mid-forties
Jeff Berk	High school teacher, mid-forties
Deborah Shannon	Waitress, mid-twenties
David Cloutier	Mayor, mid-fifties in 2013
Adam Croteau	Housing manager, late fifties in 2013

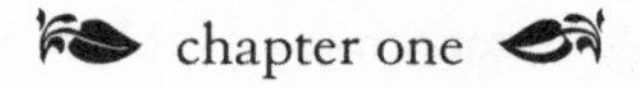

BLACKWELL

Rigid Classes and Corrupt Politics in Appalachia's Coal Fields

It is early morning on the last day of June and we are making our way deep into the mountains to Blackwell, an Appalachian coal county long plagued by poverty and labor trouble. An old truck piled high with large chunks of coal, lacking the cover required by law, strains to climb the hill up ahead, slowing our progress. Two new Chevy pickups, gun racks in the windows and dogs in the back, creep impatiently behind the coal truck, followed by an old Ford crowded with grandparents, teenagers, and small children climbing over the seats and peering out the back window. The drivers, holding their first morning Cokes, lean out their windows, anxious for an opportunity to pass.

The hillsides are blanketed in green leaves—the irrepressible kudzu vines start at the road and climb the hills, covering trees, abandoned cars, piles of dumped garbage, and the dilapidated coal tipples of deserted mines. The road dips down to follow a creek bed littered with plastic bottles, rags, washtubs, and other debris, and around the bend a precarious wooden bridge stretches across the creek to a faded trailer and its rusty prefab outbuilding.

As the road rises again to clear the mountain, an old coal camp emerges in the narrow valley below—company housing long since sold to the families who have lived here for generations now. A few houses have bright new aluminum siding and tidy chain-link fences that guard small lawns adorned with yard ornaments and painted tires filled with petunias. These are the homes of retired union miners with good pensions. Other homes are run down, their wooden clapboards peeling and covered in coal soot, children's tricycles and old tires lying in mostly dirt yards. Each small house has a front porch, some with a glider or rocker and hanging begonias, others with discarded washing machines or broken televisions. Overalls and sheets hang on clotheslines, providing hiding places for young children running from each other and their skinny dogs. The narrow, rutted dirt road is partly obstructed by cars parked alongside the houses. Most vehicles are decrepit, but at the end of the road an older couple loads suitcases into the trunk of a new Chrysler with Michigan plates and a Shriner ornament on the rear bumper.

The coal truck turns off the main road toward the railroad tracks, where its coal will be weighed and loaded on a train, and the pickups and old sedan speed ahead. A sprawling, modern, yellow brick home with a carved wooden front door and shiny brass light fixtures sits on the hill to the right. A new red Blazer with a boat trailer is parked at the end of the long, walled driveway, and a rolling lawn stretches to the two-lane highway—all a monument to the fabulous riches a local strip miner amassed during the brief coal boom in the late 1970s. Rounding one last hill before Blackwell's main town, the road widens into four lanes, and down in the valley the two- and three-story buildings marking the county seat are visible above the morning mist hovering over the river.

The new mall built by the Parkers, a leading coal family, is on the left, anchoring a commercial strip along the main highway. Only about half the storefronts facing the parking lot are occupied, and there is no sign of activity this early in the day. On Friday nights the mall parking lot comes alive with cruising teenagers, reminiscent of a scene from the 1950s—bright, recently waxed cars creeping bumper to bumper through the lot, guys calling out to one another and to girls in other cars, honking, music blasting. Just behind the McDonald's and Kentucky Fried Chicken restaurants two big discount stores are under construction. Studies by distant marketing firms have confirmed what local merchants have known for decades—this area has a solid captive retail market, including a steady flow of public checks that will be spent locally.

The large regional hospital lies just beyond the mall. It was built in the 1950s by the United Mine Workers union but is now owned and run by a large statewide health corporation. Employment here means a highly desirable union job, no matter whether you work in the cafeteria or out front admitting patients. *We're the best-paying employer in the county other than the mines—the unionized mines—when they're working*, says a hospital administrator. The hospital employs about three hundred workers, mostly women, and there is little turnover. When there is an opening, the administrator says, *it pays to know somebody. It pays to know me. It pays to know the dietary manager, or the housekeeping supervisor, or the maintenance engineer*.

Along the stretch of highway before town a few roadside vendors open bedspreads on the hoods of their cars, lay their freshly picked tomatoes and used clothes out neatly, and set up folding chairs where they will spend the day. A teenager nearby, cigarette hanging from his mouth and hands stuffed in his back pockets, uses his boot to nudge the stiff body of a dog killed by a car more than a week ago.

In the early morning light, the imposing stone courthouse that dominates the square in the center of town casts a shadow on the World War I memorial. The young men from Blackwell are renowned for their bravery in foreign wars and for their strong work ethic in urban factories in the Midwest. The courthouse is where county business transpires, where the magistrates and county judge administrator who make up the fiscal court haggle over where the county gravel will be spread and, as one exasperated assistant complained, *who's going to get the opportunity to do the job rather than what the whole project will do for the county*. Out front, the park benches where old-timers spend the day trading political gossip are still damp.

"GOOD RICH PEOPLE" AND "BAD POOR PEOPLE"

Surrounding the square is the usual small-town mixture of stores, lunch counters, florists, smoke shops, and the two banks that have been rivals since practically the turn of the century—one of them run by an octogenarian president who knows all the families and their reputations. According to a young man just returned from Ohio, *When I came back here I went over to the bank and said I'd like to borrow a thousand dollars. Old man Carver, who is about a hundred years old, he comes out and he goes, "Well, who are you?" And I said, "My name's Greg Benton." And he goes, "You any kin to Matthew Benton?" I go, "He's my great-grandfather." And he just gave me the money. I didn't even sign a note. They just handed me a thousand dollars cash because my grandfather used to own a lot of land up here*.

Secondary streets, lined with parking meters whose timers are notoriously unpredictable, are crowded with furniture and appliance stores, shoe stores and barber shops, and several old hotels with their names painted high on the brick walls above the tangle of electric and telephone wires that drape from building to building. These are the stores where not too long ago an irreverent member of the elite dressed as a poor mountain woman, with old clothes and blackened teeth, and knocked on the doors seeking handouts. She found, as she suspected she would, that most of her good friends slammed the door in her face.

There is an astonishing number of lawyers' offices, all offering "no charge for initial consultation" on black-lung benefits, workers' compensation, injuries, and Social Security. More than one fifth of the county's working-age population is disabled from work, and large numbers of children receive public funds because of their mental, emotional, and physical disabilities. *A child's disability check can support a family down here*, explains a lawyer who works these cases.

Farther down Main Street, beyond the new Department of Mines offices and the old utility company, lie the sprawling welfare offices where child support and foster care are arranged and eligibility for food stamps and Aid to Families with Dependent Children (AFDC) is determined. Like the lawyers' advertisements, these offices are reminders that the town will be transformed tomorrow when the "first-of-the-monthers" flood in from the hills and hollows to collect and spend their public assistance and disability checks.

Many will also pick up prescriptions for pain and nerve pills. Old Jackson Jones has his medical practice in a small house two blocks from the square, and patients are already parking their cars up and down the street to get in line to see him. For ten dollars he will look you over and most likely write the prescription you desire. People with little money rely on him. He comes from a powerful old-line coal family, people say, and is reputed to be a fine diagnostician. Those who seek his help have usually been treated disrespectfully at the hospital, and they appreciate his price, his straightforward manner, and his kindly advice when their children are hurting. *That's the best doctor*, says one patient. *You tell him what's wrong and he'll give you some medicine. If you was really sick you wouldn't want to go there, but, he's like ten dollars and he'll always give you some medicine*. No one refers to him as Dr. Jones—he is "Jackson Jones" to everyone.

This isolated coal town is nestled in a small river valley, and although there are pleasant small homes up and down the streets near Jackson Jones's office, most well-to-do families live up on Redbud Hill. *We always say they live up there so they can look down on the rest of us*, jokes Gwen Boggs, who works in a fast-food restaurant. Redbud Hill is indeed a world apart from the bustle of downtown, far removed from the rumbling coal trucks and trains, the small shacks, rusting trailers, and littered streams out in the county. Here freshly blacktopped roads meander gently over the hills, with long drives leading to homes set back from the road by broad lawns with dogwood and redbud trees. These are the homes of the lawyers, physicians, and business owners, the elite families who play golf at the country club, worship at the Baptist or Presbyterian church, and whose children attend the independent public school for city residents.

Conveniently, the city's public school is at the base of Redbud Hill. It is an educational oasis in a county and region infamous for corrupt, patronage-driven school boards and high school graduates who cannot read or write. Donna Campton says that when she graduated from it in the 1950s the city school could boast that more than two thirds of its graduates went on to attend college—a remarkable statistic for a rural public school even today. In the 1990s, a proud teacher reports, as many as 85 percent go on for more education. This public city school serves the elite and professionals and makes it possible for them to avoid confronting the politics that cripple the county schools. It is, with their church, the focal point of community life for their families. Sons play football and basketball, daughters vie to become cheerleaders. Making the cheerleading squad has become a big social status marker, and competition is keen. But like sports generally, it is kept in perspective here in the city, unlike in the county schools. One parent explains, *Lower-income families emphasize sports more, like in the ghettos. Your higher-income families deemphasize sports, and are interested in more academic, country-club-type things. There's a divide there*.

The divide in Blackwell is clear not only between families but also between the community institutions that serve them. Life is family based and church based, and families and churches are grouped by social class. As one minister tells it, *I see people very, very concerned about their own families, and their concern stops there. Let's just say they are very defensive about the rights of their family. They don't want to be criticized. I've talked to my congregation. This concern ought to go beyond family*. Living in the county seat, sending their children to the city school, participating in the parent-teacher organization and school events, and attending the old established churches, the professional- and business-class families are insulated from the poor in their county.

Jim Campton, a coal executive who lives on Redbud Hill, observes, *People tend to stay together by church. I don't think there's a whole lot of interaction between the social elite and others. Same thing with our schools, although that's more diverse than it used to be. At one time the city school was considered the rich kids' school. At least that's the way most of the county people look at it*. County residents concur. A restaurant worker says, *It's a different caliber there—lawyers, professionals—those are "county seat" folks, and they think they're better than the rest of us*. A truck driver's son comments, *The kids in that school are always trying to act upper echelon over the other people*.

The population of Blackwell County as a whole is 32,000, but the city that serves as county seat, where those with wealth and power and security live, has a population of only 3,000.[1] Around 50 percent of the households in the county had incomes below $15,000 in 1989. Median family income was $18,000, compared with around $36,000 nationally. Close to 40 percent of households receive Social Security benefits, which is partly an indication that those over sixty-five and eligible for retirement can come home to live—"have a dog again," as the song goes—regardless of how scarce jobs may be.

Work is hard to find. Only half the working-age men are employed, only a quarter of working-age women. *These days you can't even buy a job*, complains one young man recently laid off from a mine. *Even men have a hard time getting work around here*, a young single mother from Michigan explains. She was told to go on welfare when she went looking for work through the Department of Employment.

The Blackwell Department of Employment is the local office of a state agency charged with tracking jobs and connecting employers with job seekers, and staff members here have considerable discretion both in dispensing the jobs that do come across their desks and in working out deals with employers to subsidize wages. For example, poor women seeking employment say the local motel requires that all applications for positions as maids come through this agency, thus ensuring that the government pays a portion of their minimum wage. The director and her staff link workers with jobs, and this means political power because jobs are so scarce. Their own children have landed good positions in recent years—driving a delivery truck, managing a restaurant or meat counter. The people who come here are the workers, the director points out, not the poor. Neighbors they have coached in Little League or known through church come to see what is available, and the department itself becomes part of the general system by which jobs are obtained through personal connections.

Dependence on public assistance is widespread. Volatile mining employment combined with high levels of coal-related disability has meant that receiving public assistance is widely accepted and not stigmatized. When coal miners are laid off for several months they get food stamps and unemployment compensation, and their children are eligible for subsidized youth employment programs and other opportunities for the disadvantaged. In fact, many young women and men from families with middle-class incomes receive subsidized housing, training opportunities, food stamps, and even AFDC in some cases. They and their family and friends view their own welfare receipt as different from the dependency of the first-of-the-monthers, who they assume have no interest in working. A teenage mother who is from a well-placed family but receives AFDC, food stamps, Medicaid, housing assistance, as well as subsidized child care and transportation while she attends college, explained. *We look down on people for whom receiving assistance is all they're going to do with their lives. My husband and I are not always going to have to have assistance because we're going to school. I think people realize that with us. My parents told me that there was nothing wrong with us getting assistance because we are paying for it in all actuality—because we pay our taxes into it and everything. We're not going to be on it all of our life. For me, personally, it would be hard* not *to look down on those who that is all they do and don't have any ambition*. Another welfare recipient whose parents have good jobs distanced herself from those who have long depended on welfare, referring to them as *scum, the bottom of the barrel, people you don't want to associate with*.

The prevalence of long-term dependency dominates descriptions of social life in the county in the 1990s. Community residents use phrases like "huge gulf," "cliff's edge," and "giant gap" to describe the distance between the haves and the have-nots. Those with jobs characterize the groups as "those who work" and "those who draw." It is assumed that those "who draw" do so by choice. *People that want to work are the same as people that do work*, says one of the employed, *because they're still trying to work. And then there's people who don't want to work at all, never have and never will. We call them first-of-the-monthers because they come out of the mountains the first of the month with about ten kids and don't wash. When I worked at the grocery store, you could smell them coming. But they just draw food stamps and stuff like that. They live like that, and I guess that's the way they want to live*.

These days coal miners at the big mines are considered among the haves. *The people who are just regular coal miners can bring home maybe thirty or forty thousand, in that bracket. And then you go from that, and the transition is like a cliff's edge, and it drops off and you got people who are very, very poor*. A newcomer can hear the same story about ambition three or four times in one week, each time told as if it happened to the speaker personally: *Why, just the other day I asked a young boy from up in the hollows what he wanted to do when he grew up and he answered, "I want to draw." I said, "Well, that's great. What kind of artist will you be?" And the boy replied, "No, draw a check."*

Few doubt that there are families here who have accepted dependency—who know nothing else and whose livelihoods depend on discovering what programs are available at the welfare office or the Community Action Agency, when commodities are handed out or coal is made available, and what churches help with light bills or groceries when the stamps run out. A minister I first interviewed in 1990, several years after he had arrived from Florida, found his parishioners and the county's citizens in general surprisingly resistant to reaching out to the "country poor." *I'm talking to them—I have for a year or two—about a soup kitchen. They give me this story about how every Tom, Dick, and Harry would come in there, and you would have all kinds of misfits. I'm sure that's true, but we could work that out. We could weed that out. I think that it would be good for our church to start that process. It would help them. It would help us. I think the word would get out and we would have a lot of people come*.

When we talked a second time, two years later, he said he still prodded his congregation to do more, but he also had developed a strategy to avoid subsidizing the same families making the rounds to his church door every month seeking handouts. *Some days it's like you need a store counter out there to wait on people as they come in for a handout. Power bills. There's one right here. Someone left it on my desk—$268 power bill. And it was $300 two months before. A few weeks ago I had one woman whom I'd never seen before come by and I gave her $80, to be exact. Three others came that same afternoon, came because they heard. You see, they have a network. There are people in here day in and day out wanting money for power bills, groceries, gas money. I've never seen it to this extent anywhere I've ever been. What we're going to do is phase out helping people, believe it or not*—he smiles at the irony in his words—*when they come here, unless it's an obvious real need. What we're going to do is reach out and find people ourselves that we know need help, through our members and through other agencies. And just go to them and help them*.

Experiences like this undermine community trust and reinforce the commonly held opinion that the very poor scheme to manipulate the system.

Because this minister's parishioners are the well-to-do county-seat residents who have no contact with the poor, they will have difficulty finding people who they can be sure "need" help. The social isolation that keeps the haves out of contact with the have-nots means that all long-term poor are stigmatized and lumped together as an undeserving group. Those with good jobs often use the pronoun "they," and speak with disdain about the dependent poor. A public employee said, *They know the system. They know how to get food stamps. They know all this stuff. They may not be able to read and write, but knowing the welfare system is like a job with them*. And the prejudice and distrust work both ways—people who have work often feel there is resentment of those who "try." *Poor kids call people who try snobs. If your parents have the drive and initiative to give you more, and you dress a little better and have a little more, then you're a snob regardless what your individual personality is*.

The poor know they are seen as a distinct, inferior group. As one teenager from a family with a "bad name" describes the community, *There are the "good rich people" and the "bad poor people," and they are segregated*. These distinctions are family based, and rich and poor alike agree that those whose "Daddy never did any good" will have a hard time getting work. A coal miner's son with a good public job obtained through political connections explained the way family names matter. *A lot of times you can hear somebody's last name and before you even meet them, you've already got the idea that they're either a good person or they're sorry as can be. Everybody knows everybody's family names. If you're a certain family, then you're this way. But if you're from that family, then you're that way. There are last names that you would just immediately associate with being trouble or lazy—they're immediately in a class*.

Employers in the private sector agree, whether they are in the mines, stores, or fast-food restaurants. Even the manager at the Department of Employment says coming from a family with a bad name is a disadvantage for young people. *Those that have a family with a horrible name, when they come in, we know them, and they're not worth two cents. They're sorry as can be—stealing, selling dope, bootlegging, picked up for driving drunk, in and out of bankruptcy court*.

Those from the families with the bad names give the same account about discrimination against them. They say family background matters for housing. *Everybody around here knows everybody, and they know what family you come from. Now my family, they've always been a bad family. There are places we can't even rent a house because of our last name. And that's just the way it is. You can't change it. You have to live with it*.

They say it matters for work. *You have to come from the right family around here. You gotta know people. It depends on what your name is. If you got a last name that is a rich name, they'll take you; otherwise, you can't find no work.*

They say it matters in getting health care. *The hospital staff was snooty until they heard what my parents did for work, and I know it was just 'cause she thought I didn't have any money. I had my hair down and no makeup on. And there was a real young girl in the bed in front of me and they treated her real bad because she didn't have any money.*

And they say it matters in school. *They make their picks on the people that's got the most money up here. They try to say it's because they achieve more, but it's not. It's because they got more money. The teacher treats them with respect, treats them right, like they're supposed to be treated—like a human being. When I was going to school, I was sent to the principal's office every day, even if I didn't do nothing, and I got paddled. And they did my brother the same way—whether or not he did anything, he got paddled every day.*

These "good" and "bad" families live and work under the eye of the powerful families and politicians who control the county's nine thousand jobs in the public and private sectors. For decades the school system has provided a large proportion of the jobs in these Appalachian mountain counties. John Martin, a counselor who over the years has worked for some of the biggest health and education organizations in the county, explains. *Thirty years ago, school boards and school superintendents were never really elected. Boards were bought. And they in turn put the superintendent in who bought them, who paid for their election. So the school superintendent pretty well ran everything in these counties, and they were pretty well manipulated by those powers. Nobody would dare do anything that would upset the superintendent. Because if you did, they controlled the jobs—and they knew who your family members were, and everyone would feel it.* Teachers and business owners tell a similar story about the present. *The schools are full of politics and it's according to who gets the most board members on their side. And of course there's jobs. People get good jobs for payoff when they go along and people get shipped to Timbuktu when they don't cooperate.*

A business manager who had lived in Georgia for years was astounded at the way local politics works. *I come here, to a county of thirty-thousand-something people in it, and the county commissioners are some of the best-paid people in the county! And most of your county commissioners are people who come from large families—an average working-type class of people—not that there's anything wrong with them, but they'll go into that county government with no expertise, no sense of how to run a big business. So, they sure in hell not going to know how to run a county. It's like that all over the region. P[illegible]tics is an end in itself.* He was also struck by how differently the apparent community leaders behave. *The people here that are the community leaders, the movers and shakers in most places, the people with the money, that own the big mines, that own the bigger stores—Parkers, Scotts—those people are never directly involved in politics. Rather, they support some guy who has a ninth- or tenth-grade education, but who has got a big family. They support him and get him elected. They're not really part of it. They're just behind the scenes trying to move and manipulate, and they're only doing it for their own benefit.*

Control over jobs is intertwined with power over property and other assets. As one older man put it, *You've got two or three families that control the money and control the county, and there's not much left for everyone else*. Many liken the way power is used to small medieval fiefdoms where the lord reigned unhampered by democratic rules. An adviser to the current county judge administrator, Bobby Lee King, recalled the most recent election. *Let's just say a couple of the coal operators control the positions on the school board. They had gotten their person in as superintendent, and so they could manipulate him. Then what they wanted was to control the county administrator again, so they tried to set that up*.

No one expects politics to be any other way, because this is what people have always known. The origins of both the class divisions and nondemocratic, corrupt politics can be found in the way social life and work were organized in the early days of coal mining in Blackwell, when operators established complete control over workers' lives.

BLACKWELL YESTERDAY: DEVELOPING APPALACHIA'S COAL FIELDS

Blackwell was first settled in the early 1800s by subsistence farmers who came from neighboring states to eke out a living on the marginal soil in these rugged, isolated hills. These early settlers did a little trading, bartering ginseng, furs, and sometimes hogs for salt and a few other staples; but almost everything else they produced or hunted for themselves. Their lives were family oriented in every dimension—work, politics, education, and religion—and making a living was hard. In the late 1800s there were about six thousand people in Blackwell County, people whom Appalachian scholars and writers describe as independent and self-sufficient. Travelers into the mountains regarded them as stopped in time, relics of an earlier era. "Quaint and peculiar" is the image portrayed by "local color writers" in their stories for popular magazines like the *Atlantic* or *Harper's*. Whether or not these romantic characterizations of a preindustrial pioneer life held some truth in the 1800s, they were soon irrelevant when the subsistence economy was replaced by an industrial coal economy at the turn of the century.[2]

By the late 1800s outside interests from the Northeast had bought and cut vast timber land in the region, and they were soon followed by other businessmen prepared to mine the rich coal reserves. These investors, with the help of local boosters, persuaded railroads that great sums of money could be made in Central Appalachia's resource-rich mountains, and by the early 1900s railroads reached even the most remote counties like Blackwell, where significant coal reserves had been identified. Mountain lawyers and merchants were positioned to act as go-betweens with the outsiders. They often managed the sale of vast amounts of land and coal reserves and sometimes became local partners and investors.[3]

Business and political leaders expressed great optimism about the potential development that would follow coal mining. The *Manufacturers' Record*, a popular business journal of the period, predicted that these rich resources would bring widespread wealth and prosperity to the region, and state governments in Appalachia aggressively tried to attract capital to develop railroads and coal and timber reserves. Historian Ronald Eller cites some opposition to the boosterism, including a report by the West Virginia Tax Commission in the late 1800s that cautioned that local wealth and control were being recklessly sold, "threatening to leave West Virginia in the near future 'despoiled of her wealth and her resident population poor, helpless, and despondent.'"[4] But the general mood was upbeat, and warnings about the dangers inherent in outside ownership went unheeded. Indeed, West Virginia and Kentucky historians describe how these business interests seized control of political as well as economic power in the mountains, even in small communities: "After the turn of the century the level of citizen participation declined, and the average farmer or laborer became isolated from the political process. . . . there emerged in Appalachia a constricted political system based upon an economic hierarchy—those who controlled the jobs also controlled the political system, and those who controlled the political system used their power to exploit the region's natural wealth for their own personal gain."[5]

By 1900 four railroads reached deep into the region's center, where the rich coal reserves had been found and bought by these outside developers. The railroads stimulated a sudden and dramatic increase in coal production. Large national steel and power companies established mines to supply their plants in the Northeast and Midwest, and coal employment in Blackwell grew from fewer than several hundred men to more than ten thousand in three decades. Blackwell's population tripled in the first decade, then doubled in the next. A small number of foreign immigrants and southern blacks migrated to the area, but most of those who came to work in Blackwell's mines and live in the coal camps constructed to house workers were the subsistence farmers who had scratched for a living in the region's hills for decades. These poor and uneducated hill people traded the uncertainty and hardships of isolated subsistence farming for the volatility and vulnerability of an oppressive coal industry.[6]

From the beginning coal companies kept a tight rein on their workers—partly by establishing clear differences between management and labor and partly by denying them control over even their private lives in the community. The companies deliberately created a divided two-class society, with management living in its own neighborhood, usually on a hilltop, and workers in small coal-camp houses. As coal-industry analyst Curtis Seltzer has put it, "there were those who provided the opportunity to dig through their investment and expertise, and there were those who dug." Seltzer describes communities with no middle class, no public sector—the community was controlled and run by management and operators: "Self-imposed segregation was the norm." Eller concludes that "industrialization . . . fragmented the social structure, creating a great and growing gulf between the lower-class laboring population and those above them." Miners had separate social institutions, and many "simply withdrew from active participation in local and county politics, leaving a truncated political system to be controlled by the managerial elite."[7]

Coal operators feared union organizing and labor unrest, and wanted to make all aspects of miners' lives "subject to the authority of the coal operator." Seltzer says, "Companies frowned on miners establishing their own institutions, be they lodges, churches, or unions. They preferred to envelop miners in a total environment, the better to control their behavior." Operators also prevented miners from owning property because ownership would give them independence. If miners complained or went on strike, operators could evict them from tenant housing as long as they rented from the company. Seltzer quotes a newspaper reporter covering West Virginia in the early 1900s who wrote: "The operators are not only the miner's employer; they are his landlord, his merchant, the provider of his amusements, the sanitary officer of the town, sometimes the source of police protection and the patron of his physician, his minister, and his school teacher. It is a paternalistic, in some ways a feudal, civilization."[8]

Thus miners had no opportunity to participate in civic life or local governance, and worker-run organizations were discouraged. There was virtually no public sector or infrastructure—in part because local organizations were deliberately blocked and in part because the taxes to finance them would have had to come from operators, and they had the power to prevent costly community investment. "Public" aspects of community life were controlled by coal operators, who also selected and controlled public officials. Eller describes how coal operators seized control of local politics in the early 1900s to ensure order and guarantee that their own interests prevailed: "The abuses of the new order were apparent throughout local government. There had always been a degree of nepotism in mountain politics, but the traditional political culture had rarely been plagued with serious cases of graft or dishonesty. With power concentrated in the hands of the coal barons, however, reports of corruption, intimidation, ballot fraud, vote-buying, and other scandals became widespread."[9]

Eller portrays a political system tightly controlled by coal barons at all levels—"industrial oligarchies" of coal operators and widespread "reports of corruption, intimidation, ballot fraud, vote-buying, and other scandals." Sheriffs and other authorities worked directly for the operators, assuring favorable tax assessments and security and cooperation in dealing with labor strife. Coal operators developed slates of company men they wanted elected, and they used coercion and bribes to get them elected. School officials became part of this local political scheme. During the first few decades of the twentieth century public education was becoming well established in many parts of the United States, but in Appalachia schools that had been neglected in the late 1800s were now coming under the control of coal companies. They set up schools in mining camps, hired the teachers, and took an "education fee" out of miners' wages. At the same time, operators made local elected school trustees part of their corrupt system of patronage and control.[10]

The prevalence of company towns in the region meant there were virtually "no public places and few public roads," according to Eller. "The company controlled or owned the land and furnished the houses, stores, churches, and schools. There were no public agencies to provide for social welfare, and residents had little voice in the management of public affairs. It was a most atypical town, one that strictly limited personal and social liberty and left its residents powerless to control their own destinies."[11]

Miners' families were required to shop in the company store, and when times were bad, the company store was where the coal companies made their only profit.[12] Across the region, operators saw the coal camp as part of their overall investment, and they expected every dimension of that investment to generate profits. Appalachian coal miners often charged their food and other household goods at the store and never saw any money or any profit for a year's work. When they became indebted they were tied to the company.

The miners also were vulnerable to cheating by the company—first, in the early days, when the coal they mined was weighed, and second when their accounts were figured at the stores and they were charged for medical care and for housing. Suspicion and distrust were deeply ingrained from the earliest days of coal development. Bituminous coal operators were in bitter competition for distant industrial customers who played companies off one another, and operators pressed miners and their families hard to maintain their own share of that market. In the 1930s Justice William O. Douglas wrote that the bituminous coal industry was structured such that "labor and capital alike were the victims. Financial distress among the operators and acute poverty among miners prevailed during periods of prosperity."[13] The exploitation and class segregation generated a deep mistrust and antagonism—as Seltzer puts it, a "them versus us" relationship— that made union struggles violent for decades to come.

During the Great Depression miners and their families suffered greatly. Work was irregular, wages were constantly being cut, and children suffered from malnutrition and disease. One analyst described the ensuing struggle to establish a union in coal areas as "both an attempt to remedy unsatisfactory working conditions and a miners' revolt against the county's mine owners' arbitrary economic, political and social power."[14] To explain the level of violence and near anarchy that erupted in the coal fields, he cited a litany of social problems associated with sudden industrialization: the disruption of traditional family ties, including a divorce rate of one out of four marriages in the 1930s, high illiteracy, the lack of a middle class, the absence of any civic or social organizations, and extreme population growth over a decade or two. A *New York Times* reporter covering a union-related trial in a Kentucky county in the 1930s observed, "It is the political and economic system of that rich soft-coal field which is at the bar. For [here], as nowhere else in the country, except possibly the Deep South, the visitor encounters feudalism and paternalism which survive despite all efforts to break them down."[15]

The industry's labor struggle continued into the 1940s. Operators believed their business ownership and success gave them rightful authority over miners and they expected their workers to obey their rules. To ensure that the system was not challenged, they bought and ran the political system, maintaining firm control over local government, including law enforcement.[16] Sheriffs and deputies were paid by operators to prevent unionization from gaining ground in the area, establishing a pattern of corruption, lawlessness, and arbitrary power that persists to this day.

Even after John L. Lewis, the powerful leader of the United Mine Workers of America (UMWA), crafted a solid contract with George Love of the Bituminous Coal Operators Association (BCOA) in 1950, lack of trust and long-standing habits of violent confrontation still characterized the industry and the region. The UMWA/BCOA agreement raised wages and provided benefits for those who stayed on at the mines, but it also permitted mechanization that meant massive layoffs.[17] Hundreds of thousands left the region in the 1950s, seeking work in growing midwestern and northern industrial cities. Coal employment dropped precipitously in Blackwell from more than fifteen thousand to around seven thousand. Those who stayed behind but did not have union mine jobs were desperately poor.

In this job-scarce environment, control over public employment became even more important as a source of power. School officials had historically been appointed by coal operators as part of their general control over county politics and community life, and from the beginning school personnel were appointed more often for patronage reasons than on the basis of merit. In the thirties public jobs and resources were frequently used by politicians to enhance their own political capital. Later, in the sixties and seventies, when jobs were declining in the coal fields, patronage politics became central to mountain life. As one coal miner told child psychologist Robert Coles in the 1960s, "Welfare is a business here, not the right of a citizen who needs help and is entitled to it. No wonder a lot of our people have contempt for welfare, even if they'll accept the money. They know that the county officials use welfare to stay in power, to buy votes and to punish enemies."[18]

Blackwell residents say the coal elite blocked new industry at critical junctures in the 1960s and 1970s because they feared dilution of their power over labor and community affairs. One frustrated organizer told Coles that people want change, but they justifiably fear repercussions: "They are former miners or people from up a creek who are fed up with things and want to see changes take place. You get talking with them, and they tell you they'll help, and they do. But after a while they find it hard to get other people to go along, because people around here are plain scared; they're afraid they'll be cut off from welfare, or their kids won't be picked up by the bus, or won't get their free lunch, or a hundred other things will happen that the courthouse crowd can do to you."[19]

The class divisions and social control instilled by early coal operators, as well as the corruption in politics and law enforcement they engendered, live on today in Blackwell—exacerbated further by the scarcity of jobs and the strains of supporting a large dependent population.

Blackwell experienced some increase in coal employment during the short-lived coal boom that followed the Arab oil embargo, but by the mid-1980s hard times, scarce jobs, and steady out-migration had returned. Thirty-five hundred were employed in mining in Blackwell in 1980, but by 1990 coal employment was down to around twenty-five hundred. Economic restructuring swept the nation's rural areas in the late 1980s, marking a shift from predominately goods-producing jobs with high wages and benefits to less desirable service-producing jobs with neither. Coal-dependent areas like Blackwell felt this impact as well: by 1990 more than half the jobs were in the service sector and less than a third were in mining. Jobs are scarce, good jobs very scarce, and virtually all jobs are controlled by a few powerful employers.

THE FAMILIES THAT RUN THINGS

Today everyone in Blackwell, no matter what their status, can name the families that "run things." These families use their considerable wealth and power to influence county affairs and further enrich themselves, often at the expense of their competition and the county in general. Their lack of attention to civic affairs and the long-term well-being of the community comes up time and time again. A community leader in a neighboring county observed, *I think too many times the elite in this region direct themselves, their work, or the things they do, for personal profit—and for right now. They don't realize that if they did something to help develop the community, to help individuals, that in the end their profits might be more.*

The elite in Blackwell and other Appalachian coal counties are often descended from independent merchants and skilled craftspeople who secured an early hold on land and opportunity. When they arrived in the county they had more resources than most people in the area, but not fabulous wealth. They may have made strategic alliances with outside investors, the absentee corporations that had bought the land and timber and coal reserves in the early 1900s. Today they dominate local economic life, controlling locally owned coal and retail businesses, considerable real estate, and most good jobs. They are reputed to have strong relationships with state-level political leaders, in part because of their economic power in the region and in part because they control the region's politics. Their families are large, and many say the ongoing rivalries and recent betrayals within as well as between families—sometimes violent and dramatic—reflect their continued ambition and inability to cooperate. When I ask, "Do you know who runs things around here?" two families are named—the Parkers and the Scotts. They are not regarded as civic minded. *The Parkers and the Scotts compete among themselves for control over family fortunes. They want power to do for themselves, not for everyone. They're in it for theirselves, for what goes into their pocket.*

These powerful families take their power for granted—as an extension, perhaps, of the complete control coal companies exerted in Blackwell's early history—and those who live and work here fear them. Their style is paternalistic. They talk about their companies as a "family," and they expect loyalty from those they employ, including not only good performance on the job but also patronage at "family" businesses. They are reputed to influence employees' political choices as well. A young miner says he hears you have to vote "the right way" to get on at the bigger mines—*you gotta be fer who they're fer up there at the big 'uns*. Several young staff workers with good jobs in a summer youth program nodded emphatically as their director explained how things work. *You have to be very careful here. You have to be extremely careful. If you're not careful, you'll make enemies, and you don't want to make enemies—especially if you don't have importance. You can make some real bad enemies here and you'll never get a job. If they blackball you, you will not be able to get a job flipping burgers*. Highly placed, cautious adults make the same point. A leading attorney in the county nodded gravely when I asked about politics and employment. *There are pressures. I know of situations right now where individuals have that threat of losing their jobs or being blackballed in the county.*

Creed Parker is the most important local coal operator. His office at the mines, where he can be found seven days a week, twelve months a year, is several miles northwest of town on a winding road barely wide enough for one coal truck. Just beyond the concrete block building of the Primitive Free Will Baptist Church, I cross the creek and climb a gravel county road for a few hundred yards until I come to a small parking area between two one-story, flat-roofed metal buildings.

Parker, sixty years old and a chain smoker of filterless Camels, wears workman's grays as he sits at his broad metal desk covered with printouts and reports on production and prices. He is tall and thin, and his lined face has a ruddy complexion set off by his thick gray hair. His blue-gray eyes are surprisingly warm, given his reputation, and he speaks in an open, direct, respectful tone. Decades of steady smoking have lowered his voice to a rumble, and at times I strain to hear his words. Outside the window, the conveyor belt on the loading ramp from the coal tipple hums and creaks. Inside, the radio through which he listens to conversations between his laborers and supervisors crackles periodically. He is interested in talking, telling his story, sharing his opinions.

In 1900 Creed's father, John, the son of a farmer in the lower hill country, came to Blackwell with carpentry skills and an ambition to make his fortune. The railroad had come the year before, bringing with it big outside corporate investment in coal mines and the promise of spectacular growth. When John Parker arrived, the population of Blackwell was about nine thousand. The population tripled over the next decade and doubled again the following decade. He built coal-camp housing for large out-of-state corporations with mining interests. He saved money and, with some financial help from his father, invested in his own "bucket mine" in the 1920s.

This was the period of dramatic growth in coal production in Blackwell, facilitated by the new railroad with its favorable freight rate structure compared with that available to northern coal interests, the area's high-quality metallurgical and steam coal reserves, and—significantly—the comparatively low, flexible wage rates.

After his first wife died of pneumonia, John Parker married Creed's mother, a bright young mountain girl who not only had completed high school at the mountain settlement school but had gone on to a regional college for training as a schoolteacher. Creed was born a year later, in 1930, when his father was forty-five and his mother twenty-five. He was raised in town and attended the city school, but he spent summers out at the mine and stayed in the coal camp, learning the business at a young age.

Creed says his father was a hardworking, fair man, *but he was sort of a womanizer*. By the time Creed was in high school his father had a relationship with another woman, his parents divorced, and Creed was sent off to boarding school. Creed never got along with his new stepmother, who he believes made a drinker out of his father. When Creed was twenty-four his father was shot to death. Creed has no doubt the murder was committed by his stepmother in collusion with her lover, a financial officer at the bank that worked with rival coal companies. *But*, he says, *the biggest political lawyer in the state got her off*. As the courts wrestled with claims and counterclaims about John Parker's death and the disposition of his substantial coal interests, Creed worked in other mines around the county.

In the late 1950s he finally assumed control of his father's much-troubled company, which had suffered from years of mismanagement and "scamming," as he puts it, by his stepmother and the company bookkeeper, who had become her second husband. In the meantime, Creed's stepmother had died—poisoned, some say, with formaldehyde by her new, alcoholic husband. With the backing of Carville, the banker who is now in his eighties, and his father-in-law, a local merchant, Creed began to rebuild and solidify the Parker coal enterprises—coal sales, mining-related construction, and mining supply companies. He introduced mechanized loaders in the late 1950s, continuous miners in the 1960s. When the union would not agree to lower his required payments into the welfare fund, he shut down and reopened as a nonunion company. *My father was union from 1940 until we went nonunion in the mid-sixties, when the whole county went nonunion. Mines just closed down and kept closed, and it just got to the point where everybody was losing money. In our own instance we tried to make a deal with the union on the welfare fight, that we would increase wages for the men (because we weren't paying union wages, and nobody else in the county was, even though we had a union customer), if they would let us not pay so much welfare, then we would pay more wages. That meeting was held right outside that door, with the men that worked here and a union field-worker, and his comment was, "Hell no." And within thirty or sixty days after that we just told them that we were through. If they wanted to work nonunion, fine, but otherwise we were out of business.*

Creed drastically reduced his labor force and then rebuilt Parker Coal. By the time the coal boom of the 1970s arrived, he was well positioned to take advantage of it. Over the years he had built a reliable customer base, companies that could count on him to deliver when and what he said he would. His two hundred miners produce more than eighty thousand tons a month. He says his advantages are quality, service, and reasonable prices. In recent years Creed has invested in retail stores and real estate development. The Parkers, including Creed, his brothers, and his five children, now run not only coal businesses but also a shopping mall, a theater, a small motel, and a miniature golf course. They have rented land and buildings to the new outside chain stores as well.

He leased land to a large grocery chain because, Creed says, it bothered him that local stores would raise prices just before the checks came in on the first of the month. *If you're here the first of the month, and you go in the grocery stores and look at your prices, and you go in a week later—now I'm not just talking about one, I'm talking about all of the large ones—the price will be down ten percent a week after the first of the month. When checks come in—they come in the first of the month—prices are raised. I thought that competition would make it cheaper for people to live here. It knocked it down a little, but not what I had hoped for.*

Creed sees little cooperation in the county—coal operators and even the banks carry competition to a bitter level, something he attributes to personalities. He says in the early days the national steel and machinery companies were good corporate citizens, but when they left and multinational energy companies came in the norms changed. And labor conflict has always marred the community, he says—when he and other smaller operators went nonunion in the 1960s it affected the politics throughout the county and reinforced old divisions. He attributes his own difficulties in getting a road built to his mines to these union politics and old grudges.

In Creed's view, the scarcity of jobs is the biggest problem Blackwell faces. He says some union members are lazy but, overall, people in Blackwell want to work. He took about eight hundred applications last year, he says, and figures fully seven hundred of them really wanted to work. He would like to see public jobs created. *If there was work made available by the government, we would get something for the money we spend on aid and those people without work could live a decent life. People will be thankful to get a job at whatever they can get, whatever wages. I've had plenty of people tell me, "I'll work a week for nothing. I'll work for whatever you want to pay me." It makes you feel bad that you can't give a guy something.*

Creed Parker's name came up during most interviews in Blackwell, often because people knew him as a power in the county and were careful not to cross him. Some had specific, personal stories about how they had benefited when he gave them a break or interceded on their behalf, while others cited examples of reprisal when workers or politicians let him down. A young woman described his call out to the hospital on behalf of her sister, who had been turned away. *Mary took her little girl out to the hospital clinic and they wouldn't see her because she owed a few more dollars, and they asked her how much she could pay on this particular bill if they did see her little girl, and she said, 'Well, maybe twenty-five, thirty dollars." They said, "Well, it's going to be a lot more than that because we have to take X rays." And they said, "You might as well go on home because we can't see you if that's all you can pay." She works for the Parkers, so they called up there to the hospital. And after that call, the woman that works up there called Mary at her house and was just trying to be so nice. "Oh, we're so sorry. Bring your child on out here." Everything here is who you know.*

Randy Perkins, who calls himself "a hardscrabble mountain man," described his understanding of Creed's power. *Now Creed Parker is a pretty good fellow—and powerful. I heard not long ago he called down to the sand and gravel company to make an order for building that new road of his, and they wouldn't bring it to him, so he got mad and bought the sand company. One time my cousin who works for him got hurt and went out here to the hospital with his finger half cut off, and they wouldn't wait on him. So Creed, he heads on out there and walks in and says, "I'm Creed Parker, and if that man isn't taken care of in less than five minutes, I'll buy this place and fire every damn one of you." And he meant it. He meant it.*

A social service worker said Creed had called the office trying to prevent food stamps being given to someone he had fired for refusing to work on Saturday. Since food stamps come from a federal program, the worker noted, even Creed Parker could not manipulate the rules. Another man heard that Parker had framed a worker who reported safety violations at one of the Parker mines. *There was one man from Wind Gap, name was Davis. He had turned in a violation on a mine which was owned by the Parkers. Turned it in to the federal mine inspectors. They had some irregularities in their mines, some safety irregularities. About two weeks later they came up with, well, this guy has been stealing from the company. What it was, he took the company truck home, just as he had been doing for ten years, and there was always equipment in it. Now all of the sudden they said he stole it. I honestly don't think he stole anything. After that, he was blackballed and it took him forever to find a job.*

Whatever the specifics might be, it is clear from interview after interview that Creed Parker is regarded as a man whose power extends throughout the county. It is better to have him on your side than against you. As for politics, Creed insists he is not directly involved, although he describes making an occasional phone call on behalf of a politician or arranging a meeting for local coal operators to discuss their interests with the new judge administrator, Bobby Lee King. *He's a pusher, and I like him*, Parker says of King. *I don't like some of the things he does, but I like him. He's a good person. Everybody was for him, the first term, in the county. Then he did some things some people didn't like, and everybody wasn't for him the second term. My brother is involved some in politics, and another guy up the road here, Willy Granger, he is involved. They didn't want him. They wanted to talk to him, and he wanted me to go with him, so I went up and they had a meeting. They had given him a hard time and he had sat there and pretty well had taken it. They told him they were going to beat him in the election, unless he changed the way he did things.*

Loads of gravel buy a lot of votes in Blackwell, and there's an awful lot of loads that go out. That doesn't particularly bother me because most of them are people that can't do for themselves anyway. But there are some things he does that do bother me. I guess ambition to go higher is natural in anybody, but I think we're letting a lot of things go in this county that would be a big contribution if we worked hard enough to get them, like roads.

When I say that people in Blackwell consider him very powerful, Creed demurs. *I have some money. I don't deal with politics. A lot of people think I've got some power. The only time I really participated was when I was with a former governor trying to get some roads. Of course I've tried to get that road of my own built for twenty years. And there was one election year that I was very interested in, and that was when it seemed we could get politics out of the schools. I thought we did, but we didn't. I think that it's better than it was, but I don't like politics. I think it's dirt.*

Creed and his family members are genuinely surprised that they do not get more appreciation from community residents—they see their real estate and business investments as a service to the community. Furthermore, family members point out, not all their investments are making money. And the roads he wants—sure, he says, they would benefit him, but they would benefit the whole county as well. *There have been a lot of coal operators here.*

A lot of them have lived here all of their life and worked hard, and have done things for the community. There have been others that have come, made a bunch of money, and left. Didn't put any, or not a lot, back. Whatever I've made has gone back into this county. I've got five kids, and they all live here. And I suspect their children will live here. I just want to see Blackwell prosper. In this perspective—as employers and investors in the county—as well as in their far-reaching paternalistic power, the Parkers resemble the other family dynasty around here, the Scotts.

The bedrock of Joey Scott's considerable wealth is the grocery business—but grocery writ large, much like the old commissary stores in the company towns. Today the Scotts own numerous diverse businesses and properties throughout the county and the region. The family business offices are located in one of the larger stores in a small railroad town out in the county. I arrive for our interview at the regular grocery entrance of the store, where shopping carts and cash registers are lined up by the doors. But then I am led through a maze of other stores within a store—dark and cavernous, room after room of furniture, appliances, toys, and hardware items, to a steep, narrow wooden staircase.

At the top of the stairs, off a crooked hallway, are the corporate offices of the Scott business empire. In Joey Scott's office, the wood-paneled walls are covered with photographs of family members and political friends, pictures of the stores in their early days, and a large glass window looking out on the checkout area. Shelves along an opposite wall are crowded with old memorabilia, including the original sign from his parents' first store.

Joey is a short, stocky man who exudes energy even when he is sitting behind his desk. He is a third-generation business owner. His grandparents on his mother's side had a farming supply store upstate, and his father's parents were in the well-drilling business in Ohio. *My dad lost his leg when he was about sixteen years old working in a logging operation. He went back to get an education. When he graduated he married my mother, and they came to Blackwell in the 1930s looking for a job teaching. So my father got a job teaching here and my mother got a job teaching here. They had taught for about three or four years, and were making $125 a month. Then they cut his wages to $100. He said, "I can't live on that a month." So he bought a small grocery store in Wind Gap, over on the other side of the county. It took all of their savings.*

Joey describes how he and his older brother Sam returned from college in the early 1960s, a period of massive unemployment and high out-migration, and remade their parents' two relatively modest grocery stores into a large multiproduct and multisite business. *Mother and Dad just wanted to break even*, Joey explains, *and the stores were not all that popular*. The family was doing well enough that Joey and Sam could attend the state college and not worry about money, but they had not amassed great wealth. Joey makes it clear that the growth in the family business has occurred on his watch. *Dad had a small grocery store in 1950, then he made it into a supermarket there, and in 1955 he put a smaller, second store here where we are now. That was about it until I got out of college. My dad never cared about making a lot of money. He gave away more than he kept.*

Joey recognized that even in hard times he had opportunities here in the mountains. At first he taught school, but he was looking for other ways to earn money and accumulate assets right from the start. *I came back home in the early 1960s and it was tough. So I taught for six years, high school, and my wife taught for five years. I was teaching and working in the stores. I had three jobs, which soon turned into four, trying to get started. I owned a coin laundry and dry cleaners, and I was working with some real estate investments then, too. We came back because we felt like the opportunity was better here for us than some other places because we had established some businesses and we had some real estate and stuff.*

Over the years "the Scott boys" have amassed a wide array of businesses and real estate. *We have three supermarkets, three convenience stores, one with a gas station. We have a department store, a hardware and auto supply store, a clothing store, a jewelry store, and a home supply business. Then we have a discount store, a wholesale lumber company, Wild Berry Apartments, and finally, Scott Incorporated, a development partnership. Sam and I buy and develop commercial rental properties throughout the region—office buildings and stuff—that we lease mostly to federal agencies like Social Security, Department of Mines, that kind of thing. Then we own the radio station in town. And, over in Harrington, we bought a sixteen-floor apartment complex.*

Sam and Joey were partners in every Scott venture for thirty years—from their college days to the year their mother died at ninety. Joyce Scott outlived her husband by twenty-some years, and spent most of that time working every day in the main store. As Joey tells it, Sam and his mother started fighting after Sam's divorce. She did not like his new woman friend and he did not like the personnel decisions she was making in the store. *She was constantly telling Sam that she didn't like this woman, but Sam dated her anyway. They kept having problems and problems. Sam and Mother just really could not get along. She just got put out with him and through anger and through some other things, Mother decided, "If that's the way he's going to be, then I'm not going to leave him anything." So she changed her will. He was the administrator of the estate. She changed it to make me the administrator. She didn't leave Sam but very little, left my sister very little, and left me the bulk of it. Well, I knew what Mother had done. She was ninety years old. I didn't care what she wanted. Parents in their eighties or nineties, you let them do whatever they want to do as long as they're not breaking the law. So after she died I gave Sam a copy of the will and my sister a copy of the will and said, "Here it is." Mother and I were very close, and I didn't do a thing or say a thing for some time.*

Joey pondered the situation for several months, and then decided he should divide the estate equally among the three of them—that way his own children would respect him. *But Sam never got over it and he still resents it. I did just exactly what I said I was going to do—split it up a third, a third, a third. But it still hasn't worked.* He looks exasperated. *I don't care. I've done everything I think I have to do and did what was right. I can live with it. I hope he can. But it just has gotten down to where we disagree on everything.* Today the two brothers are going their separate business ways. Joey is still expanding, diversifying, and hoping to bring his own children, who are just graduating from college, into the business.

Scott Enterprises employs hundreds of men and women, young and old, full and part time, semiskilled and unskilled. About 70 percent are part-time workers, and the majority are young or female and earn minimum wage. *We employ an awful lot of young people. A lot of young people and a lot of women, because of the pay scale, that is about what we can get.* Joey sees himself as giving a first opportunity to the children of the respectable upper middle class who make up the haves. *Mainly the people who work for me are high school kids. A lot of them are pretty industrious. They want to go on and make something of themselves. Looking for a first-time job, learning about work and what it's all about. And their parents are either the doctors or the lawyers, schoolteachers—the kind of professional people in town that are pushing their children out to work. In fact, a lot of people down here that are in those professions have worked for me at one time bagging groceries. They'll say to me, "That is the most valuable experience I ever received. I learned to deal with the public. I learned what work was all about." So we get a pretty good turnover with kids like that. Like I said, women—a lot of them are just a second income.*

Neither the adults nor the children from poorer families are interested in working, according to Joey. *They don't really want to work. They'll come by and say, "I have to apply for the job to get my welfare check. Will you sign this card saying I've come down and applied for a job?" Not really apply, in other words. They've got to have me sign that they've made the contact, but they don't want to work*. And as for those who do want to work but are not going on to middle-class, professional careers, Joey says, *Let's face it, if you're going to bag groceries or something like that all of your life, you can't be the smartest guy in the world. So the ones that stay with me who are like that, if they have two or three children, they probably have some kind of government card for insurance. They're not making money. They're making minimum wage. You know, they may be married and have two children and make $4.25 an hour, and they still would be eligible for food stamps, public assistance, and things like that. I've had employees before that were in that position where I've offered them a raise to $5.00 an hour, and they said, "You give me a raise and I'll lose my benefits."* The part-time laborers in Scott Enterprises earn so little that they are still eligible for federal public assistance. They piece together a living with their welfare benefits and the part-time hours at minimum wage they get from Joey Scott.

Joey sees a large group of persistently poor men and women in the mountains, and he does not expect that their children's lives will be any better. *I've seen this class all my life. There has really been a lot of interbreeding. Daddies and sisters, mothers and sons, daughters and fathers and stuff. So we've got an element out there that is really low. You go up to some of the hollows and meet some of these people. You really have got some problems. We've got some people that have grown up in families where their parents did nothing but beg and would get whatever they could wherever they could. When I was growing up, these people were coming by and begging, wanting assistance. They had grown up and had too many children—ten or twelve children. Now their children are back here doing the same thing*.

But not everyone chooses the dole. Joey and the people who hire workers for his businesses see demand for jobs far outdistance supply. In recent years Joey has run a day-labor business that contracts out to area coal mines to do manual labor for which the operators do not want to pay union-level wages and benefits. This is hard physical labor paying low wages, but people want the work. *It's strange. Once the word got out that we were doing work around the mines, a lot of men would go down to our office and stand out there and wait for a couple of hours, hoping to get some work*. Confirming what every person seeking work tells me, Joey explains that he hires based on knowing the families or having a solid recommendation from someone already working for him. *I would not hire the first person through the employment office. I take referrals. If his brother works for us, or his daddy works for us, or a friend works for us—they'll tell him about the job and then he'll come in and apply.*

The day-labor work is grueling, and there are many who choose not to work at hard manual labor for minimum wage. But some stick with it. *Some of those guys that we provide work for are hard men, tough, but they know the value of trying to make a living and doing better. Those people are making eight, nine, or ten dollars an hour—those are the operators and the electricians, the people that are given more responsibility. Of course, they know the work is hard, but they're going to work hard. Most of them have dropped out of school, maybe in eighth grade. Maybe they've never done any high school at all.*

So although Joey shakes his head about the large dependent population that chooses public assistance over working, he also knows from personal experience that there is demand for even minimum wage and hard-labor jobs. He would like to see a minimum wage factory come in and employ a thousand women. Then, with the women working in an apparel or bakery-type factory, he says, *you would have two people working, or even three or more, when the children start working too. There is a lot of women here that would like to work and they need to work. Every day we'll have probably five to ten women apply for a job*. Of course, few are hired as there is little turnover, even in the grocery business.

When the Scotts do hire they are looking for people who are good with the public and can fit in with the company. *We try to interview everybody that comes in and applies for a job. After scanning their application, if it looks like they would fit into the family here—you know, it really doesn't take a lot. We would like them to be a high school graduate, pretty fair family background, and stuff like that. It doesn't take a lot to be a cashier. We've got a little math test we give them*. He elaborates on what he means by "fair family background." *I know most of the families. And I'm looking for people that, of course, their names are not constantly in the newspaper for being in the courthouse, fighting, shooting, drinking, and drugs, and stuff like that. There are some families that I know, if their name pops up, I just won't consider it. That is what I'm talking about. If they apply to us, I trash that application*.

He reminds me that he is looking for the future lawyers, doctors, and teachers. *Of course, we're really looking for women and young men who have some ambition and want to make something of themselves, who are service orientated. Basically, we've got to give better service than the chain stores. We've got to be friendly. We've got to have something that is unique to this community and it's got to be a community store, and we're looking for people—we don't always get it—who will remember the customer's name, greet that customer and make them feel that they are at home here.*

Creed Parker and Joey Scott talk about the workers in their businesses paternalistically. A young man who stocked shelves at the Scotts' larger store says Joey would look after him and his young wife. *If something happened to you or someone in your family, let them know and they would try to help.* As Creed's daughter put it when asked about her social circle, *Most of our key people at our operations have been with Daddy since they were young, so there is a bond there with them and their families. Yes, we became larger, but we have what I term our old-timers, and we are close to them. Now, we don't socialize with them.*

Both Creed Parker and Joey Scott live out in the county, rather than on Redbud Hill, but they paid tuition to send their own children to the city school. Like Creed, Joey tells me he deplores the politics in the county school system. He sees the corrupt school politics as the responsibility of the same poor families who are doing manual labor, bagging groceries until they retire, or choosing dependency over work. He acknowledges some involvement, but no responsibility. *When you speak about politics, school board kind of politics, you're looking at people there on the lower end. They're looking for jobs. They've got about 450 jobs that they can control. Unfortunately. That doesn't mean a lot to me one way or another—their politics. I think they're foolish for having any politics at all in our school system. It is very distasteful. I would much prefer to see people out there donate their time in order to see that the children get a good education and to heck with politics. Who gets a job? The best person gets a job. Someone who will teach our children what we want them to learn.*

When jobs in the private sector are scarce, jobs in the public sector take on huge importance and become part of a patronage system. *In our county school system, the people on the board are more interested in the politics—who they can get a job for, that kind of stuff—than they are in the children. The city school is just the opposite. The board members there are not interested in any money or any influence. It's just, "What can we do for the children? What is the very best job we can do?" That is what we're interested in—a lot of good quality people have been on that board and they push the school to do a good job. Academics is number one. Sports and stuff is fine, we have them, but that is not where we put our interest.*

In contrast, in the county schools sports are all-important, and there is chaos and violence as well. Joey Scott elaborates. *I mean, girls are afraid to go into the bathroom, because there are going to be muggers and they will get beat up or something. Even the guys are afraid of that! The principal doesn't have control of the school system, and it's crazy.*

THE POLITICS OF WORK IN THE MOUNTAINS

There are four basic kinds of work in Blackwell: mining; service-sector jobs in retail stores or fast-food restaurants; public jobs in the schools, social service agencies, and working on the roads; and, finally, odd jobs such as mowing lawns, shade tree mechanic work, hauling away trash, painting. According to census statistics, only about half of the nearly ten thousand working-age men in the county are employed, and nearly half of these are coal miners. More than three thousand working-age people have a disability that prevents them from working, and these are probably mostly men, probably mostly coal miners. One thirty-year-old welfare worker said, *This place is SSI crazy. We get a lot of people in here that are younger than me claiming total disability. They worked in the mines and their back hurt a little bit, and I tell them, "Maybe you can't get back in the mine, maybe you can get a desk job somewhere or something like that." But they say, "coal mining is all I know." And I'll tell you, eventually they do get a check.*

Work is particularly hard for women to find, and the region lags behind national norms; elsewhere, over one half of women in the 1990s are working. In Blackwell, about one fourth of working-age women are employed, and we can assume that most of these three thousand women work in the service sector and the public sector. Joey Scott and the hospital employ a good number of them, and many combine public assistance with work in a fast-food restaurant.

Everyone my colleagues and I interviewed in Blackwell insisted that you get work according to whom you know. Once they get on at a place, people help get jobs for family members, and they will put in a word for friends. *You don't get jobs on merit—it's on who you know. I've lived away from here and I know what's on merit. Other places it can be merit—qualifications, your education*. One consequence is that certain families are "job rich," with several family members working, while almost a third have no one working.

Coal mining is considered the best job for pay and benefits. Steadily employed miners can earn more than $50,000 a year, including overtime. Community residents recognize that coal employment is declining, however, and the old notion that good boom times would return has been replaced by recognition that coal employment is unlikely to grow. Many miners were laid off permanently in the 1980s and 1990s. In 1950 eight thousand men were employed as miners, but the mechanization agreement between the UMWA and the BCOA cut that number in half, and by 1960 there were only thirty-seven hundred miners in Blackwell. The decade of the sixties saw that number cut again, to less than twenty-five hundred. After a high of thirty-four hundred in 1980, the figure declined once more to twenty-five hundred in 1990. *'Bout all the long-term jobs around here are took. The only thing to go into is the coal mines. Ain't no hope in that, though, in goin' into the coal mines. They is layin' so many off, back there, right now. There was two to three mines closed down up there where I live, here recently. Knocked people outta work.*

Two large outside-owned coal companies produce the most coal and employ the most miners, several hundred each. They are followed closely by three or four smaller, local companies like Creed Parker's that employ around two hundred men, pay competitive wages, and produce about 800,000 tons per year. In addition to these larger operators, the county has many subcontractors who work for the big mining concerns, and many "dog-hole" mines—small, often unsafe operations that pay low wages and have no benefits. One hard-pressed small operator working a couple of dog-hole mines said he considered federal black-lung payments a kind of benefit package available to his employees, since his small outfit could not afford a company pension plan.

Even when mines are owned by outside corporations, jobs are obtained through friends and family. *These coal mines, it's usually generation after generation, father to son, uncle, nephew*, Creed Parker explains. Those who hire are local, and local rules apply. *If we got somebody that's worked here for years that has got a son that wants a job, he would probably get a little break. I think he ought to. That's my way of looking at it. If his daddy did well for us for years, why not give his child a job? You've no way to really measure people, because most of them you don't know. You look at where they've worked and what experience they've got, if they've got experience. But in this day and time, we can generally try to hire somebody that has some experience. Two or three years at least. And then we try to train them in our way of doing things.* Jim Campton, a longtime Blackwell resident and manager at a large outside-owned coal operation, explained that his company gives priority to sons over "outside" applicants because miners have such a high degree of dependency on one another.

Today fast-food and retail jobs make up over one fourth of the jobs in the county, about as much as coal mining. But as Joey Scott pointed out, these are low-wage and often part-time jobs, jobs that workers supplement with public assistance or see as only a portion of a family's income, with one or more other workers. These twenty-five hundred fast-food and retail jobs are made available through word of mouth and whom you know, but the fact that there are relatively more of these in the county means that they are more "open" than other jobs. The men and women I interviewed who work only in fast-food restaurants really struggle to make ends meet. They generally get fewer hours than they want, and they all say customers can be cranky and demanding.

Social service workers point out that the new fast-food restaurants have made it possible for more women to work for the first time. In the 1970s many low-income women saw welfare as a way to stay home and be a mother, but now women want to work, and these jobs offer some the opportunity. The welfare director explained how changing times have affected the mountains. *Nowadays I think there are more that want to do better. Back in the 1970s it was just get out of school, even drop out of school, get married and have children, then divorce. And that was going to be a way of life because their ambition in life was to be a housewife and take care of their children. Nowadays they want to do something. They want to have a job and become a nurse.*

Employment in the schools—which includes not only teaching but also working as an aide or in the cafeteria or janitorial services—provides a significant portion of the jobs here, and the allocation of these jobs, as we have heard, has long been a matter of patronage politics. School board members are elected to represent small communities in the county, and it is widely agreed that they are elected to look after their constituents' job needs, not the education of their children. Corruption and patronage in Central Appalachian schools are well known. Many deplore the situation, as Creed Parker and Joey Scott do, but most despair about changing it.

John Martin, an educator and community leader, has concluded, *You can't break the whole web. You can maybe break strands of it, and you hope, somehow, when they get rewoven, that they're different people with different ideas and things change a little. But I haven't seen it change.* In recent years Blackwell's system has been taken over by the state, but students still report chaos and employers still say graduates cannot read or write. The cost of these politicized schools is literally the future of the region's children. In 1990 only half the adults in Blackwell had completed high school, compared with 75 percent nationally.

The body politic in Blackwell has been corrupt since the turn of the century when coal operators seized control. Elections have been declared null by state officials on more than one occasion, and the area's violent reputation dates back to political battles over school trustee positions. Labor struggles in the mines became virtual wars, wildcat strikes have been common, and the area has been known for high homicide rates since the early 1900s. Some of those I interviewed recalled dangerous times when coal companies and unions were in bitter conflict. A former company man said, *There was a strike up there at the mines, and it was a very, very bad strike. We had to go in on armored trucks. I wore a pistol everywhere I went. As a matter of fact, I had two of them on me at all times. There was a time when I was involved in planning several things where we said, "If the union did this, we were going to do this." And I'm talking about some destructive things. That didn't bother me at all. Here were people that were trying to do something to us, if we're going to do it to them. That's revenge, we'll get revenge. If they kill one of ours, we're going to kill two of theirs.*

A union organizer described the threats he received, and his own reputation for toughness. *Well, I was vulnerable. They threatened to kill my kids and blow my house up. They said, "You've got a little girl that gets off the school bus at such and such a time." Oh yeah, they tried all of that on me. They operate everywhere from bribery and killing, and lying and slandering. But in everything I ever do, I play rough. But make no doubt about it, I was scared a lot of times. There were times when I carried a gun in my lunch bucket. Get me a small gun, I would carry it in my boot in case anything came up. You know, underground somebody could knock you in the head and pull a big rock down on you and call it an accident.* He also described making deals with a local judge, trading union support of the judge in the next election for a favorable outcome in a case.

School politics is rarely violent, but it is nearly always corrupt. Control over jobs and contracts in the school system is still a source of power and wealth, and the scrambles for them have compromised social relationships and undermined civic institutions throughout Blackwell. Schools are concerned more with the politics of jobs and contracts than education, and politics is not about civic participation or working for the common good—politics is for gain. *They're not into it to help anyone. They want to hoard up everything—they're scared of losing it. People are uneducated so they don't trust anybody; they're scared.* Professionals' and merchants' families who live in the county seat say, *"Nice people" don't get involved in the county schools because "that's politics."* Like Creed Parker, they say that *politics are dirty*.

Willy Granger, a wealthy coal operator and owner of several businesses, including a construction company, a truck dealership, and a coal equipment supply operation, is in politics. *He's illiterate, but he's filthy rich. He pulls a lot of political strings. The county gets all their trucks from him*, according to a schoolteacher. Willy controls the governor's "patronage man," the person connected to the governor's campaign and administration whom you need to go through to get any kind of state job. *The patronage man here is one of the most powerful men. The government gives him the power to divvy up jobs here in the county, and with jobs the way they are, that is a lot of power*. But people say Willy also wields power over county jobs in law enforcement, administration, and the schools. As a leading political operative in the county, his power is based on his ability both to give and to take away. If you and your family have voted with the right faction you may get jobs in the school cafeteria, on the roads or sanitation crew, or in the classroom. If you have voted with the wrong faction, you will lose those jobs or, if you are a tenured teacher, you may be moved to a less desirable, more remote school. He and the school superintendent and board members determine who gets what public jobs. Some suggest that he and his political allies "ran out" a newspaper editor several years ago who was covering county affairs too thoroughly, attending hearings and meetings and writing complete stories in the weekly paper. The current paper is in no danger of violating the norms of silence—it consists mostly of advertisements and coverage of some high school sports events.

Everyone knows Willy Granger, just as they know the patronage man at any given time and the whole cast of political operators in Blackwell. *They meet down at the Shadyside Restaurant for lunch and they all talk, and they're all very powerful people. They're* very *powerful people. They have money—they've made it in the coal business or they've made it someplace, and they have lots of powerful friends*. Greg Benton, the return migrant who described how his good family connections got him a bank loan, also had good qualifications for a state job. He had scored the highest on the state exam, yet he was passed over time and time again for a job in the Welfare Department. Finally, his girlfriend's family told him that he needed to speak to the patronage man. Within a week of doing so, he had a job.

Another public employee who needed the patronage man to appoint him said, *Oh, yes, there is a patronage man and I know who he is. Now I have never done more than nodded my head, never spoke to him. When all of us in this office go out to Shadyside for lunch, he'd be out there. I didn't talk with him directly. My manager did. My manager said, "Look, I have to have him in order to operate." So I didn't have to go to him and say, "Please give me this job and I'll vote this way or I'll vote that way." But it certainly happens that way.*

Supervisors of government offices and school principals explain that they have to take the people the patronage man recommends, but in the better agencies or institutions the administration has the patronage man's agreement that they may let go those who do not do a good job. Everyone takes this system for granted, and even those who criticize it do not see any way to bring about change. *It's like a big wheel. You can't change it.*

The effects on the quality of education and the honesty of the justice system are deep and far-reaching. Teachers who are hired because of their political connections are often neither interested nor skilled in teaching, and the whole dynamic of relying on power and politics rather than merit extends even to how students are evaluated and rewarded. Some powerfully placed parents expect their children to receive passing grades because of who they are, not what they have accomplished. *If teachers try to enforce discipline they get calls at night—parents calling and hollering and stuff if little Janie doesn't get on the honor roll, or if privileges are taken from their children. It's the wealthier families, because the poor people don't hardly go into the schools. But the wealthier ones, they think they should be able to buy everything their child needs, including its education.*

A retired teacher recalled, *If the child made a grade that was not what the parent thought the child should make, it was never the child's fault in lots of families; it was always your fault. I had one student whose father was a board member. They had five children. I think I had four of them; three were good students and one wasn't. They were given the benefit of every doubt because of who they were. But I did not give them anything. I just could never do that. And on report-card day the mother came in and said to me, "My son made all Bs except in your class and he made a C." I said, "Well, I had to stretch it for him to have a C." And she said, "You must not be a very good teacher." They are very wealthy people. They are very into politics and they control a lot of the schools.*

The most significant impact is on the quality of teaching in the classroom. Student after student talks about just passing the time in class rather than studying or learning. Those who attended schools in other regions remark on how much lower the expectations and standards are for learning and behavior here in Blackwell. Greg Benton, for example, who went through his sophomore year in Ohio, found a dramatic difference. *Where I lived in Ohio was pretty much a middle-class town with excellent schools. You just didn't get up and walk out of class if you wanted to and go into town. There's no doubt in my mind that teachers were much better trained and they cared a whole lot more. I think that the county system has been the good ol' boys' system for far too long. A lot of them say, "Hey, I have a job and I'll never lose this job." And they just get lax. I think they just don't care.*

The disarray of the school system reflects a more general corruption and disorganization in the political system. The people I interviewed insist that votes are bought here still. A political middleman, now "retired," described how he would work with the larger families. *I pick the families, and I'll get thirty people working for me over there, for say forty dollars apiece. They're all working for the same thing. They all have families. You get them out of big families, you know. I had families I relied on, whom I taught how to do this.* A nineteen-year-old boy whose father and grandfather have long been involved in the politics of their little coal camp, delivering votes to the right people at the right time, said it looked as if he was going to have to get involved in politics. *If I'm ever going to have a job, I'm going to have to get into it, get to know the right people and stuff. The only way you can really get a job is to know somebody, you know, real good.* His father had backed the wrong person in the previous school board race. *Well, the guys that my dad was for the last time didn't get in, so my dad just changed over to the other guys and they just talked and stuff and they told my dad they'd help me and my older brother get a job. A couple of weeks ago I went up there to put my application in at the school board, they told me to go up there and put this guy's name, so I put his name down. They're supposed to get in touch with him and they said they'd help me get a job. This guy's best friend is on the school board.*

Throughout the county I heard detailed accounts of voting fraud. Some people were paid, $150 in some cases, $50 in others, and some were given liquor for their votes. Since the laws have been tightened in recent years, the tactics have changed. Money might accidentally drop on the driveway when people get out of the car, for example. But men and women of all ages had stories of buying and selling votes. Some activists think they detect a change. People take the money but then vote according to their choice, newly confident that their vote is private. But others are less sanguine. *There's no doubt there is vote buying. I mean this place is historical for elections being bought and this last election was no exception. It's been like that forever.*

The corruption extends directly to the legal system, where people say that the way traffic tickets, driving without a license or tags, drunken driving, drug offenses, child and spouse abuse, and littering are dealt with depends on your reputation and your clout with the powerful. Justice is often dispensed according to political allegiances and family alliances rather than the merits of the case, and currying favor for vote-getting erodes law enforcement in everything. One police officer, for example, who refers to those from bad families as "scum, pure scum," explained how people are dealt with when they are caught with marijuana. *It depends on who you are. Some people we'll just let go, but there are others that we'll scrape off their roach clip in order to get them on possession. It depends.* Candidates spend more than $20,000 to run for a position as sheriff that pays $38,000—*and it wasn't that they needed the job, it was just where it would put them and how they could benefit in the long run.*

A schoolteacher described a serious, obvious case of child abuse that was not prosecuted because the adult involved had a large family and an election was coming up. *We had a child here one time that the mother's boyfriend got drunk and put whiskey in the child's milk and it cried and he burned it with cigarettes, burns all over its body. It was brought to this same pediatrician I was talking to, and he said, "I will have something done about this if it is the last thing that I do. Something will be done." This has been years ago. He turned it in, I don't know to what official, but they wouldn't do anything because they had an election coming up and this fellow had a big family.*

A minister explained the reluctance to prosecute littering. If a large family that brings a block of votes is held accountable, the official will suffer retaliation and not be reelected. Indeed, there is no commitment, even from public works, to remedying the situation. *A member of my congregation has a lot of garbage in his creek. People throw things in there, and when it rains, garbage washes up against his bridge, and it all won't go through. So he'll call them to clean it up. The county or somebody else will send some people up there with a truck and some shovels and pitchforks. But instead of putting it on a truck and hauling it off, they just pitch it over the other side of this guy's bridge!*

Greg Benton, after living away for many years, was shocked to see the way every dimension of the public sector is enmeshed in politics. *We have not been real good at enforcing the laws. People have been allowed to build substandard structures and substandard homes, substandard sewage, you know, everything. Until they start enforcing these laws it will never get cleaned up.* Property assessments vary according to political positioning rather than house value, and the county gives farm tax exemption status to several times the number of farms counted by the state department of agriculture. *There's a lot of tax dollars out there that aren't being collected. It is all politics.*

A newcomer from Ohio summed up her impression of local justice this way: *There's no law here. It's not like anyplace else in the world. A few people just run the town the way they see fit. If somebody commits a crime and they know him, or he is a cousin's brother or somebody's sister or such crap like that, then he's free. But you can't say nothing, you can't do nothing. They'd probably kill you or you'd have an accident somehow.* In the absence of reliable, neutral law enforcement, family members look to one another for protection and security. Women rely on family members rather than the police to protect them from violent ex-husbands, and stories of law dispensed according to family names and influence abound.

A forty-year-old woman whose husband and sons have been stopped for DUI (driving under the influence of alcohol) complained that they paid larger fines and stayed in jail longer than many others because they do not have political connections. *I don't think it's fair. Now my Jerry got stopped for drunk driving, and he got fined and plus he had to stay a few days in jail. Our neighbor's father-in-law knows a lot of people in the courthouse and stuff, and he paid like fifty-nine dollars and that was it—no jail. If I go to town or whatever without tags on my car, I'm gonna get picked up. But others get away with it.* The punishment extends beyond the fine and time served in jail, since her son can no longer get a job anywhere because his name has appeared in the paper for drunken driving.

Willy Granger is one of those who oversee this political fiefdom—and when he is personally attacked, he invariably gets even. An earnest young police officer who violated the norms by arresting Willy's nephew for wife beating was later denied a promotion based on a small technicality that most agree would never have stopped him if he had not made an enemy of Granger. *That boy, Granger's nephew, he said, "I'll have your job for this." And sure enough, they waited and they got his job*, says a person familiar with the case.

Some managers in public offices or agencies insist that they would be set up for sexual harassment, discrimination, or even embezzlement complaints if they were found to be disloyal. *If they decide to get rid of me, they would find somebody who would come up here and say that I tried to sexually assault them. I'm ruined for life and I've done absolutely nothing. People are that way here. If they want to get you, they'll get you hard and they'll get rid of you. And that could follow me far outside of Blackwell. Then all of a sudden them or nobody else will hire me.*

Everything is run according to the will of those in control, and every violation carries the risk of repercussions, not just for the individual rebel but for his or her family members as well. The result is a lawless social world, a world run as if by the mob, where favors and political allegiances determine access to resources, merit is irrelevant, and no one trusts public officials. When this corrupt civic fabric is combined with a deep prejudice against those from "bad" families, the opportunities for moving out of poverty are virtually shut down.

BLACKWELL'S HAVE-NOTS: SCRATCHING A LIVING UP THE HOLLOWS

Gwen Boggs is a slim, pale complexioned thirty-year-old woman with green eyes and strawberry blond hair drawn back in a bun. She sits at her linoleum kitchen table, still dressed in her restaurant uniform. A fan blows toward us from the open, screenless doorway in the old trailer that she and her husband rent from her uncle. Her uncle and aunt live up the road in the old family place, and her mother lives with Gwen's youngest sister and brother in another trailer down below hers. The dirt road is rutted—*we have tried for years to get gravel up here but we don't know the right people*, she explains.

The Boggses' trailer is small but neatly kept, with children's toys piled in a plastic milk crate in the corner and the day's laundry just off the line and folded in a red plastic basket nearby. In the summer the family spends most of their time outside, sitting on the steps or in lawn chairs under the gnarled apple tree. Gwen has geraniums growing in extra-large pear cans on the stoop, and children's bikes and other toys are scattered around the yard. A vegetable garden with knee-high corn, full tomato plants, and beans tied to a homemade trellis lies just up the hill beyond the apple tree. There are two rabbits in a homemade cage at the end of the trailer near the stream that runs down the hillside.

Gwen grew up in this hollow, in a small house with her parents and seven brothers and sisters. Her father, like both her grandfathers and her husband's grandfathers, worked in the mines from the time he dropped out of school in the sixth grade at fifteen until his death. He died four years ago, after twenty-five years in dog-hole mines where work was intermittent, depending on the spot market for coal. There were times when he would be out of work for a month or more, and during the 1970s they would use "stamps" to put food on the table. When Gwen was about eight her father hurt his back badly in the mines and was out of work for months. She recalls that they drew some kind of check during that time.

Although her father worked hard in the mines, Gwen remembers many weeks during the 1960s and early 1970s when they did not have enough to eat. And there were never any extras. *My childhood was hard. We picked wild apples and stuff, and Mom would make hot little apple cakes. We would gather berries. In the winter it would get even harder. We had mostly beans, potatoes, and corn bread. I would come home from school and complain. Mom would say, "Well, we're not having beans and potatoes, we're having potatoes and beans." She would say something like that. Biscuits and gravy, grease and water and flour. I told her we were going to get rickets, with no juice and fruits. But we couldn't afford it. It was rough.*

Gwen's parents could not read or write, and neither drove a car. Their social circle included close family members, aunts and uncles and cousins. *They didn't really go out and go to anything. Church—you know, we would go to church, but as far as going out and associating and meeting with people, they're not really talkative. They were quiet and withdrawn.* Both her parents were very traditional. Her mother, who had dropped out of school in seventh grade, was deeply religious, committed to the small Little Shepherd Primitive Baptist Church just down the road. *My mother—I love her and I would turn the world around for my mom—but she was really strict. I got to go to camp once, a Christian camp, and when I got back she burned my bathing suit. No shorts, no makeup. She was real old-fashioned and really, really strict. And Dad was the type of man that a whipping was all he knew. To straighten you out, it was a straight whipping. Nothing but a whipping—with a belt, a switch, he would give you a good one, one you wouldn't forget, even when I was a teenager. In my life I guess I had more fear of him than really loved him.*

Gwen enjoyed school. She liked her friends, and she remembers it was a great treat when they had juice and fruit. She is creative, and these days she invents art projects with her own children using everyday materials. In school she especially liked history. *I loved learning about the pyramids, you know, reading through the history books and seeing how they would make things out of gold. I really got into history*. But other children were hard on her. *Kids made fun of me because of not having decent clothes and things. Most of what we had was hand-me-downs, this one to that one, to make ends meet. You just never fit in*.

Her teacher confirmed that many children who came to school in poor clothes, or in some cases, dirty, were ridiculed. *If a child is well dressed and is a little blond princess, she is going to be treated different by the other kids, and sometimes by the teachers, than a very poorly dressed child. I think my one big contribution was I could get closer to the children who didn't have much, who needed help. But they were treated different, sometimes by the teachers, and by the children. I have seen children who came very poorly dressed, who didn't smell good, just treated horribly and it always broke my heart. They were courageous to be there*.

When Gwen was thirteen she visited her aunt on the Chesapeake Bay. *The very best time of my life was when I went to spend the summer with my aunt in Virginia. I stayed the whole summer and it was different from here. That was the first time in my life I had ever seen a lot of water. To me it was like the ocean, but it's just a big bay. And we went out on boats, we hunted sharks' teeth, we had cookouts. The first time I ever saw crabs, and clams, and things like that. All that was new to me*.

Through grade school Gwen studied hard and received good grades. Her mother always insisted that she and her brothers and sisters come right home after school. In high school she learned that there were "good rich kids" and "bad poor kids," and she found herself left out of social activities until at fifteen she began to run with a bad crowd. They would stay up all night, drinking and smoking pot, and on several occasions she was picked up by the police and spent a night in jail. *That kind of got me out of school*, she remembers with a smile.

At seventeen she met Billy, her husband, and got pregnant with her daughter. Her daughter was born out of wedlock, but Gwen and Billy married afterward. In quick succession she had Jack and then Danny. *Having the children made me grow up, turned my whole world around*. Today the children are thirteen, eleven, and nine.

For the past year and a half she has worked forty hours a week at a fast-food restaurant, but for eight years before that she worked on and off at a half dozen restaurants. She would work for a while, with her mother or sister taking care of the children, and then she would stop and stay home. She earns minimum wage, and last year her income was $5,400. *I would like better, but it's really hard to get a job in a small community like this. Most of the time it's not what you know, it's who you know. There's a lot of family business here, and it goes to kin—cousins, brothers, sisters and nieces, nephews.*

Billy works in timber, running a skidder and a bulldozer for a small logging operation. Since his work depends on good, dry weather and machines not breaking down, he averages about three or four days of work a week. He has to go on unemployment every winter. Last year he earned $12,000. They have no benefits and pay cash for medical care, and Gwen cannot get ahead enough to put together the money to go back to school. *Well, now if you're married, it's hard to get help. But if you're divorced, or you just have children and you're not married, then you can get welfare, food stamps, hospital card, bills paid for you to go to school. That's the way with my sister—she didn't go, but I wish she had went. She has got three children and she is not married. The government housing program pays for her house, they help pay half of her electric, she gets stamps, a medical card, welfare, so much a month, and they offer her the opportunity to go to the college up here and let her get training and so forth. But, like if you're married and he is working and if you're working, it's really a struggle and it's hard. It's very expensive with three children. And then as far as the hospital and all of that, you don't get anything. You pay cash. Whatever we get is straight cash or we don't get it.*

Gwen and Billy have had hard times from the beginning, always pressed by bills and unstable income, and the marriage has not been smooth. *At first, oh, I thought he was everything. Then after the kids came, pressures got hard, and we had a lot of problems. We've come really close to separating quite a few times. Then as the kids—I guess it was pressure from the kids, and then me putting it on him. Then he would be working and I would be sitting at home taking care of the kids. The kids need this and that. Money was barely reaching, stretching all the time. So it put a lot of pressure on him. It got really bad for a while, then it would get better, then it would get worse. But lately, since the kids are a little bit older, it has been better.* She sighs. *Billy and me, I guess we will probably stay together now.*

Gwen sees her children as the most important part of her life, and she invests her dreams in them. *My kids are my life. I have built my world around my kids. I want better for my kids than what I have.* Her voice softens as she talks about what makes her feel good about herself. *I don't really know how to explain that. I guess when I see my children doing well. When they come home with a test and we have studied and studied, and it's over and they do well. When generally things go well for them, you feel that you have done the best that you can do.*

But I try not to let anything get me down too much. I don't do it. I feel you need to face every day one day at a time. You have to learn to work your way around the bad times, or make the best of the situation that you're in, because you've got to keep going. Gwen admires those who have the ability to survive when times are hard. *I admire people who—I guess women in particularly—like my mom and a lot of other ladies that have really had a very hard life and have come through it with still a smile on their face.*

There is an independent streak in Gwen. She rebelled in a destructive way when she was a young teenager, and regrets that time and what her "messing up" cost her. She has thought of going to talk to high school classes about the high price she paid for running around wild, and she would like to see some kind of recreation center where young people can go and be supervised but on their own a little too. As an adult, she is active in her children's school activities. Last year she organized a petition to make the school bus safer. She is confident now, and does not feel inferior to people who have more than she does. *Okay, as far money goes, I put myself in the poor community. But as far as feeling goes, I feel I am just as good as the person living on Redbud Hill.*

She still holds on to the hope that she can go back to school and get a degree in early childhood education. *Well, as far as the waitressing job, the job is okay. I don't particularly love it, but I would rather work than sit at home, and I have my own independence. I have a car, my husband co-signed for me so I could get my loan to get the car. I'm now making the payments, it's all my money. It gives me independence. We go together as far as the bills and so forth, but there is some things like you just need inside of you to know that you are doing it on your own, that you're not depending on him every time you need something. Before I started working, it's like, "Can I have this?" Or if you buy someone a gift, you have to ask. I know it's our money and even then I was doing my share, taking care of the kids and the house. But inside, it's still not like you are getting it yourself.*

She has ambition for her children—and keeps her dreams for them in her head as she helps with their homework or makes up art projects with them. Above all, she wants them to avoid the mistakes that she made and not have to struggle the way she and Billy have. And she hopes they will not give up and fall into the trap of those who have lost hope in Blackwell. *I want them to not drop out, not to end up sitting on the porch all day. I want my girl not to marry and get pregnant too young, but to have a good family when she is ready. And then my boys, I don't want them to have children, and go to work, and barely be able to feed them, or barely be able to put diapers on them, and just have to scrounge, like Billy and myself. My daughter, if she does marry, that's great. But I would like her to have her own job and a car of her own, know how to drive, and not be totally dependent on a man. My boys, I don't want them in the mines. I want them to do better for themselves. You know, they don't have to be doctors, lawyers. They can be teachers, nurses, social workers. Even like the restaurant work, maybe they may want to get to be the operator or owner of it, but not just work in it as a hard, scrounging, everyday job to get by.*

For now, she puts her own dreams on hold and looks to the future her children can have. Of constantly struggling to make ends meet, she says, *It puts a strain on your relationship, and you may do and say things that you don't really want to do or say. But you do it out of just frustration, when you want to do better and can't do better. Like Billy has told me many times after we fight and argue, "Well, honey, I want to do better. I want you to have better to wear. I want the kids to have better to wear. I want us to have better to eat. I would like to take us somewhere too." Then he gets frustrated on himself because he can't do that for us. And you may say and do a lot of things you don't mean.*

More than likely I probably won't get to do what I want to do until really later in life, and even then I may not get the chance. But what I see for myself is seeing that my children—not live my life through my children—but see that my children do have the opportunity in their life to do something, make something out of themselves.

Gwen and Billy live right on the edge, with no security and no cushion. They are surviving, but they are not getting ahead. They both dropped out of school, and their limited education and their parents' low status and lack of connections have limited their job prospects. Local institutions fail them—the schools, the health care system. Even though Gwen is supporting her children and helping them with homework, the schools themselves are so bad that her children may graduate without the skills they need for work. But national safety-net policies also fail them. The Boggses are the working poor—uninsured, unprotected, and struggling to keep a marriage and family together against the odds.

Wanda Turner, only twenty-six, has also had a hard life. Her once pretty, china-doll-like face is drawn, and there are big circles under her blue eyes. As we talk, she holds a cigarette in her left hand, chain smoking, and nervously runs her right hand through her shoulder-length blond hair. We sit on the wooden steps that lead up to her run-down trailer, way back in this hollow that was once a thriving coal camp. Her seven-month-old baby is napping inside, her four-year-old is wading in the creek, and her twins, now eleven, are playing up in the woods behind the trailer.

This cluster of trailers is back at the end of a rough, winding road. The creek that runs alongside it is littered with plastic bottles, and large trash bags hang from low trees on the banks. About fifty yards from where Wanda's son plays, an old rusty car straddles the creek before a bend. Wanda's own yard is full of debris and trash, discarded toys, car parts, an old armchair with the stuffing coming out where a cat curls up with two kittens.

Wanda spent all her teen years on welfare with a mother who drank heavily and moved from town to town in this coal region. Her father was a coal miner who had gone through the third grade and into the mines as a teenager. He was ten years older than her mother, and after they divorced when Wanda was twelve he lost contact with the family until four years ago when he was dying of cancer.

There were eight children in the family, and there was often not enough to eat. Her father and mother were both alcoholics, and one of Wanda's few memories of her father was when he was drunk and used a gun to control his children. *He would just make us sit down on the floor and hold a gun on us. He said he was going to kill us if we didn't sit still. He has hit me with his fist a few times. I got real aggravated when I was eleven and I ran away. I was walking down the road and he came by in his truck and he said, "Get in." So I got in. He pulled a gun out from behind the seat and he said, "If you don't be quiet the rest of the day," he said, "I'll shoot you." So I was quiet.*

She and her sister and six brothers were close and supported one another during these rough times at home. They still pull together. *In our family, if somebody needs help, the others will always pitch in and try to help them out—financially or physically, whatever it takes. That is the way we all work. Because all we had was each other growing up. Mom and Dad drank. We all had each other to lean on. We would get in the back room and try to figure out what would be best to do.*

Moving around as a teen meant that Wanda sometimes attended three or more high schools in one year. She and her brothers dropped behind and lost any connection to school. Like Gwen, she describes a school with two kinds of students. *There were the rich kids, who had things, and they stuck together, and then there was us poor kids, and we stayed away from the rich kids.* When she was fifteen she dropped out, pregnant, and married the nineteen-year-old with whom she had the twins. He began to drink and "lay around," sometimes getting rough on her, other times disappearing for days. They moved back in with Wanda's mother and depended on her check and on his parents, who had a miner's pension, for money.

When we first got married he had a job, but that didn't last too long and when we moved back in with Mom, we stayed with her maybe two months. Then we moved back out again and he held a job at the mine supply downtown. He worked there maybe a month, but it just got too hard for him to handle. He wouldn't work, he stayed drunk all the time, and he roughed up the boys, so I just got out of it. She moved back with her mother and younger sister, into an old trailer that had an extra room added on by a previous tenant. It was crowded quarters, especially during the winter months when they had to be inside so much of the time.

Over the years Wanda has suffered from "nerves," and often she will go see Jackson Jones and get a prescription to calm herself. Because her experience at the hospital has been so negative, she also goes to Jackson Jones when she can for the children, even though she cannot use Medicaid there. *There's one doctor over in town, Jackson Jones, and you can see him for ten dollars and that's the only place I know to go. The hospital up here will not let you in unless you have the payment with you to pay them for whatever you do—an office visit or if you have surgery done, you have to have it paid, they have a right to refuse you. One time I didn't have my medical card, and my boy had pneumonia and the hospital refused to let Dr. Harris or Dr. Stanley see me. They said, "If you people all would have your card or pay your bill, this hospital wouldn't be in the shape it's in." My child was refused and I came back up later that evening and went through the emergency room, because the child was about dead if they didn't see him. He was admitted and stayed in for seven days. I had a card and I just couldn't find it, and if they had just taken my social security number and runned it through, the state would have paid for it. They act that way to people who are on welfare and who have those medical cards, poor people that have to be pushed back and waiting.*

Wanda has been on AFDC since she left her husband five years ago, and she and the children also use her mother's food stamps. She has tried to get child support, but she says the county attorney provides no help if you are not connected with someone big, and she has no ties. At the time we talked, in the early 1990s, there was a new child support program to help women like her try to collect, and she thought it might help.

There were other changes in the welfare system in those years as well—including the creation of a series of education and work programs collectively known as JOBS, part of the Family Support Act passed in 1988—and the possibilities they offered made Wanda cautiously hopeful about change in her life. Her caseworker, Marlene Combs, seemed to really take an interest in her and what she would need to get off welfare and into the workforce. *When I first talked with Marlene, she just came right out and told me things. She didn't care, she just said what was on her mind. That's what I liked—she was a real great friend. That's what you need, someone to turn you over, give you a boost in this world, like me being so backwards and shy.*

At first she was intimidated by Marlene's demands. *Marlene threatened me big time, and that got me scared.* Last month the program bought her new teeth, replacing the rotting, broken ones she had had for many years. And Marlene has given her tips on how to wear makeup and suggested she make her hair more stylish—shorter and curly in front, instead of the more old-fashioned straight style most people associate with traditional, poor mountain women. Marlene is encouraging her to earn her General Educational Development (GED) certificate, perhaps get some training as a nurse's aide, so she might find work out at the rest home.

Wanda knows there are very powerful people who control opportunities. *The Parkers and Scotts run things. Mostly they got the money and the power, and everybody's kind of afraid of 'em 'cause they know what they can do. They have a lot of pull in Blackwell.* People seem to be out for their own family. Even those in charge of the local food bank and secondhand clothes projects seem to keep the best things for their friends and family. *People try to keep you down,* she says. *I don't really hardly look ahead anymore. I used to did, but I got so disheartened, I just thought, "Quit dreamin'."*

Randy Perkins is a solid thirty-five-year-old man with red hair, green eyes, and a rugged face. He lives way up the mountain in the southern end of the county with his young wife and two boys in a house he built himself on family land. Like Gwen and Wanda, Randy had a hard childhood in a poor mountain family. His father was disabled in the mines when Randy was a small boy, and the family of eight depended on the garden and, often, the charity of relatives. When the food stamp program was first established you had to buy the stamps, and Randy's father worked at odd jobs to earn enough money to get them. But Randy remembers the same tiresome potatoes-and-beans menu that Gwen complained about.

During the 1970s students in Blackwell's public schools were still required to buy their textbooks. Like many children in the poorer mountain families, Randy did not have the money for books. *My daddy, he couldn't afford my books. Books was high. I went into what they call a special education class where they furnish your books and I stayed in that for four years. We didn't do nothing in school. We didn't have to go to class. The teacher would take us out and we played baseball every day. I got around. Sometimes I would pick up garbage in the house, chase women, but I didn't learn nothing. I'm afraid I was smarter than that teacher was anyway.*

Randy worked part time while in his teens, and he gave the money he earned to the family. When he graduated, still unable to read or write well, he started to put more time into work. For ten years he worked whatever hours he could get at a hardware supply store, combining the $150 he earned there with food stamps. Hours were irregular and pay was low, but he liked the job. There were no benefits, but he is confident that Lester Jones, the store's owner, would have paid any doctor bills he ran up. After all, when he broke his glasses the old man paid to repair them.

For the past ten years Randy has run a small business trading used car parts. If he needs to buy gas or a Christmas toy for his boys, he might ask for cash, but generally he trades without money. He considers himself a pretty good carpenter, electrician, and plumber. People who know him trust him, so he can run up charges as high as $300 a month at the little country grocery store at the bottom of the mountain until his AFDC check comes in, and even the utility company will let him go two months if necessary before he pays his light bill. In the early 1990s, he was getting about $300 in food stamps and $285 in AFDC for his two boys each month, plus a medical card. In the winter he can get coal delivered from the Community Action Agency. So from various sources—food stamps, aid for the children, odd jobs, and whatever else is available—Randy manages to piece together a livelihood. Although he appears in census statistics as a "nonworking working-age male," he is actually working in an underground economy.

The hours he puts in on junkyard business vary with the customers and the flow of the day. *It all depends. One customer, he may come up and he may have nothing to do and he may sit around and talk for half a day. I love to sit under the shade tree and talk. If I make ten dollars off him before he leaves, I'm happy.* Randy values the flexibility he has. He would like to eventually own a junkyard himself, but he would need funds for insurance and start-up costs that he does not have, and in the meantime he enjoys trading. *A guy come down the other day and wanted a transmission, but he couldn't afford one—they're on food stamps too. Jobs is hard to get here. He didn't have no money and he needed a transmission and he couldn't go to the grocery store. He had an old truck sitting around that I wanted. The truck wasn't worth anything but I wanted to deal. If I want something, I want it. So I take the man's truck and charge five dollars. My trucks was a little low on fuel—I had to put in two dollars' worth to get up here this morning. I built me a wrecker. It is an old '65 model and I built it piece by piece, but I ain't got enough money to go on the road with it. I got a sixteen-foot trailer, so I put it behind my truck and had him put his truck on it. Took two hours.*

Another advantage Randy sees in his current work arrangement is having the chance to spend time with his wife. When he was twenty-two Randy decided he ought to get married. *I got to looking for a wife and her brother knew me well and he took me home and introduced me. She was a little blonde, a little doll, and she was sitting on the bed and I decided, "Hell, I can't do nothing with this girl. I'm too ugly to date with something like this." We set there for a few minutes and I decided, "Well, if I can kiss her, I'll stay, and if I can't, I'll be on my way." I reached over there and kissed her and then I started taking her out.* They were married in a short time, and she dropped out of school at fifteen. *She is my onliest pleasure. We hardly ever fight. I don't see no sense in it really. I've seen men and women fight and knock each other out and all this.* He wouldn't change his life now because *I get to stay home with Momma plenty. I treasure her—and*, he laughs, *we 'bout wore out that waterbed of ours.*

Randy is content with his life on and around the mountain. He is related to all the families up the hollow. *There is something you have to understand about this community. We are all kin, everybody. The whole community where I live at, unless some outsider moves into the neighborhood, we are all kin. So everybody on the mountain is just kin. Dogwood Branch has got about seven hundred people in it; Pine Valley has got a couple of hundred; Milton has got a couple of hundred. You can look in the phone book through all the Perkins and there are about thirty-five sets of Perkins in that book. There are more Perkins than anything else in the whole county, Perkins, Combs, and Bledsoes, and we are all kin. And we pretty much live all together.*

They vote as a bloc for their magistrate, Ira Bledsoe—*a good ol' country boy*, Randy says, *who will set and talk with you on a lawn chair no matter who you are.* When Randy needs gravel on his road or the weeds need cutting so he can see around the bends when he is driving, he just gives Ira a call. The hollows have some bootleggers, but the police do not bother them much since they just do a local business—buying beer and liquor over the line and selling it here in Little Pine. *It's local boys mostly and they don't bother nobody. They don't set in the middle of the road and pee in front of women. They will buy it, and then go down in the hollow and get drunk. It really doesn't matter because the people that bootleg, they are not causing any problems, and the cops don't bother you if you are not a problem. Just every once in a while the cops have to do their job and get some names in the paper*. Randy himself does not drink anything but RC Colas, but his grandpappy and brother are heavy drinkers and often spend the money their families need on liquor. *We don't drink or smoke or take dope or nothing like that. We can't afford it if we wanted to; don't drink no coffee. That's it*. He raises his eyebrows and grins, *I do go through a carton of RC in a day*.

Randy and his family can get by when they combine public assistance, trading car parts, and some odd jobs. He gets along with everyone except his mother-in-law, and he likes to think a lot of people would come to his funeral if he were killed. He would like to have a little more money—to buy a better truck and to be able to put a few more things under the tree for his boys at Christmas. He would like to get his own junkyard going and not depend on food stamps any longer. He is a self-taught handyman who can do odd jobs—so he says he does not miss the learning he never got in school. He is a devoted husband and father, a good son and brother. He is engaged enough in politics to get gravel for his road and coal from the community assistance service. As long as public assistance programs are available, he can provide for his family even when there are no jobs.

Things are not going as well for Virgil Bratcher. Virgil, thirty-six, is a large man, six feet tall, with a weathered face, a broad, once-broken nose, and distinctively floppy ears. Like Randy, Virgil lives up in the mountains and pieces together a living doing odd jobs and collecting public assistance. When he married in the late 1970s his wife's mother gave them a little piece of land way back in the hills in the northern part of the county, and he used scrap lumber from an abandoned coal tipple to build a little house. They have electricity, but no phone, and haul their water from a nearby spring. *See, right now I own my own home, my own land. I don't pay no water bill, all I pay is light bill, TV cable. And burial insurance, you know, in case anything happens to me or my wife*. Since he lacks the political connections Randy has with his magistrate, Virgil's road is rough and rutted and hard to get up in the winter and during rains. The Bratcher family has a bad reputation—his father drank and was picked up for DUIs time after time, and his brothers have been picked up for possession of marijuana. People gossip that his cousins up the hollow are involved in incest. Virgil struggles to rise above a "bad" name and no resources. *Every day, right today, there's people that make fun of people just because they can't afford to wear the same fancy clothes that other people wear, go barefoot or something, live in a shack or something. I don't see nothing wrong with how I live.*

Virgil grew up in a large family way up a hollow in the northern part of the county. When his daddy lost his job as a mechanic, he moved the family here and joined the "Happy Pappy" work gang, as the regional public works program was called, where he looked after park vehicles. His father never attended school at all, and could not write his name; his mother had gone through third grade and could read and write a little. The family struggled, and with ten children there was never enough. School was hard for Virgil because he was so poor—he felt he never received much attention from the teachers, and the other children scorned his poor clothes. *It was a hard time. We didn't have no, what you say?—no fancy clothes to wear. I can remember from first grade up to about the sixth grade I made practically honor roll. When I hit seventh grade, where they kept changing classes and I was in a different school, people were making fun of me because I would have to bring my own lunch to school, wear shoes with holes in them, whatever. That's when my grades went downhill. In the eighth grade they passed me anyway to get rid of me.*

Virgil began to fight with others in high school, and the principal gave him a choice. *They said, "We can expel you for the rest of the year or give you fifty licks." I took the expel because I really was ready to do odd jobs and work around the house to help Mommy anyways. It doesn't matter to me. I could have gone back later, but I decided not to. I couldn't study half the time. I would have to go out and do odd jobs to help pay on the family bills and stuff. Wasn't easy . . . if I had gone back to school, it would just put that much more on my parents and make them have to buy stuff for me. Back then you had to buy your high school books and everything else.*

Today the Bratchers and another family, the Johnsons, live up the mountain from the hollow where Virgil grew up—Johnson Hollow. Virgil thinks they should change the name to Bratcher Hollow, because "anymore" there are more Bratchers. *I own on the mountain I live on right now. My brother and his wife live in the house over from us, on land my wife and I give to them. We got about two, three acres, but their neighbor out from them is really my wife's and her sister's second cousin, and down the mountain from us, my wife's grandfather lives down there, and on the other mountain, his son lives down there. And down the mountain from them, they got another second cousin who lives down there. All of them are neighbors, but really, there ain't none of us that gets along.*

Finding work has been a constant struggle for Virgil and his family members—they have no connections, and when they do get a job their grasp on it is tenuous. Virgil worked for seven months in the Sanitation Department as a garbage man, but they cut back and let him go six years ago, and he has not found a regular, steady job since. *There ain't no work. My sister lives in Blue Orchard. Her old man was working coal mines, but he got hurt in the mine and then the mines got shut down too. Now he ain't got no job. Ain't none of my brothers got no job but one; I got one brother who still works for the sanitary department. He's a garbage man. He's worked there off and on for about ten years. He's been off about as much as he's been on. Things get low and they lay him off, things pick up a little bit and they call him. Me, I'm just doing odd jobs every now and then, cut brush, mow lawns, trim trees—whatever*. He has filled out applications two or three times for the Sanitation Department, but they never call.

Virgil says his biggest obstacle is transportation—he cannot afford insurance on his car, so he cannot get to jobs regularly. Although he does not say so explicitly, the insurance premiums he faces likely reflect high rates after an accident or DUI. *A poor man, if you ain't got the $500 or $600 to pay insurance, in my case every six months, you can't make it here. If you can't afford that insurance, then you might as well forget it. There is no work you can do, unless you are going to walk to it or hitchhike to it, and if you are doing that you ain't going to be able to carry a lot of garden tools, yard tools*. He gets a ride with a relative or neighbor when he needs to pick up his $300 worth of food stamps or his $285 AFDC check. With those checks and the income from odd jobs he gets when he can hitch a ride, he makes it through the month. He can charge groceries at the tiny store at the foot of the mountain, and pay off Mrs. Combs with some work around her place.

But when asked what has been the happiest time in his life, Virgil gets tears in his eyes and says, *There really ain't been no happy time*. His daughters make him proud, and he loves his wife, whom he married when she was seventeen and he was twenty-one. He says he wants more for them, but he feels trapped with no vehicle, no work, and little prospect for either one. As a young man he tried working in other places, in Florida, Georgia, Ohio. But one thing or another would push him on—the place would close, he would get laid off after coming in late, living was expensive, and he just really felt like a country boy who was not accepted.

He is pessimistic about this county's future. *Why would anybody want to stay in Blackwell? They going to be just like me. They ain't going to have nothing unless they had it when they first got here or they had enough money so they could keep it. Anyway, that's the way it works, looks like to me. That's the way it has been happening so far. I don't know if that's the way it works or not—that's the way it looks. Scratch is all you can do. I'm making it scratching.*

BLACKWELL'S HAVES: THE GOOD LIFE ON REDBUD HILL

Those who "scratch" are far removed from the elite who live in the county seat. The Camptons' lives of privileged isolation are typical. Although their work brings them in touch with unemployed coal miners and welfare recipients, the Camptons' own social world is protected from the hardships and uncertainties of those lives. Donna, an attractive woman in her late fifties with classic southern features, runs a division of the Welfare Department in Blackwell. Her lightly streaked, graying hair looks fresh from the beauty parlor, softly curled and perfectly in place. She wears a green A-line skirt and ruffled blouse with a light sweater draped over her shoulders in anticipation of the cool air-conditioning in the new annex to the welfare building. We talk in her private office as the morning sun streams in the window over leggy geraniums and framed pictures of her children.

Donna's father came from eastern Ohio in the early 1900s to set up a hardware store in town. He married a young woman whose father was a skilled electrician in the mines, and they raised three children—Donna and her two older brothers, both of whom are now lawyers in town—in the comfortable cocoon of the county seat. During the 1920s, 1930s, and 1940s violent labor struggles and political battles swirled around them, while deep, persistent poverty plagued those in the mining camps and mountain hollows, but these children barely knew they lived in a coal-mining area. *I really knew nothing about the county. I remember as a child, there was a house next door that was rented to families where the man worked in the mines. We were fascinated as kids to see these men come in with black faces. After their shower or bath, they would still have the little black rings around their eyes. All of this was just really new to us. We really didn't get much of it right here in the town. The children we knew from the county who came to our school paid tuition, and were the engineers', foremen's, and commissary manager's children. Later I learned that those out in the county thought we were "uptown" and called us "county seat" in a mocking way.*

When she went away to college years later, a professor assigned her a paper on her own home county, knowing it had a rich and turbulent history, but Donna knew nothing of it. She realizes now that the teacher was looking for an account like the one a friend of hers might have told. *One of my good friend's father had been county attorney and he had been killed when she was a baby. He had gone home for lunch here in town, and he was involved in some way with, maybe, the union. Some people who were opposed to his views put dynamite in his car, and when he went out to have some lunch the car blew up and he was killed. Her mother then became very active in politics and was assistant to the county judge for years.* As an adult Donna became more aware of the violence, poverty, and politics in the county, and she says she is sympathetic to mountain women who are trying against the odds to bring up children alone.

When Donna returned from college she married Harold Campton, a third-generation post office worker. She stayed at home while her children were growing up, giving private violin lessons to the children of the town's elite and volunteering in the church and the women's club. Reading a history of the area a few years ago, she realized that the father of one music student was accused of having numerous union sympathizers killed—but even then she lived in a world removed from political battles. When her own children were older, she wanted to go to work, and, like her friends who are part of the haves, she found a job through personal connections. *The welfare supervisor was a lady in the church, and she was a good friend of my family and of my husband's family. She just knew that I was getting ready to go back to school, and she asked if I would be interested in working as a social worker.*

During the 1960s, social workers like Donna made home visits. She was surprised—despite journalists' coverage of the poor in Appalachia when John F. Kennedy visited the region—at the depth of the poverty. The poor she visited and assisted were mostly miners' families whose lives were controlled by the company. They lived in crowded coal camps with no grass or space for a garden around them. Some homes were clean, especially those up on the mountain; others were dirty, with chickens running in and out. What struck Donna was how much these families lived from day to day, without any planning. *Our clients were women and children, women whose husbands maybe had worked in the mines and were hurt, and then they were disabled, and not able to work and therefore getting AFDC.* She cannot resist a little moralizing. *But I was fascinated with the fact that when they were working, they were making a lot more money than my father ever made at the hardware store, and yet they had no money. They had much less than we did as kids, perhaps, in looking back, because when they had it, they ran through it.*

These coal-mining families often came out in debt at the end of a pay period. And they had to rely on the honesty of the managers of the coal-company commissaries. *They had gone to the company store—you know the old song about how you owe your soul to the company store? There's just an awful lot of truth in that, because they were encouraged to charge and get in debt. The mines made those people trade in the commissary. They were not allowed to pick up their check. They were to trade at the commissary and meat would be maybe a dollar more a pound at the commissary. Food was so much more expensive at the commissary. And the children or the wife would go in and just get what she needed for the day, and probably go there daily. They had no idea there was any other way. They bought their clothes and all there, and at the end of the month they owed the company instead of clearing any money.*

Donna is cautious when she talks about the "powerful families," but she does mention that grocery store employees are required to shop at the store where they work, no matter whether prices are lower elsewhere. And she knows there is blackballing, although she hears that it occurs when miners get lazy, influenced by the overzealous do-gooders from outside who tell people they are owed a job and a paycheck. *Now I have been told that you cannot get work once your name gets on this blacklist of goof-offs in the mines, such as they're not really working—if they're going from place to place, or just troublemakers, you know? And I'm not so sure how I feel about that either.*

Do you remember the Vistas?[20] *Well, they were very active here when I first started working. I know that the whole purpose of that organization was good. Originally, the thought was good. But they came in and just put these ideas in people's heads, "You are owed this." And they told Blackwell people, "People are putting you down." So, miners now just could go into a mine and think, "I'll sit. I'll get my bucket and sit over here on the side and not do anything, and draw my pay as long as that big continuous miner machine is operating. It will produce coal." This is where some of these people have gotten on blacklists. I've heard that there was a list, and once you got on that list, that it would be just about impossible, once you caused trouble, or had been pretty well known as a trouble-maker or a goof-off in the mine, that it would be pretty hard to get a job.*

Donna and her family are involved in the social world of the county seat. Her husband has had the security of a solid post office job his whole working life. She worked her way up to become a top administrator in the welfare agency, where she, too, has security and a regular pension to look forward to. She deplores the politics and patronage out in the county schools and says she regrets that she always has to hire the person designated by the patronage man when she has an opening. Her family has always lived in town, sent their children to the independent city school, attended the large Baptist church, and been busy in various town clubs and activities, including the country club, which her father helped to establish. Some who have worked under her supervision over the years complain about her. *She is one of the hottie-tottie type women who go to the big Baptist church and are part of the women's club. Their attitude is "I'm up here and you're down there." And, "Me and my husband, we get along so good and we've got this nice little house up on the hill up here, called Redbud Hill." She wouldn't actually say that, but that's the attitude: "I'm up here and you're down here."* One woman called her "classic county seat." Certainly her day-to-day life is pleasant here in Blackwell, and her own family has always done well.

Jim Campton, Donna's eldest son, works as an executive in one of the biggest coal companies in the area. The buildings and entrance appear humble from the outside. I drive up a gravel road, pull up to the right not far from the tipple, go through a metal door with a handwritten sign that reads "Not hiring" taped to the glass, and enter a low-ceilinged building to be greeted by the receptionist and secretary in a very utilitarian entry. But here at Big Iron Coal Company, the windowless corporate offices tucked behind this entrance are expansive and furnished by a decorator from Harrington in popular purple tones. Jim has made some time for our conversation before his usual Tuesday-afternoon golf game out at the club.

Childhood and school days were good for Jim—he was a second-generation Boy Scout, captain of the high school football and basketball teams, and a reasonably good student. *It was just a very pleasant, small school. I met my wife there. I was in several clubs, was president of my class, got along well with people.* He was accepted at the naval academy—one of the few children of Republicans in this Democratic county to be nominated by the congressman of the staunchly Democratic district. But he decided to attend a well-regarded private college in Harrington rather than risk a lengthy military obligation in the heated days of the Vietnam War.

After college his parents urged him to come home, and his fiancée, his high school sweetheart, was eager to live in the mountains where her family lived. His mother's cousin offered him work in a coal company that was expanding in response to new strip mining and renewed deep mining opportunities in the booming coal market of the 1970s. *It just sounded too attractive and I was engaged and I felt a social obligation to my parents. If I had gone on to graduate school they would have been very instrumental in financially support-*

ing us. I felt like they had done that long enough. I was sort of tired of school, too. And, when you're in college you reach a point when it's time to earn some money. So, especially since I was engaged to be married in the fall, I felt like I better do that. When he began he worked long hours and did a little bit of everything, including manual labor, but since this was a period of big growth in coal he was earning twice what his college classmates were.

Big Iron Coal secured lucrative long-term contracts with several power companies in those early days during the energy crisis. The company's combination of management of reserves—stoker coal for metallurgical markets and steam coal for utilities—and long-term contracts brought explosive growth and high profits. Some businesspeople in Blackwell say that company officials bribed environmental inspectors during this period, in part by procuring prostitutes for them. Whether or not such extreme violations occurred, things have changed in the 1990s. New, "crusading" public utility regulators are scrutinizing the high prices in the old contracts Big Iron had negotiated years ago, and now a sizable share of its business is subcontracted out to crews whose men earn lower wages, have no benefits, and will work "low coal" (coal from mines so low-ceilinged that miners must work bent over). Furthermore, Jim's mother's cousin is now being investigated by the authorities for some illegal business deals. The old security has vanished. Now in his early forties, after more than twenty years in the coal industry, Jim finds he must worry about his future.

Family is most important to Jim now. He hopes his children can find work in the county through old contacts once they acquire professional training. He was recently elected to serve on the city school's board of education, which reportedly is immune to politics, but he recognizes the political machinations out in the county schools. *I don't think you could change the way it works even if you wanted to, It's power. In most of the region, especially where there's not much coal, it's the biggest employer. It's that way in Blackwell, even with the coal jobs we have. When you consider teachers, bus drivers, and mechanics, and janitors, and cafeteria workers, everybody is trying to get their kinfolk a job.*

But he is not so sure that the way politics governs the schools, how you need to know someone to get a job, is any different in other places. He sees people choosing dependency over working in minimum wage jobs—in part because they all compare their earnings to the good coal-mining jobs that are now so scarce. Unlike Creed Parker and Joey Scott, he thinks people would turn down factory jobs even if they were available. *I think it's unique here in that you're either exposed to the mining industry, which is high skill, or nothing. Or welfare. We don't have a lot of work that's in between the two. I thought a lot about trying to get some sort of industry in here. I think it's apparent to everybody that we could use something other than coal. But I wonder if you could get five hundred people that would work for a wage lower than the miner? Maybe they would just say, "The heck with it, I'll draw welfare," and maybe get a bit less and not work.* In Jim's view, companies like Big Iron that must compete mightily with other coal operations do a good deal for the area just by providing jobs. *Really, coal is about all we got.*

Jim and his wife, Valerie, are raising children in the county seat, where life is sheltered from the poverty and politics for which the county is known, just as it was when his mother was growing up and when he was growing up. Jim's own job may be less secure—indeed he regrets not specializing more and going on to business school twenty years ago—but he has contacts here and could likely find a position. Family and church, his regular golf games, and his responsibilities on the city school board and in Kiwanis are important to him, and even a downturn in the coal market would be unlikely to unravel the life he has here. He is concerned about the problems out in the county—poverty and dependency, the corrupt politics, some lawlessness—but his life is focused on his church and his own family right now.

BRINGING CHANGE TO BLACKWELL

While Jim's world is far removed from the poor who are scratching and scrounging, a small number of teachers, social workers, and community organizers work to encourage those like Gwen Boggs, Wanda Turner, Randy Perkins, and Virgil Bratcher who are struggling. Joanne and John Martin, in their respective professions as nurse and education counselor and in their ministry of a small, newly formed church, prod and lend a helping hand to those who cross their paths. They grew up poor themselves, and they benefited from thoughtful people who recognized their potential. They have little patience for those who will not help themselves, but they also recognize the importance of cultural broadening and the need to have independent resources to overcome the politics governing opportunity in a place like Blackwell.

The Martins live in a modest home on top of a hill outside town, up a long, winding gravel road. Joanne and I sit on the wooden swing hanging on their front porch on a hot July afternoon. The renovated garage, still smelling of fresh paint, serves as her husband's little church. Joanne's new herb garden is just below the house, and a chicken coop sits out back by the fruit trees. Joanne is a large woman whose sweet smile and apparently shy demeanor belie her determination and forthright, even opinionated, approach to life in Blackwell.

The oldest of eight children, Joanne was born in 1940 on a small, marginal farm in the next county. Her mother worked hard to put food on the table while her father was in and out of jail. *My dad had probably a first-grade education and my mom had like a fifth-grade education. So they just lived off the land and farmed and did odd jobs. Neither one of them were ever employed for any particular length of time with an organized place.* When Joanne finished grade school, at the age of twelve, she was sent off to a settlement school established by two Boston missionaries in the early 1900s. *At that time they didn't run school buses. You either lived there or didn't go to high school. I was the first person in my family to finish high school. My mother valued education, even though she didn't have any formal education herself. But the high school that I would have had to go to was like twenty miles from home and they didn't run a bus, due to county politics at that time.*

Boarding school was a good experience for this skinny, independent little girl. Teachers took an interest in her, she made good friends, and she was exposed to things she never imagined—including the idea of going to college. But even getting to boarding school took all her mother's determination and the encouragement of a teacher who knew the family. *It was really not scary to me because I'm the oldest of eight and I've always been allowed a lot of independence. I don't think it was a big decision for my mother. My dad probably did not see as much value in my leaving—and being the oldest I had always cared for the younger children. But a grade school teacher who was our next-door neighbor had attended that boarding school, and she helped my mother understand what school was about, and the importance of my going. She played a really big role.*

The opportunity changed Joanne's life dramatically, opening up new horizons for a mountain girl who had known only her family and the people on her road. *To me it was an excellent experience. I really hate that those boarding schools are no longer available because I think they were more instrumental in more people going to college and to high school than anything else. It removed you from the only environment you've ever known. I had never been more than twenty miles from my home until then. If you grow up with everybody being the same, you don't know that there is another way of life or another goal, or anything to aim for.*

Joanne went to the same college Creed Parker's mother had gone to—a regional college especially catering to bright mountain youth with ambition. *I learned about college through the boarding school. They had someone who could take over and wade through the paperwork and the bureaucracy. Most students today really can't figure out all that's required and don't understand the importance of all these deadlines. You've got to meet this and you've got to meet that. Without someone really intervening or seeing to it that it happens, then I don't think a lot of these kids will ever go to school.*

Joanne was eagerly drinking down every opportunity to learn at boarding school, and then she discovered, in a way that seems almost accidental to her now, that she could go on and do more. *When I was a junior in high school, the girls were sitting around talking about who was going to do what. They assumed I was going on to college because I made good grades. That was the first time it ever dawned on me that grades had anything to do with going to college. They said, "Well, I'm sure you're going to college." And I said, "No." But then the people at the boarding school, every time I said, "No," they said, "Yes." When I found an obstacle about why I couldn't go, they always found a way that I could go.*

She would never have gone to college herself without that intervention—the whole idea was outside the family's idea of what is possible. *Number one, your parents aren't educated; number two, there's no money; number three, you don't have a car; and number four, you don't know how you'd ever get there. It never entered my mind that I would go to college, but I think the people at the school had that goal for me from the day that I entered the school.*

She recalls the teachers fondly and thinks of them when she acts as a mentor to young people in this county. *Now that I've had children of my own, and work with other children, I think back about how those women at that school were amazing people. To most people it would have appeared that I was obstinate, that I didn't want to do anything with my life. I didn't want to go to school. I think they could see through all of the things that were going on. I think that's what happens to a lot of children today. The teachers, or counselors, or whoever, are there more for a job and not for the real purpose of what they can do to help those kids. It's so easy to write off those stubborn children.*

Joanne believes poor children need a combination of cultural exposure and programmatic opportunities. She believes children should be taught more discipline and not be "coddled." *These days, the rule is "you can't spank a child, you send them home." You know, I don't see how that's ever going to help to get these kids to go on to school, because if you already tend to not want to be in school, it doesn't take long to learn how you get to go home. It just sends them right back to that environment that's not going to encourage them to go to school anyway.*

This kind of thinking is characteristic of Joanne's strong opinions about the need for discipline and opportunity combined. She thinks teachers and welfare programs expect too little of their students and clients, limiting their potential by not demanding more. *I really think from grade school on they spoon-feed the kids too much. They're never given an opportunity to be independent, and maybe going to boarding school accounts for part of my feeling. You know, I left home at twelve years old and did fine.* Her main concern is the quality of education and how it is undermined by the politics that drive teacher hiring. *It goes back to: the majority of the people are teaching because it's a job and not because of the desire to help, or to make sure things happen.*

Although she values independence and criticizes what she sees as pampering, she has no patience for stigmatizing the poor. *When our son was in first grade he came home and told me that he felt real sorry for some of the kids who couldn't bring money to help buy the paper towels, because the teacher wouldn't let them use the paper towels to dry their hands—that they would have to stand there and just let their hands dry, or you know, shake them dry. So I went to that teacher and offered to pay for those people. I said, "Eddy told me this and I really think that's wrong. If that's the issue then I'll pay their money." And she would not allow me to do that. Her thing was that these kids' parents could pay if they wanted to—they just wouldn't.*

Joanne recognizes how important institutions can be—that both her boarding school and college experiences were turning points for her—but she insists that individuals must have the motivation to take advantage of opportunities like these. *That desire to succeed has to be there. People have to motivate themselves. You can pass any law you want to, you can give me ever how much money you want to, but that desire, and work ethic, and all of that, has to be within that person. I've lived in the mountains all of my life. I grew up in real poverty, but I have felt freedom all of my life. My mother had no education, but she taught me that I was no better than anybody else, but I was as good as anybody else.*

Joanne worries about how isolated the poor are in the mountains, and how that prevents children from developing an image of an alternative, from dreaming bigger dreams. They need someone looking out for them, opening doors for them, pushing them to aspire to more. *To me what brings you out of poverty is not anything that the school system does. It's not anything that bureaucracy does. It has more to do with a mentor. You have to have somebody there. I don't think that person necessarily knows they're a mentor at the time. But there has to be something introduced to that person's life before they can see that there's a different world.* Joanne sees poor people become accustomed to the marginal lives they are leading. *A lot of these people that live in poverty with nothing think that's normal, that's expected—because that's all they've ever known. If that's all you've ever known all of your life, how can you know there's anything different?*

At sixteen Joanne went to college, and during her first year there she met John at a folk dance. He was an older student of twenty-five who had served in Korea before coming back to college. John recalls, *My sophomore year, this thing comes along. The prettiest thing I've ever seen. A tall, skinny, good-looking woman who was a good folk dancer. You never saw anything like that, I tell you.* They secretly married during her second semester, when she was seventeen. Within three years they had two daughters, and Joanne took some time off from school to work as a nurse's aide out in the mountains while John began a job with a small boarding school nearby.

John was a true mountain boy, having grown up in even more remote circumstances than Virgil or Randy, way up on top of Oak Mountain, in the 1930s. *We lived in a place called the Cliff House. There was an actual house built out in front of it, but the cliff itself was a big overhang rock, and underneath it people had lived in the past. We used it as a stable. It was a place for the cows, and the mule that we used for plowing while we were up there. We were squatters. It was all company land, but they left us alone most of the time. We raised all our food. The only time we came off the mountain was for things like salt and coffee. Almost everything else we raised on top of the mountain in the garden we had up there—the field. We raised corn and all your different vegetables. Sometimes we would kill rabbits or squirrels for meat. We raised pigs and chickens.*

Theirs was a single-parent family living a subsistence life, scrounging in the woods. John was one of five children. *I really don't remember much about my father. He was an alcoholic and just never was around that much.* His mother was an independent, hardworking woman. *My mother was quarter Cherokee Indian. She was only about four foot six. She could stand under my arm, and I'm short. A beautiful woman with the darkest black hair you ever saw, long black hair. But she was just independent as all get out. She would not cater to living close to people because they try to tell you what to do. So she lived on her own up on the mountain, and until I was about nine she would only go down the mountain to trade for some supplies every so often.*

When John was nine his mother became very ill, and some loggers who had watched out for them informally—bringing candy and sometimes coffee when they made their way up into the mountains—grew worried about her and the children. They notified people in the county seat, who came up and put the family in jail—the only place for indigents at the time. After about six months, John and his younger brother were sent to an orphanage in Pittsburgh, far from the mountains, where he finished high school. They were wild children. His brother would sneak out and steal food and bicycles and keep them in a secret hideaway under the school's swimming pool, And they were bright. John skipped several grades, and the orphanage's minister worked to get him into a boarding school and steered him toward college. He went into the service and spent time in Korea, an experience, he recognizes, that broadened his horizons.

Joanne and John have spent their working years in the mountains, she in various health programs and he in education. They came back at the crest of the War on Poverty in the 1960s, and its experimental programs were often the vehicles through which they worked to improve the lives of the people they encountered. Later they were involved in implementing expanded federal social welfare programs like Medicare and Medicaid. They managed mountain volunteer programs that brought northeastern middle-class youths to do Peace Corps–like work. They started health programs of all sorts, and projects that involved visiting young mothers, visiting the elderly and helping families care for them—nutrition outreach, housing improvement programs, skill development programs. Joanne and John worked in all aspects of community development, writing grant applications and seizing opportunities wherever they were available.

They have seen enormous changes in material conditions—from one-room schools with coal stoves and broken windows and no books in the 1960s to modern facilities in consolidated high schools and a new community college, from clinics run out of a van to a big hospital with a large staff. They worked to bring medical care to mountain families who had never had any at all. But the changes in the mountains have not all been progressive. Joanne and John are highly critical of programs they see as condoning lazy behavior or resistance to progress. They also deplore the politics pervading every local institution—undermining not only the schools but also the hospital and other civic establishments.

About welfare, John says, *Well, if you get money, you don't care what you do. That's why Joanne and I have always said, "Do not give people money. Give people an opportunity to earn money." Tell them, "You can have these kinds of things, but in the meantime we're training you for work and if a job becomes available you're going to take the job that you're trained to do. Now if it doesn't give you an earned living to where you can make it, okay, we'll keep your medical card. Until you get to the point where you can survive and do better than you can on welfare, we'll subsidize."*

They see selfishness in those managing important community institutions, people who are too worried about their own jobs, their own future, their own families. *People are selfish. They will not replenish the things that need to be done. Then it deteriorates down the line because you hire people, and they're there only for exactly what that job description says. They aren't accountable. They don't want to answer your questions. In fact, they don't expect that you will ever ask any questions, ever question what they do. This is one of the things that fragments our community. All these organizations have their own internal politics, in addition to the other politics. But unless you brought in a large number of new people at one time, you're not going to topple anybody. Most new people don't stay long enough.* And, Joanne adds, *The ones that do try that are usually so radical they turn people off.*

The Martins give informal counseling to people who have learned about them through word of mouth. *Kids that he's known at school may get married real young and they end up in trouble. We talk to them. We buy schoolbooks for people, help them find ways to go to school. John hauls them back and forth to school. We've been real blessed when we intervened with families who have never had a child finish college, fought the battle with the parents about letting them leave, and saw them go to college. After that first child went, then they let the others. We've seen several first college graduates in a generation with our work at the church.*

Joanne and John are close to formal retirement, but they will continue to act as counselors to those around them—partly through the little church that is like an extended family, and partly just doing what they do and folding in those around them. *I hope to continue to be a mentor to people, like people were to me. But I don't ever intend to just give people things. I intend to make it possible for them to work, but I think you do a person a disfavor to hand them money.*

They carry out small, personal measures of social support, and in doing so they can change people's lives, just as teachers and ministers changed theirs when they were young. But they cannot change the economic or political context. They and the handful of people with whom they work feel isolated even as "do-gooders" who treat have-nots with respect. There was, however, a recent federal social policy "experiment" that affected the institutional resources used by the poor people in Blackwell—briefly, and with interesting results.

In the early 1990s, the Family Support Act, a revised welfare program emphasizing work passed by Congress in 1988, was just being implemented in Blackwell. Social welfare workers involved in its Job Opportunities and Basic Skills training program, or JOBS, as it was called, were upbeat about this new direction in welfare. The JOBS program was designed to get people off public assistance and into the workforce and included numerous support programs to help them do so. It was based on policy ideas developed primarily by David Ellwood, a Harvard University economist, and Senator Daniel Patrick Moynihan, a longtime poverty scholar and policymaker. The general idea was to provide support to welfare-dependent families that would help them find and keep work. There were educational components, child care and health insurance assistance, and even provisions to help people obtain eyeglasses, false teeth, and good interviewing skills that might build their confidence and improve their self-image to help them find employment.

In Blackwell the Family Support Act programs were introduced as an experimental change for some welfare recipients from the county's large caseload. The ten or so social workers selected to work in the new program had spent years in the regular Welfare Department, where they worked with fifty other caseworkers to handle thousands of AFDC and food stamp cases. The new program transformed the content and purpose of what they did as welfare caseworkers. In the JOBS program they each had 60 clients, instead of 350, and a private office in which to counsel them instead of a cubicle in a large room. But most important, under the new program their task was to get their clients off welfare, not to deliver public checks and cross-examine people to ascertain that they were not cheating, as it was in the regular welfare programs. Welfare workers like Marlene Combs and Greg Benton, bitter that their own low salaries of $20,000 practically made them eligible for the programs their clients got with no effort, had found themselves resenting the welfare recipients. Now they were forging new, mutually supportive relationships with clients. I interviewed six social workers before and after they joined the JOBS program staff.

Marlene is the social worker for Wanda Turner, the twenty-six-year-old mother of four who has been so disheartened. Marlene herself grew up poor, the daughter of an illiterate coal miner and his wife. Despite their own lack of education, they pushed Marlene and her sisters to finish school. Fortunately, the principal of the school the girls went to was a now famous anomaly in the county—a dedicated and effective school administrator who held teachers accountable and did not go along with the politics raging around him. He saw many students in his school learn well and finish their high school education. Marlene was among them.

Marlene married at seventeen, right out of high school, and had her first child at eighteen. She was a substitute teacher in the county system and then held a few appointive political positions in county government. She spent twenty-four years in an abusive relationship with an alcoholic spouse until finally, helped by a counselor she met while seeking medical care for one of her children, she found the courage to leave her husband.

She has been a social worker for fifteen years, and in 1991 she was one of those selected for JOBS. Like her colleagues, Marlene thinks the program is great. *Now you get to know the people and you feel like you're doing something. Before it was just get them out of your face, get them what they need, make sure they were not cheating. But with the JOBS program you can see an overall future, an outcome. Before I didn't feel like I was doing anything. I really didn't. Now I can tell them that they are not just a name and a number. We have plenty of time to spend. I've got sixty people, and any type of problem you got, we work it out. We talk about it. We help in any way we can.*

She and her co-workers say that when social workers were being selected for the JOBS program their attitudes toward the poor were the focus of the interviews and the criterion for selection. *They wanted somebody that could be compassionate. Somebody that didn't see this new program as a job. They wanted somebody that was willing to do whatever it would take to get these people out of the welfare system. To reform them.*

She has seen hard cases. *Like mom and dad, they've been raised up in hollers and stuff, and nobody has an education, and the family just sits on their front porch and "pick and grin," all that stuff. Even then, I find if you just push and pry just a little bit and show them a different way of life than that, then they'll run with it. The majority will. I'll be interviewing a woman and look at the date of birth, and look at her, and try to figure out, "Why do you look like you're fifty -something years old, when you're only twenty-five?" Their lives have been so hard. And then they have no teeth. They tickle me to death. I can buy them teeth. I can buy them glasses.*

Marlene's colleague Greg put it this way: *These are the same people I used to resent, but instead of them being a number coming in the office wanting the food stamps and AFDC, you see that they're people who really want to better themselves, but don't know how to go about it. They've lived here all of their lives. A lot of them lived on welfare all of their lives. They have no idea how to better themselves, where to go for help. All they know is how to "go get my food stamps and AFDC." So you kind of learn that, yeah, they do want to do better, but they don't know how.*

Marlene gives this example. *There was this one lady who is in the GED program and she is struggling. It's been almost two years. Her husband doesn't do anything. He was one of these that was laid off, lost his self-esteem, and just sits at home, fusses at her all day long. He really doesn't want her to go to school. He resents her studying at home. She's a very attractive lady, thirty-six or thirty-seven years old. She came in one day—her teeth are real bad. I said, "Laura, honey, if you want to get your teeth fixed, we can buy your teeth. You have $300 that you can spend." She jumped right on it. She got her teeth in. She came in here one day, had her new teeth in, had her hair fixed, had makeup on, and she looked like a doll. I asked her, "How's your GED going?" And she said, "Well, I'm having a hard time with math." I said, "Well, that's a problem for a lot of people in this area. You just keep working." She reached over and hugged me and said, "Thanks for everything you've done for me. I'm so used to doing stuff for everybody else that I never thought about anybody ever doing for me." And I didn't do nothing, I barely didn't do anything. But that little bit was so special to her because nobody has ever done for her before.*

These programs institutionalized, for a moment, the kind of social support Joanne and John give people. Caseworkers became allies and advocates, rather than enemies, allowing them to stay in touch and continue encouraging low-income people battling to get a GED and a job. Under the previous system, welfare workers like Marlene and Greg could spend only fifteen minutes processing paperwork for public assistance; now they became counselors who could reach out to clients and guide them. The new structure and rules transformed the relationship between social workers and clients from one of suspicion and resentment to one of trust and support. Caseworkers and clients alike praised the program. On their own time, the welfare workers in the program organized a graduation celebration—including getting local businesses to donate flowers, invitations, and sandwiches—for their clients who have completed GEDs.

In 1997 the Family Support Act was replaced with state-level programs designed to "end welfare as we know it." While these programs may offer comprehensive support in some states, many poor states will be hard-pressed to provide the close supervision and support that Marlene, Greg, and their colleagues were able to give clients in the JOBS program. And, of course, even those who successfully learned new skills and acquired new cultural resources in the JOBS program still found a job-scarce environment when they were ready to look for work. As Marlene says, *The economy here is what is going to be the drawback to the JOBS program. There are no jobs.*

Community leaders, as well as social workers, believe that political change must occur if Blackwell is to create a community climate in which economic growth can happen. Some say there are hopeful signs in county government. The county administrator, Bobby Lee King, is widely regarded as a friend to the poor, and the majority of those I interviewed felt positively about him. Some, like Creed Parker and Randy Perkins, thought he might be more interested in higher state office than in the well-being of the county—but even Creed is basically supportive. Willy Granger has had problems with him, in part because Bobby Lee will not do as he and the governor's patronage man command. Creed had described how he arranged meetings for Willy Granger and the county judge administrator several times in the previous year to help him "see the coal operators' point of view."

The county judge himself views the coal operators' selfishness as a key problem—although an understandable one. Bobby Lee puts it this way: *I have this philosophy that all coal operators have had such a tough time staying in the business surviving that the ones that are left are such rugged individuals that they just can't get along. Their competitiveness in business on their own little ground just prevents them from agreeing; they can't even agree sometimes on the Clean Air Act—which is what they ought to know. So they don't form good allies. And they are also used to being in command. It's hard to have ninety chiefs and no Indians. Maybe this attitude is a little in all of our people, because it has been such a struggle fighting against obstacles. If you stay here and you survive—I think you are pretty tough. You get to be opinionated sometimes, and used to having your own way.*

A new county attorney who won by a narrow margin several years ago is considered honest and law abiding—a dramatic change from the past.

Both the judge and the attorney represent a new generation of elected officials, ambitious for themselves and each other, and for their county. As young people growing up in the 1960s and 1970s they took an interest in local politics, became involved, and, inspired, they say, by John Kennedy's presidency, idealistically envisioned forging a more public-minded local government in Blackwell.

But jobs in Blackwell are still largely controlled by a few powerful people, and these once idealistic young leaders are the first to admit that few have the economic independence necessary to challenge the political status quo. Each of these "new" leaders has become hostage, in small ways, to the traditional means of getting things done, making their own deals and arrangements with the powerful. When one of them, a state legislator, worked to bring about school reforms at the state level that might begin to break the patronage system in Blackwell, he was not reelected the following term. Several have compromised their principles, done what it takes to get support from powerful people—actions that in this climate mean they are becoming part of the old way of doing things in spite of their intentions as young, idealistic political activists. It is hard to be optimistic about countywide change until the economy diversifies.

Diversification itself is held back not only by isolation and poor transportation but also by the corrupt politics and lack of civic cooperation. Roads might be improved if the county's elite could come together for the common good, many say, but Creed and Joey and most businesspeople are discouraged about the prospects. Each player wants the new roads to benefit their business or their constituency, distrusts the others' motives, and is not interested in compromise. And it will be hard to bring good jobs to a place where the schools are so bad, although the factory managers might settle comfortably in the county seat. Some say tourism offers a development strategy, perhaps combined with historical exhibits on the coal industry and its dramatic, colorful labor history. But promoting tourism would require cleaning up the litter and the coal camps and beaten-down hollows where so many poor people live—and perhaps reforming the legal system, as well.

Litter, the law, the welfare system—these are entangled in corrupt factional politics, and until the many residents who are poor and uneducated acquire an education and a modest job, independent of controlling bosses, significant change seems unlikely. The Martins and others who have worked for change for decades see a vicious circle, as the cliché goes, and rich and poor alike say, *You can't do anything about it; that's the way it is, and the way it always has been*. So while some might say political change is needed before economic change can occur, others will tell you it is the other way around.

There was a brief period of hope in Blackwell during the late 1970s and early 1980s. Coal regions in the Appalachian Mountains experienced a boom, as the Arab oil embargo created new demand for domestic coal. This was the same period when midwestern steel and automobile industries were undergoing restructuring—when their region was said to be "deindustrializing" in the face of increased global competition. Coal counties saw a wave of return migration, as those who had left the region in the 1960s for jobs in automobile factories in the industrial Midwest returned for new coal-mining jobs created by the boom in the coal industry. Coal employment in Blackwell increased from around twenty-five hundred to thirty-five hundred, and the population increased by about six thousand. Things were looking up.

Those who returned brought higher expectations for their communities and their social institutions. They found work in the mines, the banks, and other support industries, and some community leaders and advocates of change dared to be optimistic. Here were middle-class families who had seen another way of doing things. They were prepared to hold public officials accountable, ready to run for the school board on a platform of improved education rather than jobs for your family members, ready to support candidates who would advocate a cleaner environment.

But the coal market began to collapse again in the mid-1980s, and experts widely agree that even the volatile pattern of years of boom followed by busts and then booms again will not be repeated. Many of those with higher expectations and experiences of a different civic tradition lost their jobs, being "the last hired," and moved on, to Georgia or to Florida, where the economy was not collapsing. Old habits prevailed. The Blackwell county school system has been taken over by the state because of bad performance and mismanagement. As one discouraged leader explained, *Until the people get fed up with what is actually occurring, I don't know how any mandated school reform is going to control some of the nepotism, some of the blatant hiring and firing practices, promotion practices. It will not change until the people themselves get tired of it and they don't want to pay the tuition to go to another school system, they want to correct it and they correct it by going to that board member and saying you either correct it or I'm going to work just as hard getting you out as I did getting you in*.

Another referred almost wistfully to a nearby county closer to an interstate where job growth was changing the political landscape. Change was coming from the inside out, but it was facilitated by the economic independence accompanying new jobs that broke the old hold of the families that run things. *In Lyndon County the people who might have left, with an education, stayed when new jobs came in. And they started to do things differently. Mothers Against Drunk Driving organized to oppose the corrupt court that was letting drunken drivers go because they had large families that voted for these officials. People who cared about education started running for the school board. People started letting the county judge know what they wanted—not jobs for their cousins, but roads and litter control, garbage pickup.*

And all of these things, all these civic concerns, brought them together. When it starts moving in a good direction, the judge had to become part of it. The district court had to become part of it. I'm talking about mountain politics generally here. You work with them, you bring them around, you let them know you want a different kind of politics. But for any of this to happen, people got to have education, and they have got to have a job outside the reach of the power structure.

As we will see, those who know the poor and politics in the Delta come to the same conclusions.

BLACKWELL TWENTY YEARS LATER: HUNKERING DOWN WITH FAMILY

It is a crisp, cold morning in February 2013, and frost clings to the tufts of brown grass on the edge of the parking lot for the fast-food restaurant where Gwen Boggs works. Nearly all of the cars and trucks in the drive-through line and parked in the lot have Friends of Coal bumper stickers. Some have Friends of Coal license plates. The bubble-gum dispenser just inside the door has a Friends of Coal sticker.

These Friends of Coal are facing hard times. With recent coal-mining layoffs, official unemployment in Blackwell is over 17 percent.[21] But the unemployment rate does not convey the depth of the economic stagnation that defines the region. In 1990 only 50 percent of men over sixteen were employed, and in 2010 less than 44 percent were, compared with 65 percent nationally. Around 32 percent of women over sixteen are employed, compared with 55 percent nationally. One third of families have no one working. Almost 30 percent of young people sixteen to twenty-four are idle, not in school and not working.

Poverty is still very high—one in three are poor. Over 40 percent of children are growing up in poor families, and nearly 40 percent of households with children rely on the Supplemental Nutrition Assistance Program (SNAP, formerly food stamps). Making a living is hard. *If you wanted to stay in Blackwell and provide for your family, you just had to go to the mines. And as the mining jobs closed out, people began to leave, just as they did in the other great migration. And the ones that stayed behind have had to scrabble for whatever they can get.*

The restaurant's handful of customers includes two groups of older women and one of older men having their morning coffee visit. Four younger men in fatigues, staff members from a regional program for youth at risk, are eating biscuits and gravy at a fourth table. Gwen, who was passionately hopeful for her children's future when we interviewed her twenty years ago, is now fifty-four. She recalls those days when we spoke in the 1990s as hard times and does not want to be reminded. She and Billy have long been divorced. Her children, now grown, have steady jobs and stable families. She is focused on the present, on her adoring second husband, Rich, and on her five grandchildren, who love their Mamaw. Gwen is behind the counter taking an order from a traveling salesman, one eye on three of her grandchildren sitting in a booth waiting for a ride to school. Her husband, their step-grandpa, will pick them up in a few minutes because their Daddy had an early shift at the mine and their Mama is just getting off the night shift at the hospital.

Sara Hensley, a slightly overweight eighteen-year-old mother of three with a long, straight ponytail, sweeps up and straightens trays. Gwen has befriended Sara, helping her learn the ropes in her first real job since she got out of a drug recovery program two months ago. Sara smokes, sometimes bites her fingernails, as we talk on the patio during her break. She attributes the beginning of her prescription drug addiction to boredom and peer pressure. *We didn't have nothing to do. Got into drugs and breaking the law. I experienced everything when I was a teenager and got a boyfriend young, children young. I started everything young. Everybody that I went to school with, they all either lost their children or have gave them up to their parents, or they are just running around doing their own thing.*

Blackwell is home—it's what she knows—and she and her young husband plan to stay. *I guess I got used to it and it's like I would feel out of place if I ever moved. I'm so used to being here, with his family and mine. You know everybody. So I would feel out of place if I ever moved. I'd rather be here.*

That's how many who are still in Blackwell feel. However, the community has lost a third of its population in recent decades. There are over seven thousand fewer people than when we were last here, 35 percent fewer families with children. The number of twenty- to early-forty-year-olds, the family-forming age group so critical to the economic and social vibrancy of any place, has declined by a third. Jobs were scarce in the early 1990s and they are even scarcer in 2013. Only 44 percent of working-age adults are in the labor force, compared with 69 percent nationally.

Jobs declined from around 10,000 in 1990 to just 8,500 in 2010, and of course, with recent coal layoffs and the ripple effect from them, there are fewer still in 2013. In 1990 there were 2,500 coal jobs; now there are 1,200. An equipment supplier that opened up recently had more than 700 applications for twelve positions. *There's no job opportunities here. It's either you're a nurse, you're a teacher, or you're a coal miner . . . There's no other jobs really.* Nearly everyone has a relative or a friend who does "three twelves" in a city a couple of hours away, sharing an apartment with fellow nurses or electricians, and then drives home to be with family in Blackwell for the other four days. A teacher whose children have left said, *There ain't no jobs here in Blackwell for nobody. You have to get out of town to do it. My son said, "Mom, the only chance I'm going to have to make something out of my life is to just get out of Blackwell."*

The biggest changes are this loss of people and jobs and a pervasive epidemic of prescription drug addiction that emerged about ten years ago. People say every family in Blackwell, haves and have-nots, has had someone struggle with painkiller addiction. *It's rare anymore for me to have a family law case where drug use is not an issue for one or the other.*

In this remote community where everyone seems to know everyone, when a man or woman becomes addicted to drugs it has a broad impact. And it has undermined the comfortable small-town atmosphere, because people must worry about theft by those needing to feed their addictions. *It's so close-knit, when it hits one person, it's affecting twenty different people. So that's really, in my eyes, the largest problem down here. It's not just affecting one or two people. It's affecting the entire community.* Jenny, a young woman just about to leave a local rehab program, described getting involved as a teen in high school, and then turning to stealing and dealing to support a thousand-dollar-a-day habit. *When I was on them I didn't think about anything else but that pill.* An uncle stretched for cash turned her in to the police for one hundred dollars, and she went to jail for eight months, a second conviction. Now she says she feels ready to move on. *I want to live. That's the truth. I want to live.*

Teachers say every student raises his or her hand in response to the question "Who knows someone struggling with painkiller addiction?" Legislators in the Appalachian region have worked to get more funds for drug treatment and law enforcement, "pill doctors" have been arrested and "pill mills" closed, changes have been made to the drugs themselves.[22] But the problems persist in Blackwell, and headlines in the local paper about drug arrests, often of men and women in their forties and fifties, as well as accounts of drug-related deaths, are common.

The local drug rehabilitation center is a valuable resource, according to some. *If they get in trouble with drugs and things like that, rather than being put behind bars, they actually basically try to rehabilitate them and reintroduce them back into normal society, and that is an awesome, great thing.* But another observer with her own addiction struggle said, *I've heard horror stories about the Freedom Center . . . my heart goes out to them, because I know how hard it is for them. . . . As they're all going in, there's always somebody there making fun of them. It is a tough place.* Sara, who has family members who use pills, found it a safe haven, and stayed on longer to be sure she was ready to return to life in a community where so many are on drugs.

Some worry that those addicted to painkillers are selling their food stamps to get cash for more pills. *I think that people who are on food stamps, they need to drug test them. They need to drug test them before they get their food stamps. Because people that's on drugs, they'll get their food stamps and then they'll sell them for money.* There are rumors that stores are in collusion with the food-stamp sellers, buying soda back at a discount and making a small profit on the transaction. Several people told us that they had been approached by someone with a SNAP card at the store, proposing that the card be used for the groceries and the shopper exchange cash with the card holder.

A critical juncture for anyone caught with drugs is the sentencing. If you get a felony conviction, everyone agrees you will not work again in Blackwell. *I had drugs take everything I ever loved in my whole life away from me: my home, my truck, my bass boat, my houseboat, my four-wheelers, my guns, everything else. And now I'm a convicted felon. I cannot own a gun no more. . . . I destroyed my whole family's name. . . . I'm a certified craftsman, but I can't get a job nowhere.* One educator recalled that several years earlier there had been a separate drug court, and people could *go through a program for eighteen months, and not have to face a felony. But a lot of them face felonies, and then they can't get a job the rest of their life*.

Many link the pervasive drug problems to lack of opportunity and the downturn in regional coal mining. *So if you're not gonna be a nurse . . . if you're a man, you basically have to be a coal miner. . . . And that's the only opportunities as far as employment go. There's really nothing else for people, and I think that's why Blackwell has such bad drug problems*. The coal economy in Blackwell, and Appalachia overall, is in trouble. *Coal is all there is*, people still say. *Coal mining is about the only thing around here, really*. Coal production and employment increased temporarily during the wars in Iraq and Afghanistan, but competition from natural gas and higher-productivity coal mines have brought local employment down in recent years. Deep-mine productivity has declined by over 40 percent since 2000, as the region's remaining coal becomes harder to mine. In 2012 alone, coal production and employment in Blackwell dropped by more than 25 percent. Coal has long been the foundation of the local economy, and coal jobs are virtually the only ones that pay a good wage. A report a few years ago calculated that coal supplied 14 percent of the jobs, but those jobs made up nearly a third of earned income in the county.

The Friends of Coal stickers represent an increasingly polarized and politicized regional campaign, financed by political forces outside Blackwell, to identify those who are "for coal" and those who are "against coal." But even in this climate of boosterism, most people we talked with in 2013, including several who either were mining or had been miners, agree with national energy experts that coal employment in Appalachia will continue to decline. An elected official observed, *The kids right now here in Blackwell are so worried about the coal industry because we are a single-industry county. They know, the ones who have enough intelligence, that their only ticket to life is to get enough education to get a job somewhere else*.

Mindful that we are here in winter, when days are gray and neither blossoming redbuds nor green blankets of kudzu cover the hillsides, we nonetheless are struck by the signs of decline throughout the county. Downtown Blackwell, the county seat, looks much as it did twenty years ago, but with fewer businesses, more empty storefronts, and less activity on the streets. Lawyers' offices abounded in the 1990s, but now they seem to occupy every other building, still advertising help with black lung or disability and, more recently, family law. The courthouse, with a couple of newer plaques commemorating this or that, is a backdrop for a current generation of old-timers on the benches out front, catching up on the news, complaining about the Obama administration's "war on coal," clucking over the latest arrests for domestic violence or possession or drunken driving reported in the police log. The notoriously unpredictable parking meters are gone. Parking spaces are readily available in the sleepy downtown.

The small restaurant just across the street from the old courthouse has been replaced by a new drug-testing business catering to the many substance-abuse cases the judges hear. In addition to a law office or two, each street around the courthouse has several empty storefronts, maybe a pawnshop. Outside the "rent-to-own" furniture store three women are smoking. In fact, outside every establishment in Blackwell, every business's doorway, including the hospital, a small group of smokers huddles together in the chilly air, no matter what time of day. Restaurants still permit smoking and, in several, these are the crowded sections. One discouraged businessman observed that people in Blackwell are dying of drug overdoses and lung cancer.

Although there are many instances of a tidy well-kept house sitting beside a falling-down trailer or dilapidated old home, there are some neighborhoods largely segregated by income, including Redbud Hill, still home for most of Blackwell's professionals—lawyers, doctors, pharmacists, and insurance people. Today the bloom is off Redbud Hill, where Gwen had observed twenty years ago that the "haves" liked to live so they could *look down on the rest of us*. The winding roads are in need of repair, homes need new paint, and more gardens appear neglected. There have been arrests for drug dealing in the neighborhood. The county seat independent school that nestles up to the Hill is busy on a winter afternoon as students prepare to go home. The school still sends a high proportion of its students to college, and remains highly ranked in the state. Those we interviewed who are living well in Blackwell attended the independent school, and send their children there. On this midafternoon there are as many dads as moms, and quite a few grandparents, picking up children.

Twenty years later the Department for Community Based Services occupies the same unimposing two-story stucco building, still leased from Joey Scott. The current director, who stays in Blackwell to take care of his aging parents and to enjoy fishing and hunting, explains that the combination of welfare reform in the mid-1990s, with its limited time for receiving benefits, and today's electronic transfer of SNAP means the building is much quieter now. Unlike twenty years ago, when waiting rooms were filled to capacity with young mothers and their children, no clients appeared while we were in the building. The welfare benefit, or Temporary Assistance to Needy Families (TANF), now aids around one hundred households at a time, compared with more than fifteen hundred before reform. Clients need only one face-to-face review a year, plus a six-month case review by mail. Gone are the endless cubbyholes of caseworkers, struggling with their ambivalence about programs for unemployed single mothers that delivered benefits worth nearly what their own salaries were. Fewer than twenty workers now oversee SNAP, TANF, and Medicaid eligibility.

Dependency and abuse of programs to help people are a constant theme. Joanne and John Martin, whose hard work and caring mentors propelled them out of poverty so many years ago, worried about dependency when I interviewed them in the 1990s. John sees their own foster child, who is smart and yet was eager to get into public housing and now lives on assistance, as a perfect example. *What I said way back years ago when I worked on the War on Poverty, under the Kennedy administration, I said then "there are some people who will never get out of poverty because they want to stay there." I know that is a crazy thing to think, but it's just the truth.* Joanne adds, *It's because somehow that's the life they know. They don't want to know any more and they don't want to get ahead because I guess it scares them or something. Don't you remember he told us that he did not want his family to know that he graduated from high school because nobody else had graduated from high school and they would think he thought he was better than they were?*

The Martins still live in their small home up the hill from their white church. The dark living room is filled with nicknacks and photographs of their own children and grandchildren and the many young people for whom they have been foster parents. Slowed down by age and arthritis, they stay close to home. Their view is that Blackwell has seen material changes—better housing, an impressive new high school facility, the expansion of the community and technical college—but that social problems and the dependency they deplored twenty years ago still afflict the county, and are worse now. *They want the government to give them a medical card, to give them food, to give them child care, and I just don't see any of that ever being a positive thing. . . . They just want it given to them, they don't want to work for it.*

Many Blackwell residents we talked with complained about dependency, even those who otherwise would clearly consider themselves progressive politically. *The women, the women have babies and get on welfare. The guys live with them.* Over and over we heard versions of the old cliché from twenty years ago about young people without ambition. *When I ask, "What do you want to do when you grow up?" they reply, "Gonna draw, draw a check."* Just like twenty years ago, people can at the same time complain about dependency and remark on the seven hundred applicants for twelve jobs at the new equipment supplier, or describe a young man who received disability in Blackwell but, when he moved to the Southwest with a new girlfriend, found work. Jobs are scarce and many who stay in Blackwell depend on whatever public assistance they can get.

Mining is hard, dangerous work. By the time miners reach their forties and fifties many have hurt their backs or have other physical disabilities. Of course, the relationship between the painkillers for those injuries and the current addiction problem is on everyone's mind. A third of working-age men report a work-related disability. Almost 15 percent of adults receive Supplemental Security Income (SSI), or disability payments, twice what it was in 1990. Blackwell has about 8,800 working men and women over sixteen, and about 3,000 over eighteen receiving SSI. A psychologist described how the process goes. *I was part of that system at one time, attorneys, doctors, and it was an economy. The attorneys would hire me, and I didn't fudge. I did the intellectual assessments and academic assessments, and here were these guys, with IQs in the 80s and low 90s. They have an educational level of eighth or ninth grade. They can barely read and write. They're functionally illiterate, and they can't get a job based on that. You know, that's my report. And then they have a doctor's report where they have a bad knee, bad eyes, or you know, ankles, back. They get that doctor's report, and then the attorney takes that to the worker's comp board or Social Security board, and they get some sort of assistance.*

Disability and other programs to support low-income households concern working people in Blackwell, who see dependency all around them. Inevitably there are also those who abuse the system, and these stories make people question providing aid more generally. *She's thirty-one and is already on SSI, and that's why she's taking the Lortab, supposedly because she's got a back problem. But she walked perfectly normally, you know, no cane, no crutch, no difficulty with our steep, crooked stairs. That's probably a case of somebody who doesn't have any education, probably can't read and write.* Rumors about misuse of assistance abound. A woman who works at Walmart tells her friends that students who receive money to help them get an education misuse those funds and flood into the store to buy things unrelated to schooling when they get their checks. *December is a crazy month because of Christmas, and January's crazy because of all the returns. February's crazy because all of these people going to school on checks bring the extra money they got from their checks that's supposed to help pay for the semester and for the gas and for . . . They bring it all to Walmart and blow it within a week. You know, with big TVs and electronics and stuff.*

Everywhere we go there are police on the street, all in new cruisers paid for with Homeland Security or coal severance tax funds. The police in one town have been heralded for recent efforts to reach out to young people, mentor and involve them in fishing or sports, but the resounding theme is that the police ignore drug deals going on right in front of them or, on the other hand, more often, overstep their authority. *Well you have uneducated guys who put the badge on and put the gun on, and they hassle people. They stop you for no probable cause. They just give people a hard time . . .* A young man struggling with addiction described the first time he was pulled over. *I had a license. But it was known that I was using. And the state trooper was a former neighbor of mine. And he just saw me, passed me on the road, and pulled me over. . . . I never was, never was drug tested. But he arrested me anyway. He had me do the sobriety field test and everything. I passed with flying colors. And he arrested me anyway, said I didn't . . . I said my alphabet backwards. I stood on one foot and said one-one-thousand, all the way up to like twenty-two-one-thousand. I mean I just kept going and going, and he still arrested me. I mean he wanted to.*

Families cluster together in Blackwell's small settlements, each with its own identity and loyalty, just as they did twenty years ago, and, as we have seen, family holds people to this place where there are so few opportunities to make a living. Certainly that is the case with Benny and Bobbie Jean Corbett. They are in their early twenties and working hard to raise Bobbie Jean's four-year-old son. We meet in a booth in the back of the pizza restaurant, away from the smoking section. Benny, tall and skinny in jeans and a cap, was laid off at the mines six months ago, and his local magistrate, knowing his father was a hard worker, got him a job with the county hauling gravel and pushing snow. *He brings home half what he did at the mines, but I am just glad that he got a job*, Bobbie Jean says, and Benny nods vigorously. Benny and Bobbie Jean say the era of coal mining is gone for Blackwell. *They think the future of Blackwell is coming out of the holler. It's past. I'm a coal miner too, and I know the future is not in coal. It's sad but true. It's not easy to let go of heritages. But if this county's going to succeed, to prosper at all, it's got to go beyond coal, because coal's over.*

Both Benny and Bobbie Jean grew up poor, though Benny's family was stable while Bobbie Jean's was chaotic. Her mother was a drug addict, married numerous times, and her birth dad could not hold down a job. She is grateful to be wrapped in the embrace of Benny's extended family on whom they depend. They all live next to one another on his uncle's property. His parents pay for their housing and heat, and help with groceries. Benny, more an athlete than a student, graduated from high school and went right into the mines. He has not ventured far from Blackwell, not even to the interstate highway that crosses the state sixty miles from Blackwell. Bobbie Jean passed all her AP courses, but then found she was pregnant. *I didn't have a car, didn't have parents to turn to. I was on food stamps, welfare, everything. And now I am watching my sister go through it.*

In reflecting on Blackwell and how things are going, they say they worry about the children who grow up in the hollows and for whom school is the only time they socialize and get a good meal. *You got some nice places around here, but when you get down our way you got kids that don't have phones, Internet, or cable. Whose houses look like garbage.* They both say they will never leave Blackwell—partly because they could never afford to live anywhere else, and partly because they want to be near family. *A lot of people really just stay here because all their family is here. I mean you are just surrounded by them. It's a family-oriented place.*

Family members support those who can't find work or have been in trouble with the law—with money, housing, child care, and emotional support. *I've been on my own. I've had to go backwards and forth a little bit, like moving back in to my mom and dad's because I'd lose a job or something. But it wouldn't take me long to get back out of there because my parents are one of my biggest stress triggers. They're very controlling, going back to where I needed them when I got pregnant early and didn't know what to do.* We talked to several young parents who were struggling who simultaneously appreciated their parents' support, a rooftop and meals, help with housing and children, and chafed under the control it involved. *When I've threatened to leave, I've had my mother get mad and threaten to take me to court to get custody of my children.*

Indeed, while grandparents have raised young people throughout rural America over the years, there is a clear consensus that grandparents are now raising more and more children as drug addiction ravages their parents' lives. A magistrate and his fishing buddy said they figured half the children in Blackwell were being raised by grandparents. Although this is hardly the case, even official census statistics, which do not capture the informal or temporary arrangements, indicate that the proportion has doubled over the past decade and now is nearly 10 percent. We heard one account of a struggling young mother selling her children to her in-laws, who later sued her for child support so they could qualify for grandparent benefits. A teacher noted, *I had a really high percentage of children that were being raised by grandparents or other family members. And it almost seems like the children who were being raised by grandparents had more pressure to succeed than children who were being raised by unemployed parents or single parents or substance-abuse parents.* The ties are complicated, and those relying on their own parents for help are both grateful and resentful.

There are some glimmers of better conditions. In 1990, 49 percent of adults had a high school degree, and in 2010 the figure was up to 68 percent (compared with 85 percent nationally). The several county high schools have consolidated. The building and accompanying sports facilities are impressive—more like a college campus than a high school. While consolidation has necessarily reduced the number of students participating on sports teams, to the chagrin of some, the newly consolidated Blackwell teams are highly competitive statewide, a boon in a sports-loving region. The school collaborates with the community college on the new dual-credit programs. Students say there is less fighting in the new building, where the grades are separated on different levels, and where it is harder to run across people from other communities with whom you might want to fight. There are hundreds of security cameras, and at least one security guard on duty at the entrance.

Over the past two decades the community and technical college has evolved into an important anchor institution, with multiple campuses and programs training miners, nurses, teachers, and even embalmers. The school includes a dynamic arts and culture program that brings a wide range of community residents into its events and encourages new dialogue about the challenges facing Blackwell. Like other Appalachian arts and culture programs over the years, it has achieved national recognition. For many the college has provided a supportive educational environment leading to training, and that training permits some Blackwell men and women to find a way to work without leaving. But people point out that the local markets are saturated, and outmigration is bound to increase, especially as coal employment declines still further.

People in Blackwell often say they love the mountains. *Mountains are almost like family here. You walk out the back door, you're gonna hit one. You walk out the front door, you're gonna see one. They're there. You drive around 'em, and they're like grumpy old family members who don't wanna move, and you gotta get around 'em. But, they're comforting, too, to me.* Some say the natural environment is improving in Blackwell, thanks in part to better regulation and in part to greater consciousness about litter. There are fewer "pamper trees" along the rivers, and local fishermen and hunters report that the bass and elk and black bears are back. *You can actually eat the fish. Really. You can eat the fish.* But at the same time local newspapers regularly report fish kills, and the debates over the environmental consequences of strip mining rage fiercely. The energetic recreation boosters are eager to see more progress on the environmental front to bolster their efforts to woo tourists and fishermen and hunters to Blackwell. The Friends of Coal complain about excessive regulation and President Obama and the Environmental Protection Agency waging war on coal. Indeed, in some ways the old "fer us or agin us" attitude that characterized labor and management fights in the coal industry has been replaced by battles between those who want to protect the coal industry and those who want to see Blackwell transition, like much of rural America, to more of a tourism and recreation orientation to take advantage of the region's natural resources.

So some educational and environmental improvements have seeped in from the outside. But overall we found that the long-standing problems in Blackwell persist, and local politics and economic hegemony are just about the same. Former county judge Bobby Lee King, who had wrestled with personal and political challenges in recent years, died recently, young, in his early sixties, just after our visit. His own children are among those who have left for urban areas with more jobs. His memorial service was well attended, and he was lauded for honest hard work in a community known for its self-serving politicians. Leonard Burns, the current county judge executive, is a voluble, well-meaning man from Tennessee who has been reelected three times. He says when he was first elected he informed the magistrates that there would no longer be gravel poured and bridges repaired according to how people voted. His wife explains that he sees his work as county judge as service, part of his faith. He worries about the marital infidelity he sees throughout Blackwell, and relays scandalous stories of bad behavior in the county, including itinerant evangelical preachers taking advantage of young girls. He is critical of the county school system, where he sees patronage as the norm. *They are more interested in getting their family jobs, and their friends jobs. It's too political.*

Judge Burns has faced challenges in this small community's historically corrupt and faction-driven political culture. An opponent had a woman with a hidden video camera come seek financial support in an attempt to make it appear that he was accepting a bribe. He was cleared. He believes the county sheriff tried to set him up, and more recently, the feud has escalated. He conducted an ethics violation investigation of the sheriff's office related to missing drug enforcement funds, and then the sheriff arrested him for theft of property from a county building. He has been exonerated on the theft charges, but the sheriff, who continues to conduct drug raids for pills, cocaine, and Suboxone, is still under investigation for those missing funds.

Down the hall from Judge Burns is the office of Blackwell's county seat's magistrate, Sue Wells, a young woman who, like most of the student body at the local community college, went back for her associate's degree in her late twenties. She balanced bringing up her two young children with looking after an elderly grandmother and helping out two younger sisters raising kids on their own. She was raised by grandparents committed to education, and attended the independent school. A couple of dedicated teachers at the college inspired, supported, and cajoled her through her degree while she held down a job at the hospital and acted as "point person" for her extended family. Like Sara and the Corbetts, she says family ties are her anchor to Blackwell. *Family means a lot more in this region than it does in other places because, you know, we're just moving so fast we don't have time to appreciate who brought you up. And here, families mean everything. That's why we stay here. That's why I'm trying to make it a better place to live right now, and I'm actually proud to be here.* Today she works with a handful of others in Blackwell to promote new tourism and recreation programs, ATV trails and a new zipline, for example, to draw outsiders into the county. *We've got mountains.* The Friends of Coal worry that these tourism promoters are more intent on promoting the natural environment than protecting coal jobs.

Twenty years ago we found a community divided into haves and have-nots, where family names and reputations mattered, and where a few families "ran things." In 2013 the have-nots are struggling still, now with the additional challenge of serious drug abuse problems. And the same few families control Blackwell twenty years later—the economics, the politics, the land, everything. People still say that they look out for themselves, and block any investments or political efforts that might challenge their power.

Creed Parker died more than ten years ago, but his four sons run the coal operations and other businesses he developed. People say you don't want to cross them any more than you did Creed. *Don't get on their bad side*. And: *If you get fired from the Parkers you will never get another job in another coal mine ever*. And: *The Parkers are very influential in the economy here. They have so, so many things going on. Politically, they control down to the magistrate races*. The Parker sons, now in their fifties and sixties, and the older Scotts, Joey and Sam, now in their eighties, still hold tight control over the Blackwell economy, along with a small handful of other coal families. When you ask people, including a class full of students, "Who runs things?" you get the same answer you did twenty years ago—the Parkers and the Scotts. Some will include Willy Granger, who continues to be influential, and a couple other prominent local coal families who were also mentioned twenty years ago.

The Parkers' coal operations now include surface mines as well as deep mines. They also continue to have very substantial property holdings, including the buildings they rent to public agencies and the big mall they had just opened when we were here twenty years ago where young people used to drive around looking for other teens on a Friday night. The Parkers reportedly had the police put a stop to the cruising, and some say young people now do their cruising on foot in the Walmart. The Parkers' mall seemed to be on the verge of some hustle and bustle twenty years ago but now has only a few tenants. Most of the early stores have gone out of business, and locals complain that the Parkers charge rents that are too high for local businesses.

While many criticize them for only looking out for how they will profit from any new development or opportunity, others give the Parkers and Scotts credit for being in the community. *You can say what you want about people who may or may not control things in a democratic way, or whatever, or operate in an open way. But at a certain point it becomes, "they're here."* Judge Burns, switching from referring to people by their first names, argues *Mr. Parker's* presence means he cares about Blackwell. *Their kids went to school with our kids, and so it hurts them to see their community suffer. That's one thing that's almost ironic. You've got this togetherness, and then you've got this rough and tumble*.

After a period of discord when their mother died, Joey and Sam operate separately now, each with his own stores and buildings. Like the Parkers, to whom they are tied by marriage, they continue to wield heavy influence over what businesses come into Blackwell, or don't, and expand, or don't. Many people told us how the profitable local Walmart planned to become a Super Walmart until the plans were thwarted by Sam, who leases them their land and has his own successful grocery store nearby. *I don't know if I should say it or not—but the community leaders want things to stay just the way they are.*

The Scotts and the Parkers own most of the land that can be developed, and people from all walks of life say they still protect their own interests and look out for opportunities for their own families. *The families own the land here, those two families, the Parkers or the Scotts.* They will allow nothing to dilute their wealth and power. *There are wealthier families that don't want there to be any economic boom . . . that could challenge their power. You have almost a—I don't know how to put it—almost like a clan-based system. Families stick together and they jockey for power.* Several people mentioned specific examples of new businesses that were blocked from coming to Blackwell in the past five or so years. *One of the most limiting things here is if you're not one of the Parkers or not somebody with money, then your opinion, your ideas would not go very far as to make substantial change. [They have] a stranglehold. I have a friend from Georgia who wanted to bring in a retirement facility. . . . They choked him out, wouldn't let it happen . . . they just choked him out.* After years of being a dry county, Blackwell's county seat recently passed a new, limited "moist" law permitting the sale of wine and beer within the city limits, and the establishments taking advantage of the opportunity are owned or backed by the Parkers.

Politics and economic control remain tightly intertwined in Blackwell. *There is a lot of politics here. If someone does not like you, you cannot get ahead in this town, and you have to leave. . . . There are certain . . . people that have a play in the politics of Blackwell, that won't let anything in. . . . It's the same families. It's just a different generation.* Although there are signs that some areas of local politics are more honest and more focused on community improvement, including the efforts of Judge Burns and Sue Wells, many people we talked with named recent examples of corruption. Judge Burns recounted a case of an odd sort of morality. *I said, "I'd sure like to have your support." He said, "I can't." I said, "Why not?" He said, "Because I'm committed to the other person. He paid me already."*

Family names continue to matter. Even in a courtroom, a judge might interrupt the lawyers to ask the defendant what his or her last name is, taking a measure of the young person's family reputation. *At one point, he stopped the hearing and said, "Young man, what is your father's last name?" And I'm going to myself, what the devil does that matter? You know, what business is that of yours? But he answered it and the judge went, "Okay, now I know who you are."* But the drug problem has added a new dimension to the role that names play in Blackwell. A teenager was one of several we interviewed to have this experience. *My dad was a drug addict and stayed in trouble all the time, in and out of prison. My big brother was the same way. My little brother's starting to get that way . . . it would be anywhere, even the doctor's office, hair salon, anywhere that would require me to reserve something in my last name, I couldn't do it. They wouldn't, they would not allow me. Just because of my brothers and my dad, they would think that I was the same way.*

The worsening jobs situation, the outmigration, the drug addiction, ongoing teen births, high poverty and dependency, all paint a dreary picture of Blackwell, aggravated and perpetuated by politics tightly controlled by a small group of families. Change has not just failed to emerge, it has been blocked. The story of Johnny Bledsoe, a native son who tried to work for change, illustrates how political forces can stamp out progress in isolated single-industry communities like Blackwell.

Twenty years ago I concluded that better education was key to improving opportunity in chronically poor communities. And, fortunately, education has improved in this Appalachian state over that period. Blackwell's county schools are reportedly somewhat better too, primarily as a result of statewide reform. Johnny Bledsoe played a key role in developing and implementing those reforms. Johnny and I talk in his small windowless office over the mine engineering facility at the community college. His accomplished woodworking projects are displayed on his shelves among the books. A couple of students pop in as we talk, but most of Johnny's students are taking his classes online these days, many from other parts of the state, some even from overseas in Iraq or Afghanistan. Johnny's great-great-grandparents came to Blackwell in the early 1800s, and they and their children and grandchildren worked in the mines and started small businesses. After graduating from the county seat independent school, Johnny went on to college, returning home in the tumultuous early 1970s. He considered teaching in the public schools, but like Joey Scott more than a decade earlier, he could not see how to raise a family on the low pay. He was eventually hired by the new community college.

Grateful for the student loans that made his education possible, he broke from his parents' Republican politics and became a Democratic activist, running to be Blackwell's state representative in his late twenties. To the surprise of many, he won by a large margin. He went on to serve in the legislature for fifteen years. He was passionate about education. He recognized how the patronage-driven school boards in the region had undermined good teaching and, in his mind, stood as the primary obstacle to development of the region. Working with his fellow "young Turks" in the legislature, Johnny took a leadership role in bringing much-needed education reform to the state. One piece of that was a new accountability office he created while he served as chair of the education committee. Somewhat to his surprise, one of the committee's very first targets was Blackwell. But he acknowledges, *Blackwell was real dirty. It was dirty and needed cleaning up*. Money had been laundered and misappropriated, hiring was based on patronage rewarding loyal voters, everything called for intervention. The state took over the Blackwell schools for a period in the mid-1990s.

Johnny also took a stand on coal. He always opposed mountaintop removal, but he supported deep mining and he had Creed Parker's financial support, if through another person, in the early days. But Johnny's concern about mountaintop removal became more urgent when he read a national news story about devastating strip-mining pollution in a nearby community in his district. *I read it, and I went up there, and I went, "Man, how did I not know this?" Two weeks after I was elected I met with state environmental people and said, "What's going on with this strip mining? Like, you know, we gotta work on it," and they promised they would.*

Over the years Johnny made himself felt, both statewide and in Blackwell. In response, local coal operators, including the Parker sons, who were heavily engaged in surface mining, joined with the school board members who were angry about his education policy and they set out to defeat him. They used the old-style political pressures. *It's a mindset. It's folks who've been outta work for years. They will still get that signal from the operators, you know, and they figure that's what you have to do. You have to go this way*. After the election, school workers stopped by his house, sometimes in tears, to say they couldn't vote for him because they would lose their jobs. *She said, "I'm so sorry, but I was afraid I'd lose my job. But I couldn't vote for you, you know, my family didn't get to vote for you." And then a person that worked at the cafeteria at another school, some cooks at the cafeteria, people, janitors, staff, and some teachers said they felt pressured.*

Johnny and his wife have made a good life here. They enjoy their family and community and he continues to speak out politically. He coaches his granddaughter's Little League team with one person who worked to defeat him. They chat about their grandchildren, and even stop for coffee after the game on occasion. As Judge Burns observed, *you've got this togetherness, and then the rough and tumble*. Johnny can make a life in Blackwell among family and neighbors even after his political defeat and the permanent civic-sector blackballing he endures. But when Johnny thinks about the future, with coal in decline, drugs hurting so many, and county schools still in bad shape, he is not optimistic. *Until we diversify this coal, and I know it sounds clichéd, but until we do something about that, it's not going to change. And there's enough wealth still among the coal operators that they will direct, direct the economic area . . . politics and economics are joined at the hip here*.

In the 1990s Blackwell was made up of two rigid classes and entangled in corrupt politics. The Parkers and the Scotts held tight control over jobs and economic development, looking out for their own families. Twelve thousand people lived in poverty, more than a third of the county, and they were looked down upon and deprived of opportunities to get a good education or steady work. People then said nothing would change until Blackwell had some kind of economic diversification that would loosen those powerful families' grip on the civic culture.

Twenty years later the base of the economy has not changed. *Coal is all there is*. But coal is down and going down further, and people are leaving, especially the young adults that every community relies on for vitality and growth. Importantly, the same few families still run Blackwell, and they still run things to benefit their own families, not the community. Poverty, dependency, and drug addiction ravage the have-nots, who scrabble and live a mean existence. Family ties and a deep love of the mountains hold many, but opportunities are few and the future is dim.

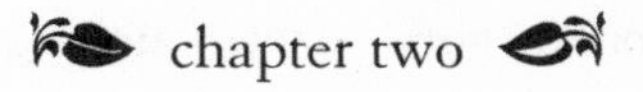

chapter two

DAHLIA

Racial Segregation and Planter Control in the Mississippi Delta

Highway 44 shimmers on this hot July day as we drive toward Dahlia, long one of the nation's poorest and most unequal counties, in the heart of the Mississippi Delta. Large plantations growing cotton, rice, and soybeans dominate the landscape and the economy of this large floodplain of the Mississippi and Yazoo rivers. Flat fields stretch endlessly to the horizon, interrupted only by the levees built decades ago to protect the crops from Mississippi River flooding. On both sides of the road, giant sprinkler systems—spiderlike pipes on wheels spewing water—are moving slowly down the fields. On the right, down a rutted red dirt road, a truck is parked near a group of workers who chop at the weeds growing up in the rows of cotton. The smell of hot tar in the road mingles with a slight odor of pesticide in the air. In the distance a small plane flies low over cotton fields to the west, then eases up over trees and telephone lines and back into the fields, leaving a fantail of pesticide in its wake.

Off the two-lane highway and down a long driveway, tucked back among high shade trees, stands a large, elegant house surrounded by manicured gardens, a tennis court, and a swimming pool. This modern plantation home is where Dahlia's Episcopalians hold their annual tennis tournament, the parish's big charity event—*tennis with a sumptuous feast*, says one enthusiast. The event raises several thousand dollars for someone in the white community with large doctor bills—last year an elderly woman with leukemia, the year before a farm manager's son who had muscular dystrophy.

Farther up the highway we pass a cluster of old tenant shacks on a dirt road near Baker's plantation store and gas station. The shacks' corrugated tin roofs are patched with odd pieces of metal and their siding is a collection of different-sized wood nailed roughly to the leaning structures. An elderly black woman is sitting on the porch steps, watching two small boys playing with an old tire near an outdoor pump.

These country shacks are becoming a rare sight because each year several more are burned to the ground when black families no longer needed on the farm move into neighborhoods closer to town. *With five good tractor drivers, they can farm three thousand acres of land. They want to get the older people out of those houses*, a white lawyer explains. *Now, people say Winston would not have just put this old nigger woman out onto the road and said, "Get down." But he kept saying to her, "I'm not going to keep this house up. I'm not going to fix the roof. I'm not going to fix the floors. If you move out, I'm going to knock it down." When I first came here in the 1950s you could have found tenant houses all over everywhere, and you can hardly find one anymore.*

All that remains of the former settlement of white sharecroppers here on the outskirts of town is a small wooden church. Its name, Little Oklahoma Church, painted under the steeple, has faded with time. The few low-income white families still in Dahlia now live in town, where well-to-do whites refer to them as "porch people" because of the clutter they accumulate on their porches. But they still come out to Little Oklahoma on Sundays to attend their own church.

DAHLIA'S TWO SOCIAL WORLDS

There are two separate social worlds in Dahlia, just as there are in Blackwell, but here the divisions are based on race as well as class. The haves are the very wealthy planter elite and the comfortable, upper-middle-class whites for whom the small-town contacts and friendly social life make the place like "paradise," as a local physician likes to describe it. The have-nots, who make up the great majority in the county, are blacks who struggle to provide for their families. Although a few working poor white porch people still live in Dahlia and, as we shall see, a small new black middle class is emerging, the social milieu is defined by the large divide between whites who have money and power and very poor blacks who have long been dependent on them.

Even today, plantation owners with enormous wealth are called "bossman" by the blacks who work for them, "farmers" by other whites. As in Blackwell, everyone—white and black, professionals and school dropouts—can name the top five or so families that run things. These powerful farmers can get you out of jail if they need you in the fields, have you permanently blackballed from work if you cross them, or make sure you and your family never get credit anywhere if you let them down. *They will cut you out*, warns a white businessman. *They will run you out of town*, a black professional cautions.

As we approach the county seat of Dahlia, agricultural land gives way to buildings that house businesses and service facilities on the edge of town—first a catfish plant surrounded by its loading ponds and a small gravel parking area, then a long blue aluminum industrial building, recently expanded, where the apparel plant that located here twenty years ago still produces blue jeans for large, low-end clothing chains. Closer to town lies the old faded stucco hospital, now a clinic, where waiting rooms segregated by race only a few years ago now are divided, with much the same effect, according to whether patients have appointments or not. Beyond the clinic is a small shopping plaza with a chain grocery store notorious for its high prices and racially biased promotion practices, and a locally owned drug store where elderly black women have the Catholic sisters do their shopping for them to ensure that they get fair prices. *They have been taken advantage of so much that most still don't trust us*, explains the white proprietor.

Farm machinery and car dealerships, their lots full of new tractors and shiny automobiles, line the highway on the north side, followed by an old drive-up hamburger restaurant where waitresses in red aprons come out to your car and a Dairy Cream shack that still has a side window where black customers are used to placing their orders. The Sunflower, a sit-down restaurant famous for its good black cooks and easygoing white waitresses, is located right on the highway where it intersects with the road into town. Cooks are told to stay in the kitchen, and waitresses are warned not to mix with them. *They said, "Your place is out here and theirs in the kitchen,"* a woman who was recently hired explained. Here Dahlia's farmers and merchants, lawyers and secretaries, come to visit and eat greens, slaw, and fried catfish or chicken. The atmosphere is friendly, as patrons talk between tables and boisterously greet new arrivals. Most days the clientele is all white, although occasionally a professional black man or woman visiting from the capital on state business may come with a local white counterpart. Even this infrequent integration is recent. In the seventies no black would have been welcome, and even now some whites glare disapprovingly when black customers come in. One black teacher says she stays away on principle, although her brother, a politician, eats at the Sunflower on occasion when he has business to conduct with whites.

The white neighborhood, where all whites except the wealthiest plantation owners have homes, lies between Highway 44 and the small downtown area. Old trees form a canopy shading streets laid out in straight lines and even blocks. Gardens are lush and well kept. Most houses are large and set back from the street, and even smaller homes have columns in front, marking their regional heritage. A few older plantation-style homes in the northernmost section of town, near the porch people's neighborhood, have a Faulknerian look of decay and neglect: peeling paint, rusting hinges, overgrown shrubbery. But new bikes lying on the driveways near basketball hoops indicate there is life inside.

The Presbyterian, Methodist, and Episcopal churches, relatively modest structures within a few blocks of each other, are mixed in with the homes in this white neighborhood, their brick walkways leading to the church and the manse. Blacks are rarely seen here, and not long ago a resident complained to one of the ministers about black child care workers parking on the street. *We have two black ladies keep our nursery during Sunday morning services and they were parking out here in front of the church. Somebody spoke up and was opposed to it, to letting them park there. They said they ought to park in the back.* The minister asked the women to park their cars in his driveway to avoid further dispute over the matter.

Downtown Dahlia, adjacent to this serene white neighborhood, has a pleasant small-town ambiance—Main Street is wide and merchants do a steady business. Next to an old Rexall drug store with a soda fountain is a dark antique shop run by the former superintendent. Farther along is Farmer's Bank with its newly renovated facade and cash machine. Just beyond the bank, shaded by pecan trees planted along the sidewalk, is a line of storefront offices, including those of several lawyers, a new doctor's office, and the main location for the Catholic Sisters' Mission, where Sisters Mary and Ruth hold sewing and parenting classes twice a week for young black mothers who have dropped out of school. Interspersed are the three family-owned furniture stores that sell everything from air conditioners to living-room suites on credit to those who have *their Mama's signature and the bossman's okay*. Down the street, at the north end of town, looms the large, imposing Baptist church with wide white steps that stretch across the whole front of the building.

Dahlia Day School, the private academy, occupies two small buildings surrounded by tennis courts and ball fields on the edge of town behind the Baptist church. Founded in the mid-1960s when integration looked imminent, the school is still not accredited and pays low salaries to its mostly female teachers, who are wives of farm managers and storekeepers. The academy absorbs all the volunteers and funds in the white community—*drains the money and energy*, laments one minister—but it is also the social hub. Dahlia's weekly newspaper features a school event organized by the Mothers' Club in nearly every issue: the auction, a bake sale, the fashion show, a carnival. The school also runs the town's other annual tennis tournament, combining crucial fund-raising with townwide socializing. Scholarships are made available through the churches, the Women's Club, and several wealthy farmers, ensuring that even the children of the few white truck drivers and waitresses can attend. These children are not included in the cliques of the wealthier white children, but at least they do not have to attend the largely black public schools, and thus the well-established pattern of segregation is maintained.

Many residents, black and white, say the original funds and supplies for the private academy came from the public school budget, made available by the powerful, politically adept former superintendent of the system, Jack Peabody. *Everyone knows our former superintendent used the public school fund and equipment supply to set up the academy—it was not a secret*, explains the spouse of a former teacher. At first the public school district kept paying the teachers who moved to the academy, but eventually the judge who had ordered the public schools to integrate required the teachers to repay that money.

Black students attend the public schools, first the un-air-conditioned elementary facility along Highway 44, then the junior high, now housed in the former white elementary school on the edge of town, and finally the large high school, surrounded by a chain-link fence, also out on the highway near the car dealerships. The public elementary and high school facilities are poor—*built as colored schools*, explains a teacher. Classrooms and hallways are chaotic, and at the upper levels cutting class is routine. As in Blackwell's county schools, teachers and administrators struggle to maintain order. *It's a free-for-all. It is unbelievable what those kids are doing—food fights in the cafeteria, holes in the walls, cutting class, laying out on the benches all day long. It's just horrible.* Some students say they come to school drunk or high, and even twenty-year-olds are punished with wooden paddles and may spend all day in detention rooms. Teachers as well as students report that knife fights are common. *They have had cuttings start in the bathrooms and spill out into the halls even when state evaluators are there*, sympathizes an educator from upstate.

Low test scores have kept Dahlia's public schools on probationary status for years. Some administrators strive to enforce discipline and to lift the schools from their bottom ranking in the state, but scarce resources, destructive racial politics, discouraged teachers, and pressure to hire "homeboys"—men and women who grew up in the county—make it hard to accomplish. A white principal explained that hiring requires extensive interviewing because he has to be sure white teachers are not prejudiced against blacks and black teachers are not racist toward white teachers.

In recent years more blacks have been elected to replace white school board members and superintendents, but change comes slowly. Black activist Harold Jackson explained: *Sometimes the elected black is more oppressive than a white can be. I believe it is a phase the community goes through. You elect the most electable person in your county, and it may turn out to be not the best representative of your community. But you do that so you can break the barrier, and then the next time around you find someone who will be more representative of our constituents.*

The stakes are high, just as they are in Blackwell, when schools often hold out the only hope for children growing up in desperately poor families, often with illiterate parents or guardians. For years white school officials avoided making investments in the black schools—hence no air conditioning in the 1990s—and resisted applying for public programs available for schools with poor children. Keeping costs down and outside interference to a minimum have been the goals of the school administrators and the elected school boards to whom they report. *When we tried to get the free breakfast program implemented in the school system, we had opposition from the superintendent, who was then white, and even from some of the teachers. It was seen as "too much trouble" and that "it wouldn't really help kids." "It would be a wasted program." "They wouldn't eat their food." "It's a giveaway program." "We shouldn't be doing that kind of stuff."*

When black sharecroppers lived on the plantations and the bossman furnished everything from housing to medical care, black children attended one-room plantation schoolhouses. These plantation schools were closed in the 1950s when school consolidation swept rural America, and Dahlia Colored Vocational School was opened with grades seven through ten.

Until the 1960s a complete high school education was available only to the handful of black children selected by their congregation to attend a church-sponsored school. In the 1980s about 15 percent of black adults in Dahlia had completed high school; by 1990 the rate had reached a little more than 30 percent. Now education is available to all black children for the full nine-month school year, but the schools themselves are deeply troubled. The few black professionals who live in Dahlia worry about their children's education, and several families pay tuition so their children can attend the Catholic school in the next county.

In the 1990s, most blacks in Dahlia, even those who work on the farms, live in one of three neighborhoods—all outside the city limits surrounding the enclave where most whites live. There is Dahlia's longtime black neighborhood called Old Town, an unincorporated area just east of downtown where the more established black families live. A few houses, well kept, with tidy yards, are those of schoolteachers and small store owners who have been able to buy homes here. But even these are small and were built at a time when blacks had no resources for housing. The majority are clearly substandard, patched over the years with bits of plywood and roofing material, their yards cluttered with discarded chairs or appliances, old cars, and leaning outbuildings. The streets are narrow and full of potholes, in stark contrast to those in the white neighborhood just on the other side of the railroad tracks beyond the water tower. Despite the presumably stabilizing influence of long-term residents and married couples, idle teenagers gather near the small cafes scattered throughout the neighborhood and worry older folks. Whites see these conditions as the responsibility of the black leaders who live in the neighborhood. Schoolteacher Sharon Carter suggests, *Maybe there wouldn't be so much drug activity if some of the trash and some of the old homes and some of the cars were picked up, if some of the places were condemned and torn down?*

In the 1970s an enterprising white businessman, who has since left the area, used federal funds from the Farmers Home Administration to develop a subdivision of modest single-family tract homes for low-income blacks, calling it Tall Pines.[1] The new development was located out in the county between two huge plantations some miles from town. Blacks and whites describe a rocky start here when very poor, illiterate country families, accustomed to wood heat and cooking stoves in their plantation shacks, were suddenly placed in homes with electric heating and thermostats, electric appliances, utility bills, and mortgages. These newcomers reportedly left the heat on high but opened windows to cool their houses; they failed to pay utility bills, missed payments on their house notes, and faced foreclosure. Several houses are boarded up to this day. Now the neighborhood has mostly younger households, many headed by single parents, and young men in gangs are said to control some streets. It is a socially disorganized and even dangerous place to live, much like a city ghetto.

Finally, there is the new public housing complex, the Fields. Built in the late 1980s, it is the Delta version of rural multifamily housing everywhere: two-story duplex apartments arrayed around a barren cul-de-sac where the metal mailboxes and a bulletin board are located. Most apartments in the Fields have at least two plastic straight-back chairs crowded on their small stoops. Despite the lack of a front porch, these are desirable, subsidized apartments, where tenants are young single mothers or older widows on public assistance. Getting into these subsidized apartments is said to be highly political. Like summer program slots or public jobs, they represent a resource that people are grateful to have, and local leaders who make them available expect to be rewarded with votes at election time.

Michael Long, a black leader, recalled, *When the apartments started coming in, the politics started. They started getting their friends into the apartments. You may have had a daughter or child who lived at home with mom and dad and they wanted them to have a new apartment. My phone rang off the hook—"We want an apartment. We want an apartment." I didn't have anything to do with the decision making about who was going to move into the apartments. But when they got an apartment, then that family felt obligated to those who made it available.*

There are just a handful of black homes outside these three settlements. The Greens and the Wrights are two of the few black families that have owned small farms or funeral businesses, preached, or taught school for more than a generation, and they have nice brick homes out in the country. They are part of the small black elite in Dahlia who have property or education, or both. Some activists like Harold Jackson and Michael Long call them "Toms," short for Uncle Toms, because they reportedly accommodate the wishes of the white power structure, even when it requires looking the other way when blacks suffer injustices. There are also several new houses near these brick homes of the black elite that Frank Pendleton, owner of one of the largest plantations, makes available rent-free to the older black tractor drivers on whom he has come to rely. Sarah Early, a black nurse practitioner, deplores the way these rent-free homes perpetuate the old plantation dependency. *The plantation owner built five or six pretty nice little brick houses, bathroom inside, all the conveniences. His guys live in those with their families and they don't pay any rent. They don't pay any utility bill. So, they own you already, okay? My cousin thinks, "I live in a nice house, no rent. I don't have to worry about my gas being turned off in the winter, or my lights being turned off. I* got *to stay here."*

Land is notoriously hard to buy in Dahlia—partly because it has high value as farmland, but also because controlling land is crucial for maintaining segregation. It is virtually impossible for blacks to obtain land for homes or businesses. In the early 1990s some white and black leaders formed a fledgling chapter of Habitat for Humanity, the self-help volunteer housing group promoted by former president Jimmy Carter. But even with several well-placed whites on its board, the group has found obtaining affordable land a major obstacle to getting a house under way for a poor family that is invariably black. A white board member gave this account: *It's hard for Habitat to buy land to build those houses, partly because of greed. The land values have gone up. Maybe some of it is fear of where they're going to put it. They don't want it too close to a white neighborhood. Those are some of the unspoken reasons. But these farmers are good businessmen. That's just the way they are. I've seen them wheel and deal, and you can't fault them for that. They're just good at that. As far as Habitat goes, land is very precious. They don't want to give it up if they can sell it for $12,000 an acre.*

Finally, just in the past several years, junior high principal Robert Wilson and his family and another couple who are recent return migrants, new middle-class black families with professional jobs in the public sector, were able to lease small tracts of land from a white who needed cash. They built modest homes in the country, not far from the Fields. But they are an oft-mentioned exception. In fact, the majority of black schoolteachers, even those who grew up in the county, commute almost an hour from suburban middle-class neighborhoods in a metropolitan area west of Dahlia where they can find a nice brick home. There is no housing integration in Dahlia in the 1990s, nor any other kind of integration.

Today there are 4,400 families in Dahlia, about 1,800 white and 2,600 black, a demographic fact with far-reaching political and social implications. The poverty rate has been over 40 percent for decades, and more than 80 percent of blacks are poor still. More than 1,500 black families live in poverty, compared with about 200 white families. Nearly half of black children live in single-parent households; of white children, only 12 percent do.[2]

But Dahlia also includes very wealthy farmers, and over the past thirty years farms have become larger and ownership more concentrated. These thousand-acre farms receive very large federal subsidies—as much as $20 million in some recent years, twice the amount of federal grants that comes in for the three thousand families on public assistance. Since large farmers disperse ownership among relatives to increase the amount of subsidy they can claim, some wealthy farm families have received more than $85,000 per year in federal subsidies. A farm manager explained: *Well, the big corporate farms that you have around here, they're still "family farms." It's just the corporation is made up of the patriarch or matriarch of the family and the sons, and as many people as they can scrape up for government purposes.* In one notorious case from a nearby county, covered in the national press, a planter with some fourteen thousand acres claimed over a million dollars in federal payments through his various corporations and family trusts.[3]

So there is great wealth for the few, deep poverty for most, and virtually no middle class, white or black. A white schoolteacher stated flatly, *There are four middle-class white families here.* A storekeeper says, *I think there are three or four of us now.* A gas station owner talked about his own decision to go into business for himself in terms of class: *We weren't advancing socially. In Dahlia there's a great deal of social pressure 'cause there are a lot a wealthy people and there is not a big middle class.* Most agree with the black schoolteacher who said, *Our black middle class are those who have left for the cities.* Census statistics show that in 1960, when there were twice as many farms, the poverty rate in Dahlia was 75 percent, and 90 percent of the population had incomes below the U.S. median. In 1990 the poverty rate was 50 percent and 75 percent had incomes below the median. Per capita income for whites in Dahlia is nearly five times that of blacks, more than $15,000 compared with $3,500. This inequality, with its glaring racial dimension, is the dominant factor shaping social relations and determining prospects for mobility and change. Race and class go together in Dahlia, and being black means being poor in all but a few cases.

Although there is complete social segregation, the black and white communities are deeply intertwined economically. Whites own almost all the property and businesses and control all the jobs, but they depend on blacks for labor and often as customers. Blacks must seek jobs, credit, and housing from whites, and sometimes from those blacks who act on whites' behalf. Blacks work for white families and farms as domestics, cooks, tractor drivers, field hands, and for white-run businesses as factory workers stitching at the apparel plant or cutting off fish heads at the catfish plant. Black workers have no recourse or rights on the plantations, according to both whites and blacks. One white truck driver's wife explained, *If one of the blacks was to piss Jimmy off—you know he drives for a farmer—he could make it hard on him if he said something to his boss. He could make it really hard on the boy, make him get fired. It's just over here the blacks don't have the opportunities that whites does. They're really disgraded.*

For years, farmers—like coal operators in Blackwell—made sure no new industry came into Dahlia, thus ensuring their monopoly over employment and wages. Many people think they continue to obstruct new industry. Farmers' fears about losing their workforce are well founded, even today, according to Diana Smith, a black educational leader. *If the guys that drive tractors now could find a job that pays decent wages, they would get off the tractor. I'm talking about a job* here—*not one that they would have to travel fifty miles one way to get to work. Tractor driving is hard work, and it's really only summer work, with long hours then. But, see, the advantage that the white guy has right now is that they may only work five or six months out of the year. So what does a guy with a family do during the winter months? He has to go back and ask his bossman for an advancement or a loan, or whatever, to help him until he starts working again. In most cases, they'll give them that loan. "I'll let you have this money or whatever, then I know you'll be back when I need you in the spring just to farm again." That kind of lending is still going on for most of your farmers.* The furnishing of advances, just like the coal company's commissary furnishing credit in Blackwell, helps maintain the old system of dependency.

As in Blackwell, the elites control not only the economic resources in the county but the political machinery as well. Even though blacks make up the majority, whites influence and control county politics, partly by exerting direct economic pressure or interfering in the process. But black leaders also lament the way dependency is ingrained among people with little education or experience outside Dahlia. Blacks who have known only the plantation and a life in which they relied on the bossman will vote with him out of habit and deference. As Michael Long explained, *Uneducated people need to go through someone, they need to get help from Toms. In every area you have two or three what we call Toms that have been there for a long time and the whites have gained control of them. Since a lot of the people living here can't read and write, when they have a problem—just like this lady who came here wanting to see me a few minutes ago—they go to those people. They depend on those people for direction. The white power structure tells them what to say, and they go out and preach in their area. So the whites don't have to say anything. All they have to do is give the money to the people they already have in place, who then go out and pass it out and take people to the polls. They get paid so much for every person that they take to the polls, and they'll give the people who they take to the polls so much money. A lot of times they help them vote. So they got everything in place, you might say*. Assuming that money is exchanged for votes everywhere, he adds, *It's not like in the city where people are educated and say, "Hey, I'm gonna go take that money over there, but I'm gonna vote the right way."*

Whites also recount stories of vote buying, deliberate coercion to affect voting, and even examples of ballot tampering. A white businessperson recalled working at the polls: *So I handled the black polls and I really learned a lot that night. I learned how they paid them off, you know, all of that. I remember looking up at the sky, and it was a harvest moon that November night, and I said, "Oh, boy, don't let my Mama and Daddy look down from heaven and see where I am." But, anyway, we won*. In the 1970s, whites who tried to help blacks living on the plantation get to the polls were told, *Do not come around our place. We will tend to our own blacks*. As recently as the 1980s there were news stories about alleged ballot tampering and intimidation by powerful whites, but nothing was proved in court.

In the 1990s blacks and whites agree that the pressure is more subtle. White control is sustained largely by long-standing habits of deference and fear of crossing whites, especially among older blacks who have always worked for white farmers. But even today, with two blacks on the board of supervisors in one county, there is great inequity, and the farmer who runs the board acts imperiously to maintain virtual control. A white lawyer gave the example of a meeting at which the county's attorney said a matter required a public hearing, and this farmer responded by saying, *A public hearing has just begun on this issue. Any comments? No? The public hearing is adjourned*.

Socially, the white and black communities are distinct worlds with separate schools, separate churches, separate Christmas parades, separate activities for children. The weekly newspaper increasingly covers news of the black community, in part to sell more papers, but its articles and pictures invariably depict all-white or all-black events. One week you might see a photo of the white academy's basketball team and cheerleaders on one page, and a photo of the black public school's team and cheerleaders on the next. The white school, with several hundred students, receives far more newspaper coverage than the black schools, with several thousand—in part, the editor explains, because some black school officials distrust the paper and provide less access and fewer news items. A minister commented, *Everything here is segregated. There is no social interaction between the races, and no trust. Whites say you can't trust blacks and blacks say the same thing about whites.*

The exception to the rules of segregation is when the panel or group being covered is federally funded, and then, as a white professional points out, someone "safe" from the black community will have been appointed. *If they want to put them on federal boards that are required to have an integrated board, they'll ask, "Now, who do you think, John, would be good to sit on that board and would be nice and quiet and wouldn't disturb us too much?"*

People in Dahlia say there are both "liberal" and "conservative" whites, and they are talking about race, not political ideology. A liberal is someone who would not mind seeing Dahlia more equally balanced and would send his or her children to an integrated school, who perhaps would hire blacks for white-collar work, who has eaten with black professionals at the restaurant, who may have attended an integrated school elsewhere. There are whites who are not seen as racist. For example, a black man described a white woman with whom he had worked as "color blind," and he elaborated: *She is a very beautiful person. She was born and raised here, but she doesn't look at color. Her husband is the same way. Anything that she can do, he can do, as a person, they do. She has helped me through some things, and that gave me some confidence.*

But racism is prevalent, and even those who are liberal on race describe prejudiced friends and relatives. *My friends say, "A nigger is a nigger is a nigger is a nigger." You know, and "They're all worthless, no good, sons of bitches."* Edward Carter, a department store owner, worries about the lesson children receive. *There's some people here who still think they ought to be, not in chains, but not far from it. They think they shouldn't be allowed to come into the restaurant. That's sad, and the thing is, it perpetuates itself. It gets passed down. They didn't just wake up one morning feeling that way. They were taught. I hate to see what they teach their children. Now, maybe you got one spouse that thinks like that and maybe the other spouse is a little more enlightened and can do a little better job with the kids as far as that goes. I mean, it is better. The attitude is better than it used to be.*

Young black men and women who have lived or visited elsewhere remark on the relative openness in other places. *When we go to Carterville, white people, you know, they treat us like we white. Down here you can't go to the same clubs that white people go to, but in Carterville you can. They laugh at the things you do, you laugh at the same they do. Down here it ain't like that. They think they better*. Or in Indiana: *Up there, it be like, all colors, they be combined together. They can either be black or white. But see, here they don't do that*.

Most whites who live in town have little regular interaction with the black community. They have a black maid, maybe a black gardener, but for those who are not managing a store with black customers or a plantation with black laborers, daily life involves limited contact with the black community. Newcomers remark on some local whites' habit of talking about their black household workers as if they were not in the room, and often whites whom I interviewed knew little about their maid's family circumstances.

A handful of white teachers stayed with the public system when integration was forced on the counties in the late 1960s, in part to keep their pensions, in part to initiate some changes. They were stunned by the grossly inadequate facilities at the black schools. *Nine hundred students and a faculty of thirty, and one functioning bathroom in the elementary building for all those children and one for all those teachers. Raw sewage was backing up half the time. The lunch room was smaller than my living room*. The daily deprivation experienced by their students who lived in plantation shacks—from lack of food and clothes, to no plumbing, books, or even magazines at home—shocked these schoolteachers. Sharon Carter, who has worked at both the white academy and the black school, was one of those astonished teachers who went to the black schools in the late 1960s. *These were definitely cotton-patch black children—bathrooms were unheard of, running water was few and far between in the homes. It was the most different and difficult thing that I had ever, ever seen in my life. That was really the bottom bottom bottom*.

These white teachers and black youngsters had to overcome decades of social rules maintaining segregation and black deference to whites. Sharon's friend June explained, *I was taught never to look them in the eye. They were taught never to look me in the eye. I was taught to stay this far away from them*—she spreads her hands two feet apart to show the suitable distance—*and don't you come any closer. And they were taught to do the same. Now how are you going to teach somebody like that, with both of us looking on the ground and both of us far apart? Particularly a little child. So I had to gradually work myself to get closer to them, and then tell them to hold their head up and look at me, and for both of us to look at each other. I had to convince them that I wasn't going to kill them and that they weren't going to melt because they looked at me*.

These white teachers found that they did not know the black community as well as they had thought. *Just simple things like my hair—they had to touch it. They used words that I had never heard. I didn't know what nappy hair was, and they'd tease other children that have a nappy hair. And now, I knew they called their mothers "Mother Dear," but I didn't realize the horrible, the intense emotional feeling they have toward their mothers, and if anybody said anything about Mother you just were in war*. Like many of their neighbors, Sharon and her friends had always maintained that they understood blacks. *People say, "I live in the Delta and I know all about black people." I can remember saying that myself. But you have to get in there and work with them to know what you're talking about. I was so smarty. I thought I did know all about them. I didn't have any idea*.

Congregations in the white churches see the boundaries of their parish's responsibility extending only to the border of the white neighborhood. At Christmas and Thanksgiving parishioners traditionally prepared church baskets for "nice white families who are really trying." But even now, when the churches sponsor charitable activities, they most often take place outside the county: sending volunteers to do home improvement in Mexican villages, sending money to national programs that help foster children, or to the handicapped. There is talk that one minister was reassigned to a new church downstate because he pushed his congregation too hard about reaching out to the black community. His replacement is careful to accommodate local norms. *I'm a conservative person so I never try to go too far in anything. I think I can still serve effectively working within some parameters that are agreed upon by everybody. I don't feel like it's necessary to go out there and be a radical to fulfill my ministry. I've never felt that that was necessary. I have an understanding of how far they want me to go in that sort of thing*. One longtime resident says, *Ministers have wealthy people in the church who just tell them outright, "You can't have any contact with blacks in this church." The congregation prevents them from engaging in any contact with the black community*.

There are no food pantries or secondhand clothes outlets sponsored by the white churches. A minister explains, *Either they would have to hire somebody to run it or they would have to have volunteers in there to run it all the time. I don't think they would do that. It's just not done. They would say, "Why should we hire somebody to go down and run a store, when it's not going to benefit us?"* A lawyer explained to me that white farmers will sometimes help blacks if they are asked to, and gave the following example. *We've had a child or two that's been run over out on the highway, across from the highway, and they wouldn't have anything to bury them with. You could go up to several big farmers and they would let go of money to bury the child. When I told them "this is a worthy cause," they'd hand over the money. They just wanted somebody to say this is not a hoax, that the money would not be used to buy a gallon whiskey.*

There are a few exceptions, including the charitable activities of Catholic sisters who work with the black poor and a small literacy effort led by a lone "professional" volunteer, who many say is considered "eccentric" but is tolerated because she is from an elite family. There is the fragile new Habitat for Humanity group. Aside from these, the local white community seems to wash its hands of the needs in the black community in its midst. Some are ambivalent, others oblivious, but most say, *You can't change it. That's the way it is.*

Several white ministers, uneasy about their congregations' priorities, give money to the sisters in the Catholic mission, *because they're going to touch people that this church will never even hear about*. The Lion's Club, Rotary Club, and Women's Club all donate primarily to the white community. *We help the school—both schools, but we basically concentrate on the private school*, says a Lion's Club leader. *We sponsor a blood drive every year and we have a club house that's available for rental for the community, so we have to keep that up*, explains a member of the Women's Club. *It is frowned upon to do activities in both the black and white schools*, another reports.

Black and white interaction is rare in town. Whites say it would be impossible to have a black friend here, and blacks find it difficult to have white friends. A white health care provider who has black friends at the clinic described attending a housewarming at a black friend's new home. *Now, one of my friends in the hospital just built a new house and had a housewarming party and I went, which, for here, is pretty damn liberal. I mean, really and truly. White people do not go to parties that black people have*. An attorney concurs. *Socially, the races don't intermix here. You have a lot of kids there in the black community that because they have no home life, no family life, they are totally undisciplined. I'm personally not going to stick my little girl in that type of environment, no more than you would.*

There are few truly public places or activities, and those that do exist are public in name only. A white professional pointed out, *There's nowhere in this town that you can go and have an opportunity to meet middle-income blacks. There is a standing rule that whites do not want to have anything public because the blacks might come. We used to have a public swimming pool. It's down here behind the hospital. But integration was imminent and everything was going on,* *so it became a private club pool. I'm talking about stuff that I belong to. I pay my $145 and my kids go swim there. It used to be a public pool, until integration came. And then it became a private pool. Then, of course, we built the "public" pool up here on the north end for the black kids.*

Stereotypes thrive when isolation is this complete, and racism persists, on both sides. Many whites talk freely about racist friends, even racist spouses. A white businesswoman told me that *all the middle-class and smart blacks left, and we just have ignorant lower-class blacks now—"agricultural blacks," my husband says.* Whites who are active in youth organizations in the white community say the black community has neither Scouts nor recreational sports teams because there are no black male role models who can lead such activities. *Their leadership turns over about once a week, because the Scout program is based on commitment, whether it's the boys or the leader. You've got to have that commitment, and they just aren't willing to make the commitment. Now the Cub Scout program works in a black community great. But it's built on a den mother, and the black women in the black community are dominant. They are the ones who run the community.*

Both whites and blacks express growing concern about troubled, poor black families headed by young parents who seem to have little control over their children. The problem of youngsters involved in drugs or teenagers having children outside marriage is on everyone's mind. Whites refer to the lack of structure in poor black families with varying degrees of sympathy or blame, but the social isolation is so extreme that even some who consider themselves liberal on race make sweeping generalizations. *The black community as a whole sees absolutely nothing wrong with illegitimate children. It's a warrior cult—"how many women can I be with tonight?" They see no problem at all with that. And it just goes on, and on, and on. They see absolutely nothing wrong with the idea of instant gratification on Saturday nights.*

The new, fragile, multiracial Habitat for Humanity group offers hope of progress, but it also illustrates the deep divide and distrust, even among those who want to work together. The group held a prayer meeting that included blacks and whites on Main Street, an event that seemed momentous to those involved. But whites complain that black churches do not donate enough to Habitat's efforts, while blacks see white authorities resisting the location of new Habitat-built homes near white neighborhoods, and wonder if white board members could do more. The group had trouble getting basic approvals from the city when it tried to locate a black family inside the city limits. A black board member said, *We got the land. I think the owners thought the land was for the Sisters, because after they found out it was to be for a black family they tried to talk the Sisters out of buying it. When we started to build, we encountered problems trying to get the foundation, pipes. We encountered problems with permits. There is resistance.*

A minister summed up what he called the white attitude about community responsibility in Dahlia. *"It's comfortable. We come and we go. Yes, we have the drugs and the people on the corner that are drinking all the time, but they're really not affecting my life." It's a comfortable lifestyle for the white community. "Why should we change?"* Blacks, for their part, take racism in whites as part of the landscape. When blacks describe a white who does not seem racist, they say, "she treated me like a person," repeating the phrase to emphasize how rare and remarkable the encounter had been. The roots of this segregated society go back to the mid-1800s, when the plantation economy was first established.

WORK IN DAHLIA: CREATING AND MAINTAINING THE PLANTATION WORLD

Mississippi's Yazoo Delta was settled in the 1830s by wealthy planters from other areas in the South who had the resources to clear the swampy, snake-infested land and buy slaves to cultivate cotton in the fertile soil. Historian James Cobb describes a socially and economically ambitious group of Delta planters who pushed their slaves hard, year round, so that they could live ostentatiously themselves. He says their ability to maintain their decadent conspicuous consumption and to meet the economic requirements of growing cotton in this harsh environment "was wholly dependent on their success in retaining and controlling a large supply of black labor."[4]

Immediately following the Civil War, the planters experienced a period of labor shortages as both blacks and whites adjusted to a social and economic world without slavery. During this time some blacks rented farm acreage and others were even able to purchase marginal land that required clearing. The forebears of some black families in Dahlia benefited from this narrow window of opportunity. The window, however, was soon closed. By the 1890s, with federally financed levees and privately financed railroads ensuring their place in the national economy, Delta planters once again had complete control over their workers. More black laborers came into the region as cotton plantations grew and workers were needed to build the levees and railroads, effectively ending plantation owners' worries about labor shortages. The planters adopted modern, manufacturing-style management techniques and, as part of this strategy, reestablished firm control over their workers.

They also benefited from growing restrictions on blacks' political rights. As Cobb concludes, "changes in the economic and demographic conditions in the region during the 1880s triggered a sharp decline in the overall fortunes of blacks and set the stage for the legal and extralegal measures whereby whites regained control over black workers in the Delta. . . . If the events of the 1880s and 1890s ultimately helped to seal the gloomy fate of the Delta's black laborers, they had precisely the opposite effect on the fate of its planter elite."[5] By the turn of the century the planter elite had diversified into other economic endeavors, reinforced its political control, and reached out for both public and private capital to feed the region's growth. To maintain their profits and extravagant lifestyles they needed the low labor costs they could derive through rigid control over their black field workers.

Between 1900 and 1930 opportunities and options available to black workers in the Delta were further eroded by disenfranchisement. Most continued to live on the plantation, subject to economic and social controls, whether their status was laborer or sharecropper. In arrangements virtually identical to those in the coal fields, they were often required to buy supplies at the plantation commissary, and most needed a cash advance furnished by the planter during the winter months when there was no work. These patterns were documented in histories of the 1920s and 1930s. As one historian put it: "Tenant farmers and sharecroppers acted as economic shock absorbers for landowners and planters. Many tenants never made a profit and succeeded only in going deeper and deeper into debt from year to year. Landlords kept the books and managed the sale of crops. Opportunities for exploitation were increased by the high rate of illiteracy among tenants and sharecroppers."[6] While tenants often moved from plantation to plantation—some say because the only way they could protest bad treatment was to move—the terms on any given plantation were likely to be the same. Delta planters were concerned about losing their labor during the first Great Migration of blacks northward before and during World War I, but they managed to retain complete power over those who remained. Importantly, that control was over every aspect of life—economic, political, and social.[7]

During the 1930s psychologist John Dollard and sociologist Hortense Powdermaker documented the rigid class and caste stratification imposed by white planters. They showed that planters maintained their complete domination over black laborers and sharecroppers not only in the workplace but also in crucial social institutions. Planters controlled all credit, stores, and housing, just as coal operators did in Blackwell. Whites blocked poor black workers from their schools because they feared educated blacks might challenge their hegemony, but they tolerated black churches because during this period churches mostly reinforced, rather than challenged, the status quo.[8]

During the 1950s and 1960s, the effects of the second Great Migration to Chicago and other northern cities swept these Delta communities. In the 1960s minimum wage laws were imposed and planters reacted by introducing mechanization to save on labor costs. But they still kept tight control over those laborers who continued to work on the tractors, in the fields, and in the cotton gins. National welfare programs established by the federal government were tightly controlled and manipulated by the elite, who ensured that the benefits reinforced rather than undermined their absolute control over the livelihood of those who remained. As Cobb showed, they were able to make federal assistance available to black families when there was no work in the field, and then have it withdrawn when they needed workers. He concluded, "Although the cumulative influences of the New Deal and World War II brought dramatic changes to the Delta's economy, the transformation of Delta agriculture left the region's planter-dominated social and political framework fundamentally intact."[9]

Despite the danger of repercussions in these small, segregated communities, some blacks took part in civil rights demonstrations during the 1950s and 1960s—and most often they found themselves blackballed from work as a result. Cobb recounts how all those who signed a National Association for the Advancement of Colored People (NAACP) petition in favor of school integration lost their jobs. The relentless and devastating punishment white employers could inflict on blacks who supported civil rights forced the NAACP to be less outspoken in rural areas. Dahlia's NAACP, like the NAACP groups Cobb researched, came to represent "a conservative, middle class orientation."

Not all whites, of course, were part of the blacklisting and resistance to civil rights, but the tone was set by those who wanted no part of integration. There was fear and resistance to change from whites. A young professional woman in Dahlia recalled that her father, a physician, had insisted that his children stay in the house for a week when Martin Luther King was killed.

He told them things were going to change. *I remember that year, in the fourth grade, my father telling me, "You can't use the word 'nigger' any more." We used it pretty loosely. I knew as a child that it was a derogatory comment and to be polite you used "Negro"—if you can understand the distinction.*

Across the nation, the decade of the 1960s was a period of rural industrialization, when manufacturing plants moved from America's increasingly troubled urban industrial areas to job-hungry rural communities where workers accepted lower wages. Cobb describes how whites in the Delta would make sure that factories interested in their communities would have no qualms about hiring only white workers. Both whites and blacks can cite specific examples of factories interested in locating in Dahlia being turned away by planters. Some acceptable factories—like the blue jeans factory—came in after they agreed to hire blacks only as janitors. Many Dahlia residents think the opposition to industry persists. As one white leader put it, *As long as the farmers' power structure is there, they're not going to let industry in. They blocked it before and they'll block it again.*

Like Blackwell, Dahlia saw significant out-migration in the 1950s and 1960s: almost half the population left the region in these decades. Those who remained often relied on a combination of part-time and part-year minimum wage work and welfare programs. Despite the out-migration and the decline in farm labor, planters continued to maintain tight, even ruthless, control over economic and political life, ensuring continuity of their privilege and power into the 1970s. When integration threatened the well-established caste system, whites set up separate private institutions to replace public ones—schools, recreation facilities, and clubs. These separate worlds persist to the present.

In 1930, when the grandparents of the twenty-, thirty-, and forty-year-olds I interviewed were in their prime working years, 90 percent of all employed people in Dahlia worked in agriculture. Nearly all the 125 black men and women whom my colleagues and I interviewed, poor and nonpoor, had grandparents who "worked on a farm." This concentration in farming declined gradually over the next several decades, and by 1960 about two thirds of all work was in agriculture.

The demand for workers changed dramatically in the 1960s, when mechanization replaced hand picking of cotton, crop reduction programs of the Department of Agriculture further reduced the need for workers, and minimum wage laws pushed the planters to introduce greater labor efficiency. By 1970 only one fourth of all workers in Dahlia were in agriculture.

In 1990, the official census statistics showed that only 16 percent of all workers were in agriculture or related industries; manufacturing now provides employment for a quarter of all workers. These statistics may understate farming's role today because they miss many part-time workers who "chop cotton"—or weed the cotton fields—in the summer, but they are indicative of the scale of change. When the 1960s began, there were still thirty to forty families working on every two-thousand-acre plantation. Today those farms can operate with five or six men, most of them seasonal workers.[10]

As the structure of the economy changed, people adapted by moving away to seek work elsewhere. Between 1930 and 1990 the population of Dahlia shrank from over 45,000 to around 20,000, while the number employed dropped from nearly 28,000 men and women to just 6,000. Every black person I interviewed had relatives who had left the Delta for northern and midwestern cities, as well as a few southern cities like Birmingham, Memphis, Little Rock, and St. Louis. Usually at least half the siblings in a family would be gone. Many poor men and women now in Dahlia have lived elsewhere at some point but returned home when things did not work out.

The 6,000 working men and women in Dahlia have jobs in stores, government offices and schools, on farms, in sewing factories and electrical assembly factories, in catfish plants, and, very recently, in gambling casinos. In 1990, 1,500 white men and 1,800 black men were employed, as were 1,200 white women and 1,200 black women. Blacks have more difficulty finding work. Only about half of black working-age males are employed, compared with two thirds of whites, and only one third of black women are, in contrast to nearly half of white women. About half of working black males have only part-time or seasonal work.

Whites run the plantations, do the white-collar and managerial jobs, and present the face seen by the public in stores and businesses. When a job becomes open, those doing the hiring call people they know socially to see if they are interested, just as happens in Blackwell. People describe a hiring process that operates by invitation only—in schools, in welfare offices, in banks, and in stores. *So-and-so called me and said, "Are you interested?"* The same process occurs for those from the handful of black establishment families.

At the same time, the farmers' ability to get people hired, and fired, is widely accepted. *These farmers could say "well, he's worth hiring" and they'll hire you. That's all you have to do is to have one of the farmers say something about you and that'll be it because you'll get the job any place. Even in a store or something.*

Blacks who dropped out of school or only finished high school work in fields and factories, while the few who have a college degree are likely to work in the schools and public offices. Even with the factories, many black women still work as domestics—although these workers often do not appear in official statistics. Jobs in the fields are seasonal—their peak is April to November—and during the winter months the farm managers go duck hunting and the farmworkers get unemployment checks and food stamps. Jobs in sewing factories fluctuate as well, as managers lay off and hire to make production accommodate the "just in time" demands of their big retail customers. A plant with 300 employees may let 50 of them go when orders are low in the spring. Managers of factories, where more than 80 percent of the workforce is black today, have as many applications on file from people seeking work as they do jobs in their plant—300 in the case of the apparel plant, 60 to 70 at the catfish plant. A new local take-out food business recently had 150 applicants for 17 new jobs. *Jobs are scarce* is a constant refrain among blacks in these Delta counties, just as it is among the have-nots in Blackwell.

Like Joey Scott, the businessman in Blackwell who figured that only women and teenagers would take his part-time jobs, a Dahlia businessman explained that he needed to hire blacks because whites would not take the kind of work he had—part-time hard labor. *My employees are colored men. I don't work anything but black because most of my business is part-time. I can't afford to pay somebody a monthly salary year round because we have a seasonal business. The whites are going to need more work that I'm not going to be able to give them.*

A political and business leader lamented the passing of the days when blacks were doing more fieldwork. *It's good to have those jobs and good menial labor. There are people who say, "just get the equipment and don't do any more hand labor." But I think hand laboring teaches the value to life—to production.* Other whites express the same view, saying it is good that the farmers are hiring more people to chop cotton since it provides much-needed work and discipline. Black men and women who have chopped describe brutally hot, exhausting, long days, *cotton stalks hitting you upside the head*, and many blacks in their teens simply refuse to take the work.

CLASS AND CASTE IN THE DELTA

The social class structure reflects racial stratification—almost all the whites in Dahlia have economic power and security, almost all the blacks are poor and powerless. Around two thirds of whites have a high school degree or more, compared with one third of blacks. Nearly a fifth of whites have completed college, but only about four percent of blacks have. These patterns of inequity were established long ago to meet the economic needs of a plantation economy, and they have been deliberately, and on occasion ruthlessly, maintained to preserve white power and affluence in a black-majority area.

At the bottom of the social structure are the black poor—many of whom work at least part of the year, even if they receive public assistance. At the top are the big farmers and their families, followed by their anxious lieutenants—the shopkeepers and politicians who control jobs and small-time politics as long as they do not challenge the status quo. People in this next echelon of whites—those with neither land nor great wealth—see their interests as best served by allying with the wealthy farmers; they keep themselves separate from the poor, preserving a segregated system that ensures their own comfort and status. Finally, there is the small, changing black leadership group, made up of the few black households with middle incomes (in 1989, 3 percent of black households earned between $35,000 and $75,000).

The black working poor in these Delta counties grew up in hard circumstances out in the countryside on plantations—some black leaders call them "first generation," meaning first generation to move off the plantation; some whites, as we saw, call them "agricultural blacks" or "cotton-patch children." They invariably refer to themselves as "country," and as adults they still struggle to overcome what growing up poor in the country has meant for them. Caroline Gage's story illustrates how isolation and lack of even minimal resources make the Delta poor vulnerable to a lifetime of insecurity, while James Hill's and John Cooper's experiences show the deep and pervasive influence of the bossman on black men's lives in the Delta.

Caroline is a thirty-four-year-old single mother who supports herself and her five children by combining work in the sewing factory, housecleaning, and public assistance. She lives in Tall Pines, the Farmers Home Administration development with single-family homes, in a sparsely furnished three-bedroom house with a combined kitchen and living area. Her possessions are old things she has refurbished—a rusty refrigerator covered in a floral-patterned sticky paper she found on sale, an old couch with a bedspread thrown over it. She is always battling to rid the house of rats and roaches.

The neighborhood is rough—young men in Tall Pines use knives and sometimes guns to fight with their counterparts from Old Town. Crime and drug use are high, and most yards and houses are run down; many have bars on the windows and doors. Caroline would rather live somewhere else. *Staying out here is like staying right under somebody*, she says. *On weekends, they always be standing on the corner and they bust bottles and all that kind of stuff in your yard. They throw paper. Every week we have to clean the yard. We have to pick up beer bottles and glass which they have broken in the yard. Dishes, old paper, cans, and that sort of thing. I just don't like it. I had to move back here because I couldn't find any other place to go, but I don't like it.*

Caroline and I talk at the oilcloth-covered kitchen table on a hot Saturday morning in July, interrupted now and then by her children, who check in as they finish chores. She is a striking woman with high cheekbones, steady brown eyes, shoulder-length hair tied back, and a soft, low, melodious voice. She has a serene bearing, a calmness that belies her age and the struggles she has had growing up herself and then raising her children. As she begins to talk about where she has been and whom she has known, she gives herself to the story, punctuating this memory with a long, whistlelike *ooo-oooh*, summing up that episode with her refrain—*I just got tired*—by which she seems to mean both weary and fed up.

She grew up in a family of thirteen in a tenant shack out on the Pendleton plantation. *Mama had us like stair steps, one then the other*, she remembers. The two-room house included one bedroom and a front room that had a kitchen but no plumbing. *In the wintertime it was drafty*. She purses her lips. *Ooo-oooh, it was cold. In the summertime it was warm, it was* hot. *All of us stayed in one room in two big beds—the boys slept in one and the girls in the other. Mama and Daddy slept on couches in the front room*. Her father, like her grandparents on both sides, worked on the plantation, plowing and planting in the spring, chopping cotton in the summer, picking cotton and then working in the cotton gin in the fall. During the winter months he was off, and he would borrow from the bossman against next season's work. These months were long and hard on the family, crowded in their little house.

She remembers one night when she was about ten and her father beat her mother, and how she had assumed that her mother had done something wrong. *I saw them fight one time, and he was choking her on the couch and I was hanging out the bed in the other room, looking in there at her. And my dad raised up and said, "You all want your mother? I'm going to kill her," or something he was saying like that. And I was just looking. I didn't know what was going on. I didn't understand it, but the next day they was talking again and everything, and I thought, "I don't know." Being a child and everything, you don't think of too many things especially wrong between Mother and Daddy, and I thought, "Well, Mother must have did something wrong 'cause Daddy jumped on her last night."*

Caroline's mother worked on the farm too, but Caroline says, *Mama was sickly with sugar. She had sugar diabetes.* As the oldest girl, Caroline was expected to stay home from school when the family needed her, to care for her sick mother or for the younger children when her mother worked in the fields. During the fall and spring, when the crops were ready or going in, she and her siblings, like other black children living on plantations during the 1960s and 1970s, were expected to miss school to help with the farmwork. Although she loved school, by the eighth grade she had missed so many days fulfilling her family responsibilities that *the principal just told me to quit coming.*

When she was not needed in the fields, this fifteen-year-old would carry water from the outside pump, haul wood, cook greens on a hot stove, or clean the outhouse, all the while watching over younger brothers and sisters. She loved being outdoors, even in the summer heat. Sometimes they would get time off and go fishing near the levee. But growing up with siblings in the country did not prepare her for the larger world. By her own account, she was shy and ignorant—*dog ignorant*, she says.

Several of the young women I interviewed described being sexually assaulted when they were young—by relatives, mothers' boyfriends, in the back of cars on "dates," by boys who came around or men who were just passing by in a car. When Caroline was only twelve an older boy from a house down the road began coming over in the afternoons and forced her to have sex with him. She says she told her mother, who went to talk to his family, and after that *he don't come no more.*

At sixteen, Caroline found a way to escape her life of drudgery. A friend introduced her to a twenty-year-old man from Chicago, and after a short courtship, *I married and left home. Set a date, married, and left home. Ooooooh, big mistake. Big mistake. I didn't love him. I didn't know nothing about what no love was. Love and all that stuff. I just married to get away from home, because he said I'd never leave if I didn't get married.* But soon after they arrived in Chicago she found that her new husband was addicted to cocaine. *He was terrible, awful. He started beating me. It was awful. Then one day—after we been there about a month—when he was high, he put a knife to my throat, said he was going to cut my throat, going to kill me. See this scar here, buried down in my neck? Then he put a gun on my forehead, cocked the gun, said he was going to kill me. I just said, "I don't care. Go ahead." I was tired. I wanted to be home. I wanted to be rid of him.*

His assault was interrupted by a cousin's arrival with some new drugs. While her abusive husband sniffed cocaine in the bathroom, Caroline slipped down fourteen flights of stairs, out the door, onto the streets of the south side of Chicago. *I just left. And I was lost in big old Chicago.* She was sixteen, pregnant, and had spent only a few weeks away from the plantation world that had been her whole life. *But being in the city! Think what that was like! You never been anywhere. Stayed in the country, hardly ever come to town. Come to town sometimes on a Saturday, taking turns, my sister would go one Saturday, I'd go another, my brother go the next Saturday. That's the way we'd do, the way we went to town. I hadn't ever come out of the country, and all of a sudden I end up in a big city.*

Caroline had no place to go, and she walked and rode buses all night long until a kindly bus station attendant at the end of the line took her home to his wife and called the police. Although at first she was taken back to her abusive husband, she eventually found relatives who helped her return to the Delta after her son was born. *When I got back home, he had beat me here! He was telling my parents, "My stupid wife don't understand life. We had one fight, and she left." And all like that. But I said, "I ain't comin' back neither. No way."*

All she knew was home, and she returned to live with her mother. The next fifteen years of Caroline's life were chaotic and unstable. For a while she worked in a place that trained her to sew, paid by the piece for sewing labels into pillowcases and mattress covers. *I only made twenty dollars every two weeks. Then some of the girls showed me how to make more by eating the labels. I chewed up them labels and swallowed them, and that time I made seventy-some dollars instead of twenty.* She collected Aid to Families with Dependent Children, sixty dollars a month for her son.

Two years later she had a second child, out of wedlock, bringing her AFDC payment up to ninety dollars. She quit the sewing job, lived with her mother for a while in the country, then with her sister in the Tall Pines subdivision, then on her own in a house in town that was flooded periodically when a sewage ditch backed up near the house. *Me and the kids just stayed up on the bed those days*. Then she moved out to the country again, to an inexpensive place with no plumbing.

She dated many men, one of them—Amory, the father of her fourth and fifth children—seriously. She considered getting a divorce from her first husband so she could marry Amory. *But then he started treating me bad. He moved us to the country, and he would take the wires off the car, and do something to the phone so I couldn't call or be called. He'd be gone all day, into the night, out with another woman. He had jumped on me, and I didn't like how he would do the kids. He used to pick them up, throw them down on the couch and tell them, "Don't you move. You set there."*

The relationship was stormy—he was jealous, but unfaithful himself, and he expected her to have his supper ready and take care of the house. *During that time my dad had cancer and he was in the hospital and the doctor said he wasn't going to live long. I went to see Daddy at seven in the morning and I got back that night at eight. And Amory came in—he'd worked all day—and asked me, "Where's the food at?" I explained, "I just got to the house. I'm fixing to fix something." He was furious. "You mean to tell me you been gone all day and you ain't cooked nothing?" I said, "I went to see Daddy." And he said "I don't care who you went to see." Well, I threw pots and pans. My daddy's dying, and he don't want me to go! I went and bought me a brand new ice pick. I told him, "If you lay a hand on me again, I'm going to kill you. Don't say nothing to me." And he knew I was fixing to leave. I was tired.*

For a while Caroline's "tiredness" with Amory extended to the rest of her life, and she lost interest in the world. *I wasn't taking care of my kids or my house. I was seeing a lot of guys, drinking, and staying in hotels. I was awful. I was miserable*. But during this time she had enrolled in a GED class. *I was going to school to get my GED. They paid me $108 every two weeks to go, and I went just to get paid*. One evening during a break from class she was drawn to the stories told by a young woman attending a revival. Caroline went along to the revival the next night, and was saved. *The man was teaching how Jesus died for his peoples. He was talking to me about continuing to come and learn and read the Bible and all that. After that, things just changed. I wanted to know more about him, about him dying for me*. Her newfound Christian faith has given her life some structure, a set of rules, and purpose. She disciplines the children and teaches them responsibility. Each has chores, and throughout the house Caroline has taped lists of instructions on the wall, often misspelled, but clear to them.

Like Gwen Boggs, she is trying to help her children avoid the mistakes she made. *It takes something to be a single parent and raise a family, especially a family of five. And they all growing up ranging from age seventeen to age nine. It's tough, it's difficult, and it takes the love of Christ to keep us together. I believe that. It takes the love of Christ too that we be able to sit down and talk.*

She is determined that her daughters understand about sex and pregnancy. *My oldest daughter is fifteen, and I had to sit down and talk with my kids about the facts of life, about womanly things. My mother never told me about things like that. I learned in school, and I don't want my kids to learn that way. I want them to know. So I tell my baby too. I tell my girls what boys want. "You have to be careful. They tell you one thing, they mess around and get you pregnant, they run off and leave you. They don't want you. If they ain't able to take care of themselves, how are they going to take care of you?"*

I use my life with my kids as an example. I say, "I'm a mother thirty-four years old. Here I got all five of you all." I say, "What do you all think?" I let them explain to me what they think about my life. Do they think I should be married or have a husband? I have five kids that need me. "You got one daddy," I say to my son. I tell my older daughter that she has a different daddy. "You all ain't got the same daddy. Do you think that should be? You know, that's not right. And I don't want you to grow up like that thinking it is. Your mother wasn't taught when she was coming up. But I know now, by God's grace, for him saving me so I could teach you. You can be married before you have a child. And before you marry, take time to know yourself and find yourself and grow. Go to school and do something that you want to do. Don't just jump in and marry. Do something that you want to do first and then later on if you decide on that, then marry. Don't listen to these little boys, because the only thing they looking for is the cream out of the Oreo." At first, I was embarrassed and wondered if I should talk to my kids like that, but if I don't tell them, no one will.

To provide for her family, she works as many hours as she can get at the local sewing factory. At the time we talked, two or three days a week was all they gave her. She was paid $4.70 an hour and earned about $200 a month on average. She was still eligible for about $80 in food stamps. When she was laid off for a whole year, she really struggled because she could only draw $35 a week on unemployment. She can get medical insurance when she is working, a benefit won by the factory's small union. When she was not working, the children were eligible for Medicaid.

She knows her previous experience helped her get the job she has now. But she is certain the Lord made it come available two years ago after more than five years of waiting to get hired there. Like many poor country women in the Delta, she did not know that the manager who does the hiring regards "checking back" as a key indication of readiness to work. When she had not checked back, her application in the manager's bottom left-hand desk drawer was dumped out with those of others who had come only once.

Now she is glad to have the position at the factory—it is considered a good job in this job-scarce region, even though the working conditions can be unpleasant. *I like the job, but I don't like being inside all day, with no windows. I like to be outside. And this time a year it be so hot in there. They have air in front, but it don't reach the back*. Even when she is not laid off, work can be unreliable because of machinery repairs. *We hardly ever make production because the machines are constantly breaking down, and we are off then*.

The family works together, and her fifteen-year-old daughter is shouldering adult responsibilities just as Caroline did as a child. *My kids take care of theirselves. My oldest girl takes care of the house—cooks, bakes, keeps the house clean. But*, Caroline sighs, *life is a struggle—a constant struggle to pay house notes, bills, a constant struggle*. Her tone is factual, not complaining. *Right now work is cut back, so I barely pay the house note and the light bill and the water bill—my last check was only $119. I am behind, ooo-oooh, way behind. I wish I had waited on buying those encyclopedias*. She nods her head toward a low bookshelf where the A through G volumes of the World Book are neatly stacked. *Also, I has to pay back SSI*—supplemental security income—*$40 a month to repay $3,000 in overpayment from when they kept sending me money after my son's asthma had got better. They got to be paid. I hate being in debt. It is hard being a mother, being a single parent. Hard financially, and hard training them up*.

Caroline is clearly independent minded and determined to raise her children well, but her options are limited by her lack of education. Her account of her life is animated and expressive, but she is not well-spoken, and her country speech limits her job prospects. She married her first husband as a child of sixteen, and she has never divorced him. She has had four more children with two other men since she bore the first. Caroline is unlikely to leave Dahlia—she relies on family and they rely on her, sharing a car, helping with child care, lending money or food stamps, often providing a room for a period of time. She would like to go up to Arkansas, where a grandfather owned some farmland, but that would take money she does not have.

Caroline does not expect to marry again. *No man wants a readymade family*, she smiles.

When she was a young girl, no one was hopeful for her or encouraged her to finish her education. Indeed, she was pushed out of school by family poverty and shortsighted attendance policies. When she faced hard times with a violent husband in Chicago, people in a bus station and on the police force were kind to her, but she felt she had no prospects for making a life there. She returned to the Delta home she knew, her mother and siblings, aunties and uncles, to do what black women with limited education do in the Delta—work in sewing factories or part-time in the fields, clean white people's houses, and collect welfare. She has been quite alone, never really talking to anyone about her life, her thoughts, her problems.

Caroline continues to live in a world separate from those who are doing better—black as well as white. She has had little contact with whites in the community, except for the woman whose trailer she cleans out at the lake. She knows the handful of powerful farmers; two of her brothers work for them. *The farmers—ooo-oooh, they have a lot of power. Winston and Pendleton and Baker. They have a lot of power, a lot of power*. She has heard rumors from various factions in the black community about leaders stealing public money that should have gone to the new cooperative community store in Tall Pines. She hears that some low-income blacks take advantage of charitable donation programs, and that those in charge of giveaway programs save the best clothes for their own families or sell the better food in the neighborhood food pantry to the highest bidder. *The people in charge would take the best stuff. When the peoples got there, the ones who really needed the money didn't get it. The ones in charge would take the clothes and have a rummage sale, and make them a profit off it!* As far as she knows, these rumors are true. She is not involved in community affairs or politics. She keeps to herself, to her family, to her small country church with its itinerant preacher.

Many of the seventy other poor women I interviewed are even more isolated and rough-spoken than Caroline is. All but seven receive welfare, fifty-eight have had children out of wedlock, and only fourteen finished high school. Some dropped out when they got pregnant; others, like Caroline, *when Mama got sick*. Some say they just got tired, that they never felt any connection to school. Many were mocked because they were from the country or wore hand-me-down clothing—*when we used to get on the bus, kids used to jump on us and make fun of us 'cause we weren't dressed like the other peoples*. Their health is often bad—they have problems with "nerves" and suffer from asthma, perhaps, some health care workers say, from breathing the pesticides used in the fields. As one young woman explained, *It take me a while at doing it because I have asthma and my head just hurt all the time and when I go to thinking real hard, it make my head hurt real bad*. Heart trouble and diabetes plague their mothers and aunts who are now in their forties and fifties.

Like Caroline, most of these young women moved as teenagers from a crowded plantation shack to a poor neighborhood where welfare dependency was high, more than half the households were headed by single women, drinking and drugs were common, and stable work was rare. Many say their boyfriends or their kids' daddies "jump on them." *He used to come over there and he had been drinking and going out, and he jumped on me because he jealous*. When they have no work they spend their days watching children and soap operas, visiting with a sister, Mama, a boyfriend, or one of their children's fathers. They distrust neighbors who gossip and whites who "try to keep us down." Like Caroline, they have limited skills and limited exposure to work. Indeed, Caroline was fortunate to have had the training she did in learning to sew.

Black men in Dahlia have even fewer options for employment, because they are not seen as suited for production work in the apparel or catfish factories. Several black educational leaders described how black men in their late twenties and thirties mainly do farmwork in season and are idle or picking up odd jobs otherwise, while those in their teens and early twenties who dropped out of school will not do agricultural labor—*they refuse to work on the farm, they refuse to work for minimum wage*. The older men work hard for very little during the week, especially during summer months, and then drink and party hard on the weekends. They are easily lured into café life, drinking and gambling, or if they are younger, sometimes gangs and drug dealing. Their opportunities for legitimate work always depend on the white bossmen, either directly or indirectly.

James Hill works at the plantation store for Jack Baker, a big farm owner who has employed James's father for more than thirty years. James and a group of his friends are hanging out at the houses Baker owns and rents out to poor families, mostly single mothers on welfare. We talk on a Sunday morning in July, sitting on two folding chairs that we move to the edge of the dirt drive, out of earshot of James's friends who are drinking beer and joking on the porch steps. The day is hot already, and flies are buzzing around everyone's heads. The smell of stale beer is in the air. These tenant shacks near the Baker store are a gathering place, and while James and I talk, old cars pull in and out of the road, young men calling to one another, looking for someone, *making a date with a young lady to "go riding," to "start talking."* Young women visit too, scolding their toddlers, fussing over the new babies too young to run around.

James is tall and lanky, and looks younger than his twenty-five years. His face is earnest, and he seems amused that I am interested in his story. He grew up in Old Town with his mother and three siblings, where he lives now, although he has his own room that he has fixed up as an apartment of sorts. His mother and father were never married and never lived together, but his father, who began working on the Baker farm as a twelve-year-old boy, has stayed in close touch with his children and has been a steady influence.

Like many of the younger men I interviewed, James was "wild" in school. He cut classes, talked back to the teachers, and sometimes would get involved in fights when his friends needed help. The school was chaotic, and his own behavior contributed to that chaos. *Don't hardly like staying in class at times. You don't stay in class at school, you know, if they catch you out, they give you a whupping or you get suspended. The principal would give you a whupping. It was too wild, like peoples, the kids, they all be fighting and stuff, fighting during school, carrying knives around school and all like that.*

Although I heard many reports about young people involved with cocaine and marijuana, James says he steers clear of drugs, just drinks beer now and then. *You got some now that love to smoke marijuana. They be trying to pass it to me, but I go "naw man, I don't need that." You know, I drink, beer. That's all. They drink certain type of little liquor, wine*. The cafés, where many drink and socialize, are wild and can be dangerous. *I've been to some, two or three times*, he says a little disingenuously, *and they be shooting and fighting. The only time I've gone is at night. They all be shooting, cutting up people. Once I was just sitting down at the table and two guys started arguing, and next thing I know, that guy shot this guy. Shot him right inside the café.*

James finished high school because his parents promised to buy him a car if he did. He likes cars, and if he could be anything he wanted he would be a mechanic. In high school he enjoyed a class in auto repair, but the class only got as far as taking the engine apart when summer came and school was out. He has seen flyers advertising mechanic schools since then, but they are in distant cities where *I don't have no family*. Right now he has his eye on a newer used car south on Highway 44, but he is worried about how he can finance it. *You got to get the bossman, your bossman got to co-sign for you, and you gonna have to have three good credits. See, like you dealt with somebody and you got credit. I ain't got but one credit and that with Mr. Carter, at the furniture store, for my air conditioner and television I keep in my room at Mama's house.*

When he was eighteen he went to Ohio for a while, where he lived with an aunt and worked part time pumping gas. His memory is that up there *people treat you like you're s'posed to be treated, treat you almost like you white.* But after a few months, he says, *Mama called me home.* He takes pride in the fact that he always has told his employers when he is leaving. *Every job I worked at, I ain't never quit. When I get ready to leave, I explain it to them.* When he did return to his mother he was out of work only a couple of weeks before he got hired on at the Baker farm. *My daddy's bossman, he came and got me to come work with them.*

James had worked for Baker when he was a young boy, and he earned a reputation for being trustworthy. This connection came in handy for him when he was picked up by the police. As James tells it, *I had used my daddy's car. It were kind of cold that day, and it was raining, and I picked up this guy I knew from school, and he said he'd pay me two dollars to take him across town. So I took him over to Smith's, downtown, and he went in to cash a check. Turns out the check wasn't under his name.* The store owner took down the license tag number of his father's car, so the police came looking for him. At first James told them he did not have a car, so they brought his father down to the station, but it was soon evident James had been driving and they let his father go and took James to jail. *My dad, he was so worried about it, he came down there where I were.* But James's father, even though he was a steady worker in his forties, could not get his son off on his word alone. It took the bossman's okay to clear things up. *Yeah, they let me go. My bossman, he trusts me for so long, you know. When I was kind of young, I usually work around the store, pick up the paper, something like that. He got to know me real good. He trusted me and everything. I ain't never been in jail, I ain't never stealing nothing. He put in a word for me.*

James is one of the fortunate few who has a connection for work, even if it is a part-time job for low wages. Many young men with whom I talked were having a hard time finding any work at all and resented the way getting a job depended on whom you know. James's friend William, who wanted a job loading trucks at the jeans factory, talked about his suspicion that "people have their picks." *I tried at the factories downtown and all those places and they weren't hiring. That's what they told me: they weren't hiring. Then about two weeks later they called my neighbor for the job but they didn't call me. And I went up there and applied in person and they told me they weren't hiring. And I asked if I could fill out an application and the lady said they don't have no applications and about two weeks later they gave my neighbor the job part time. That's the reason I say they got their picks on who they hire here.*

Chopping cotton and working in the fields is about the only option for young black men, and it is available for only about six months. Those who are fortunate—or well connected—get hired at the cotton gin after the fieldwork is completed. But even getting on a truck to chop takes connections. As one young man hanging out with James explained it, *For chopping cotton we bring home $160 a week, working fifty hours a week. But see, the lady who's taking us out there, she get like $25 from each one of us every week. We have to pay her for taking us out there. They call it hauling. She charges $5 a day for taking us and bringing us back. It's her truck. Her truck, her gas, her ice, her water. I found her through my sisters, and she let us go, and we've been chopping ever since. The only thing I know about farmwork is chopping cotton. We was practically raised up on a hoe.* Men in their late twenties and thirties, like those hanging out near Baker's store on this hot Sunday morning, often rely on chopping cotton for income.

Those in their thirties and forties were part of a generation of people who, like Caroline, had to miss school to work in the fields, and they resented seeing the white children go while they were heading out to the fields to work. *We lived right on the highway, and you'd always see the white kids riding the buses to school, while we would have to stay out of school. It just didn't seem right.* Many blacks and whites feel that there are farmers who still do not want to see blacks educated. *They was against us going to school. I wanted to go because I didn't want to be no farmer the rest of my life like my father do. I think I can do better than that. They think because you're black, you can't read, you can't count. I can read just as good and count just as good as anybody.* The white literacy volunteer agrees that there is resistance from the big farmers. *Oh, there are some who perceive reading as a threat.* Her son says, *Mom thinks they don't want them educated. I hope she's wrong.*

John Cooper, hardened and discouraged at only thirty-five, struggles to get by on what work is available. His mother died when he was three, and he and two siblings were put in a foster home in a distant county where they were treated terribly. I interviewed all three children, and they described a hard life of abuse—sleeping on the floor, eating leftovers when the foster parents' own children were finished, and being forced to work hard in the fields. They escaped when John was a teenager, helped by an aunt who found them and went to the authorities. John then went to the Job Corps, a program established in the War on Poverty days to give low-income youth skills and training in a craft. John learned to be a concrete mason.

Those years, and the several following his training when he had a masonry job at a veterans' hospital in St. Louis, were the best times he has known. *I ain't really had a real great part in my life. The best part would be when I worked for the Veterans Administration and I didn't want nothing. I didn't need nothing. I didn't need nobody to help me or nothing. I had my own place. I had everything that I wanted. I didn't have no pressure on my mind to worry about bills or anything. I was just living free. It was after I come out of Job Corps. I got up and went to work. I had my own transportation. I had money in the bank. I had my own little old house. Kept my bills paid up and everything. I wasn't married then. I hadn't even met her yet. That was the best time of my life. Other than that, it has been hard.*

Against his aunt's advice he married an older woman when he was in his early twenties, and they had a rough time. He lost his job at the VA hospital because they hire only veterans for long-term jobs. He worked at a steel factory for a while, but he was injured on the job, caught up in machinery. When he returned from recuperating, they treated him badly and he left. His marriage dissolved then too, and, like many young men, he came back to family at home, to his aunt and sister and brother in Dahlia.

It has taken him nearly five years to find steady work here—and even that work is seasonal. He thinks one problem has probably been his inability to fill out an application accurately. He has found that employers ruled him out for full-time work over and over, although he would get called for short-term work, a few days here, a few there. *I tried to find a job. But I didn't have a car, so I walked, you know, the limit that it was to find a job. Wasn't nobody doing nothing, no hiring or nothing. I'd sit around and drink. Until last year. As the years went on, as I stayed here longer, I made more friends, I met more friends with cars. So I got them to take me more further out so I could find a job, and I finally found a job on the Mayberry farm, way out.*

The job lasted until winter. *I was driving tractors last year. If it didn't rain and I worked every day, I would make something like $290 that week. I paid bills, helped my sister pay bills. I helped the man break his land, plant his production, and when it come to harvest time, when the crop come up, when he got* *everything did that he needed to be done, he laid me off. I couldn't do nothing. It was wintertime then. I drawed fifty-six dollars unemployment for three months.*

John struggles to make it. When he is out of work, people treat him badly. Like many I interviewed, the prejudice and disrespect he has endured bothers him day in and day out. *If you colored and you got money, white people, they will talk to you. If you ain't got no money all they want to hear is "yes sir" and "no sir." I believe everybody should be treated the same whether they got it or don't got it. That's the way I feel about it. A whole lot of people around here got no other choice whether they're poor or not. There ain't nothing they can do. It is hard.*

Now he works when he can, sometimes doing fieldwork, sometimes helping out at a plantation store, but it is barely enough to get by. *Do you know how much it costs to rent one of these houses here without a bathroom? Sixty-five dollars. Without a bathroom. Sixty-five dollars. Then you have to pay your utilities, your gas, your lights. You're making $168 a week, and then you got to buy groceries. How can you save some money?*

His dream is to get a regular job like he had in St. Louis, using his trade as a mason, keeping up with the bills, not depending on others. There is no way to get ahead here in Dahlia. *After Christmas and New Year's, I'm planning on moving back to St. Louis and try it all over again there. I seen now that I can't make it here. I been here this long and I don't barely have enough money to buy a pack of cigarettes. I've been here over five years. I will try to get back into masonry. I done learn a lot by coming back down here and seeing how it is. I seen how my people get treated.*

At this point, John looks up the road to where a car has turned in. *And now, there's somebody to come see me,* he smiles, excusing himself. The lady friend he had been waiting for drives up, and John climbs into the car with her to go riding.

The difficulty John had in finding work plagues all the young black men here in Dahlia. Although a few work in the factories—in shipping at the sewing factory, outside with the ponds at the catfish factory—I was told time and time again that they generally do not hire many black men. They reportedly like to hire black women because they are seen as more compliant. *There's a few black males out there, but you have to be very docile, you gotta get stepping. That's the training, that's the training.* One thirty-year-old man, angry about being called "boy," was convinced he had lost his factory job because he raised objections about working conditions.

Others, in their forties and fifties, were clearly blackballed for speaking out against racist treatment. *That's why you have a lot of them that back off, simply because, if you do have a job and you're outspoken, you can be blackballed. And I think that is what happened to me when I was terminated down there. I couldn't find a job—nothing. I tried all over, just about every place they had work. Nobody would hire me. I was blackballed. After I was fired I think that they meant for me to get completely out of the county*. Although factory managers deny it is the case, most blacks, and some whites, believe that white farmers can influence hiring at the jeans plant as well as on the farms. *The people, whoever got the money, they runs things here. Whoever got money, they can get anything they want*.

But even apart from possible blackballing, jobs are scarce and hard to get without a connection. Knowing people is important for all kinds of work, but especially for the good factory jobs, and eventually some get discouraged. *I don't have no bad record or nothing. I finished school and I be trying hard. Every time I try hard. I told them I'd work seven days a week and anytime, day or night. I don't be seeing no way why they can't give me a try. More like they pick their family members, they give to them quicker than they would somebody else. There are so few jobs*. Others have been told, much like people in Blackwell, that their family's reputation is the problem. *They say that if your parents no-good workers, you won't do no good work. They won't hire you*.

The poor black men and women in Dahlia look very much like the inner-city poor described by William Julius Wilson in *When Work Disappears* and Elijah Anderson in *Streetwise*.[11] They are socially isolated, outside the mainstream, often idle and often behaving irresponsibly. Those in their twenties and thirties grew up on plantations with parents who had little schooling. They went to disorganized schools, sat in classrooms with uninterested teachers, and rarely were drawn into studies. Girls dropped out, had babies, drew small welfare checks, and worked in the fields or factories. Poor men were often rowdy in school—*full of liquor, cussin' the teachers out*—and were kicked out by exasperated officials after many years of failing until they were in their late teens in eighth and ninth grade. They say that teachers favored the children of other teachers, preachers, store owners—*name-brand people*, one called them. There were few male role models in the school. *To see a man teaching was rare. When I was in high school, to have somebody actually take time out to tell you about how things are, and what you can be or what you can do, that was sort of a rare thing also. There wasn't anyone who pulled me aside to say, "Hey look. You can do it." We didn't have it*.

Men cannot draw welfare checks unless they have a disability, but these young men frequently live with girlfriends, mothers, grandmothers, and aunts who receive public assistance. Some younger men do odd jobs for money, and others say they sell "rock," or cocaine. They "go riding," hang out with their friends, and some say they get rough with their girlfriends when they have been drinking. *Lately I been getting into a lot of trouble*, says one young man. *Done been in jail six times. Me and my girlfriend got into it one day last month and we had to go to court Monday. I just give her a black eye. That's about it. Her side kept hurting, you know. That's all.* They are fathering children out of wedlock with different women, and then their mothers help care for the babies. Like inner-city youth, they have grown up outside the mainstream culture and remain disconnected from it, often fulfilling their relatives' worst expectations.

Despite their isolation from opportunity, these poor black men and women are deeply entangled with the whites who control the economy in Dahlia. Bossmen running plantations still need labor they can depend on, although they need fewer workers than in years past. But the livelihood of other whites also depends on the black poor, just as the haves who are merchants in Blackwell depend on the have-nots to use their public assistance checks in their stores or to get credit from them while waiting for those checks. Here in Dahlia, like in Blackwell, store owners sell groceries and other consumable items at inflated prices to those who lack transportation to distant cities or have no savings and need credit to buy appliances and furniture.

WHITE PLANTERS, POLITICIANS, AND SHOPKEEPERS

Within the white upper class there are two groups—the very wealthy who have owned land and large farms for generations, who make up a true social elite, and below them, politicians, store owners, and some farm managers who emulate and ultimately defer to these big farmers. There is a well-understood hierarchy—*everyone knows their place*, says a lawyer. Social rules are strict, and social status carefully observed. A farm manager sees clear distinctions. *Lines between classes and races are clearly drawn, so no one guesses what they can and cannot do. Nobody worries about it. They know the lines are pretty well drawn and there won't be much crossing over one way or the other.*

The farmers who own the largest plantations primarily grow soybeans, cotton, and rice, but some also have catfish farms, farm equipment dealerships, and other land development investments. *These guys are in agribusiness and have sophisticated, diversified investments*, explains a black leader. The men in these top five or six families supervise farm managers who run their operations on a daily basis. Some have direct, visible political roles in Dahlia. Others work behind the scenes.

The total control customary under old plantation norms still guides some planters, younger as well as older. A forty-year-old farmer, filling out a Welfare Department form for a worker seeking unemployment benefits, stated that the man had worked for him "since birth." This same farmer told me, *These people are poor because they don't like to work. They just want to be on the dole*. There are reportedly bossmen who still insist that their black tenants seek permission to have visitors on the plantation. Recently, a farmer chased a literacy teacher off his property, telling him not to return. *Stay away from my people,* the bossman warned.

Those who work with farmers are cautious in choosing their words, but they describe men with considerable power. *I would say those people that have controlled things for years and years still pretty much control things*, a feed-grain dealer says, choosing his words carefully. *Maybe not to the extent that they once did—maybe not day-to-day life or anything like that. But there are still certain things that they control. Either through persuasion or monetarily, they still have that power to control, whether they use it or not. Many have used it from time to time. And they still have it*. Others are less cautious. *They are rich and they run everything, and they let you know it*, declares a young waitress. *There is one guy, he's a big-time farmer and owns the dealership, too. He's got more money than he knows what to do with. But he's got this attitude problem. He thinks he's better than everybody else and he is always telling us "you all are nothing."*

These potent, wealthy men are accustomed to power in all realms—and are widely believed to control the law, the voting, and the hiring. I heard many stories of farmers getting people off a criminal charge because they needed them on the farm. One white businessperson said he would not want big farmers, customers he relies on, to know that he would favor a county where the population was "fifty-fifty"—half white and half black—and integrated schools. He was convinced such a stand would cost him business because it would threaten the status quo and those farmers' absolute control. Whites and blacks believe powerful whites can ruin your life if you oppose them. A church official worried about a black activist. *He has a nice home. That home could have been burned down. We've had some fires around. Who knows why they burn down? A couple have been sturdy brick places, and yet they have burned to the ground. Somebody does these things.*

There are planters who have a reputation for fairness. *The guy who my daddy worked for, my hat is off to him because he would always have a good house for us to live in.* And some see change. After years of blocking all industry, several farmers have recently begun efforts to promote development that will bring new jobs: a retirement home, casino gambling, other service industry businesses—investments that are in their interests and that no longer jeopardize finding and keeping field workers. But remnants of old plantation-style dependency linger—the rent-free homes for tractor drivers and their families, wage garnishing for loans during the off-season or to pay creditors who might come to the bossman rather than directly to the borrower, furnishing of advances or help with health care expenses when the worker has no income in the winter months.

Even though the farmers with the largest holdings control the big decisions, they cede much of the daily business and politics to the farm managers, lawyers, and politicians who cater to them. A black leader described this group of lieutenants. *They got their little power—they operate below these guys. They're careful not to do anything to offend the status quo. When they go to church every Sunday or whatever they do together, they're a part of each other. It's a small, tight-knit community. I'm talking the white community—and if you hurt one, you hurt the other. That's their concept still.* The small-business owners, bankers, farm managers, and locally elected public officials in the white community see themselves as part of the upper class but distinct from the wealthiest farmers. *They are part of the power structure themselves. They are the lower echelon of power, you know. They're free to do little things—whatever they want to do within a certain realm. But if the big farmers don't approve, it's not going to fly. They have to sanction it.*

In Mississippi, supervisors are elected to run the counties and a school superintendent and board of education are elected to run the schools. A handful of white farmers hold elected positions as supervisors, although others are said to work behind the scenes. But much like Willy Granger in Blackwell, lower-level politicians may wield considerable power in these counties, and most notorious is the former superintendent of schools, Jack Peabody. Today Jack runs a real estate and auction business. Many blacks and a few whites believe he still has the ultimate say in the schools in the county, that the current black superintendent serves at Jack's pleasure and does his bidding. Whether or not this is true, there is little question that at one time Jack Peabody had great influence in Dahlia. *He was like a dictator*, said one white teacher. *No, he was a dictator*. Another summed up his style as *oppressive—racist and sexist*. I interviewed a number of people, white and black, who owed their jobs to his patronage.

Jack and his wife came to the Delta in the 1950s as newlyweds, and Jack began teaching history in what was then an all-white public high school. He worked his way up in the school, serving as assistant principal, then principal, and finally he was elected superintendent just before integration was forced on the Dahlia schools. He made all the hiring and all the purchasing decisions, and he expected people whom he hired or did business with to support him, both in his daily business and at election time. And he did not like interference. When Shirley Jones, a black activist, attended a public school meeting during working hours, Jack called her employer and asked what she was doing off work that day. The employer recalls the conversation with Jack. *He called and wanted to know what Shirley was doing at* his *board meeting during* my *office hours*.

Whites praise Jack for his skillful management, and black schoolteachers are grateful for opportunities he has sent their way. White property owners appreciated his ability to keep their taxes low, *holding a lid on school spending out there*. But others decry the way his racist and sexist management of the school system undermined morale, and deplore how his lack of commitment to the education of black children set the district back several years. A former school administrator recalled working under him. *There was a lot of oppression from the former superintendent. He was well known throughout the state. Still is. Highly respected across the state. And he's a brilliant man. He had over a million dollars in savings for this district, and then the new superintendent went in and spent it all. And, now, we are $300,000 in the red. I take nothing away from Jack Peabody as far as the money. He built the money up*.

He not only failed to invest in the physical plant—some buildings still lack air-conditioning here in the Delta. He also failed to bring in state and federal resources for educational programs—programs that parents are sure he would have known about because he had such extensive statewide ties in education. *He hates blacks and he is not too fond of women. He's your basic good old boy. Black and female teachers were always put down, and I don't know how long it will take before they can get a faculty built up that truly believes in the kids and that loves the kids. People proud to be teachers*. Jack Peabody has a reputation among blacks and whites as a ruthless politician who plays the patronage game well—rewarding supporters and punishing opponents and critics. Like Willy Granger in Blackwell, he is a lieutenant rather than a general, a petty politician whose actions have created an atmosphere of fear and distrust.

Merchants and professionals are not exactly lieutenants, but they have an uneasy, dependent relationship with the elite in this small, status-seeking social world. They regard the big farmers with envy and awe, but they also may ridicule them for not working hard. *The farm managers farm. I mean, they don't just ride around in a pickup truck like big farmers*. These professionals and business owners are all part of the haves, as in Blackwell, but in Dahlia there is well-recognized hierarchy within the group.

Everyone parties together. *We have lovely, beautiful parties—the upper class does*, says one white schoolteacher and doctor's wife. A factory manager who had moved to this community from a midwestern town where he and his family *were just plain middle class*, as he put it, described how he and his wife and children were deliberately drawn into the upper class, into tennis, into the social circle of the academy, into picnics and other social affairs of the elite. An old-timer explained, *We all go the same recreation club, the same swimming pool. Everybody sunbathes and talks together. We all go the same parties*.

One farm manager's daughter who works in a bank complained about those who emulate the very rich and snub her. *They just act like they're up there with the big-time farmers. It's the way they act—they won't have anything to do with you at certain parties, when they have summer dances, summer parties or just the New Year's Eve party. Oh, you go,* she explains, *anybody can buy tickets and go. But you have that group of people there that think they're better than everybody else, when really, they're just like us. I guess those women figure their husband goes out and makes all the money and they're rich enough they don't have to work, so they're better*.

As in Blackwell, clothes are important in Dahlia because social status matters so much in day-to-day interaction. The farm manager's daughter says the big farmers' wives would go shopping in their *raggedy old jeans*, but these *uppity women* get all dressed up just to go the grocery store. A newcomer described how difficult it was for her children to adjust to the social distinctions and status-conscious behavior among the children at the academy. *It was tough for them when they first came because there's so many cliques in school. Where we lived before there weren't these different groups—everyone was pretty much the same middle class. I don't think they felt like they fit in with the uppity-ups.*

The key to acceptance is to go along with the well-established rules of behavior. An accountant who came to the area in the 1950s said he and his wife did not worry about not being invited to the big parties or tennis tournaments. They were just glad for whatever opportunities for inclusion were made available to them. *We didn't try to change anything. We came and we just tried to be a part of the community and they allowed us to be a part. So, we're grateful.*

It is a community that imposes its social rules and norms on newcomers. A minister pointed out that he had learned that *everybody in the white community is either upper middle class or they're lower class. And, if you're lower class, you're not a part of this church, because the church caters to the upper middle class. A lower-class person would not be accepted. That's why the porch people still go out there to the Little Oklahoma Church. The white community is pretty well close-knit. They all associate with one another. But there are rules.*

Although whites rarely have social contact with blacks in Dahlia, the local newspaper owners, pharmacists, doctors, furniture store owners, grocery store managers, and other retailers all depend on captive black business. In many cases these local businesses are just now being turned over from parents to children, who represent the newer generation of haves. Edward and Sharon Carter are a good example. Their livelihood depends on business from the working poor in the black community.

Edward, now thirty-six, grew up in Dahlia, the son of a furniture store owner and grandson of a farmer who sold his medium-size farm during the 1970s. We talk across his cluttered desk in a windowless office in the back of the store. Later I interviewed his wife, Sharon, in her freshly redecorated kitchen, where we had coffee under a window full of nicknacks. Edward attended the private academy after the forced integration—he and his classmates felt like *pioneers—we were starting the traditions*. Sharon, daughter of a postal worker and a nurse, attended an integrated public school in her hometown on the Gulf Coast. They met at college, and when his father was ready to retire they returned to run the family furniture store, finance company, and rental property.

Although Dahlia is a small community, there are several furniture stores that compete for business. *We've got an established business, as long as I don't run it into the ground,* Edward says with a nervous laugh. *What has concerned me over the last several years is that too many of our good customers are ei-*

ther dying off or moving off and are not being replaced. The younger generation is coming up and you can't count on some of them being good customers. His clientele for furniture and appliances is the poorer black community. *The white people you can't count on being customers, period. And part of it is just economic. You know, they just can't afford not to save a hundred dollars or fifty dollars on something.*

Whites drive to nearby cities to shop, where they can pay less using their cash or credit cards. Blacks often lack transportation and usually cannot pay outright for something, so they come to Edward for credit. He calls around to find out about their work habits, talks to their bossman to see if their wages were garnished for other lenders, and confers with other store owners about the would-be borrower's credit history. If the applicant checks out, he has their mother co-sign, gets 20 percent of the cost as a down payment, and then makes up a loan agreement from his finance company for the balance. It is a good business, but lending is stressful—it wore down his father. Edward himself has had an ulcer for several years.

Customers often buy several big items at once. *They might buy new furniture and an appliance, or furniture and a television, or living-room furniture and bedroom furniture. So it can add up pretty quick. Like I said, a lot of these people's incomes are not real large. There's no point in making it too tough for them to pay because you're defeating the purpose. You want to get paid, so you've got to work with them. We charge interest of a little over 22 percent, which is high, but it's not that much higher than what some of the credit card companies charge, and they're a lot bigger than we are.*

Older blacks are more reliable bill payers because they have their steady Social Security income. *There are some families that the parents never paid worth a dime and their children don't pay worth a dime either. Sometimes it doesn't work like that. More often the parents, the older generation, pay better than the younger ones do. We've had some customers who, before they got on a fixed income, a regular income, they didn't pay well, and after they get on Social Security they pay on time. It's odd. With farming, you didn't always know. I mean, you could always find work, but it might not always be the same place. Also, there were very unscrupulous landowners who would take advantage of them. But, once they have their fixed, set income, they know what they're going to have and they can plan around that and they do okay.*

When borrowers do not pay, Edward has several options. *If you sell something on a contract, a secure contract, then you can legally repossess it if they don't pay for it, or, if they have a job, you can sue them and garnish their wages.*

So that's always an option. You don't like it, but that's the two last resorts. You have to do a lot of calling and some letter writing and yelling from time to time. We also have a fellow that does collecting for us. He goes around and sees people who are behind. I say "collector," but I use a couple of guys that work here. And then there are some you just lose. Either they move off with the merchandise, or they tear it up, or they don't have a job, or they don't have the income that you can get. So, sometimes you take a chance, and sometimes you come out, sometimes you don't.

Although the store can be stressful, life in Dahlia is good for Edward and Sharon. They know everyone in town, they are active in the Lion's Club, the Women's Club, the school. Lately they find they get asked to do things—to serve on the school board of the academy, to help out with the library committee, to help organize the tennis tournament—and this recognition makes them feel even more connected to the town. It is a safe community, people watch out for each other's children, will even reprimand them if it is called for, and the children can safely bike from one end of the town to the other.

The private school takes a lot of time, but it is also where families get together. Sharon says, *It really is the focal point. There are constantly ball games—two to three ball games a night sometimes! We are constantly working on them. A big moneymaker is the country fair. Constantly Mothers' Club, constantly at the athletic banquets and booster club drives, and constantly at moneymakers for one thing or another. It is a never-ending thing for the school. It wears me out.*

Edward regrets that supporting the school has made it impossible to organize a country club in the community; there just are not enough resources—time or money—left after the school's needs are met. He describes the work that goes into the New Year's party alone. *It takes five days and you change the gymnasium into a ballroom. The women all get together and change the gymnasium into a place that really is something special for one night. And then you have to tear it all down that night so they can play basketball the next day! But it's fun. It's just an awful lot of work. We have a good band that comes in and plays. The revenue goes to the Mothers' Club, which buys things for the school, and holds different types of fund-raisers and sponsors things, and constantly gives money to the school for the people who don't have the money, for the scholarships.*

But he, too, sees the school as the center of family life. *You've got your kids there. If it's a boy, he's going to play football. If it's girl, she's going to be playing basketball, or maybe she's going to be a cheerleader. If they're going to be real smart in school, then there's that. It just provides a place for everybody to be. It's a good little school.* Not everyone agrees. There are parents who worry about the poor preparation their children receive, especially in math and science once they reach high school, and those who can afford it send their children to elite boarding schools for the summer so they can catch up and get the scores they need to get into Ole Miss.

Edward and Sharon and their friends socialize with the big farmers. There might be a big Christmas party at a country club in a nearby city. And there are weddings with lavish receptions, the tennis tournaments with elaborate picnics. Sharon's minister figures that everyone in his parish attends them. Just as the wealthy farmers are known to run things economically and politically, their wives are known to run things socially. Edward and Sharon are not wealthy, but they appreciate the contact they do have with members of the richest, most powerful families. In fact, Sharon insists, *We associate with the upper echelon, really, as much as we do with anybody. It's kind of like a circle of friends. I think it's maybe divided into age groups. The richest of them aren't in my age group, so we wouldn't have anything in common anyway. Their kids are around and we socialize with them.*

Sharon names the bigger farmers—*Jack and Betsy Baker, Joanie and Bill Winston, Frank and Gigi Pendleton. Well, Gigi and I play bridge together but Betsy and I are best friends—that's Gigi's daughter. Joanie and Bill Winston's daughter lives right on this street. Lila and George Taylor don't have children my age, but we see each other at parties. I get Christmas cards from them. And Joanie and Bill sent us a beautiful Christmas card with a note on the back of it saying how dear our friendship was. It is just that we don't see each other socially. Sally and Don Waterstone—Sally and I were "arm and arm" at Habitat—on the Habitat family selection committee. We spend many hours together. I've been to her home and feel very comfortable with her. And Ed has the greatest respect for Don Waterstone.*

Recently Sharon has become good friends with Betsy, wife of one of the big-farm owners, who was slightly ostracized when she had an affair and eventually divorced. Sharon is feeling some pressure to keep up. *Betsy has never looked at a price tag. She's never* thought *about looking at a price tag. She's never had to.* In contrast, Sharon feels she has to watch her spending. *We may have a nice income, and,* she is quick to add, *I don't have to work. But usually every penny that I make, I can find some place to put it.*

It is not always easy for people in Edward and Sharon's income bracket to keep up with the elite in the community. Sharon describes their decision to buy a Lincoln Town Car. *I drive a Town Car and that was a real big—that car weighed a lot on me and Edward. We even looked at a Mercedes before we bought the Town Car, and he really wanted that Mercedes! That car cost more than what we paid for this house! But the Town Car, I wanted it big time. I really wanted the Town Car.*

The friendship with Betsy brings more than a new shopping partner and the need for a new car. Sharon has taught at both the white academy and the black school over the years, most recently the academy, and she thinks she may give up the job so she can travel and shop more freely with her new friend. This opportunity coincides with a kind of weariness as well. She is tired of having parents think they can tell her how to teach just because they pay tuition, and her energy for all the school activities is waning. Also, the money might work out, because Betsy's new husband is going to invest in a business venture of Edward's, a fast-food restaurant franchise out on the highway.

Sharon and Edward's world is small, sometimes to the point of feeling confining, but generally the fact that everyone knows everyone is an advantage rather than a disadvantage. A farm manager likes being able to dash into a farm machinery shop and leap over the counter to help himself to the part he needs, everyone likes having a lake nearby for boating and water skiing, bridge and club activities keep both working and nonworking women connected and busy, and the men love the easy access to good hunting.

A country club would be nice, but the academy takes all the money of those in the shopkeeper group, and the very rich do not seem to need or want it enough. An older resident recalls, *I cannot tell you how we have tried to get a country club going. I don't know why it's failed. We just haven't understood that. My husband tried years and years ago to get one started—he even had the land—five acres of land. And we have wonderful black cooks here. We almost had it off the ground at the time that the private school was organized and that took everybody's money. That was the end of it. The rich people really would have had to put money out to get it built.*

Some of the more liberal men and women worry that their children are growing up in a segregated and racist environment, and Edward and Sharon are among them. They feel ambivalent about race. Sharon speaks sympathetically about some poor black women who try hard, especially one she knows who *has worked from sundown to wee hours of the night trying to keep four or five sisters and brothers together, but she has not been around, and now the kids are nuts. No discipline, no supervision, in jail—been in trouble over and over again. Not good students. And bless Mom's heart, most of the moms are trying real hard. It's just the odds are so much against them. It's just the pits. And there might be a father in the picture and they're both working their butts off trying to make ends meet and trying to keep everything together and trying to instill some values into their child.*

On the other hand, she thinks there are poor families who cheat the system. *There is a group who want Christmas baskets, who say they don't have the money for the food. Where are the values? Where are the ideals? What are they doing with the welfare money? What are they doing with the food stamps? If you have fifteen kids in your home, you know you're getting a thousand dollars a month in food stamps. Why do you need a Christmas basket? I've got a lot of questions. There's a lot of deception that's going on.*

She also talks about middle-class black families whose children are in medical school and law school, varsity players on college teams, or football queens at the university—although she can't resist mentioning two cases of such teenagers having children out of wedlock. Part of her sympathizes with these accomplished, middle-class black youths. She knows their parents are instilling the same values for education and family that she believes in. Children get "sucked in," she says. But there is another part of her that is critical. She sees the failure of her own Scout troop as due to lack of interest, for example, and the failure of a black troop as a lack of leadership. *It seems it's gotten—I know you probably think I'm awfully cynical—and I think I've probably turned this way just recently. I'm getting real tired. I'm getting tired of pushing. And I know this sounds racist when I say this too, and that disturbs me because I'm not that kind of person—or I don't want to think about myself as that kind of person. But I've been having more of these feelings as time passes. It seems like any program that is successful are programs that the whites start and then they die when the blacks take it over. Like the Scouts program. There was a black Scout troop and as long as there was a white man from Mayflower came down and encouraged the group, it went on fine. And then he got transferred somewhere else and somebody came in and he didn't nurture so it died. Now ours died because the interest died.*

And, as her friends remind her, these are "agricultural blacks"—not people you want your children associating with in any case. One of her friends told me, *I wouldn't want to put my freshly bathed, nicely dressed daughters in the class with what I see on the streets every day . . . Bigotry? Racism? I don't know what you call it. You got to educate people on the street to take care of themselves*. Some newcomers, even those from other parts of the South, are surprised by the way whites here talk about blacks. *"Nigger" is a common word here. I was amazed, and my children were taken aback*. They worry about the lessons their children are learning. *I had a station wagon piled full of children and I was delivering and dropping, and had some of them in the car still, when we passed a black walking down the road. One of the children in the back said, "I just stuck my tongue out at that nigger." I just pulled over and turned around and said, "No, we're not going to say that." I didn't do it because I was correcting this other person's child. I did it because my own child was with me*.

Some, like Edward, see small signs of progress. *I am encouraged because I see more black men moving into leadership and I think that's healthy for the black community. They were just invisible when my sister worked at the Welfare Department. Today, there's more leadership from black men. They're getting involved in recreation for the youth and trying to lift the children out of trouble and providing some opportunities for the children. A lot of interest in the school and what kind of education the children are getting. That's got to be healthy. I mean, any kind of interest is better than none at all.*

For others the racial imbalance stands out as the key impediment to progress. *I think it would be easier, the structure would change in some way, if the balance of the races were more equal. The white community would feel less—I don't know what the word is exactly—but they would be freer with their associations and there would be less competition. That's probably not the right word. I just think that everything would sort of balance out better. We would have a school, have a public school, that would be better for everybody. People would know each other and we could help each other better. If I could hope for anything, it would be for more people coming in here. We might see the makeup of the community changing, the whole county. Sometimes I feel like we spend so much energy trying to get "one up" on everybody*.

The ministers whom I interviewed are frankly discouraged. One said, *It's a mentality that blacks are inferior to whites. They have their place and we have our place and never the two shall meet. That mentality is still prevalent here*. Another sighed, *Some of us can work toward it. It's a long thing. I don't know*. In the 1930s local writer David Cohn observed, "Disturbing ideas crawl like flies around the screen of the Delta but they rarely penetrate." His words still seem apt for Dahlia's white world, despite Sharon and Ed Carter's ambivalence about race and racism, despite the occasional colorblind white who tries to relate differently.[12]

LEADERSHIP IN THE BLACK COMMUNITY: THE OLD AND THE NEW "TOMS"

Black leaders who work to improve conditions for the black majority have had to battle not only whites' efforts to retain control over Dahlia but also divisions and distrust within the black community. Many say that whites deliberately fan factional infighting among blacks. They believe that whites, especially those in political power, deliberately create rumors to prevent coordinated efforts to bring about change. *In this community, the white can put out a rumor to start a rumor, and there it go. Nobody checks on whether it's true*, a seasoned organizer sighs.

A black schoolteacher notes, *When you have ambition here the whites are not the only ones who come out and attack you. They use blacks to do so. They get other blacks to come out and do it.* The black community is divided, most agree, and old habits persist. *First of all, you go back to the plantation mentality,* Michael Long explains. *It's very much in evidence here. A leader, he's got to have some followers to make an impact. So they get to his followers. And it leaves him out there exposed, naked. He's ineffective. If he goes out there, he soon falls down on his face.*

Factionalism spawns suspicion of leaders' motives and undermines efforts to improve institutions in the black community. Just like in Blackwell, distrust and lack of cooperation also spring from envy of those who do better in an uncertain environment where jobs and resources are scarce. Some whites call it "the crab syndrome," saying the ones below hang on to the legs of the ones scrambling higher. Most blacks see it as the jealousy that is inevitable when there is too little to go around. A black mechanic says, *You might just be a plain old person who gets up and works like hell for what you have, but people will tag you as a "big shot." It becomes a problem when people get satisfied with their condition, and resentful of those who are getting up every day working hard, so they call them "big shots."* Political distrust and resentment of those who better themselves make it hard to bring about change. But black leaders persevere nonetheless, and there are signs that opportunities for cooperation are increasing.

I found three leadership groups in Dahlia's black community. First, there is the older establishment with long-standing ties to the white community, the "Toms" who are criticized by some for being overly deferential. Second is an older, "radical" group that challenged white authority during the civil rights movement and has continued raising social justice issues up to the present. Many of these men and women have paid a high personal price for that resistance. Finally, in recent years, there is a new group of professionals, some children of the older establishment and radicals, others who scraped and scrambled their way out of poverty and returned to Dahlia. This new middle class bridges the two long-standing black leadership groups in Dahlia and offers a glimmer of hope for change.

Clare Green is an older, established black leader who is a politician and funeral director. The "radicals" Harold Jackson and Michael Long are grassroots organizers who have spent their lives resisting the racism and oppression in Dahlia. In recent years they have been working more with Charles Smith, a younger "establishment" politician, and his wife, Diana, who is also a local leader. Harold and Michael and the Smiths are doing more and more with recent return migrants like Coach Wilson and Sarah Early, a nurse, members of the new middle class in Dahlia who combine pride and ambition in their professions with a dedication to improving the community.

Clare Green is in his early seventies now, a distinguished citizen in the black community. A white business leader called the Green family "upper-class black." Clare runs one of three funeral home businesses, is deacon in his church, holds an elected political office in the county, and is active in the NAACP. His wife of forty-some years has been a schoolteacher and leader in the community, and his many children and grandchildren are doing well, some in the Delta, others in Chicago. He drives a Cadillac and has a brick home in the country.

Liberal whites hold him up as an example, while black "radicals" see him as a henchman for the whites. As one leader explained, *In the plantation system, if you want to go talk to the big man in the house, you had to go through old man So-and-so—you got to talk to his black man. If he thought it was all right, he would tell the bossman and get you in. And that's the same thing today. If you want something, they figure that you have to go through people like us.*

But Clare's situation as "the white man's black man" is complex, and his choices reflect how he gauged his options given the circumstances when he was young. We talk at the funeral home in a dark, wood-paneled room, sitting across a large mahogany-like desk, with an air conditioner churning noisily in the background. He often refers to himself as "we" during the interview, perhaps thinking of the whole Green family and its considerable stature and influence in the black community.

Clare was one of eight children born to his farm-laborer parents, but he was the only one of them raised by his maternal grandparents. They were very strict—*too strict*, he says gravely. But they taught him to be punctual and responsible, and they insisted that he go to the Baptist church high school, though such a path was rare indeed for a young black male from a poor family in the 1930s. As a child and young man he worked in the fields and on the new highway—hot, physically demanding labor that paid sixty cents a day in the fields and, later, thirty cents an hour for the highway work. When he left high school he rented land from his future in-laws and farmed. When he returned after serving in World War II, he began working for neighbors who ran a local funeral home, picking up bodies of the dead and selling burial insurance to the living while he was on the route. *I went into the service in 1944, stayed there until 1946, came back, and started back working for a funeral home, and I farmed. I rented land and farmed. Then later I went into business for myself. My first job was thirty dollars a month, and it was a little better . . . The second funeral home I worked at was mostly on commission. You only get paid so much for picking up bodies, making visits. And then I had an insurance ride. I worked that on commission—doing all that work,* he recalls, *and they didn't pay you.*

In the early 1940s he married the daughter of black farmers who owned land and whose high status in the community elevated his own. Soon after, he was able to borrow $250 to start his own funeral business. It was difficult competing with two established firms, but Clare concentrated on burying babies. *At one time, I was burying so many babies that they called me the baby undertaker.* People to whom he was selling burial insurance would "try him out" with the children. *When you start with writing the burial insurance, sometimes they put the children in, and they say maybe we going to give you a trial with the children; maybe they come later. A lot of time they did,* he says with a little smile. As people came to know and trust him, his funeral business grew.

Clare is cautious with his words, says little about black-white relations, and insists that anyone with drive and ambition can "make it." *It's not too bad if you get out and try to make something out of yourself. We have quite a few that have welfare on their mind. They don't mind living on assistance. I've always been told, and I've always been taught, that a man can do anything that he wants to, if he wants to. Like I said, I made it well here and I started out low.*

He and his family have done well. His children have become lawyers and doctors and leaders in the schools. They make opportunities available to other blacks, overseeing the distribution of summer jobs, public jobs, subsidized apartments, and other resources. Leona Wright, a young woman from the other leading black establishment family, described how she got her job as an administrator in a government program when she came home from college. *When they first started getting [the program] together, Mr. Green's son, he knew me. He knowed my family and stuff, and he needed somebody with a degree. He asked me, would I like it? I told him, "Yeah." It was like somebody was just watching over me.*

Clare Green is conservative and does not cause trouble. His strategy is to play a role in the existing system, not to change it. He promotes his family and his friends, and he works with the white power brokers. They recently appointed him to a political office, and he is proud of his affiliations and positions on various boards. Noting that financing for black home buyers is a problem, he suggests—a little disingenuously—that local banks do not have enough funds to make loans to blacks who want to own homes. But he also is candid, at times, about the hardships blacks have endured historically at the hands of powerful white landowners.

He recalls the sharecropping system and the limited options for black workers. He remembers when the only black employed at the apparel factory was a janitor, even though most white employees had to commute from neighboring counties. *Years back, we didn't have many poor whites in this town. No, they were all what you might call middle class or rich—some were millionaires. And that's the reason why they didn't have any whites from here working down there. I guess they were above that type of work. Black labor, most of it was farm work, domestic work. Oh, and we had schoolteachers, too.*

Clare rose from humble beginnings to prominence at a time when few black men in the Delta had any power at all, when crossing whites was very dangerous. Few in his generation who escaped poverty stayed in Dahlia, especially after seeing the outside world during the war. But he chose to make a life here. His children are carrying on the leadership role he established in the community. The Greens, and the reportedly conservative NAACP they represent, are scorned by the "radicals" for accommodation with the white power brokers. Over the years the conflict has undermined many efforts to organize the black community.

Several of those known as radicals in Dahlia grew up in black elite families—children of schoolteachers, destined to become counselors and advisers in their community—"Toms," they would say. But they chose to carry out their mentoring role without acting as liaisons with the white community. Others were farm laborers' children who were inspired as teenagers by Martin Luther King on the radio, resisted the way they were treated, organized civil rights and labor organizations, and then were blackballed as troublemakers by the white employers in the community. They are a tight group. They have endured real hardship as a result of their efforts to bring about change in this deeply segregated society. They all describe the most difficult part of their lives as the period when their children were young and they could not find work because of their political activism.

Harold Jackson, now a grandfather and in his fifties, recalled, *The hardest part of my life was when I couldn't get work day by day. You didn't know where your next meal was coming from. You'd go off and cry. You'd be so angry. If the people only knew what you had to do just to survive, I guess people wouldn't believe it. I would sit up all night sometimes, just thinking. But we survived. I thank God for that. Sometimes you can sit back, right now, and think about all of this that's happened to you, and you realize it was so hard. I just pray. Praying has helped me through the years. I would bet you that there's not ten people here in the whole county have been through as much as we have, the handful of guys right here.* He has tears in his eyes, remembering the hard times and the solidarity they felt. *We didn't gripe. The people probably didn't know we were that bad off, but we were.*

These "radicals," in their late forties to fifties now, combine their political and social activism to improve opportunities for blacks in Dahlia with concerted efforts to rein in the young people in their community. *The way things are now with the drugs, and the gang banging and the killing and all the deaths, I believe we are going to have to show our children tough love. We have asked the supervisors to set up a curfew for the county, for the entire county. If the kid is caught one or two or maybe three times, his parents will have to be responsible. If they don't have any money to pay a fine, let those people get out there and do community work, you know what I am saying? If they have to get out there and do community work, I guarantee you they will know where their kid is next time around.*

Shirley Jones, a retired schoolteacher, is one of Harold's longtime partners in activism. Her name came up time and time again in interviews, with the poor and with some who left poverty behind, because her help and advice changed the course of people's lives. Even former residents who now have professional jobs in other parts of the country recall her influence and guidance when they were young—advising them to stay in school, helping them interpret college scholarship offers, convincing their wary parents that they should seize an opportunity to leave home. She worked tirelessly on political issues, organizing and speaking out for decent housing, for better schools, for social justice. Today she spends as much time with her grandchildren as with social issues, working in her living room full of family graduation pictures, framed diplomas, news clippings, and books in a tidy house on a side street in Old Town. She is wary about an interview and prefers to chat about the issues and share newspaper clippings, not talk about her own life. Her children, Frances and Arthur, are adults with families of their own who have made the Delta their home, and their names are mentioned by young people in their teens and early twenties. They are carrying on the family tradition, organizing Scout troops, ball teams, and working to get a teen recreation center.

Michael Long also worked with Harold Jackson to bring about changes. Michael was born to relative privilege in the black community. *My grandmother was a teacher. She taught school forty-some years. I was raised up in a group of people—I could have been a "Tom" if I'd wanted to be a "Tom." I know them—the Greens. I was raised up with them. But once I became grown and I saw the things that they were doing, I just couldn't do it.* Michael was troubled by the way other black leaders would tell him to withdraw support from those who challenged the system. *They were telling me that "hey, we're going to get rid of So-and-so because he ain't doing right," or "he's this and that." They would try to tell us that black people really don't need better housing, or really don't want a new educational program. They'll tell you that black people here really don't want this. But that's not true. They try to use the influence and power that the whites give them to keep things the same.*

Under his grandmother's close guidance, Michael finished school and went into an officer training program for the army. While he was in training he injured his arm in an accident, and was honorably discharged. He receives a small pension, and this source of steady income acts as a kind of buffer that enables him to work as a community activist, somewhat outside the economic reach of the white power structure. With a handful of others, including Shirley and Harold, he has worked over the years to improve housing, working conditions, and schools for blacks in Dahlia. His time in the service gave him not only a vision of how things could be better but also skills to bring resources together from outside the community. Several times he has brought media attention and some grant money to focus on the problems poor blacks face in Dahlia.

Although he went to school to become a computer technician after his discharge, he wanted to work at home, so he took a position with a local public social agency. His community organizing and work with young people led to an interest in politics. Drawing on the base he had from his grandmother's status, his own achievements, and his volunteer work with young people in Tall Pines, he ran for public office, as supervisor, against Bill Winston, a powerful white candidate who had held the position for years. *A lot of those younger guys, they looked up to me because I used to be one that would go out to the park and play ball with them and that type thing. Now they are young men with families that live in Tall Pines, where I live. So not anybody can come in and tell them lies about me. They know I was raised decent. The same thing with the girls. I taught them how to play softball. Now they're young ladies. So that's what helps me out there.*

But despite this community base, Michael was defeated by a slim margin. He had resigned from his public-sector job to run for office, but when he lost the election and another position at the agency was advertised, he reapplied. *After I lost the election, I went back to apply for my job because it was posted. When I resigned for this race I had received a notice saying that if in any time within two years that the position came open—a year, that's what it was, a year—that I could go back and work for the agency, because I left in good standing at that time. So I went back and applied for the job, filled out my application. I had nine and a half years' experience and I never had a rating lower than 4.5 on a 5-point scale the whole time I worked there. When I went in for an interview, the director broke down and cried. She told me, "I can't hire you back. They told me if I hired you back they're going to cut my budget. Won't be any money here." She said, "Michael, I can get you a job in another county, but I can't hire you back here. It will never work out."*

When I spoke with this director, a white woman, she gave the same account, although when I pressed for details she said she "just knew" she could not rehire him, that no one had told her not to do so. *See, I couldn't hire Michael back after he ran against Winston. I believe it was the hardest thing that I've ever had to do businesswise, was to sit in a room and tell him I couldn't hire him back. No one told me not to. I told Michael, I said, "You're smart enough to know." And I says, "Just you and me talking, this agency will not be funded sufficiently." I wanted him to know. "It's not on my account. I don't care what they do to me, but I've got to be in a position to ask for the things that this office down here needs." See, he had to resign to be in politics because we're under the Hatch Act. And then, when it was over and he lost, I didn't really think he'd come back. But he came back and asked for the job back, and he had been one of my most valuable employees. Good worker. I had to tell him I couldn't—that the ax would fall on my head and it would be me as director, not me personally. And he understood that.*

Michael continues his work as an organizer and activist. Like Harold, he is worried about young people, and he and his wife work tirelessly to educate young people about sex and drugs, to offer opportunities for further education and for job training in construction or nursing, as aides. But he keeps his eyes on the larger picture as well. His efforts to organize politically have made him realize that the black community needs economic independence. *A political base without an economic base is no good to you. You need to have an economic base in place before you get a political. You got to be able to give the people something to pull them away from the power structure.* So he and others are trying to develop some community-owned businesses that can hire blacks and be trusted, alternative outlets for food, gasoline, and appliances at fair prices. They have a small store out on the edge of Tall Pines, but he and his co-workers constantly battle suspicion and lack of trust from the black community. Caroline Gage, the young mother struggling to provide for her children, had heard bad things about the store and Michael's motives, and she believed them.

According to Michael, *People will say, "Well, I'm not going to shop there. I'm not going to make them rich." They think we get the money off of it! They don't realize that we work for nothing. It's just run by volunteers. But you can't get a person to believe that. They think, "I just can't believe that. They probably get something out of it." But we are trying to show black people that you can do for yourself. They don't understand it, they just don't understand it. They think that everybody's out to benefit themselves, and that's the biggest problem we have here—jealousy.*

He believes that local merchants like Edward Carter prevent regional distributors in Carterville and other large metropolitan centers from selling to them—that he cannot get access to air conditioners and other big appliances local black families buy on credit because then his store would challenge the white merchants' monopoly. The store fights for survival on both fronts, against the suspicions within the black community and against the power the white shopkeepers still hold over all economic activity in Dahlia.

Harold Jackson is a tall, lanky man who has worked with Shirley and Michael and the handful of others, organizing politically even when it would jeopardize his job. He grew up in the country, son and grandson of poor sharecroppers who never came out ahead and who were subject to constant harassment from the foremen. When he was a child, Harold wondered, *Why is it just blacks chopping cotton? I wondered, why wasn't everybody? My grandparents told me not to worry about that. They said, "Just do what you're supposed to do." Later on I began to see that we were really in poverty and the whites had everything. I also remember how my grandparents used to work the whole year and come out in the hole, as they call it. They owed—they did all the work, and they owed.*

As young men growing up in the sixties, even in places as remote and controlled as Dahlia, Harold and his friends heard and were inspired by Martin Luther King. *Coming up, there were about five of us who went to high school together who used to always sit around and talk about the wrongs and how hard it was to make it—for others to make it. The influence that came over me was Martin Luther King. King not only had a good voice, he had a good message. We used to sit and listen. And even though my grandparents were illiterate, the message got to them. I guess I really started listening, hoping. I also began marching, to try and make things better here. It was dangerous to do. But then you also have to look at how you're working yourself to death and you're still not accomplishing anything.*

Harold won a partial basketball scholarship to college, but he could not make ends meet and dropped out to work. He was drafted and sent to Vietnam. The wartime experience devastated him. *I don't like to go back to it. The only thing that I could say is that when I went to Vietnam I experienced things that I'd never experienced before. I did things I'd never done. I made it back alive.* When he came home from the war he had lost his drive, lost his hope, and he drifted from place to place. His grandparents called him home in the mid-1970s, just as the apparel factory began hiring black workers, and he got a position there for a while. But conditions in the plant rekindled his anger about the injustices blacks endured in the rural South.

Down at the plant, the place I worked, there was still a form of plantation work. Still a place where the supervisors and management treated people not like humans. Like Michael, he observed black leaders accommodating white control, and he fought against it. *If there's somebody they really didn't like, they'd want you to make them do something that would get them fired. I couldn't see it. You have a few groups of blacks here who are not really concerned about blacks or equality. They're the group who can talk to some of the big white guys. They can get special favors. They're not interested in equality.*

And like Michael, he. can understand why most blacks in the area are afraid to stand up for their rights. *You have fear in a lot of black people. Black people are afraid of white people. The whites control everything—everything that you do, everything that you try to do. They control the banks, so you can't borrow anything. They control the jobs, control the businesses, everything. A person has to either fall in line or be willing to suffer the consequences of not being allowed to make a living here. So people fall in line.*

Harold dreams of having his own little business one day—and that is his hope for his children as well. He wants them to be free, he says, and that means economically independent. He sees even the leadership in the black community fearful and grateful in a way that undermines freedom. *I think some of your black leaders feel that they owe an obligation. They're indebted for life. Someone has given him a job where he can make a little more than the rest. He can see a few dollars more than the rest of the people, and his standard of living would be up a little higher. Not a whole lot, but a little higher. He may be able to buy a new car every four or five years, live in a nice house, where most of us can't do this. He is willing to keep on doing whatever he's been doing, and some more, to keep what he's got.*

He sees this attitude extending to the political realm. *During the last election votes were going for five and six dollars. "Mr. So-and-so gave me this and I'm sure going vote for him." That's the way it goes.* And he sees the control the elites have reaching into law enforcement, just as it does in Blackwell. Those working in law enforcement told stories that corroborate his views. Harold sums it up: *The law is who you know. I could go out there in the street and stagger as though I was drunk or whatever, and a policeman would come by and put me in jail. You have a big-time farmer, he goes for a ride in his truck and runs into somebody and crashed the car and the truck, they'll take him home. It's who you know or who you are, you understand? The county itself has been run based on the little, little bits of fines that black people pay. Very few whites pay fines. I've never seen them paying. White people do not go to jail, even when they do illegal things, they do not go to jail.*

Like all the black leaders in the area, and many whites as well, Harold worries about the young people. They have nothing to do, are getting into trouble, and children are raising children. *The kids here have absolutely too much spare time. They don't have some kind of center or something to go to where they can do something, skate or something. Maybe there wouldn't be as much going on as there is going on, if they had some place to go. The kids just don't have anything to do. They go to school, they stay there until 2:30 or 2:45, whatever. Then they have from that time until 10:00 or 11:00 at night. The parents, they aren't into the life of their kids. They work. They don't have time. They let the kids mostly raise themselves. Then we have another problem, possibly the worst one, when you have kids raising kids and having kids. How can a kid raise another kid? They don't know right from wrong.*

Charles Smith and his wife are also working on ways to involve youths in constructive activities and to fund programs and a center where activities for them can occur. They represent a new kind of establishment in Dahlia. They work not only with Clare Green and his grown sons and daughters but increasingly with other segments of the black community as well. Charles grew up the son of black landowners. This asset provided protection that, combined with his father's lessons about being independent, prepared him for leadership. Diana was born poor in a large family out on a plantation. But then, very much like Clare Green, she was raised with just two siblings by a grandparent, benefited from family support and some key educational opportunities, and lifted herself out of poverty, marrying into a landowning family. Today Charles is a leading local politician, Diana a successful education administrator. Like most of the black leaders in Dahlia, their current status was earned through hard work combined with some crucial support and resources made available along the way.

Charles and I talked one Sunday night in midwinter at the Smiths' pleasant brick home out in the country, interrupted now and then by calls from former residents hoping he could help them—in his new role as a real estate agent in Dahlia—to find a place to live in their hometown. Now in his late thirties, Charles recalled how he had to miss school to work in the fields when he was a boy; unlike Caroline and most others of their generation, however, he was mostly working on his family's own ten acres.

I went to school when I could. I didn't miss a lot of days, but we all missed some school, because with my dad working in a manufacturing plant in Boyd County, my eleven brothers and sisters and I had to pick the cotton and harvest the crops. He would come home in the afternoon and help us out, and tell us what we needed to do the next day. But we had to stay out of school. The teacher would always get on us about missing so many days of school. But we had to, because we had to harvest the crops. At times we would miss a whole week out of school just to pick cotton—not for somebody else, for ourselves. Charles's parents would wait until the cotton blossoms were open before they kept the children out of school, but then they would have to miss from fifteen to twenty days in October and November.

Still, land ownership gave them independence. Charles's father, who had spent almost twenty years in Baltimore working on the docks, had learned how to be his own man in a white-dominated world, and he taught his children. *I guess my daddy really taught me how to work, to work for him. Then when the family got larger, all of us couldn't live off of that small farm, we would work on the outside some time. We would go over here and chop cotton for this man. We picked cotton for a few years. But we would always take care of our own cropping and harvesting first, and then we would go out and work for this guy and he would pay us at the end of the week. I got plenty of work.*

Charles's father instilled a sense of independence and self-worth that has served Charles well over the years. *If there was something that I didn't like about this guy I was working for, if I didn't like the way he was treating us or I thought he wasn't paying me right, I could just quit and go home. But so many peoples couldn't do that, because not only did they work for him, but they lived in his house. We didn't live in his house.*

He is clear about the importance of land ownership and his father's training. *I don't have any fear of white people. My experience coming up was that my dad was such a strong man and he provided a lot of guidance and leadership, even when it came to dealing with other people, especially white people. He used to kind of educate us about how to act around them. What to do and what not to do. If you didn't want to pretty well do what they wanted, then you avoid that situation.* He gives an example. *Say my dad didn't want me to work for you. He wouldn't tell you, "My son is not going to work for you because you're not treating him right." But he wouldn't give you an excuse either. He would tell you, "He is not going to work for you."*

Charles was the fifth oldest child but the first to finish high school and the first to go on to college. His college was mostly white, so he had the opportunity to interact with whites outside the segregated community where he grew up. After college he joined the army, where he had an even broader exposure to other worlds thrust upon him. *It was different. It was fast-paced and it was challenging. You come in contact with so many people from all over the country and that was different. For me, being a little country boy like that, it took some adjusting.* Charles believes that all these experiences—his father's training and the freedom their land ownership gave them, contact with whites at school, and exposure to discipline and diversity in the army—made a crucial difference in his life.

In his roles as politician and businessman, he works hard to improve Dahlia. He recognizes the obstacles posed by undereducated workers and years of dependency on the plantation. People wonder, he says, why these counties with black majorities are still controlled politically by whites. *It's going to take years to change this. People don't understand that. When you've got people that has been in politics for years and years, you can't just come in and vote them out that easily just by having a black running. I mean, they're ingrained in the community, in the black community. They've got a large share of black people depending on them for housing, for jobs, for Christmas bonus. In other words, they provide things to these black people that they need. Black people figure if you put Mr. So-and-so out of office, you are cutting your own neck off. It's economic power. How can you defeat a guy that has got half of the people working for him or that benefit from him, whether through a job, living in one of his houses, or going through him to get loans? How are you going to defeat him? They feel obligated to him because they've worked for him or he's provided them jobs.*

Like Michael, and like change agents in Blackwell, Charles recognizes that economic power is the crucial underpinning to political independence. He wants to develop black-owned economic resources, perhaps by extending his new involvement in real estate to a business. *I would like to be a businessperson, self-employed—to work for myself and then be able to employ other people. I don't have any big ideas about money. But I want to be able to see that I have succeeded and accomplished something. Not only for me to look at, but for other people to look at and say, "If he did it, I can do it."*

Although at first Charles was seen as the same kind of establishment person as Clare Green—*someone put in place by the white power structure to do what the whites want done*, as one unconvinced activist put it when I first came to Dahlia—over the years he has begun to show even his harshest critics that he does not just go along with the power brokers. Charles says these things take time. *When you move into a position like supervisor and you've got a millionaire there and another millionaire here, it takes some time for you to really know your way around. Once you learn your way around, you are going to count on more conflict with them. But starting out, you're just trying to find what is what. Then when you formulate opinions about how things should be done and so forth, then you start having conflicts with some of your board members. But usually, when you first start out, they're going to treat you nice. That has been my experience. You're gonna get some of those small things you want. But as you grow in knowledge and job responsibility and so forth, then you begin to get into a little bit more conflict and disagreement with some of the board members that have been there for years and years in power.*

On a personal level, Charles's story shows the impact of having even modest economic resources and outside experience. His wife Diana's background also illustrates how important resources are for mobility in poor places. Diana and I talked half a year later out at the old high school, where she runs a summer education program for pregnant teenagers. It was a hot July afternoon, and there is no air-conditioning at the school although the temperatures run into the nineties most days. An old fan ticked rhythmically in the background as we talked during a break from classes.

Diana was born in 1960 and grew up poor in a sharecropper shack in the country. She was one of three out-of-wedlock children born to Caddie Winslow, who died giving birth to her twelfth child when she was thirty-three. When Diana was four years old, her mother married a man who ran a café, or "juke joint," in town. When she moved to town with her new husband, she left Diana and her two other out-of-wedlock children out in the country with her grandfather. Diana's great-grandfather, whom she calls Papa, raised them until they were grown. He worked into his late seventies as a groundskeeper for a white family in town, providing well for his three eldest great-grandchildren, and they did not feel poor or suffer scorn for lacking what others had. *I always stayed with Papa. From about first grade through high school and college, it was just Papa, my two sisters, and me. We didn't have much, but I never felt deprived. We always had something to eat. You might have raised it, but you didn't go to bed hungry.*

In these small communities where appearances define your family background, shoes and neat clothing are very important. *We never went to school ratty. We never went to school without shoes.* Poor rural children often missed school events because they did not have the right clothing, or did not participate in clubs or sports teams because they could not afford equipment or uniforms. But Diana's great-grandfather made sure his three charges had what they needed to hold their heads high. *We never missed out. I didn't miss my high school prom. I wore my class ring. Now Papa may have had to suffer trying to raise three kids all by himself, but he made it so that we didn't have to suffer because he was suffering.* She smiles as she remembers. *That man did have four of us sleep in the same bed, but he always made sure we had shoes on our feet and food in our mouths.*

Unlike Caroline Gage, who had to share scarce resources with twelve brothers and sisters, where the older children took care of younger siblings and often did all the housework while parents worked, Diana grew up in a household of four. But perhaps most important in shaping Diana's future were her summers in Chicago with her father, Ernest, and her stepmother, Sherry. Ernest and Sherry took responsibility for her in the summers after her mother died, and it was there that she was exposed to a wider world as the beneficiary of city-run recreation programs when she was young and teen employment programs during her high school years.

The programs kept her out of trouble, but they also expanded her horizons in deliberate, important ways. *One year I remember we would go to this nearby Baptist church and people came in and talked to us about careers, foreign places, even personal hygiene. Just whatever they thought young people needed to know*. But they received more than lessons. They were exposed to widely varying situations and people. *We had two teachers who taught us all these different songs, and then we went all over the city, to different things all over Chicago, and we would sing—at nursing homes, hospitals, clubs, other projects. Sometimes the mayor wanted us to sing downtown, and we'd do that. They introduced us to a lot of cultural things. They would take us out to dinner. We went to a dinner theater—it was a two-person play, summer dinner theater, one night. They took you out around and introduced you to all kinds of things*. Her stepsister would sign her up for a work program in the spring, and when summer arrived Diana would take the train to Chicago, where she would assume her summer job.

These opportunities gave her a vocabulary, habits, and experiences that made her comfortable holding a job and working with other people. Later, in college, she used this confidence and know-how to find her own summer job in Chicago. *After my freshman year at junior college, I went and got this job on my own and I worked downtown. In the Hancock Building downtown, fourteenth floor. I worked for a federal bureau that investigated banks, and that was fun*.

Chicago's urban youth programs widened the horizons of this sharecropper's granddaughter, gave her new skills and prepared her for work in the mainstream. But she also benefited from a firm commitment to education on the part of her stepmother, and from the example she had set by returning to school for her GED and then going on to become a nurse. *My stepmother, whom I love dearly, had babies early, and she ended up in Chicago. When I first met her and started going to Chicago, she was going to night school to get her high school diploma. Then she finished her high school diploma and she went into a nursing assistant program, and then into the LPN program, and got her LPN. When she finished that, she went to her RN program. So my stepmother was an inspiration. But also she made a big to-do about* us *going to school. She stayed on us about going to school. She always pushed you to go to school. That's where I got my push.*

Diana first went to a local community college. *I went to Southwest Junior College and, you know, you just see things [when you go to college]. I met people and I talked to people. You found out that there was just so much more than what you were used to.* Then, although she was accepted at the University of Mississippi, she decided to attend a regional institution as a kind of private protest against the racism Ole Miss had shown when Medgar Evers tried to attend.

When Diana moved back to Dahlia after college in the early 1980s, there were few jobs for educated black women in the community. With her experience working for the bank investigating agency in Chicago, she went to a bank and asked for an application. No black had ever presumed to apply for a position at the bank, and in this small town the bank didn't have application forms. The receptionist assumed Diana, a black woman, was seeking a loan application. Even today, when each bank in Dahlia employs one black woman, getting the job depends on whom you know, much like in Blackwell. As Diana explained, *If you get any professional job here it's because you know someone. A job at the bank, it's because So-and-so told Mr. So-and-so or Mrs. So-and-so asked Mrs. So-and-so to hire you. After I explained I wanted a job application, not a loan application, she told me, "Well, we don't have any. Maybe you want to talk to Mr. Wood." Mr. Wood was the president there. I waited a long while. Then when I went in and talked to him, he told me they didn't have applications, but if I wanted to put my résumé on file, he would accept my résumé.* She raises an eyebrow as she looks at me. *So that was pretty much the end of that, you know. Since then, over the last few years, we have one black at each bank. I know the girl that got hired at Cotton Bank got hired because her daddy talked to his boss and asked his boss to ask So-and-so. That's how she got her job.*

Like Joanne and John Martin in Blackwell, Diana is disturbed by the poor men and women who are satisfied with what they have and show no ambition. *They just seem like they don't realize that there's something else out there. Their attitude is, "I'm kind of happy where I am. Everything around me seems just fine. I don't know that I'm missing out on anything." They're just happy as a flea lark,* she says—*satisfied with nothing.* Her strategy is to visit, to talk, to hear them out and give them a picture of more. *I spend a lot of my time just trying to talk with young men and young women. Not trying to push any ideas on them or anything, but just talking with them and trying to see what they have on their minds. When you hear something, or you can see that she's going to fall into the same trap that her other sisters did, you try to talk to them and gear them toward other things. You just try to make them see that it has to start right here. You have to get this education first. If you're going to get anywhere, you have to get everything that we can give you right here first.*

But economic dependency on the bossman and the closed political system present serious obstacles for those trying to convince young people of the value of an education. Diana believes that the success of these students, and of efforts like hers to widen their exposure through new programs, ultimately depend on larger political changes. *It's such a divided community. I mean, there are all the political factors. It was just really the last two elections that blacks have had any part of the government in this county. Before that you knew nothing about what was going on or how they let things go by—what opportunities you could have had, had somebody put forth a little effort. So those have been some of the barriers, or some of the things that probably held this community back for so long. But, you know, education is one of them too. For a long time, the farmers just did not want industry in this county because they felt like it would take away all their farmworkers. Which, I'm sure, it would have. And so, they just never encouraged education and never even wanted it.*

Today Diana and Charles have a comfortable brick home in the country on Charles's family land, near Clare Green's house. Her great-grandfather lived with them until he died at the age of ninety-nine. They have three children who are doing well, frequently appearing in small articles in the *Dahlia Weekly News* for academic or athletic accomplishments. When their children seek summer jobs, they will know Mr. So-and-so who can ask Mrs. So-and-so. Diana escaped a background of poverty, finished high school, then junior college, and college. She married a leader in the black community and is one of a handful of black women in these counties who have professional jobs in the public sector. The Smiths are at once part of the old establishment and part of the new professionals who make up a more progressive middle class. When whites need an integrated board for a federal project, they have traditionally looked for "someone who would be nice and quiet," and the black establishment would be tapped. Charles and Diana have come to present a more complicated choice. They have their own minds. More and more often they find common ground with the "radicals" who have criticized Clare Green and his family. And they have the backing of a growing cadre of civic-minded black professionals who are ready to turn up the pressure on black leaders and white power brokers.

DAHLIA'S EMERGING MIDDLE CLASS

Dahlia in the 1990s is still a world divided by race and class. A few whites are ready to move beyond the old habits and customs of segregation. A few blacks, through determination and often sacrifice on the part of their families, have escaped the poverty to which they were born. But, just as in Blackwell, cultural isolation and corrupt politics perpetuate poverty and hinder efforts to strengthen local institutions and create a community receptive to change and development.

A black single mother like Caroline Gage, or young black men like James Hill and John Cooper, live in separate social worlds from Edward and Sharon Carter, and the Carters know little about them and their daily struggles to bring in enough money to pay the bills. Whether in school, at work, in stores, or on the street, black men and women in Dahlia encounter disrespect every day in their contacts with nonpoor whites, reinforcing their isolation and disaffection. If Edward and Sharon's friends go out driving on Sunday morning, they will pass James and John and their friends drinking beer on the porches near Baker's store, and they will assume that these are lazy men and women who do not value work or family. If Sharon goes to a meeting where Harold Jackson or Michael Long argues for funds to improve housing in Tall Pines, she finds herself thinking, "Why did they let it run down in the first place?" Ed Carter is aware that there is a new group of black men taking initiative in Dahlia, and he applauds their actions. But he and his friends have no idea how hard these men struggle, not only with the troubled kids but also with the whites and blacks in authority in Dahlia, when they undertake this community work. They live in worlds apart.

Those who escape poverty have certain cultural and political resources in common. Diana was lucky to be left with a great-grandfather who was a good provider, and who had only three children to care for. She was lucky to have a father who assumed responsibility and kept in touch with her after her mother died. She was very lucky that her father married a woman who was herself determined to get an education, and pushed the children in her life to do the same. She also benefited from public programs and opportunities during her summers in Chicago—programs that exposed her to a new world, expanded her cultural repertoire, giving her skills, experiences, and habits that shaped later decisions she made about school, work, and family. Not only could she see a better life, she could imagine herself in it.

Opportunities to develop cultural resources may benefit a few individuals here and there, but these stories, like those in Blackwell, make it clear that political resources derived from economic independence are crucial too. Charles's father had been, and succeeded to some degree, in a white working world up north. He instilled values and confidence in his son—not only to work hard and finish school, but also to believe he was equal to any white man, to not fear whites or people with more money. Importantly, he could afford to teach this lesson because he owned ten acres of land and had a factory job in another county.

The longtime black establishment in Dahlia, the teachers, preachers, and funeral home directors like Clare Green, have political clout within narrowly circumscribed boundaries. They have cooperated with the white power structure and are scorned as "Toms" by the more radical social-change activists. Even Charles Smith has been criticized for apparent accommodation to the white elite. Politically the black community has been divided into these factions and whites have effectively used the dissension about political goals and strategies to maintain their own control. Steadily employed members of both the establishment and the radical leadership groups are often derided, "labeled as uppity-ups," as they say, by the poor, uneducated majority. Deep-seated distrust and long-standing dependence on white planters have made organizing for social change a formidable task, even in a black-majority county.

But in recent years, more and more educated blacks have chosen to undertake it, staying or returning to find jobs as social welfare workers, health care professionals, and school personnel. Like the return migrants to the coal fields in the 1980s, they have higher expectations of civic institutions and politicians. They are ambitious, conscientious members of the middle class, and their interests as professionals and as parents coincide with what their communities need to fight the isolation and dependency of the chronic poor. The majority come from families that had modest resources in a region where most black families had no resources at all. Their families scraped and saved to make it possible for them to get an education. They benefited from greater opportunities after the civil rights movement and the Economic Opportunity Act in the 1960s. As Carol Stack demonstrates in *Call to Home*, black women and men who have worked outside the rural South can become a potent political force for change. They return home with a different vision of what is possible, and with practical experience running programs they use in their professional and volunteer work.[13]

In the mid-1990s when I was visiting Dahlia, I saw members of the establishment, like Diana and Charles Smith, and those who call themselves "radicals," like Shirley Jones, Michael Long, and Harold Jackson, begin to work together instead of against one another. They were being pushed and pulled by members of this newly emerging middle class—schoolteachers and principals, coaches and counselors, nurses and even a black lawyer—men and women coming home again. Sarah Early, a nurse practitioner and health clinic director, and Robert Wilson, a middle school principal, are deliberately working with friends and colleagues to bring about changes in Dahlia. They want a community with good schools and safe neighborhoods where they can raise their own children and grandchildren. They want to build stronger institutions in the black community to battle the drugs, idleness, dependency, and violence they see destroying the young people in their neighborhoods and schools.

Sarah is a thirty-three-year-old nurse practitioner who is married and has two sons, aged nine and five. Both her maternal and paternal grandparents owned small farms in the northern part of the county, so she grew up in relative privilege here in Dahlia—a member of the black elite like the Greens and Michael Long. When she was two years old, she and her sister went to live with her aunt and uncle. Her uncle farmed the family land, and her aunt, who had been sent away to a boarding school in the 1950s, was a teacher. Her family was part of the solid middle class, well-educated property owners who put a high value on education for their children. They were strict but supportive.

We talk in Sarah's cool, dark office at the clinic, sitting across from each other at the desk crowded with patients' folders. The phone interrupts now and then as staff members seek advice about how to handle a difficult patient or a pestering supplier. At one point, Sarah excuses herself to go calm an older patient, anxious about new medicine. She is poised, confident, and matter-of-fact throughout the interview.

Sarah enjoyed school and was involved in activities and clubs. She did not have to work during high school, but after graduation she was able to get a job through a summer youth program. The family assumed she would follow her aunt's path and become a teacher, but she decided as a sophomore in high school that she wanted to work in medicine instead. She wanted to be a doctor. *We had physicians here, but at that time no black physicians, and I just wanted to do something different for my community. Back then, the hospital still had blacks on one side and whites on the other side. I always wanted there to be a change*. With help from her aunt and uncle, she went to a historically black college in the state capital—a step taken by only a few in her class. She completed a degree in nursing, planning all along to return home to practice her profession.

After graduation she married Henry, a computer specialist in the military, and they moved to Carterville, about an hour from Dahlia, where she found a good job as a staff nurse in a hospital. But she also commuted to Dahlia to work part time in the local hospital until it closed, partly to "pay back" her home community and partly to get the additional experience and income the work provided. After her second child was born, when she was twenty-nine, she began studying for a master's degree. Soon after she completed the degree, a private health provider contacted her about helping to set up a new clinic in Dahlia. She leaped at the opportunity, and she and Henry moved home to Dahlia. He found work at a casino, and she rolled up her sleeves to improve health care in Dahlia.

People in Dahlia often named Sarah as an effective community leader whom they admire. She, too, sees herself as a leader, both professionally and as a community volunteer, and she takes her role seriously. People come to her because they know her and trust her, she says, and that has meant early success for the clinic. But she finds it hard to reach the very poor. *Sometimes you have to carry your programs to the people in a place like this. They don't come to you*. She has formed a "health coalition" of workers in the Health Department and the Welfare Department who share ideas about what the community needs and coordinate their various programs. The group organizes the exchange of information for clients and patients and provides social support and collegial relationships for the providers.

She plans to start an after-hours health clinic to serve the poor in these Delta communities. *I thought about doing an evening clinic on my own with some of my physician friends in Carterville, to come to do two or three days a week, just in the evening time*. She feels confident that her idea will work and is now investigating funding sources. *Everybody knows me and they know that I've been doing this type of work for some time. They trust me because I'm from here, and that makes it easier to organize. I knew what the community needed and that is the reason I wanted to do it, not so much for just the money, but because there is a need*.

Although her professional work is in health care, she devotes volunteer time to education and teenagers, in part because she sees the problem of idle teens in the young pregnant girls who come to her clinic, in part because she wants to see more opportunities for her own teenage daughter. She adapts programs she has seen elsewhere to work in Dahlia. She recalls that when she was growing up, her only role models were in the schools. *We have black public officials now, on the county board, in the sheriff's office, but when I was growing up we did not have any. When I was growing up, your role models were inside the school system because becoming a teacher was about the only professional option at that time. Now you have a lot of blacks working in administrative positions, like the Welfare Department, the police. Things are changing.*

She is concerned that so many people look down on those who are not educated. She hears even her own friends make disparaging comments about people whose parents were "only farmers," and she believes this attitude discourages country people from coming to the clinic and staying in school, and from aspiring to more education and better jobs. Like Joanne Martin in Blackwell, she takes a respectful but demanding approach to patients and teens and emphasizes practical solutions. She is working with other parents to improve the schools and encourage the adults to be more involved. *We're going to start a PTA meeting, start a parents' and a mothers' club, and try to help our kids. But the parents got to be helped too. A lot of them are really young and they just don't understand. Sometimes they don't understand the homework themselves, so they can't help their kids with it. My cousin started a program in Chicago where they go out and teach the parents in the home, so they can help the kids with their work. Something like this has to happen here.*

Sarah pushes all the organizations she is involved in to do more outreach—her church, the school, her teen recreation projects, and, of course, her own clinic. *We sponsor a lot of community programs for the youth in our church. But generally we're just limited to our youth, the youth in our own church. We really need to start to reach out a lot more.* She serves as a board member for a youth recreation program that is trying to expand and build a facility. *It's a program that was started almost eight years ago by an assistant teacher who works in the school system and sees what goes on. During the summer, she takes a group of kids places and does things with them. Eventually the word spread about what she's trying to do, and other organizations are helping now. It's been chartered now as a nonprofit organization. But we're having a problem finding a place to really set it up. Land is so hard to get.*

Sarah and her friends have a sense of moral obligation to their community as members of the middle class relatively unfettered by the white elite, and they have a kind of self-interest in making this community a better place for their own children. She and her husband were taking their son back to

Carterville so he could participate in Scouts, but last year they started a local troop through their church. Sarah and her friends and co-workers volunteer substantial time to work with young people—overseeing Scout troops, starting a Pathfinders group, establishing and coaching out-of-school sports teams, and working to raise funds for the recreation center. But they are also getting active politically, encouraging those with whom they work and volunteer to turn out at the polls, and they are prodding elected officials like Charles Smith and Clare Green to be more responsive to the needs of the black community, middle class and poor.

Robert Wilson is part of this group. Now in his late thirties, Robert grew up in a family with six children on the Waterstone plantation, way out by the river, where his grandparents were sharecroppers and his mother was a housekeeper. Today, with ten other men in Dahlia, he is working to reach out to young people. They call themselves the Dahlia Men's Club, and they meet regularly. They coach ball teams outside school, have started Scout troops, and quite self-consciously work to be mentors and role models for young men in these poor communities where for decades black men have had little status and few options.

Robert and I talk at his dining-room table in his new brick home, interrupted now and then by his son's requests for help with a math problem. There are occasional phone calls from teenagers hoping he will come down and open the gym so they can play a little basketball on this cold Sunday morning in January. Robert is thin and tall with an athlete's build, although his hair is graying. Growing up in a poor sharecropper family out in the most remote part of the county, Robert and his siblings made do with little, taking hand-me-downs and fixing them up. *People would give Mama old bikes that might be missing a wheel or something may be broken, or a chain or something. We would fix those wheels or chains, and then we would have this bike from there. So, not only did we just make ends meet, but we saw things that we could fix and use. It would put us on a level, maybe, with some of the other kids. Now, when I look back, I just say, "Man, how could somebody survive those times?"*

Times were hard, and as a schoolchild Robert worked in the fields during the busy seasons. He was a bright child in an environment that often missed bright children. But he was also an extraordinary athlete, and he attributes his social mobility to his talent as a ballplayer. *I always tell my students that my right arm got me out of poverty. Just my ability. That will take you a long way, along with a pretty good attitude.* Robert was swept out of these hard times because when people saw him play ball they were impressed, and they wanted him on their team.

A key supporter was Shirley Jones's son, Arthur, who worked long days in Carterville driving a delivery truck but spent his time off working with youngsters in the area. Arthur Jones gave Robert rides from way out in the western part of the county, where he lived on the plantation with his mother and siblings, into town for practices and games. Arthur encouraged him and went out of his way for him. There were no publicly sponsored sports activities for black children at the time, just pickup games in sandlots. *We would get together on Saturday or Sunday. Well, it would have to be Saturday afternoon, because we worked Saturday morning. I worked in the fields on the levee, picking up hay, gathering and putting hay up for the winter for the cattle and all the livestock for the guy whose place we lived on.*

Going to the new central school for black students was a big step for Robert, just as it had been for Caroline. *Getting off the plantation way out in the country, going to the big school, it was something. Getting to meet and be involved with different people, people other than the ones that you had grown up with. It was just a new life for me. I kind of took it up on my own and tried to fit in with them. The people here, the coaches especially, saw that I was a pretty good athlete and they helped me along. And that eventually brought about a scholarship to college.*

During the first two summers he came home from school and worked long hours on the plantation, planting beans, chopping cotton. But after his sophomore year, a Carterville man interested in baseball found him a hotel job for the summers. After college he found that the privileges continued, as sponsors in a professional baseball league arranged a job for him in their city so he could play ball and try out for the team. *I worked there for a year, but then I was contacted by the principal here at home. He asked me if I wanted to come back here as a teacher. I hadn't taken the teacher's exam, so I took that and passed, and came back.*

As a coach and teacher back home, and more recently as middle school principal, Robert works hard to make the same opportunities that he had available to his students. Since the children are scattered all over this rural county, and parents work, he has to do much of the transporting to and from practices himself. *I just decided that I would drop them off, or we would get them home one way or the other*, he says. He works regularly with Michael Long, Charles Smith, and eight other men—the welfare director, the county farm agent, a black lawyer new in town, the parcel delivery truck driver—to sponsor and coach teams and to keep the pressure on local political leaders for help in getting a recreation center built. They have far more boys interested in the Scouts and ball teams than they can accommodate, but they do the best they can. They often buy baseball gloves and shoes out of their own pockets. But the children they work with are up against greater obstacles.

There are great temptations for young people to get into trouble, these men feel, to join the oppositional culture of the teenagers who "run wild," and there are few alternatives. *It's so tough for those kids. I tell my wife, I'm glad I grew up the time I did. It would be awful hard to grow up as a kid now. There is so much temptation out there now—drugs, sex, hanging out, loitering around with nothing to do. It's very tough. I don't blame the kids, because I think environment and circumstances have a lot to do with the way a person turns out.*

Although he acknowledges that there are some they just will never reach, Robert sees a number of young people he thinks of as "borderline." *Their environment is such that they get used to drinking, to using drugs. It becomes second nature. It's hard to change attitudes then, and it's real frustrating. I don't believe there are actually, at this age, bad kids. There are kids that have just seen so much and just got bad ways. I don't think the kids themselves are bad, but for some reason or another their environment is bad and they learn through association with bad things. They come to think that doing drugs is all right. A lot of adults influence their kids the wrong way.*

These men are also fighting a constant battle against those who either do not believe in their work or are outright opposed to it. Robert does not consider himself a radical, but he has well-formed ideas about how he and his colleagues need to work toward change, to make more opportunities available to young blacks in the area, and to overcome the old prejudices. He repeatedly runs up against obstacles, old habits of segregation and distrust, just like the others. For example, the junior high school where Robert used to teach and coach—the old white high school that became the junior high after integration was forced on the county in the late 1960s—is in the white neighborhood in Dahlia. *We had to be out of there by 5 P.M., out of that neighborhood. My principal at the time, a white man, wasn't in favor of being in the neighborhood later than 5. If a team arrived after 4 for a game, the principal met them on the walkway and told them to turn around.*

These days the Dahlia men plan programs to help young people and strategize about how to keep the pressure on the politicians and the white elites who control resources. *We meet every chance we get. Now we're getting ready to talk about how to get things set up for the coming summer. Basically it's the guys, the members of this little committee that we have, people who are really pitching in and trying to help. We're struggling, and at times it seems as though we're not getting anywhere. But we're not just going to stop and give up just because*—he grins—*maybe we'll get to the end of the rainbow one day*.

Robert is a savvy political leader. He realizes that making change happen is partly a matter of persuading the community that what they want can be had, and partly a matter of keeping the pressure on the officials they elect. *I'm not convinced by the argument that because Dahlia is one of the poorest counties in the nation you cannot expect much. I've always been this way: if you sit around and expect something to come to you for nothing, if you don't get out and work and push for it, you're going to continue to be poor. If you have an idea that you want to present to the authorities in the county, take that idea to them and let them make that decision as to whether they can afford it or can't*.

Robert does not give up easily. *I talked to some elected officials the other night. They were saying "we can only do so much." They said that we just can't go out in the community and say, "Hey, we have some money available for a community center." We said, "We know this. But we voted you guys in to keep us informed on things we could and couldn't get. Every time we come here you tell us what we can't get. Now tell us what we can get."* This kind of bold pressure, holding elected leaders accountable, is new in Dahlia. *I get kind of angry and I tell them so. They say, "You can't do this," and "You can't do that," but something has got to be done now, and they know it*.

The efforts of these activists are focused on the young people in their community, working with them to provide guidance and confidence, organizing to offer them sports or scouts or other activities that can keep them busy and away from drugs and sex. Nonetheless, Robert and the others are constantly battling those in authority, black and white, who see problems when they try to initiate new programs. Recently the Dahlia Men's Club has been promoting the idea of keeping the school gymnasium open when the school is closed to offer young people a place to play. Board members find objections: "*Are you going to pay the light bill?*" "*Are you going to be responsible for this, and responsible for that?*" But the demand is there. *Even now, all morning, the phone has been jumping. The kids want to go down to the school and play basketball, or Ping-Pong, or something. I have all of those things available for them to play. The only time they get to play them is Monday through Friday*. Robert is putting his own reputation behind this effort. *Saturdays and Sundays, I just go down on my own and take a chance—not really a chance, because if I'm confronted with this by one of my board members then I will give them a good explanation—but they resist giving us permission. I know that I'm maybe going against school or county policy, but all we're doing is playing basketball! We're letting some kids come in and let a little steam off. That kid, that same kid who is in that gym playing, could be going to break into your house. Then you'll be mad. That's my argument.*

He and the others in the Dahlia Men's Club have been outside this county and have seen what has been tried in other places. *As you get older, you see some things that could be done, things that should have been done, and you start questioning. "Why this?" or "Why that?"* Recently he met with the recreation director in a neighboring county and found out that they keep their gymnasium open all summer. *All summer round! All they have to do is keep it clean, housekeeping and stuff, look after it. I brought that back to the people in this county. I was able to get it, but I had to go to the board of education.*

Robert and his friends want the county to seek out grants to make new recreation programs and opportunities possible. They have little patience with old-time deference and fear among black leaders. *Some of them say, "I don't want to do this because I would jeopardize my job, or I would lose my dwelling where I live."* Like Diana Smith, Robert recognizes that information has been unavailable to black leaders in Dahlia for years—that even learning about federal programs that would benefit their own kids or neighborhoods is a recent phenomenon. *Ten years ago, people just didn't know about some of these things that they could get, that were available. A lot of people say, "County money is to build roads, clean up ditches, buy county equipment, all of these things." But there is other money there, too. You ask, "Who built this?" The county built this.*

Robert and others now have an image of what's possible. They have information and independence. They hold elected officials accountable. *The time is right for the persistence that we are putting on our county supervisors. We are constantly on them now. If they tell us, "Well, come back and check with me in two or three days," we check with them the next day to make sure he or she hasn't forgotten. We say, "Hey, have you gotten anything yet?" Then, when that two or three days are up, then we check back with them again. We're very persistent with them, getting on them about things. Even if they tell us yes, then we're going to ask them, "When can we get started?" If they tell us no, then we're going to ask them why. We just stay on all of the supervisors. That's what we call the key to changing the county.*

He recalls talking to Charles the other night about the fact that a building they had been promised was given instead to the white volunteer's literacy program. *We said, "Since you all gave that building away, we know that you all have something for us coming now. We just want the other one that you're going build for us." He said, "Well, if you all want a center, the money is here. The money is coming in and will be available. You come down and you put it on paper. Get your plan down and bring it to them." He works real well with us. Not only him, most of the other four or five members on there too. Next month we go talk to them about building this community center, or some kind of athletic complex. He and a couple more of their guys say, "Hey, we can't do nothing unless you people of the county ask for this."*

Robert and Sarah are members of a new middle class in Dahlia made up of black professionals in the social services and public sector who know their jobs, know their rights, and have higher expectations for their communities and their own roles in them. Like Joanne and John Martin in Blackwell, they have high expectations for the young people with whom they work, but they also devote hours to encouraging and making opportunities available.

Whereas their predecessors were often constrained in what they could do to initiate change because their livelihood and status ultimately depended on the white elite, these new middle-class men and women are not so vulnerable. In part, they have more protection against arbitrary retribution than they did in the past, thanks to changing laws and mores. But they also *believe* they have other options, and through education and wider experience they have a different view of how the world works than their predecessors. Whites still have the power to stop some efforts to bring about change. They control land and can prevent development of crucial black middle-class and low-income housing, as well as a youth recreation center or black-owned businesses. Michael Long was not rehired after challenging a powerful white at the polls. But the effects of the civil rights movement are gradually reaching even these isolated communities, and the sacrifices and investments of an earlier generation of working- and middle-class black guardians are bearing more fruit in the good works and jobs their children are carrying out as adults. Professional work in human services and the public sector offers some economic freedom in rigidly stratified and segregated rural Delta counties, and their knowledge of their rights, learned through education and experience outside Dahlia, enables these new activists to exercise them.

DAHLIA TWENTY YEARS LATER: NEW JOBS AND NEW POLITICS

With Gemma Beckley

These days when you drive down Highway 44 from the airport nearest to Dahlia you still travel through large expanses of cotton, soy, and rice fields, and now some corn. The big farmers, who have received more than $188 million in crop subsidies from the federal government since we were last here, flood their fields in the winter to attract duck hunters, and the low water shimmers on this gray winter morning. There are rumors that the powerful regional commission of business leaders wants to turn more of the Yazoo Delta into hunting preserves and retirement developments catering to upper-income whites—that they would like to see poor blacks leave for northern cities. Certainly there are more hunting areas. Uncultivated stretches of low shrubs and trees that attract wildlife for hunters are evident in a neighboring county, and local black state representatives have been surprised to hear that their white colleagues in the capital often come here for hunting weekends.

There have never been workers in the fields in February. Even tractor drivers are idle and rely on unemployment and other public assistance until planting season. But now locals tell us that in the heart of the growing season you no longer see the "cotton chopping" crews, water jugs in hand, going after weeds with their hoes. Farmers are using new machinery, and new herbicide-resistant crops mean they can control weeds more easily without field workers. Plantation owners were gradually tearing down the tenant shacks twenty years ago, to avoid responsibility for elderly field workers, and now there are no shacks to be seen. Low-skill, uneducated workers are redundant. Flat brown fields stretch out in all directions, just as they did in the 1990s, and the same spiderlike sprinklers now sit idle on the edges of fields for the winter.

But there is something new on the flat landscape. Highway 44 has been expanded to four lanes to accommodate visitors to the huge casino operations that emerge from the brown fields like a mirage in the western part of the county. Glitzy neon lights flash on billboards advertising coming performers and special deals for seniors, signs of urban life on otherwise barren agricultural fields covered with last season's dead stalks. Dahlia and its surrounding communities became one of the country's top gambling destinations, at one time third in the nation, providing employment for locals as well as those from nearby cities and towns and attracting gamblers from the three-state region and beyond. There are more jobs than there are adults in Dahlia. The number of employed men and women has doubled since 1990: 64 percent of men and 54 percent of women over sixteen are employed. Whereas Blackwell has lost 20 percent of its population over the past twenty years, Dahlia has grown more than 30 percent, and almost half of that growth has been people in their twenties through early forties. For more than fifteen years as much as $40 million per year in revenue has poured into Dahlia's roads and infrastructure and agencies, employing large numbers of public-sector workers. Taxes and water, sewer, and garbage fees were eliminated completely. Salaries for the five members of the county board of supervisors more than doubled to $50,000—plus benefits. Indeed, salaries in most county departments have doubled since 2000.

The casinos are legally required to "float" on the Mississippi River, as if they were boats, a requirement that poses hazards to their operations when flooding occurs along the river. The first operations were near the county seat, but later expansion occurred at the far northwestern end of the county, closer to the nearby metropolitan area. Like Dahlia's schoolteachers twenty years ago, some workers commute from Bates County, Dahlia's neighbor, more a suburb of the city, where they find better schools, better health care, and ample middle-class housing. Bates County, which rejected gambling when the state first legalized it, is not weighed down by decades of high poverty and underinvestment in education. A Dahlia leader explains: *The thing is, we didn't have a whole lot of housing, so a lot of people moved to Bates County. We got a lot of people in Dahlia, young people, who live up in Bates County. They have excellent schools in Bates County. So the ones who were able to break away, and kind of re-adapt, because everything was new, you know, did. Dahlia, we were kind of living still like in the horse-and-buggy days almost, when it came to things, in a way*. Some quote James Cobb's characterization of the Delta as the "most southern place on earth," saying Dahlia is the most southern place in the Delta.

Surprisingly, Dahlia's county seat has not seen significant local business expansion or other private-sector investment follow the casino development, although there are new street signs, a big carillon clock, and "Watch for squirrels" signs. Neither the white nor the black neighborhoods have changed much. The stores and other businesses on the highway look about the same. But everyone—black, white, poor, wealthy, churchgoing, and even the Catholic sisters—sees the casinos as a boon to Dahlia. A black leader marveled, *I just thank God for the industry coming in here. I'm not a gambler myself, but I thank God for it*. Poverty has been cut significantly. It's fallen from nearly 60 percent in 1990 to 26 percent in 2010, from almost five thousand people to around twenty-six hundred.[14] Where 80 percent of blacks were poor in 1990, 30 percent were in 2010. Still very high, but a big positive change.

The casinos and the drop in poverty are two of three significant changes that have occurred in the past twenty years. The third is the very recent dramatic turnover in local political control from the white minority to the black majority.

The white farmers who ran things when we were here twenty years ago are still powerful players in the local economy. The same families own the land—the Bakers, Winstons, Pendletons, Taylors, and Waterstones. Now it is mostly the next generation that oversees the farms. *It's even more so in the hands of just a few people. That was happening, but now some of the younger ones who maybe were sons that came into the business, they're consolidating, getting more and more, renting more land*. This control by a few white plantation owners over land and economic assets has remained the same. Whites' median income is still twice that of blacks. But the white farmers are no longer the only game in town, and economic diversification has, after fifteen years, had the political impact many African Americans hoped for when we were here twenty years ago.

In 2013 the big farmers who hold the land no longer control Dahlia's powerful board of supervisors. Twenty years ago Charles Smith was the only black supervisor, but now he is one of five. Back then Michael Long ran against one of the farmers, Bill Winston, and lost. Winston served on the board more than forty years. Recall that Michael's former employer said he could not return to his public-sector job because the agency would be starved for funds by the white-controlled board in retaliation for his audacity. White power ran deep, even in a place where African Americans always made up three fourths of the population. Just as in Blackwell, everyone said economic power meant political power, and they had many examples to illustrate their point.

In 2012 political change occurred in Dahlia. For a number of years two of the five supervisors were African American, and some would say those two were under the thumb of the white majority. But one year ago three more blacks were elected to govern Dahlia, including one of Clare Green's children. *When we told people we were working to get three African Americans on the board of supervisors, they laughed at us, told us we were crazy, and it would never happen. But not only have I been blessed to see three, we got five. Everybody in the county, with the exception of the county prosecutor and the attorney, are African American.* The county clerks, the sheriff, the county administrator, the school board, the school superintendent—and now, in 2013, the county attorney as well—are all black. Several are people whom we interviewed twenty years ago, longtime leaders in the black community who now have more official leadership roles.

The sheriff's department is large, with many black employees. A white business leader says the sheriff hires people he knows, or is related to, like others in the public sector do. *He's trying to give his community some skills and experience that if they want to go somewhere else, they have those skills. And he tends to promote people that have worked there for a long time, that have roots in the community. And those people are valuable to him, because they have that family relationship. This is a very relational place. Everybody is related either by marriage or by birth in some way. There's a lot of that kind of ties.* As in Blackwell, family connections matter for getting opportunities, but now blacks have more chances to share with family members and friends than they did twenty years ago.

There is a new jail and a large new recreation center, also employing African Americans in decent-paying public-sector jobs. These new public-sector workers represent a social change as well as a political change—they are the professional middle class we saw the beginnings of twenty years ago, some who left and came back, others who made the choice at a young age to stay. One white observed, *It started with the sheriff who at that time was in his early thirties, so he's forty now. He said, "I've been here all my life. I've stayed here all my life, and I want to see this place be successful." . . . We were coming off two sheriffs who had been convicted for bail bonds embezzlement and all sorts of horrible drug trafficking.* Sheriffs are elected in Dahlia, and have long been powerful local players in this southern state. There are some blacks in Dahlia who see the new sheriff's success as part of the old order, where whites put in place blacks whom they could control. Harold Jackson reiterated the point he made twenty years ago. *The main thing that the farmers and the whites in Dahlia want is control over the sheriff's department. And I think that's what they got. . . . If you check the records you'll see that nobody in Dahlia ever does a crime that's white. And nobody ever goes to jail that's white here in Dahlia.* It is true that the roster of inmates in the Dahlia jail includes only a handful who are not African American.

The leading white farmers, who facilitated the coming of the casinos in Dahlia while religious groups in other counties were able to block casino development, have made certain their families benefit from the new economic developments. They sold land to the casinos, developed related service businesses, and profited from public investments like the expansion of the airport. A white businessman described how an energetic young reporter at the local newspaper had, perhaps unwittingly, exposed some shady dealing by a powerful plantation owner who had arranged to reap profits from the operation of the publicly owned airport. *Actually it would have meant that we practically gave them [the plantation owner and his business associates] the airport. They would have everything, get all the revenue from the fuel and the storage, the hangar stuff, all of that. The paper sort of ran afoul of some of the people who were in the county administration . . . They didn't like it [the paper's story]. And Frank Pendleton is a very controlling person. He had, and probably still has, a lot of political power in the community.*

When the casino revenue first became available, whites were in control, and over the first fifteen years they invested in infrastructure like roads around the casinos but also out to the big farms, in a new arena named for Bill Winston, who has passed away, and in a museum showcasing Dahlia's history. From the black community's perspective, the revenue was doing little for the black population. A black leader told us, *If the intentions were to improve the quality of life for all of the citizens, when we first got this money, when you came back here, Old Town wouldn't be looking like that. But that wasn't the intention. They were trying to force as many African Americans to leave the county and turn it into a more of a retirement-type community. They had no intention of wanting us to stay here.*

Dahlia's white leaders focused the casino revenue on physical infrastructure, not human capital development. Doing so increased the value of their own property and that of their friends, and some say they believed the strategy would bring more economic development to the county, and perhaps more white in-migrants. To get the white political leadership to invest in the black public schools, African American activists had to protest, form a coalition, and hire a lawyer. *We had a big fight before they finally gave in. I mean, we marched, we demonstrated at the courthouse, we filled the board meetings up and made them dismiss some board meetings. We just stayed the point that we wanted money for education. I don't care what else you do with it, but you are going to give us some money for education. And so they had to give in, because it started pulling us together as a people.* Now 12 percent of the 3 percent of the casino revenue that comes to the county goes to the schools.

But even during the period when whites dominated decision-making on the county board of supervisors, the old system of white control and black disenfranchisement was beginning to unravel. The jobs at the casinos not only gave Dahlia's black workforce options beyond fieldwork for the white farmers. The economic diversity also meant that black voters, especially younger voters who have never known work on a plantation or lived in tenant housing on farms, could choose their leaders without fear of blackballing or expulsion by the once all-powerful white families. *Before the casino, they could put a person off their place, you know, if you were too radical or something, or [remove] your children [from plantation housing]. You might've had your mother, your grandparents, living in one of the houses on the plantation. They usually could go by and tell them, "You need to find you somewhere to go."*

In addition to economic diversity undermining white planters' control over black voters, the state's elected black officials, in both state and national offices, patiently and deliberately coached local political aspirants on strategy. Explicitly taking a page out of the Obama campaign's book, and taking advantage of the turnout his campaign generated in the black community, local black candidates registered new voters in a grassroots effort, and organized broadly. Churches were key. As one white observed, *The root of everything political in the black community is the churches, believe it or not. I kind of feel that's how this new group got their start*. A black elected official put it this way: *Dahlia is really a faith-based place, you know? And I am at every church at all times*.

Race and politics are understandably deeply intertwined. In 2013, redistricting proposals are clearly race-based, one drawn up to benefit whites and another to benefit blacks. Public debates readily acknowledge the racially based voting patterns. *Now with this redistricting, it's going to be so powerful that we're going to crack the districts up and we're going to have it where we'll be in a position to elect an African American in each of the five districts, you know, for the next ten years, 'til the next census come out. So it's going to be really historical*.

There are still two social worlds in Dahlia. But there are changes in them and between them. Whites still mostly live in the county seat and are the majority there, but some African American families have moved into white areas of town. *Two doors down from me, a black family lives. And then across the street another black family lives. And next to that, another black family lives. And we all live, for the most part, very happily together. We're out walking the dogs and gardening and things like that.* But population overall is down in the small county seat, and most blacks still live in Old Town and Tall Pines.

Retail establishments have struggled in the county seat in recent years, and many storefronts are empty. *There's been a lot of businesses come and go. . . . They're not able to hang on when the times get bad.* Some of the bigger farms have set up offices in buildings that might otherwise stand empty to try to anchor the downtown. Jack Peabody's auction business is still on Main Street, with its blue and yellow awning over the windows. Local white business owners often gather in his dimly lit office for morning coffee, where they gossip and occasionally scheme; indeed, that's where the idea for the new Dahlia museum was hatched. Ed Carter's furniture store business has contracted some, since the combination of Internet shopping and blacks having cash from non-agricultural employment means Dahlia's black families no longer need his high-interest loans to buy furniture and appliances. As whites have always done, many black families now travel to nearby shopping hubs to get what they need at better prices. A black interviewee said, *It's not like the old time, twenty years ago. It has changed from what it used to be, from when you really used to have to depend on your bossman saying certain things for you so you can get credit or whatever. All that has changed.*

The Catholic Sisters moved to a building next to Ed's store, and once a month, to the consternation of some, they organize a big free food distribution event right in the middle of town. Despite the new jobs and revenue, 35 percent of children are growing up poor, and more than a third receive SNAP benefits. Even many of the employed need assistance—Dahlia has one of the highest rates of earned-income tax credit receipt in the nation. The Sisters will have "pre-qualified" hundreds of still-poor households whose old vehicles snake around the grassy downtown median strip to pick up the bags of food that the Sisters and some volunteers from one of the casinos have put together. A white minister, noting that some wanted the food drive to move from downtown, considered it a good reminder for the white community that there is still great need in Dahlia.

People complain that there is little retail competition in Dahlia—one grocery store, one gas station, only a handful of restaurants—but out on Highway 44 there are now four Dollar Stores serving this still poor community. A few Middle Eastern families have come and started small businesses out on the highway. There is a popular new Mexican restaurant, owned and run by a couple from Mexico who live in town and send their children to Dahlia Day School. The Sunflower is still the place to meet for lunch or a weekend breakfast out, mostly for whites, but blacks do come in, and not only for meetings with whites. There are tables of both blacks and whites more regularly. *It's not out of the ordinary to see a couple of white guys and black guys all having lunch together. When I was in high school that didn't happen.* The restaurant has expanded to include a counter and a function room, but it is never crowded when we are there. The wait staff includes a young African American and a young Hispanic, but Dahlia's "good black cooks" still man the stoves in the kitchen. The white staff commutes in from a neighboring county because, like twenty years ago, there are few low-income whites living in Dahlia who would take waitressing work.

Along Highway 44 there are several big buildings that represent the public investment from the casino revenue—the huge arena named after Bill Winston, the new museum complex, and farther up the road the expansive aquatic and recreation center. Boards of directors govern the arena and museum, but the board of supervisors must approve the revenue that subsidizes their operations. The newly elected board of supervisors has recently moved some funds to the rec center, which mostly serves black children, that previously had gone to the white-led museum, a move that bothers some whites. *They cut the museum's budget in half and have given it to the recreation department's budget. They say that it's because Dahlia has an obesity problem. Well sure, that is true, but most of the people that have an obesity problem aren't gonna do anything about it. They're content with their obesity problem.*

The public schools in Dahlia are still almost entirely black. As in Blackwell, the district was taken over by the state in the early 1990s and even now is under "academic watch," once again in danger of being taken over by the state. The schools struggle to succeed with a student body in which 90 percent are eligible for free or reduced-price lunch, many, people say, from latchkey single-parent households. The number of female-headed households in Dahlia has more than doubled since 1990, and many of these single mothers must be working. Just as in Blackwell, there is a full-time security person at the high school, dispatched from the sheriff's office. Whites complain that the increased revenue made available from casinos has not made a dent in the low performance and high dropout rate, and bemoan the fact that the middle school must provide day care for young mothers attending school. They say teachers are well paid yet fewer than 50 percent of students finish at the public high school. Actually 53 percent graduated last year—a dismal outcome for Dahlia's black community and its youth.

Another black leader described how the county schools fail the community's children even when they do graduate. *They're up against it. The young people have, you know, not being able to read and write going through school, and getting to think they're honors students, and they graduate and go to college and find out they don't even know how to write a decent paragraph, and dropping out, and not being able to pass the test to go into the armed services. Our kids are hurting. Then they work at the casinos. First thing they're going to do, is do something they don't have any business doing, you know, with a felony. But we got to, we must, and this is the last thing I'm gonna . . . It has to come, it's no doubt in my mind, education is one of our ways out, but the other way is that God is going to have to send us a minister into this county, that our people can hear.*

In spite of the schools' poor record, even the white community appears to be giving the benefit of doubt to John Brown, the new, very young black school superintendent elected recently on a platform of change following the three-decade tenure of his ineffective predecessor. A lean, energetic, well-dressed young man, he observes, *It was clear that people wanted change. It was clear that they wanted a leader with a vision for this education system and for this community. And it was clear that they wanted something different.* A white leader active in education and literacy work reflected, *He's a real nice fellow. He came by here a lot, and he came as our speaker at our annual meeting. We had a nice crowd. I like him. I think, personally, he's maybe jumped people a little bit further than they're quite ready for. I've heard a lot of that. I just keep my mouth quiet about that. . . . But he's a breath of fresh air, I think, which everybody needed.*

During the race he stressed his intention to change things, including saying he would not be hiring people because they are friends or former classmates. He is a graduate of Dahlia's high school, and knows the community. A white business leader recounts how he said publicly: *"I'm going to find the best teachers, period. So if you're one of those, that's great. But if you're not, I'm not going to hire you just because we're friends."* He has introduced greater transparency in all aspects of the schools, pushed for higher standards, and rewarded the most effective teachers. He has let teachers go *who should have been gone long ago*. While he is adamant that poverty is no excuse for low performance, he also invests in programs to support those from struggling, socially isolated families. The school board, also black, resists some of his initiatives, arguing *that's not the way we do things*. Some say they want to reduce his salary so he will resign. Change is hard. But board members may also be hearing from longtime teachers whom the new superintendent no longer selected to teach summer school. He is hiring the teachers getting better results during the academic year.

On the other side of town, in Dahlia's other social world, Dahlia Day School's buildings seem a little worse for wear, but the small academy continues to serve most local white families. Parents say they are looking for smaller "college-prep" classes and a Christian environment. Sports are important at the school, and in recent years, like other white academies in the region, the school has recruited a few black athletes, girls as well as boys, who play basketball or football well. More and more white families are looking for alternatives to Dahlia Day School, however. Some carpool to private schools more than forty minutes away, while others buy or rent condos in the large city to the west, where mothers stay with children who attend private day schools during the week, coming home on weekends.

Indeed, there were innuendos about white flight. Whites saw the black community organizing for the last election and realized, as one white businessman put it, *change is coming*. Another observed: *Politically we've had a humongous change. All our supervisors are African American. We've lost a lot of white population. People have moved. We will not move, because my husband, his family's always been here. . . . We know everybody, and they know who we are*. Census figures show that the small county seat population declined by about 10 percent over the past decade, and it is down among both whites and blacks. *I'm seeing it already. People that we know, they're moving to Buford. A lot of people are moving to Buford. It's expensive living over in Buford, too, but it's the people that have the money that are moving over there. And then a lot of people have moved to the city*.

Some say the leading farm families are less engaged in Dahlia community affairs than they were twenty years ago. A white business leader said that *the Winston family has really gradually withdrawn themselves from the community. Some of them still live here, and they still own their businesses and farms and everything here. But for the most part, they're not part of the community. . . . Maybe, like me, they saw a change coming, and they've made a life somewhere else in another community*.

Many black leaders see continuity in the attitudes and behavior of the leading white farm families, generation after generation, just like Blackwell residents see the Parkers carrying on the practices of their father. *Most of them are dead. Mr. Pendleton is still living, Mr. Baker is still living . . . Bill Winston, he's gone. But see, his son took over in his position, and it was still the same, because of the way that they had taught their children how things should be. . . . So it didn't make any difference whether it was the father senior or the son. The way of doing business with African Americans in this county was still the same.*

There are some signs of change in the county seat. There is a new park honoring veterans, and some new housing on the edge of town, with both black and white residents. The big trees that line the streets in the mostly white neighborhoods give the town a comfortable ambience, just as they did twenty years ago, still shady lawns, white columns, even on smaller homes, screened wraparound porches. But even as this world looks much as it did twenty years ago, there are changes. Casino revenue built a large new jail on the southern outskirts of town to hold the increased number of casino-related offenders, often transients. The sheriff's office and county administration buildings downtown are large, all housing expanded public workforces. As in Blackwell, everywhere you turn you see a police car, parked or cruising, well-equipped vehicles with the latest technology that officers are allowed to take home. Nonetheless, with the empty storefronts and quiet streets, Dahlia's county seat feels sluggish, in decline, not vibrant, despite the Chamber of Commerce's claims to the contrary.

Old Town also looks just the same as it did in the 1990s. There is the mix of well-kept brick homes as well as dilapidated small shacklike houses, mostly wood, interspersed with empty lots and burned-out houses. Stray dogs roam the narrow pothole-filled streets, and lanky boys hang out on the corners with their sweatshirt hoods pulled over their heads on a cool winter's day. Several funeral homes line one small street, including the large Green funeral home, now one of three the Green family operates in the county. Outside a small flat-roofed bungalow, a middle-aged woman is having her hair straightened while an older gentleman rocks on the legs of his straight back chair as he visits with her. Down the other street three men hunch over the engine of a rusty old Ford truck, absentmindedly kicking at the stray puppy trying to get their shoelaces.

The Tall Pines neighborhood, with its small brick homes and scraggly lawns, seems a little less rundown than Old Town. But young men in hooded sweatshirts are hanging out on corners here too, and some older men are gathered near the store Michael Long started so many years ago. Dogs roam loose, and old cars are parked on lawns.

Caroline Gage, now fifty-four, like Gwen, lived in Tall Pines when we talked with her in the early 1990s. She was working hard to raise her children to not follow in her footsteps twenty years ago. Her children are grown, some here in Dahlia, others in the large city to the west. She is still deeply religious. Her cell phone message warns callers to prepare for Christ's coming. We had difficulty connecting with her. Maybe she works for a casino, in the kitchen, perhaps, or in a hotel as a housekeeper. One of her sons now lives in her house in Tall Pines, and we understand she stays with him on occasion. The house, like other homes on the block, has bars on the windows, curtains drawn. A large truck sits in the driveway under a carport. There is a new recreation center on the edge of the neighborhood, funded by the casino revenue and arranged for by Bill Winston, the white supervisor who long ago defeated Michael Long, but we don't see any children playing there on this weekend day.

On a Sunday morning we visit with John Turner, one of Michael's fellow youth organizers and coaches who still lives here in Tall Pines. John, a wiry, bright-eyed man in his fifties, was a successful high school athlete and went on to college downstate, but a bad injury ended his athletic career early and he came back home. Soon afterward, with the encouragement of his high school coach, he began organizing young boys to play baseball and girls to play softball, and this youth work has been his focus for nearly two decades. This weekend his sister is visiting from Atlanta, where she works as a health care professional. She is helping her aunt cook a big dinner for family members who will gather later in the afternoon. All of the houses we visit have a big Sunday dinner under way. Extended families visit in the kitchen or in front of the television, babies on hips, children playing on the floor.

Like Michael Long, John ran for the board of supervisors in the past, losing to Winston Junior by only twenty votes. He deplores the lack of development in the poor Dahlia neighborhoods, and attributes that missed opportunity to long-standing bad race relations. *I mean trillions of dollars have been thrown away, and nobody knows where it is. Now, we're struggling because the casinos are struggling. . . . We never could sit at the table with the white to make our community better. I lived in the upper Midwest for years, so I know what it's like to be with whites, that if you're capable of doing it, you can do it. There isn't a color barrier there. But this place, it isn't like that. We could have had one of the best high schools, the best hospitals, everything. But they just won't do it with us. . . . They just always think that if they couldn't control it, they didn't want it.*

A white businessman says there still are two groups of black leaders in Dahlia, *the young, "Let's change everything," completely radical group and then the ones who want to see Dahlia quietly succeed.* He says the radicals are those who were active in the civil rights movement. *The ones that want to see the community succeed are the ones who have their own business. They know you can't spend more than you make, whereas the other group, "We want it all, but we don't realize the price to get it all could lead us to bankruptcy."*

It doesn't really break down that way, however. Although he is now a grandfather, John would be considered one of the radicals, as would Michael Long, also a grandfather. Former principal Robert Wilson, supervisor Charles Smith, and the younger generation of the Green family might still be considered among the more reasonable, the more cautious. Indeed, the lines appear to be more blurred these days, even though disagreements about policy or strategy between the groups may air in public at meetings. Factionalism among blacks is no longer the norm.

Many see changes in black leadership emanating from the impact of the continuing flow of black return migrants, retirees as well as younger professionals now able to make a living in their hometown. *We have seen a lot of our citizens that have gone away, and after they have retired, now, they are coming back home. Very politically active, because they remember how it was in the past, and it's still eating, eating up inside of them. So they're coming home and saying, "I'm going to speak up and speak loud, to make a change in my hometown."* We sense that there is more collaboration among black leaders, more deliberate mentoring of younger leaders, and a broad sense of responsibility now that the African American community has control of the county and the casino revenue it receives.

Michael Long, recently appointed director of public works, comes to his office on a rainy weekend day to talk with us about the changes Dahlia has seen over the past twenty years. He has gray hair now, and a trim gray beard, and still moves with ease despite the injury to his arm long ago. Michael is sitting in this office overseeing all of Dahlia's public works because the new board of supervisors selected him, much to the astonishment of some in the white and the black establishment, in acknowledgment and appreciation of the years of organizing and support he has dedicated to the poor youth and families in Dahlia. *Michael has always been one of the ones encouraging us, making sure we do not forget about the struggles that black folks have had. He's always pounding it and pounding it. Every program, every church program, because that was the strength of our community.*

A year into the job he has earned the provisional confidence of both whites and blacks.

He is determined to invest in the neglected black neighborhoods. *When I got this job we started cleaning. . . . We built parks in the subdivision over there that had been torn down, and we cleaned out the ditches. We now have some board of supervisor orders where we can go out and clean off lots, like in Tall Pines, where houses are old and desolate. We are going to clean them up . . . and then this is going to help improve [these neighborhoods]. You see, we got this old elevator been sitting there for years. They finally got it torn down. All these things will help up our area. And then, we are going to have to look at redeveloping Old Town. The streets are too small, too narrow, using a sewer and water system that's aged and needs to be replaced.*

Michael, like many others we talk with on this return visit, recounts his stories of the coming of the casinos to what was once the poorest county in the United States—to a place where large, powerful landowners controlled most aspects of the majority black workers' lives. Everyone sees value in the casinos, black and white, young and old: this remarkable phenomenon of new opportunities for work available equally to whites and blacks, in a place where African Americans had been isolated and excluded from education and living-wage work for generations. Yet it was difficult for many to seize those opportunities. *See, there was no way that our people in Dahlia could be fully successful. They could gain employment, but maintaining and keeping employment? You have people who had only worked in the catfish industry, or at the compress doing seasonal work, or at a gin doing seasonal work, and in agriculture—that's just flat-out farm labor. How is it possible for those people to get into the casino industry and maintain their job without any training? They hired a tremendous amount of people from Dahlia when they first got here.*

Many of these new workers had been living in multigenerational households surviving on eight thousand dollars a year in public assistance. Now, Michael points out, if two daughters got minimum-wage housekeeping work, the household has seen its income jump more than fourfold, to thirty-six thousand dollars. *What kind of impact did that bring? It brought about a lot of jealousy within the families . . . helped destroy the love we had in our households, because Mama might feel that the daughter wasn't paying her enough to keep her children while she worked the eleven-to-seven shift.* There were transportation problems, child care problems, relying on family or friends who might be jealous and settle small disagreements by not showing up to drive or to care for the children. And the worker would lose the job. *No show, no job, automatic termination*. Others point out that work for poorly educated blacks was historically on a day-laborer basis—you showed up and you could get work for the day, and if you failed to show up one day there were no consequences, so holding a job was new to many.

Workers did not know how to be clean, Michael explains, and he and his colleagues would have to speak to them, coach them about holding a service-sector job. *You got to talk to Ann, tell Ann she must take a bath. She got to brush her teeth. She can't come here with mud on her, her uniform must be clean. . . . Look, you cannot dip snuff and keep this job. You can't do it. . . . Same thing with the men. They didn't know. We assumed that they did, but they didn't know. You didn't want to embarrass them, but we had to address it*.

Not long after the casinos opened, they started instituting drug testing for employees. *The very first random drug test that was done at Good Fortune wiped out almost the entire department for cleaning. Hundreds were terminated*. Michael, like John and many others we spoke with, saw a lost opportunity to train and support workers who had so little understanding of working with the public in a large organization, who lacked so many basic supports like cars or cell phones necessary for getting to work and communicating with an employer. Nonetheless there are many longtime residents who had the education and life skills to find and keep a job at the casinos, and the training the casinos offered them was adequate. It is hard to say how many have then moved to Bates County, where there are more housing options, more stores and health care, and most important, good public schools.

Harold Jackson, like several others we spoke with, described how he sees those terminated for stealing from casinos get along without jobs. *I'm pro casino. I'm glad they came to Dahlia. I'm glad they offered jobs. I'm glad they paid decent salaries. But the black community, the black people, just weren't used to being around all of that money. They weren't ready, and they start picking up what they should have been leaving alone. And quite a few of them lost their jobs. They're still here in Dahlia scratching*. . . . I ask what that means, to be "scratching." *It's extremely hard. Barely making it. You're doing pretty much anything you can, you're coming to neighbors saying, "hey, can you give me help," you are asking the Sisters, "can you pay a bill for me?" You're doing different things, like, that's scratching. . . . Men and women are doing it. You got women that are scratching and hustling. And you got men that are sitting back, and the women are scratching and hustling for them*. Scrabbling in Blackwell, scratching in Dahlia.

When we were here twenty years ago, blacks and whites alike worried about Dahlia's young people, the borderline kids, as Robert Wilson called them, because he thought they could be mentored and grow up to have a good life despite the challenges they faced at home and in their poor neighborhoods. Like Michael and John, Robert and his Dahlia Men's Club were trying to get young people involved in productive activities, away from drugs and crime and gangs. They spent a lot of time building and coaching teams, *teaching them not to fight with one another*. James Hill, the young man who wanted to be a mechanic, now works for the water department and has a family. John Cooper fell into alcoholism. Both Michael Long and John Turner recall young men and women who have come to thank them for their mentoring, who are in good jobs and attribute their success to the attention these community leaders paid them when they were children. Both men get a little choked up talking about the words of appreciation they have received.

The recreation and aquatic center represents a significant answer to these longtime organizers' dreams—a large complex with basketball courts, fields, a swimming pool, and diverse youth-oriented programs like Boys and Girls Club, Dahlia Teens in Action, and many others. Some hoped it would be a place where white and black children could come together, but few whites use the facility. A black leader at the center confided, *The white swim coach shared with me that he just can't believe the prejudice, that he went over to the white school and tried to recruit, and they said, "No, our kids won't swim with blacks."*

When we are at the recreation center one afternoon to talk with the Boys and Girls Club director, buses of children are dropped off fresh from school, all African American, all dressed in recently instituted school uniforms. Each day these children attend the after-school program, where they must finish their homework before they can play basketball or chat with their friends. The coordinator complains that they have to wait around for parents to come pick up their children after the recreation program is over. Robert Wilson's son, who was doing math homework with his father at the dining-room table when Robert and I talked twenty years ago, now coaches here as a volunteer. While he loves coaching and the young people, he is hoping for a position at the one new manufacturer in Dahlia, a foreign-owned factory that leases a county-owned facility (and therefore pays no local taxes) and promises growing numbers of jobs. This factory comes up in every interview because it represents the hope for diversification that many assumed the casinos would spawn. Some say they will hire people from Dahlia, blacks included. Others claim they do not, will not.

In some ways the recreation center is like the jobs at the casinos—great for those who can take advantage of the opportunity, new workers with the right cultural tool kit, young people whose parents or grandmother or aunt attend the small churches where word about the center's programs are shared, who will find the small fees and get transportation arranged. But most recognize that just as there were those who could not keep work without substantial training and support, who are illiterate and have never held a steady year-round job, there are children in fragile, chaotic families who are not reached, whose mother does not belong to a church, who need transportation and scholarships, and who need the staff to come out and get them. *If a mother is working, and she got four kids, she can't participate. You got to transport those kids, keep 'em outta trouble. For children, you have to really go and get them.*

During the winter of 2013, the casinos faced a serious downturn after a couple years of declining business. They laid people off, and revenue over the previous three years for Dahlia was down 30 percent. Dahlia's board of supervisors raised county taxes 30 percent in the fall of 2012 to meet a deficit of nearly $3 million in the almost $50 million budget. Dahlia has a large payroll that must be met. In 2013 revenue from gaming taxes was down to just under $30 million, from $43 million in 2006. When the budget deficit mounted to $5 million for 2014 the newly appointed county administrator, African American like his predecessor, made plans to cut budgets across all departments and asked the local paper to publish his statement to the supervisors. It began, "The excessive expenditure mentality that has been pervasive in Dahlia since the inception of gaming must come to an end." Since the state also relies on casino revenue, the governor has set up a commission to look into the downturn and make recommendations for revitalizing the casinos. Many people, black and white, observed that there is both more competition from casinos popping up in neighboring states and the problem that Dahlia's casinos have not been upgraded in recent years and do not have amenities that appeal to families.

Unemployment in Dahlia was 20 percent in February 2013, and of course, as in Blackwell, those counted as unemployed are those who are still looking for work, are likely collecting unemployment, and have been in the workforce in recent years. It does not count those who never found or could not keep a casino job, or those on disability or scratching along on SNAP and other small public assistance benefits. Both Blackwell and Dahlia have had the highest unemployment levels in their respective states in recent years.

In spite of the casino jobs and revenue, black adolescents and children still face formidable challenges in Dahlia. More than a fourth of young people are idle, not working or in school. Very young parents are raising children. Just as twenty years ago both black and white leaders worried about Dahlia's youth, today everyone is concerned that there are too many latchkey children getting into trouble. Worst of all is dropping out of high school, when a degree is essential for any kind of work these days. Lack of education and unstable families still dampen future opportunities for Dahlia's children. As one black coach put it, a poor family he was trying to work with was *not "educational," not "a together family."*

A white businesswoman described the way she sees the challenges in a summer program she supports. *It's an uphill battle because most of the kids that we're working with are second- and third- or fourth-generation welfare. Their parents have never worked. Their grandparents never worked. Even their great-grandparents never worked. So how do you break that, that mindset? The graduation rate in our high school is less than 50 percent. I think 41, 42 percent, and the largest single factor that keeps these kids from graduating is teen pregnancy. They have a child-care day care set up in the middle school.* Of course the parents and grandparents she describes worked, but they worked in the fields, part-year, dependent on white farmers, and they attended ineffective schools, most often only as far as eighth grade, and missed school when the white farmer's crops needed attention.

Like Johnny Bledsoe, many black leaders talked about the need to change the "mindset," but in this case they mean both the mindset of being satisfied, even apathetic, personally as well as for the community, and also the mindset of being vulnerable, even inferior, to whites in Dahlia. A black professional described her father's perspective. *A way of thinking, it's that Delta mentality, you know. Like my father, my father was, I guess you call him a sharecropper. He did the fields and everything, and he was kept in debt, and his mindset had gotten to the point, "This is all that I can do." He didn't have a high school diploma. He didn't have anyone around to say, "You can do something different. You can move your family. It's going to be a struggle, but you can work somewhere else." And my mother, in turn, caught the slack, because she worked two and three jobs, but my father, it was just that mindset of "This is all I can do."*

The school superintendent talks about his challenges in turning the school around in terms of changing the mindset. *I realize that there are some things that have historically been done in a way that's comfortable, but it's not best for children. And my greatest challenge is shifting that mindset of everyone to truly do things that are best for children even though it may hurt some adults. . . . We're talking about mindsets about policy. We're talking about mindsets about accountability, that's what we're talking about. We're talking about those types of mindsets.* He recognizes and names the politics of education in small communities. *In small towns you have people that have built relationships. My task is to make sure that the best decisions are made for kids, regardless of relationships, regardless of politics, regardless of all the hoopla. It all boils down to how well is this preparing children.*

An elected leader talked about the political dimension of the "mindset," describing the efforts to get the black community out to vote, and to vote their conscience. *But that's what we had to do, because they think they are inferior, you know? It's just so depressed in these black neighborhoods, not having jobs so long and having to depend on welfare and food stamps and not being able to be sufficient on your own. And also taking the black men and giving them felonies, locking them up, without having a system where they can have a diversion on their record so they can be productive. Our men have taken a backseat, so we have got to empower our men at home. That's a big problem. So I would say the influence of the white community on our people, we're trying to change that mindset. That will be the only thing that holds us back from growth, [being] scared of change.*

In the mid-1990s we concluded that the new professional and skilled African American return migrants might be instrumental in bringing real change to Dahlia, working with other black leaders in business and professional services. We thought that a black middle class that would invest in community-wide institutions might be emerging, a group that could begin to provide opportunities for Dahlia's poor children and families. Several black professionals described their plans back then to reach out to poor black children and provide better opportunities. But there were limited professional opportunities in Dahlia then. *Back then most of the supervisors were farmers. Millionaire farmers. African Americans just lay dormant. We had the worst of the worst. . . . They had family friends, the whites in all these positions. So, we didn't have a chance to hire anyone to get the jobs, so we had to go outside of Dahlia to get jobs. We were locked out of everything, and also deprived educationally. On an education level we were deprived.* When white farmers ran community affairs most black workers were excluded from all but menial jobs. Schools failed black children, whether led by Jack Peabody or his incompetent black successor who reigned for decades, leaders who were apparently satisfied with a very bad status quo.

But politics and control have changed in Dahlia. Longtime organizers and business leaders in the black community have combined with new leadership to take the reins in Dahlia, and they are determined to extend opportunities to blacks and to improve the schools. The new board of supervisors reaches out to the community. A white observer praised the approach of the new board. *Yes, it's gone from, "We are the leaders, and we will make all of the decisions. And if you want to talk to me about it, then I may or may not hear what you have to say," to "We try to involve the community." The supervisors have moved their board meetings . . . to try to give working people the ability to come. They're reaching out and trying to make that effort to try to engage the community a little more*. The supervisors themselves describe how they engage people they meet in the supermarket or on the street, how they hold public meetings.

The board recently set up a community affairs office, led by a young African American woman. She and Michael Long are two of a long list of new black appointees to public-sector jobs. They are planning to set up a human resources department so the hundreds of public employees can be managed efficiently and fairly. Some black leaders worry that the changeover in appointees will undermine the new board's ability to move forward. Their concern is that it will look like retaliation, that whites will think the board is only interested in changing the color of Dahlia's management, and they will therefore not join in building for the future. But even so these leaders who are concerned about the appearances say they are prepared to work with their black colleagues to broaden opportunity in Dahlia.

The long-term grassroots organizing and mentoring that Michael Long, John Turner, and their colleagues engaged in over the past thirty years, combined with the deliberate nurturing of young black politicians by statewide black leaders and the economic freedom black workers now enjoy, have been key to bringing about change in Dahlia.

The political dimension of poverty and development is starkly visible in Dahlia, where once whites held all the economic and political power in a black-majority county and used that power to keep opportunity from African Americans. Those young blacks who were pushed to finish school had to leave to find further education or good jobs, removing the threat they might have posed to the status quo. As one black leader noted, whites did not anticipate return migration. Nor, of course, did they foresee the powerful political change that would come with the new job opportunities at the casinos. Perhaps they thought more whites would move in and shift the balance; perhaps they thought they could control the politics nonetheless. In fact, some journalists with national papers and magazines reporting on the casinos' impact in the mid-1990s and early 2000s speculated about whether the new employment would bring white in-migration and change the racial balance in favor of whites, further disenfranchising the black community. But even with population growth, today the racial balance is about the same as it was in the 1990s.

This is a time of transformation in Dahlia, and both blacks and whites are assessing the process and the potential outcomes. The new African American leaders seem to be focused on building opportunity for the black population as a whole in Dahlia, not just blacks with good family names and stable homes, not only *the name-brand families*. The young superintendent, with his commitment to change in the schools and to preparing his students, is working to gain the confidence of the new black leadership and many whites. Some worry he is moving too fast, or moving with too little consultation, but he does seem focused on those struggling students. *We've been successful in kind of rallying all our productive and most effective teachers and meeting our issue head-on, taking the best we have and using it to improve the ones we have who struggle the most.* Given the historical performance of the schools and the depth of poverty even now, the challenges are enormous. But as Michael Long and other African American leaders in Dahlia often state, the schools are ground zero in addressing poverty.

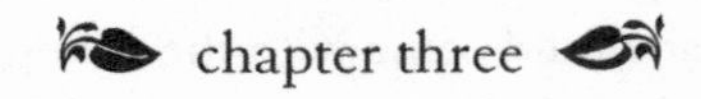

GRAY MOUNTAIN

Equality and Civic Involvement in Northern New England

A new professional middle class is emerging in Dahlia, its leaders pushing for community changes that will benefit their own families and the large number of poor families that have been struggling in isolation. They are a tiny minority, and their efforts seem fragile in the face of decades of oppression and control. They work one-on-one with young people, prodding and encouraging them, much as Joanne Martin and her husband do in Blackwell. But they also are working to transform and build collaboration among local black organizations and established institutions to expand outreach. They push their elected officials to be more responsive and more aggressive in creating opportunities, trying to make Dahlia a community that will better reach the have-nots.

In Gray Mountain, a mill town in northern New England, blue-collar mill workers, civic leaders, and business owners have worked together and invested in community-wide institutions for many decades. Unlike Blackwell and Dahlia, Gray Mountain has had the benefit of substantial income equality and, until the late 1980s, decent, stable work opportunities. Nonetheless, I went to Gray Mountain in the 1990s expecting to find a remote rural community similar to Blackwell in many ways. The two areas have about the same population, are both isolated by mountainous terrain, and their economies have depended on industry, with a unionized workforce. I knew Gray Mountain had long had lower poverty rates and greater work opportunities, but the way people talked about the limited aspirations accompanying a mill-town mentality implied a kind of country backwardness that sounded like how people "from away" summarize the coal fields. I was surprised to find fundamental, important differences in social structure and civic culture.

Beginning in the late 1800s in northern New England there was steady work in the woods and the pulp and paper mills, and later in other manufacturing enterprises and recreation-related jobs. A large shoe factory closed in the early 1980s, leaving more than a thousand people out of work. But other small stitchery and electronics firms had opened in the 1970s. Unlike coal operators in Blackwell and plantation bossmen in Dahlia, the mill owners in Gray Mountain did not oppose new employers coming in. In fact, even in the 1960s and 1970s there was an industrial development committee of citizens who worked to attract new businesses. While particular companies have come and gone, Gray Mountain has had a diverse group of small manufacturers providing employment in addition to the mill over the years. One consequence is that there has always been more work for women here than in Blackwell, although it was not until the 1940s that women were allowed to work in the mills. In 1990, more than half of Gray Mountain's working-age women were employed, adding to family income and stability.

Since the early 1900s, working-class men and women in this New England mill town have participated in a multitude of ethnic-based support organizations, and in addition, since the 1940s, in a vigorous—and apparently honest—union formed in the paper mills. They have lived on the hillsides in town and on the river and been involved in the decision making in civic organizations, unlike the Dahlia sharecroppers and Blackwell miners who lived out in the country, completely dependent on their plantation and coal bosses and vulnerable to their arbitrary power. As we will see, early paper-mill owners invested generously in educational and cultural activities for the community, including a kindergarten for workers' children. For decades summer people and others from away have brought new ideas and resources, both human and financial, to Gray Mountain and the surrounding area.

Together these factors have made Gray Mountain rich in what sociologists call social capital—widespread trust, inclusive participation, and longstanding investment in community organizations. When social and economic problems have emerged over the years—and they have—people have come together to debate and to argue, but also to forge a responsive program or project. Among the tangible results have been a family planning initiative that brought the rate of teen pregnancy down significantly in the early 1970s, a public playground and a hockey arena built completely with community labor and local business donations, youth and recreation programs like hockey and skiing leagues that deliberately make room for those from families "at the end of the road" who are having a hard time, a citizens' task force whose job it is to sell prospective mill buyers on the assets of the town, and numerous programs to help poor young adults, mostly women, find training and work. These patterns of inclusive, participatory governance and community investment are in stark contrast to Blackwell and Dahlia.

A BLUE-COLLAR MIDDLE-CLASS MILL TOWN

Once again we are on a two-lane road, this time surrounded by mountains on both sides, following a rocky, rushing river, as we make our way through the state park west of Gray Mountain. Birches and hemlocks line the riverbank, and fall colors are just beginning to show on the oaks, maples, and beeches up on the hillsides. No homes are visible from the road, just the occasional dirt road leading off into the woods. There is a chill in the September air, and hikers piling out of a late-model Volvo station wagon parked at the entrance to a trail are pulling on hats and gloves before donning their daypacks over fleece jackets. Over the next month and a half, the fall foliage will bring hikers and motorists from all over the Northeast, and the roads as well as these small parking areas at the bases of maintained trails will be crowded with out-of-state license plates. Months ago, the mountain club's lodges sold all their accommodations for late September and October, including even the more remote huts on difficult trails.

At the crest of the notch we can see Round Valley stretch below us, mountains on either side, and in the distance the sky big and deep blue. A large ski resort sits atop a gradual slope to the east, its lifts open for mountain bikers and early "leaf peekers." Like the other larger hotels and resorts in the region, facilities in Round Valley are open year round and include some time-share and single-owner condominiums whose owners live in Boston, Portland, and even New York City. These destination resorts have been an important part of the local economy since the late 1800s. The first large hotels were built to draw members of the growing urban middle class from Boston and Portland to the north woods, lakes, and mountains for long stays of several weeks in the summer. Today visitors make weekend trips for hiking and fishing in the summer, the stunning foliage in the fall, and skiing in winter, and, of course, they arrive by car rather than train. The old hotels, in combination with the well-kept trails and lodges of the century-old mountain club, suggest a comfortable world of moneyed outdoor enthusiasts and vacationers accustomed to leisure in a grand style—perhaps a world apart in its own way.

This image of grandeur is quickly dispelled as we wind through the last pass to the town itself and encounter the powerful rotten-egg smell emitted from the paper mill right in the center of town. The Abenaki River on which the mill has always depended for power and transporting logs starts up near the Canadian border and meanders through New Hampshire and Maine before emptying into the Atlantic Ocean. In Delta and Appalachian communities the county seat is the province of the elite, in many ways an oasis removed from the poverty and chaos experienced by those living out in the country. Here mill workers set the tone and are the backbone of the place. *This is a very working-class town. You have the mill-town background. It is very sports oriented, even for older people, not just kids. The men are still over there at the hockey rink playing in over-thirty leagues. And the work ethic is very much alive here in Gray Mountain.*

Most people describe a tiny upper class, a tiny lower class, and a huge middle class. Census statistics on family income confirm their perceptions. Since the 1930s, the middle-income group has included more than 70 percent of the population, in contrast to the extreme income inequality of haves and have-nots in Dahlia and Blackwell over the same period. Poverty rates have always been much lower than in the Delta or Appalachia, averaging 18 percent over the past forty years, compared with 43 percent in Blackwell and 62 percent in Dahlia.

Income differences that do exist appear to have little effect on everyday lifestyles. *People are either General Paper, the union people, who make a decent wage, or they're working-class people who make a rotten wage. That's the only real class distinction. But they're in the same families, and they do the same things. If you make good money working in the mill, you still buy recreational vehicles and snowmobiles, you just buy more of them. You have a camp, but you have a nicer camp. People who make a middle-class salary in the mill are still working-class people.*

Both the poor and the nonpoor in Gray Mountain say people are not treated differently according to their income or the work they do. Those with good steady jobs see the poor as people who are having a hard time—*as the bottom of a continuum rather than another continuum*, a social service agency director explains. *It's shades of difference between groups rather than an absolute difference. There is no sense of isolation, or of a separate culture. There's really no sense of class. There's a kind of a bond, a membership of the valley and the region, that is more important than other kinds of distinctions*. Parents and teachers, mill workers and welfare recipients all agree that the kids from Northern Avenue, the poorer section of town, generally have the same opportunities, friends, and contacts as everyone else. A woman receiving AFDC who grew up in a poor family explained, *We're not called "welfare people," you know what I mean? We didn't have a lot, but some of my friends' parents were quite well off. It doesn't really matter about your social standing*.

While social segregation is the rule in the Delta and Appalachia, here people from diverse backgrounds interact freely. *The guys I play golf or broom hockey with might make half what I do or they might make twice what I do*, says Jeff Berk, a local schoolteacher. Surgeons eat lunch with maintenance men and plan the fishing they will do together on the weekend, a hospital administrator observes appreciatively. *The lunch tables in the cafeteria are always a mix of different-colored coats, not like other places I have worked*. A lawyer's wife similarly observes, *One of the things my husband loves about this place is that he can go out to the public golf course and pick up a game with anyone, from a logging trucker to another lawyer*.

In Appalachia and the Delta, when asked "Who runs things around here?" residents would name particular powerful families. In Gray Mountain the question strikes people as an odd one, but in response they name elected and appointed officials—the mayor and town administrator—or apologize if they have forgotten their names. People know the leading local businessmen but do not see them exerting power over economic or political affairs. *There are a few people that are outstanding, that are always doing volunteer work and leading things and doing things. Peter Luntz is one big man, with a big business. Sean McCay, he is involved in a lot of things. But it's not like these people think they are a lot better than the others. There's no separation. It's not like some people are higher than the rest of us. Our kids play baseball together, they're probably in scouting together and stuff, so they talk and get along*.

Mill workers and carpenters are as likely as mill managers or teachers to describe volunteering on the hockey arena or for the United Way. And school officials are held accountable by parents. A mill worker, for example, described his own and his wife's involvement in local affairs. *Well, I served on the board of the United Way for three years. I'm also involved with the arena in town, the ice rink. I'm on the board of directors of that organization, along with being on the board of directors for the youth hockey organization. And my wife spends a lot of time volunteering at our sons' school for cafeteria work, to help the school along. Our children are involved with dancing, bowling, playing some middle school sports also. So we get involved in all that. Right now we are involved with the controversy with the local schools. Our parent groups are trying to ensure that sports stays in the school, that the education system doesn't get tampered with and run down to where the quality of education is not any good.*

These habits of participating in community organizations and investing time on boards were established early in the growth of this mill town. Economic development here in the north woods did not require absolute control over workers; mill owners needed skilled workers and invested in their employees, and blue-collar workers from numerous ethnic groups sustained diverse community organizations.

Northern New England's Abenaki Valley was settled in the early 1800s by small-scale family farmers, some coming north from Massachusetts and Connecticut, others coming south from Quebec and New Brunswick. One narrative, noting the lack of gentry, capitalists, and white-collar classes, describes pioneers who arrived with "diverse handicraft skills, a commitment to providing schooling for their children, and little more than the clothes on their backs and the contents of a gunny sack or two and the pioneer spirit."[1] Historian Richard Judd describes farmers who supplemented their agricultural work with entrepreneurial ventures in woodworking, carpentry, or boat building, all activities that depended on access to the woods. He argues that these "small-scale, land-based enterprises sustained egalitarian values that had been forged in the American Revolution and reconfirmed by Maine's deep and abiding commitment to the cause of the Union." Local memoirs describe these settlers' compact, busy farms, often with little sawmills and gristmills attached, buildings that were frequently destroyed by fire and rebuilt. Unlike the subsistence farmers in Appalachia, who were more likely to maintain a household economy and do only minimal trading, these New England farmers apparently engaged in business and trade from the beginning.[2]

Local histories speak of generosity between social groups even in these early settlements. There were "two classes of persons," according to one account, shrewd men of property determined to make money, and poor pioneers with only the clothing on their backs who "without the aid of the more prosperous . . . would have perished."[3]

Woodsmen came soon after these early farmers and began to set up logging camps. According to New England historian Charles Clark, the men lived in camps in the forest from at least December through March, sometimes longer, cutting and moving logs to rivers by sled. When the ice broke up, the logs would be sent downstream, eventually to shipbuilders.[4] They were a rough, hardworking, and hard-living group who would come to town "to have their teeth fixed," as they put it, in drunken brawls after their long winter in the camps.[5]

By the mid-1800s the railroad had reached these northern settlements, and along the river businessmen and investors from Portland and Boston set up larger sawmills, textile mills, and some boot and shoe factories that could use the waterpower. Before the Civil War, sawmills produced timber for shipbuilders in New Hampshire and Maine ports, establishing fairly significant trade and an export-oriented economy early on. In 1888, after new technology for making paper from pulp was developed, the mills turned to producing paper. In many cases the owners moved their families from Portland or Boston to the mill towns.[6]

These were savvy businessmen, geared toward the future and interested in discovering new methods of processing the cheap wood all around them. S. D. Warren's paper company, as well as several others like it, was also notable for "cultivation of good relations with its employees and the community." As historian Clark describes these benevolent activities, "Warren paid relatively good wages, led the way on the eight-hour day, encouraged an employees' Mutual Relief Society, lent money to employees, started a profit-sharing plan, and became a benefactor of the town by building a library, financing a church building, helping the town with public works, erecting 150 company houses that were comfortable and well-equipped for their day, and taking other charitable and essentially paternalistic measures."[7]

The large mill operations drew immigrants not only from Canada but also from Scandinavia, Ireland, Italy, and Great Britain. An Irishman described this period of growth in Gray Mountain when the Peterson family built up the paper mills: *When my father was growing up they probably had five or six ethnic groups, and it was a real melting pot, a mini United States.* Each group had skills and experience for particular kinds of work. *The Canadians came down here, a lot of them to work in the mills, a lot of them to work in the woods—more French than anything else. My relatives in Ireland had been told there were jobs here, that the United States was growing. "They're making paper and it's labor intensive. They need people to run paper machines. They need people to work in the woods."* The Italians came first as stone-masons, settling in what is now called the Falls. *They lived within sight of the mill in little tents, and those tents grew to be homes, so today you've got the Falls Village or Little Italy.* Germans came to build the machinery and run the machine shops that supported the paper mill industry. *There was a section of town they called Little Germany, with German-named streets, where several people owned machine shops. Then the Irish came. They didn't cut the wood,* says this Irishman, *they were the woods bosses.* Others say the "Yankees" were the bosses, the French Canadians were the foremen, and the Scandinavians were the laborers. Most people, however, agree that the groups got along well, and in the late 1800s the city's early charter was signed by men from diverse ethnic origins.

Each ethnic group had its own organizations and religious traditions. The list of churches in Gray Mountain in the late 1800s indicates this diversity and the rich base of social institutions: the Congregational Church of Christ, where many early settlers and mill managers worshipped, St. Catherine's Roman Catholic Church, attended by French Canadians, St. Mary's Roman Catholic Church, home of the Irish, the Universalist Church, the Protestant Episcopal Church, the Scandinavian Lutheran Church, the Methodist Church, the Norwegian Methodist Church, the First Baptist Church, the Christian Science Church, the Greek Orthodox Church belonging to the Russians, and the Beth Israel Congregation, the place of worship for Jewish residents.

There were more than twenty benefit and fraternal organizations—Scottish, Irish, Scandinavian, French Canadian, Jewish. There were Masons, Knights of Columbus, the Scottish Clan, Loyal Order of Moose, Fraternal Order of Eagles, Sons of this and Daughters of that—groups that provided not only social cohesion and identity but real services like life and burial insurance, mortgage loans, homes for the aged, lodges for the sick, reading rooms, and social activities. The Scandinavians started a ski club; there were theater, opera, and symphony groups, and a hockey club that thrives to this day.

Civic and service organizations were plentiful as well—the Child Hygiene Association, the Parent Teacher Association, the Women's Christian Temperance Union, the Women's Club, the American Red Cross, the American Legion, Rotary Club, Kiwanis, Chamber of Commerce, Musicians of

Former Days, the Gray Mountain Athletic Association, the Scientific and Literary Club, the Girls Club, the Girl Reserves, and the Young Men's Christian Association (YMCA).

There were numerous schools, and the mill owners, the Peterson family, made an early commitment to education and recreation. They provided a kindergarten for workers' children long before kindergarten was widely accepted, and schools received direct support from the mill. Reading rooms were established for mill workers and recreation facilities were built for the town. Mill owners brought in community nurses who went out and visited the sick. The YMCA, built in the early 1900s, had a gymnasium, swimming pool, lobby, dining hall, recreational and reading rooms, classrooms, offices, bowling alleys, tennis courts, and an athletic field. *The Petersons raised the money for it, gave the land for it, put the deal together*. They brought cultural events as well. *The wives got very involved in bringing artists and musicians and concerts to the area. They really felt they had a duty to the community because the community had built them. They felt they had a duty to put these things back into the community*. The Peterson family wanted to make the community rich culturally, in part for their own enjoyment, in part to attract and retain the engineers they needed to work in research and development at the mill, and in part from a sense of obligation.[8]

Whereas coal operators and plantation bosses had deliberately kept themselves apart from their workers, these paper-mill owners chose to be part of the mill community, and people I interviewed frequently mentioned their integration into community life. *The Petersons lived right in town. This was home to them, too. And they had a very strong social conscience. We grew up in the shadow of their big house*, businessman Sean McCay recalls, *and my father grew up with their kids*. Company owners lived in town beside mill workers, and sent their children to the local school. *When the Petersons were here, they were* here, *their family was physically here. It gave you a sense of belonging to something, something that you could, in a way, feel and touch, even though the house was up there on Cherry Street and you knew the guy was way above you in income and so forth. But it was visible and it was present*.

There are some dissenting views about the benevolence of the Peterson family. *Some of the real tough union people said, "Ah, they were tough on their help." But my father worked for the Peterson Company—I know a lot of people who worked for the Peterson Company thirty, forty, fifty years ago—and they all said those people really had a heart*. There were differences between the mill owners and managers and the mill workers—ethnic and religious, as well as class differences. *The Peterson family and the senior managers were WASPS, and they went to the Congregational Church, which was unusual in this Roman Catholic community. People would say, "Who are those odd people up there and what do they do when the doors close?"*

Others say the French Canadians always felt that they were discriminated against and less likely to get promotions. A retired mill manager recalled, *I came to realize that back then there was a fairly strong strain of inferiority feelings by French Roman Catholics. I was appalled. I didn't make that observation myself but as I began to talk to people and they said, "Well, the guy who's running the mill, ya know, is not one of us and all of that." This is not true because my mother's father ran this whole mill and he certainly is French Catholic. But there was a feeling that if you were a French Catholic, even though they were overwhelmingly large numbers as a percentage of the population, there was this feeling that "we don't get all the breaks," that when promotions come, it's the non-French people who get it. Even more particularly, people thought if you were a WASP, you had a better chance at moving ahead, I think that there is less and less of that nowadays, but back then that was a fairly strong feeling.*

Nonetheless, overall there was a good deal of mixing, and most lists of those affiliated with public entities have names reflecting diverse backgrounds. Children played with everyone. *My uncle, who never graduated from high school, could speak Russian, Italian, French, and English.*

In the early 1900s the paper and pulp companies' research teams were developing products and new ways of manufacturing paper that positioned these northern New England businesses in the national market. By the 1920s, the northern mills in Maine and New Hampshire were considered the "capital of the papermaking world, renowned for cutting-edge forestry, research, and papermaking." It was labor-intensive work, even with capital investments, as a former mill manager describes. *This mill runs on wood, and they consume, last I knew, about 450,000 cords a year. That is a lot of wood! Back then, every stick was manually handled. It was cut in the woods and moved from what they called the stump when it's first cut, then into the yard, then into the river, or onto a truck, or onto a railcar. When it got here, it had to be unloaded again, and when it was taken from the pile and put into the mill it had to be handled again.* The mills employed some five thousand workers at their height, and they made work available to another six thousand woodsmen with whom they contracted to bring in the logs.

These good times gave way to bad when the Great Depression came, and sales declined precipitously, eventually throwing the Peterson family into bankruptcy. One historical account reports that managers kept workers on after sales had collapsed, even when it meant unsold paper was rotting in railway cars. The mill faced hard times. World War II reinvigorated business and, in conjunction with some help from the state government, saved the mill from closing completely. But competition in the paper industry only grew after the war, and eventually the Peterson family sold the mill to new owners who trimmed operations.

Importantly, the railroads that had been built to haul out the timber and paper in the mid-1800s had also been passenger trains, unlike Blackwell's railroads that were for freight only. The trains brought tourists into the mountains from the region's big cities as early as the 1800s, stimulating a recreation industry that diversified employment opportunities for locals and helped buffer some of the stress on the area's small farms. Historian Dona Brown describes deliberate efforts to market northern New England as a tourism destination. Boosters stressed the healthy life as well as good morals prevalent in the northern woods. Local color writers had painted Appalachian farmers as "quaint and peculiar." Their portraits of life in northern New England invariably were sentimental and nostalgic for traditional values and simple living, qualities tourism promoters believed would be appealing to urbanites in the late 1800s.[9]

Tourism also affected the politics of development. Brown describes the success of joint efforts between farmers and local boosters to build a summer tourism industry that helped sustain small farms as well as support new, larger hotels. According to Judd, when paper and pulp industrialists in northern New England pushed for water development projects and rights to timber under the general rubric of economic growth, small-scale farmers and loggers joined with these growing recreation interests to thwart big industrial development projects that would have threatened the region's natural resources.[10]

Conservation has been strong in northern Maine and northern New Hampshire for decades, in part because of this early investment in tourism, and the natural beauty it protects has supported a recreation industry and drawn newcomers who have chosen to make northern New England their home. Thus the tourist industry created diversity in employment opportunities—and importantly, employers—that was not present in the Delta or Appalachia. It meant that mill owners did not have a monopoly over jobs like coal operators and plantation bossmen had. Also, the influx of summer people and new residents who came to the mountains for retirement brought some of the same kind of benefit provided by early diverse ethnic groups—new ideas and energy that could blend with the strong ties and community commitment of longtime residents.[11]

There were efforts to organize a union at the mills as early as the turn of the century; workers succeeded in doing so in the 1940s, and it has been a strong presence ever since. The struggle to form the union was contentious, but it did not reach the violent extremes seen in Blackwell. Ironically, it was the mineworkers' union that successfully organized the mills. *There is a very strong union here. The union was started under the United Mine Workers' John L. Lewis, who was a firebrand if there ever was one. So that was militancy right from the word go.* A retired mill worker recalled, *Management-labor relations back then were difficult and strained. They had a fair number of strikes that were very difficult. As a matter of fact, Taylor Paper Company used to have a mill here, right on Main Street, and when workers went on strike, they just abandoned the town.* A man whose family was always heavily involved in union organizing and politics remembered how tense it was when union mill workers decided to leave the UMWA. *Some of the original organizers became upset with the corruption in the UMWA, and despite strong threats from John Lewis that they had better stay in, the workers here voted to switch to the AFL-CIO. My uncle told him, "Maybe John L. Lewis had the membership, but I've got the members." He came back and they voted to affiliate with AFL-CIO. It was gutsy.*

While the plantation crops and coal of the other regions were exported without any further value added, here the economy grew when logs were processed into pulp and paper. Employment in the coal fields has fluctuated with booms and busts over the years, generally declining over the long term, and employment in the Delta began a steady downward slide in the 1950s when planters began to mechanize operations. The paper industry has experienced slight fluctuations, and other manufacturing enterprises such as shoe making and electronics assembly factories have come and gone, but overall employment levels have been stable over the decades.

Steady mill employment, both inside the gates and out in the woods, supported a stable working class. There were other industries providing economic diversity as well—shoes, apparel, tourism, a little farming. Over time, this stability and diversity produced and sustained a large, blue-collar middle class. The Peterson family's early paternalism, combined with resilient ethnic and religious social organizations, and later a strong union, established a vibrant and inclusive civic culture in Gray Mountain. Economic diversity, employment stability, and worker participation have created a community characterized by integration rather than segregation, trust rather than suspicion, public investment rather than selfish gain. These patterns of equality, inclusive, participatory governance, and community investment have continued into the 1990s.

PARTICIPATION AND INVESTMENT IN THE 1990S

When the Petersons owned the mill, people said, "the mill is the town," and everyone expected mill management to provide business and social leadership. Mill managers were always appointed to the school board, and community investments and initiatives often came from the Petersons. But since the mill was sold to an outside multinational corporation in the 1970s, the mantle of community leadership has fallen to locals outside the mill. Sean McCay and Peter Luntz operate the largest local businesses, and although they are not identified as "running things around here," along with a handful of bankers and the owner of the largest car dealership they are considered the leaders of the town's business sector. Mill managers are usually involved in community task forces and included in discussions about the town's future, but they are no longer looked to for community leadership and they no longer live in town. Instead, today's mill managers are corporate employees who are likely to live in a more affluent town with others who are from away.

Both Sean McCay and Peter Luntz have always lived in town, and people perceive them as committed to the place and the people who live here. They have inherited the Petersons' role, on a more modest scale and without the paternalism. Their business and social lives are intertwined here in Gray Mountain. They contribute time, money, and in-kind donations to a myriad of projects and programs.

Both men established and built their businesses with a combination of personal drive and material support from people who knew them and their fathers. Both now serve markets all across the region, and sometimes beyond, because, they say, customers value their reliability, flexibility, and demonstrated commitment to responsive service. Sean McCay has a lumber and construction company on the north side of town, while Peter Luntz manufactures pipes and has a regionwide plumbing business located on the southwest side—bookends on a town in which the paper mill is the center, physically and economically. The mill was an important early customer for each of them, a kind of anchor account when they were getting under way.

Sean McCay is a redheaded Irishman in his mid-forties. His grandfathers came to Gray Mountain as boys in the late 1800s to work in the mills and retired fifty years later. His father and his uncle were mechanically skilled and entrepreneurial, and together they started and ran various businesses until the Peterson Mill drew them into management during World War II. Sean and his brother and sister grew up in a house in town, midway up the hill, went to the local high school, and then attended college downstate. They grew up during good times in Gray Mountain. As a youngster Sean made friends with whom, thirty years later, he still has close ties. He always valued his relationships back home and hoped to return in some kind of professional job.

We talk in a partially finished loftlike office over the retail side of the lumber business, a new phone the only item on the desk between us. Sean frequently gestures out the window, toward town and the mill, as he talks. When he first returned, like Joey Scott in Appalachia and Diana and Charles Smith in the Delta, Sean taught school. Like many small-town haves in Blackwell and Dahlia, he used personal connections to get his first job—he called the school superintendent and was able to get a temporary teaching certificate. But teaching was not the right career for him, so his father, who was near retirement, drew him into the lumber business with the idea that Sean would help close it down and make some arrangements about the property. But Sean found he loved the work, and after a solid year of discussion he convinced his father that his commitment to the business warranted keeping it going. In the early 1970s they began to make the critical capital investment required to update the little operation that had thrived in the forties and fifties and died in the sixties.

Both Sean McCay's personal life and business operations are sustained by long-standing personal networks. His father and his father's partner were in their seventies when Sean came home after college, and both died within a few months of each other during the first year that he was building the business back up. But the relationships they had with other mills, loggers, and customers, combined with Sean's own boyhood contacts who now worked in the woods, meant that he had steady sources of information and, importantly, business backing.

Two business deals were particularly crucial, and while they were based on expectation of profit all around, they were made on the basis of trust and personal support. In one case a longtime business friend from southern New England who came up for his father's funeral offered to buy the lumber he produced through the hard winter months. *He said, "If you want to keep sawing"—because we hadn't run all winter yet, we'd run summers only—"if you want to keep sawing, I'll give you a price. I'll take all your lumber."* In the other case, a connection with a Canadian customer who needed pine provided crucial cash flow and demand in the winter months. *We used to send probably five or six loads a week right to him. He was very good on pay. And as the contract got bigger and the years went along, we ended up carrying him and actually financing him. But in the beginning, he was paying us net in ten days, and that's what we needed.*

Sean also benefited from his father's reputation. *People knew the name, so we could get credit. When we called a mill supply house and we needed to buy something, they would say, "Sure, we know who you are." Then, if you perform well, you're in.* Those early days were not easy, but Sean had contacts and relationships that gave him the opportunity to make the business survive. *You had to be competitive to get the people to work in a lumber mill, and in the beginning you had to fight to get your suppliers and fight to find your markets. But growing up in town, you have friends who go into the woods business, and they'll tell you just what they're getting at other mills and what they don't like and do like about other mills.*

Today he is clear about his advantage in the marketplace. He holds out three fingers and ticks them off: *flexibility, service oriented, customer focused.* Customers throughout the region value those qualities, and they will buy his lumber that is specifically cut to serve their needs. *We go to Portland and Boston regularly with wholesale lumber. The biggest use of our lumber is probably in commercial or heavy construction in the Boston area. And we sell a lot of our own product retail right here, out of the building.* People in town see McCay Lumber as one of the better places to work—pay is decent and fair, there are health benefits. If you work hard, you can stay in the company and move up. The thirty-five workers make between five and twelve dollars an hour—not what people make at the mill, but good wages. And there is a sense of belonging, of solidarity, among the workers. Everyone comes to the annual company picnic, and Sean always sends a van to the nursing home and to houses around town to pick up the retired loggers and woodsmen.

He also volunteers in the community. He donates company resources to projects, and serves on numerous boards and committees. *You get involved in a lot because you've been here so long. I am on the hospital board, on the board of directors of one of the banks here, on the industrial park authority, historical society, ski jump committee. My wife is a volunteer too. She was a history teacher and then worked in the library in the school system for twelve years. And now she volunteers two days a week at the school where our children go, and she helps run the library there and does reading programs with them. She's also in a crisis intervention group in the public school system, where if they have a child that has some severe problems or something blows up at home, there's a group that will be available to that child, to whom the child can go. Oh yes, and I work with the hockey arena.*

The arena's board swung into action to respond to needs there, according to Sean's description. *A couple of people on the board said, "You know, we've needed new ice, and the pipes are rotting out." We had to raise about $150,000, and then we needed renovations.* Sean donated the lumber, and a carpenter who serves with him on the board donated the labor.

He values the way people treat one another here and, like many others, specifically brings up the lack of class distinctions. *We're a working community. We're an industrial-based community. There's very little difference between people. It is integrated here in the town itself. That's one nice thing about the town, that there doesn't seem to be any class-level distinctions. Most of the people who live here feel that they're part of the community. If they don't feel they are a part, they move to the outskirts. And that's because they don't like the smell from the mill.*

Sean likes living right in town. He points out the window. *I live on the other side of those smokestacks. I wouldn't trade in-town living. I have four kids who are involved in a lot of school programs, and there's too much time lost commuting, running back and forth. I like neighbors, and walking down the street to go visit somebody or go to the store. I don't want to live out in the country. My sister and brother live in places that are more of a second-home community, with a lot of well-educated, wealthy out-of-staters who summer in the mountains, but I like living right in Gray Mountain.* He enjoys the comfortable, open relationships he finds in town—the lack of guile or manipulation. *You really feel good talking to people. You don't have your guard up, you're not in there trying to negotiate something, you're not looking for something. There's no hidden agenda. You know the people next door and you trust the people next door. We're a small, somewhat isolated community, and therefore, people tend to get along, are open with each other.*

In recent years, when the mill was up for sale by its distant owner, several community leaders got together to ensure that the town was ready to win over a new buyer. *The mill was for sale, and we formed a task force to sell the noncorporate assets of this town. We'd tell them what the community was like to do business in and live in. Our message was, "Gray Mountain is the place you want to be. There's community support. We like paper, we like working, we want to be in this town. Sure, it's up in the corner of the country, and the transportation network isn't great. But there are some big advantages in being here."*

Peter Luntz, the plumbing businessman, spearheaded this effort to promote the town. He is in his late fifties, and only in the past few years has he begun to slow his work pace a bit. We talk in his spacious, newly decorated office in a building he put up on the southern edge of town several years ago. His conference table and desk are surrounded by signed photos of state politicians and crayon drawings by grandchildren. Peter is casually dressed in a flannel shirt and corduroy trousers, and his demeanor is easygoing and direct. Occasionally a phone call interrupts us and he lays the groundwork for his bid with a contractor in a distant city on a large job. Then we resume his story, which includes some striking parallels to Sean McCay's.

Peter's mother's family were merchants in the booming, prosperous days when several mills were running and the town was the center of north woods logging operations. *They had a clothing store. And of course back in those days, with the loggers and the woolen clothes, they made a good living and did all right.* His father had more humble beginnings. He came from Poland as a young man and made his living as a trader of foods and scrap metals. Peter went through high school here and always planned to be a mechanics teacher, but when he got to college he did not like the training. Like Sean, he tried working with his father at first, but they could not see eye to eye, so he went to work at a small manufacturing firm owned by a friend of the family's. As a young man of twenty-two, he filled in for a manager who was ill for a short period, and when he increased the division's profits threefold he was soon in charge of all out-of-state buying for the company.

He decided to go into business himself and saved enough to buy out his father's scrap company. Like Sean's business, it slowed in the winter, and when he was looking for a way to sustain operations year round, his father suggested he contact a cousin in a neighboring state who manufactured steel and plastic pipes. *In the winter, the scrap business was really dead around here because come November, you get the snow and the cold. At that time I didn't have some of these commercial accounts that we have today. It was going on your own to someone's home and taking an old stove or an old furnace or an old bathtub. It was a different type of operation*, he says with a smile.

Within a few years, with some help from bankers who knew his father, customers who could pay him on time, and suppliers that let him pay late, he transformed his father's business into a large operation. *You know, just about any large project is going to need plumbing. I was a real whiz back in those days. I was offering something nobody else was*. His father's reputation helped him get established with customers and the bank. *The name of Luntz had a very good reputation, and I hope it's as good if not better today. That definitely helped.* Like Sean, Peter figures his edge is flexibility and reliability—good, responsive service and custom work. His pay scale is similar as well—around six dollars to start out, up to nine for the more skilled and long-term workers.

He, too, values the friendliness and scale of the mill town. *I like it here, and I'd rather be a big spoke in a small wheel than a small spoke in a big wheel. I don't like the idea of living in the city where you don't know your neighbor, probably don't care, and your neighbor doesn't care to know you. I don't like the idea of traveling fifteen, twenty minutes to work*.

Peter is involved in community affairs, although in his case the roles are more often regional. After he organized the task force set up to present the town's best face to potential mill buyers, he became active in trying to bring better roads and transportation to the area. *There's a team effort, a tremendous, tremendous amount of capable people in that group of ours. I didn't do it alone. In some instances my personal connections with the political machine definitely helped, but all I did was bring the people to the room*.

Relations between the mill's management and its union were strained in recent years when jobs were cut, and the local businessmen were drawn in to help reach an agreement. *The company was not dealing straight with the union, and the union was suspicious. So, how do you deal with people when they got that attitude? The situation is serious—the salvation of the largest industry in the valley and 75 percent of the economic base up here. You can't let that just fall apart!* He insists it was a group effort, not him alone. *I'll admit I was instrumental in putting this all together. But I'm only one cog in that wheel because I'll tell you, it was the whole committee*.

He serves on the Private Industry Council, an industry advisory group for government agencies that oversee on-site training opportunities and assistance. This work has brought him in touch with people on public assistance, about whom he is at once pessimistic and optimistic. *You got your AFDC people. They were born in that environment and they are going to die in that environment for the most part. There is a few that start to see the light and have some interest and do try to get themselves out of that financial situation. Those that have tried have done well for themselves. I have a lot of involvement with these people, and there are certain ones that are really out there trying and struggling and working hard at it and making good, and others who do not.*

His company became involved in training six people who came through the program, and several are still with his firm. While Joey Scott in Blackwell says he only sees people remaining dependent on welfare, Peter Luntz has seen some success stories here in Gray Mountain. He recognizes that single women are particularly vulnerable and need programs to help them get skills they can use in the workforce. *There are a lot of very intelligent, very capable young ladies who may have had a family, had a marital problem, had to divert to welfare as the only means of income. When their family is grown up enough, they can find time to go through the community college for some special training, and they can go into the nursing field or into accounting or secretarial or clerical work, or whatever it might be. Some have pulled themselves up and got out of that rut and made something of themselves.*

Peter says there are two classes in Gray Mountain. *You got your white collar and you got your blue collar. And the blue collar, there's some very capable, competent people, but they're frustrated with some of the things going on, and don't want to get involved.* He is concerned that working people have given up on the process, and will just put in their workday and then *get in their car, take their boat and go up to camp. They don't want to get involved. They're either discouraged with the process or they don't care. In the winter they get out of work, take their snow machine and go snow machining. But they are not interested in doing a lot in the community to support things—not like they used to be.*

Peter is known for his role as a large employer in Gray Mountain and for his community involvement. A nurse out at the hospital said, *Peter Luntz—his name is mentioned a lot. He's a very influential person, in a positive way. He's on various boards, including up at the hospital. He's interested in social causes. Now he is the type of person that expects people to work for what they get, but he is not unreasonable, either.* Sean McCay and Peter Luntz are in many ways the northern New England counterparts of Creed Parker and Joey Scott. They have built successful enterprises on a base established by their fathers, reinforcing the family reputation for reliable products and energetically paying attention to customer service. They make opportunities available to their own families and play leadership roles in their communities. But they operate in entirely different social contexts, and this difference in how their communities work, what the civic norms and practices are, affects their behavior and the impact they have on their communities.

People fear and distrust Creed Parker and Joey Scott, and perhaps partly as a result, neither of them has become visibly active in Blackwell's civic affairs. For almost a century business leaders in the coal fields have wielded power without accountability and have maintained firm control over the lives of those who work for them. Creed and Joey carry on this legacy. Sean McCay and Peter Luntz are seen as good, if demanding, employers, and Gray Mountain residents recognize and even praise their active community role. Some critics resented the "closed door" nature of the task force organized to welcome new buyers of the mill, but no one would say Sean and Peter "run things." Community norms emphasize investment and participation, standards that were established in the early days by the Peterson family's generosity and the great number of working people's organizations. Sean and Peter carry on this tradition in the business world, while a remarkable group of women plays a parallel role in the nonprofit sector.

Five women in Gray Mountain who are friends and co-workers form the nucleus of a group that has created innovative social programs to address community problems and strengthen existing institutions. Their programs have brought down teen pregnancy rates, lifted women out of poverty and dependency, linked middle-age women to teenage girls as mentors, broadened the scope of the college and the hospital, and improved access to family health care. These programs and the women themselves come up spontaneously in interviews with those who are on public assistance or in low-wage jobs here, just as the names of the coal barons or powerful planters would come up in Blackwell and Dahlia.

They are like Diana Smith and Shirley Jones in the Delta, Joanne Martin and Marlene Combs in Blackwell, in that they have personally inspired and counseled poor women, helping them see the steps necessary to take control of their lives. But in Gray Mountain they have also been able to create social institutions that outlast their own personal involvement and have become part of the social landscape: clinics, day care programs, parenting and counseling programs. The resources are here, as well as the civic norms of investment and community service. While in Blackwell the ministers cannot round up volunteers for a food bank and in Dahlia the literacy program is always short of tutors, here food bank volunteers sometimes outnumber food recipients. People do not suspect that volunteers are out for personal gain or political capital when they work on a community project.

The women share a moral and political commitment to social change, a commitment that found resonance in the women's movement of the late sixties and seventies. Their shared vision combines with a mutual respect to create a social support network that they each rely on and draw strength and inspiration from. *They come in and see the problem and size up the situation. I think that's one of the skills I admire so much about Cassidy Morse, Jennifer Casey, Sister Anne, Katy Chambers, and Beth Sharpe. They don't see the problem as insurmountable, nor that "it's okay" and we can live with it. There are things that can be done, or places that you can go for money, or there are ways to help—to make life better for people.*

Cassidy came as a paralegal in the local legal aid office in the early 1970s. When she first moved here, she was part of the group that addressed high teen pregnancy rates by developing a family planning program. She married John Morse, an engineer at the mill, and they have three children. While her children were in elementary school, she worked in volunteer activities that revolved around them and their school. Today she is in administration at the community college.

Jennifer was raised in an upper-class suburb of Chicago. Her father was a successful publishing executive, her mother a "professional volunteer." She was swept up in the women's movement at her small women's college in New England, and later worked in a feminist clinic in Cleveland while her husband attended medical school. They came to the mill town in the early 1970s so he could repay his medical school debt by working in a medically underserved rural area. She immediately set to work talking with other women and physicians and church leaders about a family planning program.

One of her early allies and close friends is Sister Anne, who grew up in a mill town in a neighboring state, the daughter of mill workers in a large family. After a number of years teaching and creating programs to support families and carry out changes in the Catholic church in other regions, Anne was assigned to Gray Mountain in the mid-1970s. Both Blackwell and Dahlia have Catholic sisters who work with a handful of committed social-change activists, but here Sister Anne is part of a strong community of social entrepreneurs.

Katy moved to Gray Mountain as a young, idealistic, newly trained child development graduate from the University of Maine. She went to work in a day care center in the late 1970s, married Jim Conroy, a mill worker who had moved into a supervisory position, and she now runs the day care program at the community college. Beth and her husband, Frank Thernstrom, came as back-to-the-landers in the early 1970s to live in the mountains he knew from vacations here as a child. She pieced together jobs in hotels, hospitals, and bookkeeping all over the region, as well as several home business projects, and now runs the family planning center.

They support one another—even explicitly celebrate one another and other women in the region with an annual service award and banquet—and have changed the social infrastructure of this mill town. As Jennifer puts it today, *I lived in a lot of different places before I settled here, and I was really amazed at how cooperative people were, and in some sense how easy it was to get things done. Maybe it's because there was a lot of need or maybe it's because people were looking for the opportunity to get together and do it. Women have done the things that I am aware of that have gotten done in this community. I don't mean that to be a negative statement about men, but when you look at the day care issues that we have started here; when you look at what has happened with the extension of family planning; when you look at the kinds of things that are being done through job training or adult basic education, generally it's women who are behind those things. Women know how to do things in a cooperative way, whereas men either want to work alone or they're competitive. There is a strong feminist thread in this community. Women in this community really care about other women in this community and will put a lot of energy into providing services for them.*

Cassidy, Jennifer, and Sister Anne worked together from the beginning on the family planning project, a radical undertaking in the 1970s in this predominantly Catholic and conservative rural community. But the high teenage pregnancy rate of 20 percent had alarmed even Catholic priests. There were no gynecologists or obstetricians in the valley, so they developed an education and referral program connecting to the area's general practitioners. They spoke at schools, starting with the Catholic schools where Sister Anne could pave the way. They counseled young women, high school students as well as young mothers, in their tiny office in the old Community Action Agency's office overlooking the river. Cassidy recalls sitting on the sink in the old washroom, amid mops and buckets, explaining family planning to a young woman who needed privacy. Jennifer recalls giving a presentation in a raucous high school classroom and turning to find the principal standing in the doorway holding water-filled condoms that had been thrown from her room and fallen past his window. But despite primitive facilities and some anxious gatherings, they persevered and cheered each other along. Within a few years official statistics showed that teenage pregnancy had declined, and their own program expanded to offer other preventive health services. Today it is a comprehensive family health center.

The health center was created with the help of funds the federal government made available through War on Poverty–related health programs during a period when the more conservative, inward-looking administration of the hospital would not have supported outreach or birth control. The funds made it possible to build a parallel, even competitive, institution that eventually prodded the hospital to change the way it operated. The women themselves say the cooperation and mutual support of the volunteers has made the difference. *I think that what has happened here is that the people who work on these things are people who have developed strong working relationships and trust so that things can happen.*

Jennifer moved from directing this program to a job at the hospital just as its board and president realized that outreach was necessary for survival in today's health care environment. She has initiated new programs to provide home health care and preventive clinics in the community. Cassidy, in her role as an administrator at the community college, recognized that more and more women were working and needed reliable child care and preschool, and she started two programs to fill those needs. She established alliances with school officials to draw low-income children into the after-school programs, and raised money for scholarships to supplement federal funds. *What we've put together is a program that gives scholarship slots to kids who have been identified by the guidance counselors as either being latchkey kids or kids that basically aren't doing very well in school, for one reason or another. Our theory was, and continues to be, that if they can have some positive experience outside the school with their peers or with kids from the school, that will help them improve in their attitude toward school and their own feeling of self-worth and self-esteem. We did it last year and it worked really well.*

There has been a deliberate effort to draw in children from low-income families and have them mix with those from more prosperous households. *The program was running well its first year, but all the kids in the after-school program, a large majority of them, were from the well-off families. It wasn't that they were latchkey kids. So we said, "Well, what's not working here? Why aren't we getting them?" Our feeling was that it was because the parents just didn't care enough. Even though they might have been eligible for public assistance through Title XX, a federal program that would pay for them to come, it was too much of a hassle to fill out all the paperwork. Their kid was perfectly okay at home at the house. We tried to do what would be the least intrusive for the parents, raising scholarship funds at first, to make it easy to hook them in, and then making the transition to federal funds.* Like the boarding school teachers who could see beyond Joanne Martin's obstinate resistance to going to college, Cassidy did not let low-income parents' apparent lack of interest prevent her from reaching out to their children. She looked for new ways to draw them in, and did.

Sister Anne continues to counsel troubled individuals as well as provide ecumenical leadership in the community. She, too, is taking a more active role at the hospital, working with Jennifer to develop a hospice program. *I think one person can make a difference in Gray Mountain. If, for instance, you are committed to family, or counseling or family issues, there is a way of developing programs. There are support systems. It is easier to get to support systems or to hear about them than it would be in the bigger city.* Men and women who were having a hard time in their families, or just barely making it financially, would describe Sister Anne's counseling as a turning point—a time when they were able to move forward and leave old troubles behind.

Katy and Beth are a "next generation" of volunteers. Beth took over as head of the family health center when Jennifer left, and Katy has worked with Cassidy to develop a comprehensive child care center at the college. I interviewed more than sixty women on public assistance in this mill town, many of whom were going back to school to learn skills that would help them return to the labor market better able to support their families. Time and time again the day care center and personal counseling came up as big factors in getting low-income women on the right track.

As in Sarah Early's health coalition, these women talk to one another, across programs, so they can better serve their clients or patients or students. Katy explained how her ties to nurses at the health clinic help her work better with families in her center. *It is really easy to do community work around here, because if I have a problem with a child, or there is something I don't understand about the child or something looks weird to me, I pick up the phone and I call Martha—she is a pediatric nurse practitioner at Family Health—and I explain the situation. A lot of the times we won't use names, but she'll say, "Oh,*

I know who you are talking about. Try this and try this and do this." The big difference between Gray Mountain and other places is that there is a group of women here who have very similar interests, and it kind of trickles down from the fact that we have women in administration who also have similar interests and similar experiences.

Katy and her staff, working with Cassidy at the college, have put a number of counseling programs in place that I would hear about from women on welfare who were going back to the college. Katy explained how their intervention works. *We give them the extra shove they need. When they come in they're really tentative—"Oh, I don't know if I can do this, you know. I want to be a nurse's aide, but I don't know how to start." A lot of them need just a little push. Someone who says, "Well, this is how." And they will say, "Well, I am glad you told me that." Because I don't think they know how to start the process.*

Margaret Walsh conducted a related study of fifty additional poor single mothers, and she found that the mentors and programs that women like Cassidy, Sister Anne, and the others provide made a significant difference for women from poor, unstable families. Not surprisingly, those single mothers who grew up in stable, two-parent families with steady work were better able to cope with single parenthood and provide for their children. But those from unstable households with erratic employment were not all replicating their parents' history. Some, who were ready to change, who had grown up and regretted messing up like Gwen Boggs in Blackwell or Caroline Gage in Dahlia, could turn to teachers and social entrepreneurs like Jennifer and Cassidy and become involved in the programs they have created to gain the skills, confidence, and stability they needed to escape poverty.[12] The women Peter Luntz saw escape welfare dependence no doubt had similar experiences. The support is there when people are ready to take advantage of it. And the people offering it prod the young women they encounter to do so.

Katy remembers the case of a woman who came to the college, forced by the welfare office to do something to prepare herself for work. She was overweight, dressed in a sloppy sweatshirt and loose pants, and even had bedroom slippers on her feet. She did not look Katy in the eye during the first interview, and she snapped at the two-year-old she had in tow. Over time in the program at the college, with her child in the on-site child care program, she gained confidence. Katy and her staff counseled her about her appearance and personal habits. She learned about parenting through evening sessions for parents with children in the child care program and through her own volunteer work there, and she finished a degree in office technology. The day after the secretarial program's graduation, Katy was driving by Brettogne's car dealership out past the Falls and she saw this same woman, dressed in a suit and low heels, securing her daughter in a car seat in the back of a recent model sedan and tossing her suitcase from an old jalopy into the newer car. Katy learned later that she was off for her new job in Portland.

Beth's center recently won the status of a full-fledged community health care provider, bringing added responsibilities and programs but also much needed federal dollars. She and her board have begun investing directly in further education and career development for nurses who have been with them for several years—sending them off to be trained as nurse practitioners in Pennsylvania, counting on their commitment to the town and the center to bring them back. *We do a lot of training with our staff. As an organization we are willing to take a chance on people like that, help them further their education once they are here. For instance, we've taken two registered nurses that worked here and sent them to school to become nurse practitioners.*

Those who grew up here and those who came from away in the 1970s do not distinguish their backgrounds any longer. As Cassidy puts it, *I think that the people who are the catalysts at this point are people who are no longer considered to be outsiders. They are people who have been here twenty years and they have gained a degree of acceptance in the community. The crucial thing is committing to the place and the place commits back to you. It's being able to, as a part of that commitment, integrate yourself as part of the community and be sensitive to not talking like an outsider, not acting like an outsider. This is good for us.*

For all of these women, the social network the others provide is critical to sustaining their energy and their entrepreneurial spirit. *Two things have kept me here, even after my divorce,* Cassidy explains. *First, I have a very strong support network here that takes the place of my family that is fifteen hundred miles away, and that's important to me. Second, I have a sense of community.* Their sense of community, of mutual investment and commitment, like Sean McCay's and Peter Luntz's, are not the province of an elite or professional group only. Rather, trust, participation, and investment are the dominant civic norms, shared and acted on by those in the blue-collar middle as well as those at the bottom.

THE BIG MIDDLE "CONTINUUM"

Most residents say this community is one big, solid, blue-collar middle class. Over and over again people describe few class differences, a place where everyone mixes with everyone else. A woman who moved to Gray Mountain fifteen years ago says the town is *working class through and through*, a place with few distinctions. *You need the people who live here because life is harder, because things are a little more difficult. Everybody needs each other. The fact that we maybe have more money or more education isn't going to help me at all in a snowstorm or when my car is broken down or whatever. There's not so much of any of us that we can all afford to live separately. There's not a service class here and the others who live on the hill. There's just not enough of us to make that distinction.*

When there are fewer distinctions, and those who are poor associate with those who have steady good jobs, children growing up in poor or troubled families have a better chance of escaping poverty because they can get support outside the family and develop the skills, habits, and contacts they need to get work when they are ready. Teachers Dan Tourneau and Jeff Berk benefited from this kind of opportunity, and from inclusion in those community institutions that serve everyone—the schools, sports, and youth groups—and allow contacts between the poor and others. More recently, Deborah Shannon, a young mother in her mid-twenties, has had similar experiences. Whereas in Appalachia the poor say *people try to keep you down* and in the Delta they say *peoples ain't for you*, here in Gray Mountain even the poor feel that *we are pretty much in the same boat*.

Dan Tourneau and Jeff Berk grew up the sons of mill workers in the fifties and sixties. Both had fathers and grandfathers in the mill, their grandmothers were homemakers, and their mothers worked part time in the hotels in nearby tourist centers. Both grew up in the shadow of an alcoholic father, and both made it through those hard times because their extended family and teachers and coaches looked out for them. Today they work in the public schools—Dan as a history teacher and counselor, Jeff as assistant principal and hockey coach—and both have their own families. Dan married a local woman, daughter of a milkman and a stitchery worker. Jeff brought a woman he met in college home to the valley, and she became a preschool teacher and melded into life in Gray Mountain. I talked with them out at the high school, built twenty years ago but still clean and well maintained. Even after school hours there are still a few girls and boys chatting in the hallways, and they pop their heads in to say goodbye to Dan and Jeff before leaving for the day.

Dan's father died when he was eleven, and he says he withdrew for several years, feeling alone and aloof. He and his sisters went to live on Northern Avenue in a three-story apartment house with his grandparents. They were strict and pushed him academically, leaving no doubt that he was college bound. In high school Dan played on several teams, and his coaches looked out for him, spent extra time with him, helped with money for shoes, lunches when they were on the road for a game, and drew him into after-school events and programs. *Some of the people who are still teaching here, I had as teachers. I had great respect for most of the teachers in school; they were hard workers. They were caring faculty, and they helped me out. They helped me out a lot. I was involved in sports all through high school—hockey, basketball, and baseball.*

He remembers a school setting in which most students seemed to be about the same. *Obviously there were some kids that didn't have as much as others. But they were, by comparison, a much, much smaller group. And there was a lot of sympathy for what those folks were going through. The groups in high school were, say, the athletes as compared to the kids who were going out and drinking, all right? Or the people who were taking vocational programs.* The school's social system, he says, was structured according to academic programs. *There was the group of kids who were getting ready to go to college and the group of kids that were going to work in garages and that sort of thing. The track you were in depended on your grades, pretty much. We were separated academically in the fourth or fifth grade, when they started pointing us in certain directions. So that decision, I think, was made for us.*

Jeff grew up on the west side of town in a single-family home. His father was able to keep his job despite his alcoholism. Jeff was close to his three brothers, and they looked out for one another, played on teams together, and even took summer and after-school jobs at the same resorts when they were teenagers. Like Dan, he remembers high school being divided into those taking college prep classes and those on the vocational track, *but everyone mixed with everyone else, you know, especially in sports. Kids all ran together.* Also like Dan, he recalls that assignments to one track or another were made based on your grades—*on merit and your interests, really.*

Both men recognize that students' "interests" were shaped at home. Dan had his grandmother pushing him on to college. Jeff's father insisted that after high school each of the boys would either go into the service or to college rather than right into the mill. But they do not recall any discrimination based on where you lived or what you chose to do. *You never heard, "Oh, you live on Northern Avenue, so you can't be smart."*

Life in the mill town in those days was relatively sheltered, and these boys grew up in homes with curfews and discipline. They both describe a wild and rowdy freshman year in college, partying and playing, but they settled down by junior year. In fact, both were married while still in college, and by the time they were doing their student teaching they had found their careers. *I don't think it really set in until my student teaching. And I realized, "Gee, this really is what I want to do."*

When Dan graduated he got a teaching job in Texas, but a month before he and his wife were to move down there they found out she was pregnant. She wanted to be near her mother, so they returned to the mill town. Like so many rural residents, Dan worked at various jobs, trying to find a niche that he could enjoy and that would last. He tried insurance sales, then a very hard stint working for a roofing company—work that he kept for many summers to supplement his teaching income. He also worked in a restaurant for a while. Finally, a local teaching position opened up. He learned about each of these opportunities through friends. *Some people in the insurance business knew me—knew who I was, knew I was college educated, knew basically that I was a people person, and asked me if I'd be interested. And when you don't have anything at all . . . I said sure*. He got his insurance license and went to work, but he did not like trying to persuade people to buy products they did not really need, nor did he like the pressure of sales.

When the teaching job came up, he leaped at the chance. That, too, arose through word of mouth. *Someone called me up and said, "Hey, Dan—." I came up for an interview the next day. They were really stuck. It was the end of August and school was starting in a few days. And they needed somebody. I was the warm body that they chose, and it just worked out real well. I've been very happy here. Very happy*.

Jeff found a more direct route to teaching. The summer after he graduated from college he came home with his young wife and worked as a carpenter for a friend of his uncle's. One evening in a bar he ran into the middle school principal, who offered him a job teaching math and coaching soccer. He recalls how friends from high school who had gone directly into the mill were earning $14,000, and he was looking at $6,000 as a teacher. But he was happy to have a job in his field and his hometown, and when his wife found work they did all right. He loves the town—*it's just awfully friendly. Everyone gets along. You rub elbows with any and everyone.*

Both Dan and Jeff coach sports in school and play hockey outside work in the "Gentlemen's League." Each told of looking out for student players "from the end of the road" whose parents are out of work or overcome by alcoholism. Dan says, *I told her the basketball shoes were my daughter's and no longer fit her, and then I went and bought my daughter another pair. No one needed to know.* Jeff has also helped out the kids who have little money. *As a lot of coaches I'm sure have done in this state, I've paid for kids' meals on the road. I've bought their shoes for them. Simply because these kids can't afford it. And they wouldn't be able to participate if you didn't do such a thing. There's a lot of people in the school have done the same thing.*

They worry about decreased community support for the schools, the decline in funds for extracurricular programs and sports. *The percentage of people that we had in the school that participated in extracurricular or co-curricular activities was much higher in the 1980s than it is now,* Dan frowns—*which means that these kids are out in the street or wherever they are. It's time that the coaches could be using to teach and to care, you know. That time we could spend is gone. These kids are losing that for the rest of their lives. That's an economic thing, the cutbacks, and it's a terrible shame.* There is a sense of alarm about the schools, concern that fiscal pressures mean the elderly population on fixed incomes will keep whittling away at what the schools need. And here the schools are widely seen as the place where everyone gets their start. Dan and Jeff did, and, in a more roundabout way, Deborah Shannon did, too.

Deborah and I sit at the kitchen table in her second-floor apartment in an old building now owned by a distant Boston real estate company. The late afternoon sun shines in the kitchen window, giving a warm glow to the old wood floors and dark cabinets, and it is easy to forget that the treads on the stairs leading up here are dangerously loose, that the place has been allowed to run down in recent years. Two dogs are curled up on a rag rug in the corner, and a large Maine coon cat the size of a terrier fills the seat of an old chintz armchair. Deborah opens the conversation by saying, *If you're going to be poor, you might as well be poor in this community, because it's real family oriented around here. I mean, a lot of family support. You know, growing up and everything. There's just a lot of family . . . they just stick together.*

In many ways twenty-five-year-old Deborah's story resembles Wanda Turner's in Appalachia. Deborah's mother came from a family with alcoholic parents and twelve children, and she dropped out of school in twelfth grade to get married and begin having her own large family of seven children. Deborah describes a chaotic home life, with her father drinking, hitting her mother, food and clothing stretched thin to accommodate so many children. Deborah's favorite time was when she visited her aunts' farm on the Canadian border, where they had animals of all kinds.

When Deborah was fifteen, her mother got tired of the physical abuse from her alcoholic husband, and she took the seven children and moved out to an apartment on Northern Avenue. Not too long after their divorce was finalized, Deborah's father was disabled in a paper machinery accident and sank into depression. She ran wild during this time of upheaval at home, eventually finding herself pregnant by the son of the local hardware store owners.

When I found out I was pregnant, I still remember the day. His mother came over with him, and she was willing to pay for me to have an abortion. My mother said there was no way that I was to have an abortion. So abortion was out. Then they said, "Well, why don't you give the baby up for adoption?" They said, "We'll help you place the baby in a good home." My mother said, "She's not putting that baby up for adoption, because if she puts the baby up for adoption, I'm gonna adopt it." So I was like pushed to keep the baby. Which I'm glad I did, now. But back then it was hard.

She dropped out of school and lived with her mother, who at the time was on welfare herself. Deborah received welfare for four years—first while she lived with her mother, then for several years when she was alone, still partying and living a teenager's life. She was in a bad car accident during those years, one that makes her fearful of driving even now, seven years later. When she was twenty she and her oldest and best friend from school, Ronnie, started dating and moved in together. Around this time she decided she was ready to move off welfare. *I kinda just told 'em that I was working, and that my boyfriend had moved in with me and he's working and that I didn't need the help no more. I dropped everything and I just made it on my own.*

Three years ago Deborah married Ronnie, son of a gas station owner and factory worker, whose carpentry skills are well known in this town. Two years ago their son was born. *When I got a little bit older and started going out with my husband, it was like I went up a stair, I went up in the world. I changed within a year, because I was really a partier and that stuff.* Ronnie recently went to work for a large contractor in the area who could ensure steady work and some benefits for the family, and they are buying a house using a low-interest loan available through the Farmers Home Administration. Deborah works part time at the restaurant out by the college and brings in a little over a hundred dollars each week.

In Blackwell we heard Wanda say she was so disheartened that she had to tell herself to "quit dreamin'." Deborah says, *Me, I got big dreams. I'm a dreamer. My husband's the same way I am. He's a big dreamer too. I think when I get to be my mother's age, I think I'll have everything I want. A nice home. Nice furniture. Happy family. Happy kids with a happy dog*, she jokes.

Deborah regrets dropping out of school. She thinks she has been turned down for jobs she learned about through the employment security department because she lacked a diploma, and she wants to be a good model for her children as they grow older. She has been dreaming of becoming a nurse for some time, and when she mentioned her thoughts to the nurse practitioner at the family clinic, she was directed to a program at the community college. There she met Cassidy and her co-workers. *They ran these outside programs for schooling. They came in one to day to talk to me, and explained my options to me and that helped out a lot. That helped me get started, because I needed a little push. Because when you're on the aid you can fall into a cycle of depending on it and staying in the cycle, and a lot of people do. I had the chance to break out of it. They told me all of the different things that I could do, and should do—where to go get child care, and where to find money for school, and stuff like that.*

Cassidy encouraged her and gave her contacts at the school. *She said, "What do you want to do? What are your interests?" I said, "I always thought about nursing but I don't think I can do it." She said, "This is what you are going to do. You are going to call the school, talk to this person." She wrote a name out for me. "You're going to go down there and they are going to talk to you down there, you are going to get interviewed." It happened in a couple of weeks. I got everything going and then when I took the test, I got accepted.*

But it is not just the guidance that Cassidy gave and the programs available that have made such a difference for Deborah. Although she came from a poor and troubled family, she was not as culturally and socially isolated as her counterparts in Blackwell and Dahlia. She is well spoken, and the schooling she did receive made a difference. She reads well and has basic mathematical skills. She dresses the same as those who have always been in the blue-collar middle class, and she was never scorned by classmates for her old clothes, even when times were roughest. She has always known people throughout Gray Mountain, mill-worker families and shopkeeper families, teachers' families and hospital employees' families. When she was ready to get off welfare and go to work she was able to get a job, partly because one was available, but partly because she could present herself as a potentially reliable and conscientious employee. Her husband, who has carpentry skills and once ran his own small rehab business, was her friend in school, and they did not feel they were growing up in separate worlds.

Deborah, and before her Dan Tourneau and Jeff Berk, benefited not only from the guidance of key community leaders and school personnel, and not only from the inclusive programs accessible to them, but also from the fluid social relations in Gray Mountain and the public institutions that serve everyone together.

DIFFICULT TIMES AHEAD: PUTTING CIVIC CULTURE TO THE TEST

These stories seem almost too good to be true. Can community life be so different in Gray Mountain? Of course, poverty has never been so high as in Blackwell and Dahlia, work has never been so scarce. Educational attainment has always been significantly higher, and people have done more real learning in these schools that are not riddled with patronage. Those who are poor are mostly not *as* poor, and even those in really bad situations, who have given up on mobility, do not face the kind of hardship and scarcity we have seen in Appalachia and the Delta. But the main difference is that when people who are poor in Gray Mountain want to do better, they can find ladders. There are more resources to go around, both because there are fewer poor and because there are more Joanne Martins, Coach Wilsons, and Cassidy Morses. The problems are less severe, the resources to deal with them greater, and the whole community works differently—partly as a result of this ratio of needs to resources and partly because long-standing habits of participation, inclusion, and investment have been nourished over the years.

Gray Mountain has problems, especially in recent years as mill employment contracts and many young families are pressed, struggling even, to make ends meet. The schools are having to cut back programs, and the tension between elderly, retired mill workers and those with families comes to the surface more and more often in meetings. But over the years greater equality and stability have supported habits of community participation, norms of community investment—rich civic capital that the poor as well as the blue-collar middle class and do-gooders can draw on when times are hard.

Stories of those who are poor in the Delta and Appalachia have shown us how important cultural resources are for escaping poverty. People there grew up in social isolation from those who control opportunities in Dahlia and Blackwell. With their own families and narrow networks as their social world, the poor never absorbed the habits, skills, and images that might help them enter the mainstream. We have seen some cases of individuals inspiring or guiding others to a life outside poverty, but we have also seen that the way the community works affects chances for mobility. The constellation of social classes, and how people define their own interests, determine the politics and level of trust in a community. These factors, in turn, affect how people treat one another, how opportunities are distributed, and who benefits from the way things work. Lack of trust and cooperation undermines the quality and purpose of crucial institutions like schools and programs to build skills or confidence.

In Gray Mountain the poor are few in number and have been drawn into community life and activities, where they develop the same habits, speech, and expectations as their nonpoor neighbors. The community is rich in supportive programs and individuals. When people like Deborah Shannon are ready to turn their lives around in Gray Mountain, they are more likely to know people who can help them do so. They are going to have the cultural tools, the skills, habits, ways of seeing and thinking, that teachers and employers value and expect. And there are institutions in place that they can use to move forward.

Today rural communities across the country face the consequences of economic restructuring, including the erosion of the "good jobs" in manufacturing or resource extraction that had provided a stable economic base since World War II. Both uncertainty and inequality are on the rise, with tremendous consequences for public life, especially in these times when we are moving greater responsibility for social policy to the community level. Gray Mountain is no exception. There have been big layoffs at the mill, and more and more young people fear they must leave to find stable work. This community, which historically has been characterized by a strong work ethic, considerable self-reliance, and mutual support, is at a juncture where changes in the economic base and social conditions present formidable challenges.

The rich civic culture and strong social institutions that have been built over the years in Gray Mountain will be tested as these economic changes take hold. The solid manufacturing base that provided the steady middle-class incomes so crucial for workers' families is eroding at the same time that government support is shrinking and greater responsibility is falling to local governments. We have seen the negative effects that inequality and scarce, volatile jobs have had on the social context in Blackwell and Dahlia —how these economic conditions perpetuate chronic poverty.

GRAY MOUNTAIN TWENTY YEARS LATER: HOLDING ON TO A BLUE-COLLAR COMMUNITY

Snow is starting to fall as we creep down the last steep hill into Gray Mountain and make our way through town on this early March morning. Unlike twenty years ago, there is no rotten-egg smell from the mill. The air looks and smells clean. After a series of owners and repeated shutdowns and re-openings, the large paper and pulp mill operation in the middle of town closed for good in the mid-2000s. *The heart of Gray Mountain was the pulp mill and the paper machine that was there. That was devastating when it closed. That was a shock to everyone here. Everyone figured that one of these days it's going to happen, but it happened very abruptly*. The community understood just how permanent the shutdown was when the Canadian owner dismantled it completely, with the exception of one valuable boiler that the city persuaded the company to spare. *This is worth more than just the scrap steel. Make sure it's the last thing that you tear down and give us a year or two*.

That boiler became the focus of a wrenching debate about the identity of Gray Mountain. There were some, including the mayor and several on the city council at the time, who wanted to change the area's image. Gray Mountain would transition to a new economy based on tourism and possibly expand the community college into a four-year school. *When the mill closed, the smell was gone. . . . It was a chance to rebuild Gray Mountain away from an industrial place, to emphasize the natural beauty of the area. Now there was an opportunity for Gray Mountain to reinvent itself and attract commercial development to that riverfront*. The city's seal was changed, removing the smokestacks depicting the mill. Many longtime residents as well as newcomers urged their neighbors to support riverside development that would bring visitors.

But as the national economy worsened with the great recession beginning in 2007, sentiment shifted toward those who argued that Gray Mountain was a working city and therefore the remaining boiler should be converted to support a biomass plant. The plant would contribute to the tax base almost immediately, and be a big consumer of water and sewer services, helping the city address urgent fiscal problems accompanying the loss of the mills and now excess capacity. Developing a new ecotourism-oriented identity faced too many fundamental obstacles, they said, including dams on either side of the mill site limiting river access and use, and, importantly, a Superfund site. *There were struggles. There were meetings. There were close calls.* After much debate and work to identify public and private funding and acquire permits, Gray Mountain moved forward with construction of a large biomass plant right in the center of town on the mill site.

The mayor and council members who opposed the biomass plant were defeated in the next election. David Cloutier, the new mayor, says his grandfather and father worked in the mills, and he himself was a leader in the papermakers' union until he lost his job in one of the layoffs. Leaning against the workbench in his clean, brightly lit garage where he rebuilds old cars as a serious hobby, he talks about changes in Gray Mountain and his work to preserve its middle-class character. David entered politics more than twenty years ago when he was in his thirties, determined to defend public education when, as he puts it, "some conservatives" were trying to undermine the public schools. He was both looking out for his own young son's education and standing up for the community's commitment to education. He and others on the council worked to make the school board elected, rather than appointed, to assure accountability. Throughout our visit, interviewees reinforce his perspective that Gray Mountain has always had, and continues to have, a deep commitment to public education. *It's been a struggle, but we've kept the schools together. People always support the schools . . . they understand the value of education. If you want to be anybody, you have to be educated.*

David attributes his long public service to his family's background as strong "FDR Democrats." He has been active as a hockey coach, a union steward, and now, once again, as an elected official, for many years. In his mind the three roles are all part of his public service to Gray Mountain. During the debates about how to use the paper-mill site, he felt compelled to run for mayor, promising to maintain Gray Mountain's blue-collar identity and manufacturing base. *The folks who were in office completely tore the community asunder. They fought tooth and nail against the 75-megawatt biomass, and I thought that was a golden opportunity for Gray Mountain to reinvent itself. So I went back and ran for mayor and won by a pretty sizable margin*. In a symbolic gesture, David restored the old logo with its smokestacks. *We're proud of our heritage*.

Tall cranes are moving on this snowy morning, with construction at the biomass site in full gear to meet a strict fall deadline and avoid late penalties. A large parking area near the site is filled with the trucks of hundreds of union workers from across the region who are building the large biomass plant. When it is completed it will employ some forty workers in good jobs with benefits. Supporters say there will be as many as two hundred indirect jobs for those supplying 750,000 tons of low-grade wood to the plant every year.

Cars and trucks are also parked behind the smaller specialty tissue mill downriver, the only remaining mill, which was recently acquired by a somewhat eccentric outside owner committed to seeing manufacturing survive in America. The mill's two hundred jobs pay anywhere from twelve dollars an hour, for those starting out, to eighteen or nineteen dollars for experienced machine operators. While some say the plant is struggling to find enough market share to survive, others took heart from the fact that in 2013 the plant hired a handful of new, younger workers, interpreting this to mean that all the experienced millworkers who were laid off over the last few years have either been rehired, left the area, or retired. *They just hired four people, really hired, not recalls, real hires*. And other openings should follow . . . *there's a group right now between sixty-two and sixty-five, they're just waiting to be eligible for Medicare to get out*. In early 2014 there were layoffs, perhaps giving credence to the skeptics who worried about market share.

But overall there is good news after years of bad news. As the paper industry restructured nationally and globally, thousands of jobs were lost in the paper and pulp mills in the region since we were here twenty years ago, and then in 2012 bankruptcy claimed two long-standing manufacturing businesses, including Peter Luntz's big plumbing business with its regional markets. Peter died some years ago, and rumors have it that his handpicked successors got overextended in the recession but kept people working—reminiscent of the Peterson paper company's actions back in the early 1900s. The other longtime employer was said to be "family-oriented" and employed a number of women who could receive benefits even if they were part-time. The loss of both companies was a huge blow to morale in Gray Mountain. *And you lose your two biggest employers. Geez, that was tough, because they were good employers, both of those companies*.

As in Blackwell and many other rural communities across America, the biggest employers in Gray Mountain are the schools and the hospital. But since we were last here, there are also two new prisons, one state and one federal, tucked out of sight in the woods north of town. The state prison hired a number of laid-off mill workers. *Because of the prison jobs, I don't think that we've felt the full impact of the mill closings. A lot of people, when the mill closed, were in their late forties, fifties, and they still had pension plans. So they went out, and they found jobs to tide them over.* The federal prison has a requirement that new workers be thirty-seven or younger because they have mandatory retirement at fifty-seven. Some complain about the rule, while others see the benefit of young families moving in or staying. In the winter of 2013, the federal budget sequester slowed hiring. With a new federal budget passed in early 2014 the prison can finally resume hiring its workforce.

As we climb the steep hills above town there are dozens of empty, cleaned-up lots in between the old double- and triple-decker apartment buildings common throughout New England. Many buildings have new outside stairs and porches, treated wood that has not yet been painted. Larger renovation jobs appear under way on several multifamily units on both sides of the river, all by the same Family Housing Company, a locally owned business that was formed to work on a public-private partnership to clean up the neighborhoods. After the big mill closed, housing values, low to begin with, fell even more as people left and demand for housing declined. Speculators bought properties and did not keep them up. Several landlords from as far away as Massachusetts, Connecticut, and Florida are believed to have encouraged their tenants in cities downstate who relied on public assistance, disability or TANF, say, to move to their properties in Gray Mountain, where the tenants' Section 8 housing vouchers would go further. Local agencies saw increased requests for free and reduced-price lunch eligibility, TANF, and the Special Supplemental Nutrition Program for Women, Infants, and Children (WIC).

Everyone worried about a resulting influx of low-income residents and its impact on the community. Some were blunt. *They come here, and they sleep all day and raise hell all night. They have children who are a product of that lifestyle. They get coded [as special needs] in your school system. . . . We were spending eighty to a hundred thousand dollars per kid, because these kids had learning disabilities, because of the way they were brought up. It wasn't just a threat. The situation was real. . . . We're cleaning up the mess. Those people aren't welcome here.* There were some who attributed the newcomers' arrival to health and human services departments in other cities in the state. *Because there's a real housing crunch [downstate], so they're sending them all here. So the first of the month, you see a new crop of people, usually pushing a baby stroller, smoking over it, walking downtown in the middle of the day. But it's like a superhighway from [downstate]. They're all sending them here.*

While everyone we spoke with mentioned the influx of low-income families on assistance, with children needing services, details about who came and who stayed were hard to pin down. Some were likely transients who never intended to stay when winter came. Others may have been living in one of the sixty-five apartment buildings that were condemned and torn down, and then moved away when they lost their apartment. Census data show that single-parent households in poverty increased by 75 percent between 1990 and 2010, although the poverty rate overall only increased from 10 percent to 12 percent. Clearly the additional 250 poor single-parent households living in Gray Mountain in 2010, and, for a while probably, more like them, moved into the low-rent buildings on the hillsides owned by landlords who were neglecting their properties.

The growing concentration of poverty in these traditionally multigenerational mill-family apartments concerned business leaders, elected officials, social workers, and school personnel. *There were a lot of problems in these apartments. Then we got slum landlords, who bought buildings in Gray Mountain and didn't put any money into them. . . . They milked these buildings. So we became leaders in the state with tearing down apartments. When this first got proposed, six, seven years ago, people in Gray Mountain said, "We can't do that. We can't afford to lose the tax on the property."* But the cost of managing their impact was real, too. *The police are there all the time. They're throwing their garbage from the second floor into the street. You have police calls because they're beating up the wife or girlfriend. And the kids are a problem in school, because they've only been here six months and know they're going to be somewhere else in six months.* Gray Mountain was looking at the kind of poverty and dependency that has plagued Blackwell and Dahlia for decades, and residents did not like what they saw. *People literally talked about putting walls up and not letting people in. They knew they couldn't do it, but that was the language that they were talking about. You know, how do we protect our piece of the world?*

As the snow mounts outside the Dunkin' Donuts windows, Adam Croteau tells a long, complicated political story about how he and other Gray Mountain leaders clamped down on absentee slumlords and cleaned up neighborhoods that were fast deteriorating. Adam had left Gray Mountain after high school and worked internationally as an electrical engineer before returning home with his wife, like some in Blackwell, to take care of their aging parents and enjoy the outdoors. When Gray Mountain officials advertised a new position to address the bad housing problems, he applied. They were impressed. *I'm a can-do and a project instigator. That's my job. It's always been my way. . . . You had to have that, be stubborn about it, bull-headed about it.*

Several factors had converged to create the housing problem. When the mill closed, in the economic and fiscal downturn, Gray Mountain laid off its housing inspectors to save money. Code violations increased. There were some fires started by arsonists that added to the growing sense of blight. More outside investors had come in to make a quick profit, with no intention to maintain the properties. And distant slumlords were just collecting rents without managing their buildings. *One hundred percent of those with four units and above were owned by outside, non-resident parties; two thirds of the three-deckers were owned by outside parties. . . . We had a problem. The first thing was we had to go change the laws.* Over a couple of legislative sessions Adam and his colleagues in Gray Mountain worked to get a bill that would enable them to put a lien on any property owned by a landlord who was delinquent on another property. *We had to be more aggressive. We're going to start evicting people and selling the properties. We're going to go right to the full extent of the law, so we started a process. . . . And we started taxing the properties. The ones that were bad enough, we decided to demolish.* At first local realtors complained to the council, but the housing cleanup had the full support of the mayor and other town officials, and when the good results started to be visible, everyone got on board.

The schools have borne the brunt of adjusting to the increased numbers of disadvantaged families. *We have way more poverty. We have a higher degree of free- and reduced-lunch programs [than before the low-income newcomers arrived]. We have way more special-needs students, as a percentage [of the student body].* But school personnel had strategies for assisting students at risk. *We attempt to be proactive. We meet once a week, here, various teachers and counselors and other people, the athletic director, for example, people in the know with what's going on. . . . And somebody in the committee is assigned the responsibility [for a struggling student], and the next week we come back and see where we are and what we need to do.* Another educational leader in the school system recalls the impact of the influx of families seeking low-cost rents. *The increase in special-ed cases was phenomenal. And I was very close to it, because I do participate in the case management of those kids. . . . It was a different group of families that really weren't participants in the kids' educations. So we've tried to engage parents more. We try to reach out more.*

In Blackwell and Dahlia we heard accounts of parents, often young parents, berating teachers when their children failed or were held accountable. In Gray Mountain we hear that parents still value teachers and education, and that perspective appears to influence their children. *Our kids are respectful, they're quiet. We've won a number of sportsmanship awards from the state in athletics. I continuously have people come in that deal in all of New England . . . always come in and positively comment on how well-behaved the students are, or how honest and open they are.* Jeff Berk, now a middle-school principal, described his students as *"please and thank you kids." They just appreciate everything that you do for them.* The schools have a low dropout rate, less than 2 percent in 2012. Whereas Blackwell and Dahlia struggle with high school graduation rates around 50 percent, Gray Mountain's is over 80 percent.

Gray Mountain made self-conscious choices to retain its blue-collar identity—going with the biomass plant instead of efforts to encourage upscale tourism. Community residents as well as leadership supported the housing cleanup. They supported the development of 150 miles of ATV trails, and allowing people to ride their ATVs into town on some main city roads to buy gas and food. As one man put it, they did not want poor families coming in, but they also did not want wealthy outsiders calling the shots. *Gray Mountain's gonna remain a middle-class community. See that big hulk out here?* he says, pointing to the boiler. *That ensures it. That alone sends a pretty significant message to the rest of the world that we are a middle-class community, and when you add other small, ancillary light manufacturing around that area, it sends a pretty powerful message. We have two prisons. Those families are mid- to upper-middle-class families that live in the area. We are probably the motorized recreation area of the state. That's a middle-class activity. Wealthy people don't drive around in ATVs.*

While the idea of becoming a "prison economy" was controversial at first, as the biomass plant was, even the opponents now accept, and even appreciate, the good jobs for former mill workers at the state prison and the younger families that are coming with the federal prison. *When I grew up here we were a strong middle-class community. Everybody worked, and everybody looked out for each other. My uncles and my dad's friends were Boy Scout leaders. They were hockey coaches. They were Little League coaches. I did the same. And the younger parents are doing the same.* Sports, outdoor recreation, blue-collar work, investing in community organizations and institutions—people who have stayed in Gray Mountain are deliberately working to maintain what they value in their community.

Sean McCay and I catch up in the same loft office over his lumber business, now fully furnished with historical maps depicting woods owned by the old Peterson Company, antique lanterns, old photos, tools, and wooden signs from the old mill lands. A stuffed bobcat peers over the old typewriter and yellow pads on the desk. There are no computers in the room.

Sean and his brother were caught in the downturn when the devastated national housing market hit their sawmill here in Gray Mountain. Rather than lay people off, they instituted a job-sharing program until times improved. This year they expect to earn a small profit. Sean's youngest son is completing his forestry studies degree with plans to come join the business, perhaps eventually take over. Like other Gray Mountain professionals and business leaders, he has some children and their spouses who are finding a way to stay in the mountains, and others who have moved downstate or away. Interrupted by calls with customers from Boston, Portland, and Pennsylvania, Sean recounts his perspective on the controversy around the biomass plant, in which he was closely involved as a strong proponent, and assesses where Gray Mountain is today.

After some real lows, with the loss of the mill and Peter Luntz's business and others, Sean thinks Gray Mountain is coming out of the hole. *So you've got the prisons, that was a big plus—both prisons, state and federal. You've got the building improvements in Gray Mountain that are happening, and they are great for morale. You've got the biomass plant in the center of town. That's a win. You've got the largest ATV park north of Virginia. That is bringing people. Growing up, Gray Mountain wasn't a recreation town. It was always a mill town.* Sean is optimistic about the future. *Now we're seeing people come into town. You go over there in the height of summer or the winter on the ATV trail, and you'll see cars from Massachusetts, Connecticut, New York, and these guys have trailers. And they're spending money. So we're returning. I think we had our low spot after you were here, and we hit bottom. And we've come back. And a lot of people point to Gray Mountain saying, "The community has turned itself around."*

The numbers confirm that Gray Mountain has turned itself around—at least to some degree. There are big changes, and a new equilibrium perhaps. Gray Mountain has close to the same number of jobs as in 1990. But the quality of jobs has changed. *I don't think parents send their kids to college or high school and say, "I hope you're gonna grow up to be a prison guard."* The population has declined by 5 percent, and there is a higher share of elderly now. Twenty-six percent are in their forties and fifties, 27 percent are over sixty. The median age in 1990 was thirty-six, and now is about forty-six. In 1990 half the family households had children, and today only 40 percent do. The schools are smaller and the athletic teams are in lower divisions, to the chagrin of some. There is talk of school mergers, as happened in Blackwell. Churches have merged or closed.

But Gray Mountain has sustained investment in public education, and the educational attainment levels still track the national average. Eighty-five percent of adults have completed high school, compared with around 70 percent in Blackwell and Dahlia. Even with the influx of low-income families, the poverty rate is only 12 percent, compared with nearly 30 percent in Dahlia and Blackwell. While one out of four Blackwell and Dahlia households receive SNAP, one out of ten in Gray Mountain do.

Although the loss of Peter Luntz's business and the mill has meant fewer leading citizens can be called upon for financial support of community organizations, Gray Mountain has benefited from a generous new philanthropic initiative, the legacy of a native who left his fortune to invest for the region's future. "The angel of the north," Jennifer Casey called the fund, which supports core community institutions, invests in young children and economic enterprises, and brings diverse groups of citizens together annually to build collaboration and stimulate new ideas. *You know the Fund is part of this story. It's an important part of this story. And the fact that the funds are out there gets people [thinking] . . . you can't think, if you don't think you can do it, you know? So the fact that the funds are out there, you get a good idea and you think, "Ah! Maybe the Fund will go for this." So it's an interesting dynamic.*

Gray Mountain is a region in transition, like much of rural America. An economy based on the extraction and processing of trees has changed. Sociologist Chris Colocousis has shown that the legacy of managing forests to produce low-grade fiber for the mills is manifest in the small-diameter woods today, appropriate to feed low-grade fiber to the biomass plant.[13] A controversial logger from a neighboring state has clear-cut huge expanses of woods, but then made the land available at a good price for the ATV trails. Several people who deplored his logging methods said they respected his honesty—a handshake will seal a deal. Environmentalists continue to push for conservation, but many say they are less rigid, more ready to work with longtime residents. *I think they have really learned a lot about how to behave in the community and be a community partner, as opposed to being the rabid environmentalists*. Locals value the woods for recreation and do not want to see gates that limit access, whether put in place by government agencies or new second-home owners from away.

In the mid-1990s we found a strong civic culture in Gray Mountain. People trusted one another, people participated in community organizations and events, no matter what their status, and people invested in community-wide institutions, in contrast to the divided, family-oriented culture in Blackwell and Dahlia. I attributed this strong civic culture to the large blue-collar middle class, compared with the heavy burden of high long-term poverty in coal country and the Delta; to diverse ownership of businesses and land, as opposed to the tightly held economic and land resources in Appalachia and the Delta; and to a history of investing in education and in the community by both the early paternalistic mill family and by the many working class–led ethnic and civic organizations. But back then we saw difficult times ahead for Gray Mountain, as the paper and pulp industry restructured, layoffs were beginning, and the solid manufacturing base that provided the ballast for the blue-collar middle class was shrinking.

Those difficult times came, and then some, with the loss of other businesses and the influx of hundreds of low-income families. But while the economy has changed and the population has aged, it appears that Gray Mountain's strong civic culture has remained. *You know that's one thing we have is the ability to work together. That is one of the strengths of our community, really working together, getting to know one another, supporting one another*. People look after one another. *The fabric hasn't changed much. Everybody knows everybody. . . . We've had some new folks move into the area, took jobs at the federal prison. And they come in here, and they're just blown away. People talk to each other. People are friendly*.

Although many in Gray Mountain let the poor newcomers know they were not welcome, the ones who left most likely did because their pattern was to be transient or because their housing was condemned in the cleanup, not because they were forced out. The families who stayed were wrapped into support services in the schools and clinics, programs at the community college and those providing mental health services. Beth Sharpe explains that the various service providers coordinate to help families, just as we saw them doing twenty years ago. *We have been able to sit around the table and say, "What services are being offered? What services are not? What and where are the gaps? Who can do it, and what funding can we find to do it?" We all work together, so no matter what door you enter, there is no wrong door in Gray Mountain.*

People continue to cross boundaries and mix with people from a wide range of circumstances. *I was at Sean McCay's Christmas party and in the same conversation was a judge, a prosecuting attorney, a defense attorney, and the defendant in the case who had gone before that judge. The prosecutor and the defense attorney and the judge and all of them were sitting around and having a drink together and talking about different things. I don't know where you could go and find that scenario happening. And all sort of had an equal . . . obviously not an equal status, but everybody listened to all of their stories somewhat equally. Nobody was dismissed, you know?* When I have lunch in the hospital cafeteria with Sister Anne, all the tables are still rainbows of coats, with orderlies, nurses, doctors, and maintenance workers eating together.

Gray Mountain is adjusting to economic change, holding on to its blue-collar identity. But whereas the people staying in Blackwell are hunkering down with family on the piece of land they call home, here people are also, very self-consciously, trying to hang on to the community they knew. They lost all but one of the mills, and the good wages that came with mill jobs, but they are adjusting to a new economy—still blue collar, and to a community that is now older and less prosperous. They value and protect that community, both its culture and the woods that define it.

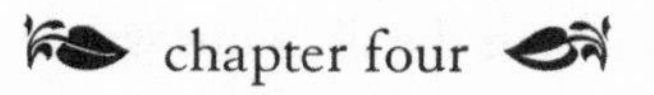

chapter four

SOCIAL CHANGE AND SOCIAL POLICY

What do the stories from the 1990s in Blackwell, Dahlia, and Gray Mountain tell us about why some people and places remain trapped in poverty in America? Do they support the thesis that poor people's destructive behavior is the real cause of their poverty? That communities like Blackwell and Dahlia have chronically high poverty rates because there was a brain drain when "those with get-up-and-go got up and went," leaving behind those without education or ambition? Or does the real problem lie with the larger structural forces in society, the way capitalism's free market invariably results in unequal opportunities? The way patterns of racial and class discrimination create impenetrable barriers to mobility?

CULTURAL AND STRUCTURAL CAUSES OF PERSISTENT POVERTY

Throughout the sixties and seventies, the persistence of poverty was explained from either a structural perspective that blames inequalities built into the economic and social system or a cultural perspective that blames individuals' values and behavior.[1] In recent years, urban-poverty scholars have begun to focus on how poverty is perpetuated by the social relationships and institutions in the community.[2]

The structural argument emphasizes the forces affecting the distribution of opportunities in the national, and even global, economy. Scholars and policymakers have long criticized the way capitalism allocates resources unequally among groups and places, and the way racism has caused persistent disadvantage for black Americans and other minorities.[3] A highly unequal two-class society was established early on in Appalachia's coal fields and the Delta's cotton plantations, and the divisions were exacerbated in the Delta by the extreme racism that condemned blacks to deep poverty. Over the years, as we have seen, the extraordinary power that employers had over workers and that whites had over blacks has maintained this inequality and long-term poverty.

Both the structure of the larger economy and relations between races still matter in the 1990s of course, and these issues have received new attention from analysts in the wake of the economic restructuring that has enveloped the nation since the late 1970s. Economists attribute growing inequality nationwide to declining employment in the goods-producing sector, which provided high wages and benefits to relatively unskilled workers for twenty years after World War II. Furthermore, the expanding service-producing sector is polarized into high-paying professional jobs in business and finance, law, medicine, and technology on one hand and low-wage, menial work in retailing, hospitality, and janitorial services on the other, available to those with limited skills and education. Minorities are especially hurt, in part because racism and segregation over the years have ensured that they are more likely to have few skills and low educational attainment.[4]

Restructuring of the economy has had a profound effect in rural areas where extractive and goods-producing jobs continue to decline and fewer high-end service jobs emerge at all. Between 1980 and 1990 the proportion of all jobs in natural resources and manufacturing declined from 36 percent to 28 percent in Central Appalachia, from 31 percent to 29 percent in the Delta, and from 37 percent to 27 percent in northern New England, while service-producing jobs increased proportionately. Good jobs continue to be hard to find, and people are still leaving Central Appalachia and the Delta.

But while the larger economy and long-standing racism have produced unequal opportunity, and continue to do so in the 1990s, the stories we have heard suggest that other factors having to do with culture and class at the community level can help us understand the persistence of poverty. From a commonsense point of view, the "culture of poverty" thesis—that the poor, discouraged by their own failures, do not teach their children the values they need to succeed—is compelling. Some of our dominant theories of social action have long assumed that our behavior is shaped by our values, that we act based on what is important to us. If getting ahead is important, then a person works toward that end. Those who are stuck in poverty are those who choose to enjoy immediate pleasures rather than behave responsibly. *I guess that's the way they want to live*, a young man in Blackwell had said about the first-of-the-monthers who depend on welfare. Most of the haves in Blackwell and Dahlia hold this view about the poverty of the have-nots.

The implication is that people are poor because they reject behavior that will help them get ahead. Anthropologist Oscar Lewis developed the culture-of-poverty thesis in the 1960s to shift attention from the "personality of the individual victim of poverty" to the "slum community and family." He saw the poor's failure to act responsibly as a rational adaptation to their marginal status in a "class-stratified, highly individuated, capitalist society" where low economic status is attributed to "personal inadequacy and inferiority," despite low wages and high unemployment. In other words, he first developed the culture-of-poverty idea as a sympathetic theory explaining why people behaved in ways that hindered their escape from poverty. Later the culture-of-poverty thesis became part of a victim-blaming analysis that attributed poverty's persistence to the poor's cultural values.[5]

For some conservative social theorists and policymakers who subscribe to the culture-of-poverty thesis, the obvious implication is that no policy will reduce poverty. Political scientist Edward Banfield, for example, wrote that the inner-city poor were oriented toward pleasure in the present, and no liberal reforms could change those self-destructive attitudes and values. More recently, Lawrence Mead has argued that inner-city youths have high unemployment rates because they choose idleness over work. Since this explanation often jibes with popular impressions about how the poor behave, it has seemed a reasonable explanation for why some people are trapped in poverty—especially when juxtaposed with the more abstract structural argument that ignores the importance of responsible behavior like finishing school, holding down a job, or waiting to have children until marriage.[6]

Sociologist Ann Swidler suggests that we can better understand why people behave the way they do if we think of culture not as values that guide our behavior but rather as a "tool-kit of symbols, stories, rituals, and worldviews" that we assemble as we grow up and experience the world. Culture, she says, is "more like a set of skills and habits than a set of preferences or wants." It is not so much our values but what we know. "People may share common aspirations, while remaining profoundly different in the way culture organizes their overall pattern of behavior." When we make a choice in life, we reach into our tool kit and select familiar tools so we can, to use sociologist Pierre Bourdieu's phrase, do what people "like us" do. Swidler gives the example of a "slum youth" who is asked why he does not do what is necessary to become a doctor. He never says he does not want to be a doctor. He says, "Who, me?" He cannot even imagine being a doctor. It would take a style, skills and habits, experiences and know-how that are not in his tool kit.[7] We can imagine Wanda Turner in Blackwell or Caroline Gage in Dahlia responding in just the same way. *Me?*

The insight captured in Swidler's metaphor is that our tool kits are shaped by what we experience in the social world, by the relationships we have and by the larger community context in which those relationships occur. As children our social world is our family, and we get our sense of who we are and who we can become from what our parents and other relatives tell us and show us. This process of socialization is something we all experience and recognize, and it is why we so often look to families to provide the foundation for future success. When we are older, we venture out into the neighborhood and into school, where friends and teachers give us more information about how the world works, what the rules are, and how we, and our families, fit. Through our social relationships—first in our families, then in our neighborhoods and social networks, later in social institutions and organizations like schools, youth groups, and workplaces, we acquire the habits and skills, stories and view of the world that we use when we make decisions about how to act.

This understanding is why we often expect schools to compensate for the lack of family resources available to poor children. It also helps explain why mentors can help low-income youths overcome disadvantages and envision a positive future for themselves. Over the past ten years, more and more scholars have applied this understanding about the important role played by the community, or the effects of the "neighborhoods," in studies of poor children and youths.[8]

Sociologist William Julius Wilson has led this theoretical development, arguing that urban poverty persists because of the combined, interacting effects of joblessness, deteriorating neighborhoods, and the "oppositional" culture these forces generate. He argues that inner-city poverty was exacerbated during the 1970s and 1980s when work disappeared from their communities and the poor became more isolated from the mainstream. Urban communities like Chicago lost good blue-collar jobs to the suburbs and overseas locations. At the same time, stable working-class families were moving out because antidiscrimination laws opened up suburban housing to African Americans and affirmative action created new employment opportunities for many college-educated minorities.[9]

Since fewer people in the neighborhoods were working, the disadvantaged had fewer connections for getting jobs and fewer positive role models. A decline in the number of two-parent families meant that children and teenagers received less supervision and needed to survive on smaller family incomes. Crucial community institutions like schools, recreation centers, neighborhood stores, and churches that depend on resources provided by stable working- and middle-class residents declined or disappeared altogether. The depressed conditions and disorganized neighborhoods meant that poor youths were more vulnerable to gangs and drugs, as well as more likely to leave school or have children out of wedlock. Wilson describes the process as a combination of structural, psychological, and cultural effects, connecting acquisition of one's cultural tool kit to community conditions.

> Social isolation deprives residents of inner-city neighborhoods not only of resources and conventional role models, whose former presence buffered the effects of neighborhood joblessness, but also of the kind of cultural learning from mainstream social networks that facilitates social and economic advancement in modern industrial society. The lack of neighborhood material resources, the relative absence of conventional role models, and the circumscribed cultural learning produce outcomes . . . that restrict social mobility.[10]

Poor men and women in Blackwell and Dahlia experience the same social isolation that Wilson describes in parts of urban America. Jobs are scarce, and people from "bad families," like they are, do not have steady, well-paying jobs. The behavior of young people in Blackwell and Dahlia is often similar to that of inner-city poor youth—they drop out of school, have children out of wedlock, "run wild," and depend on welfare. But despite their segregation by class and race, they are embedded, as we have seen, in social relationships with the haves.

CLASS AND POLITICS IN RURAL COMMUNITIES

The social structure of these chronically poor Appalachian and Delta communities is made up, fundamentally, of two classes: upper-class families that control the resources and participate in mainstream economic and political life, and lower-class families that are powerless, dependent, and do not participate. The poverty of the have-nots is inseparable from the privilege of the haves. As historian E. P. Thompson has put it, class is

> something which in fact happens (and can be shown to have happened) in human relationships. . . . The relationship must always be embodied in real people and in a real context. Moreover, we cannot have two distinct classes, each with an independent being, and then bring them *into* relationship with each other. We cannot have love without lovers, nor deference without squires and labourers. And class happens when some men, as a result of common experiences (inherited or shared), feel and articulate the identity of their interests as between themselves, and as against other men whose interests are different from (and usually opposed to) theirs. The class experience is largely determined by the productive relations into which men are born—or enter involuntarily.[11]

Studying rural communities offers advantages for making the connection between the face-to-face relations and common experiences people have and larger social processes involving structures of class and power. Rural communities like Blackwell, Dahlia, and Gray Mountain are a "micro" social world where we can see people from different social classes and racial groups interact, and even track the evolution of these relations over time. Class and race relations "happen" within the boundaries of a coherent place, and people have direct experience with how they matter, with their consequences for the families they know.[12]

Contemporary social patterns and norms in Blackwell and Dahlia are anchored in the way the economy was organized a century ago. The extraordinary power of coal barons or plantation bossmen played out in actions that became part of social life and eventually social history. One day a coal operator set up a company store and required miners to shop there, or a plantation bossman told his workers their children would continue to pick cotton, and miss school, even after the plantation schools were closed. Maybe during an election in Blackwell the owner of a coal company handpicked the sheriff, who then ran out unruly laborers interested in organizing a union. Maybe a sharecropper who questioned the bossman's handling of his account was evicted and blackballed from employment. Over time these decisions, rules, and experiences that are grounded in the structure of class power and racial oppression and define how people relate to one another become patterns that people expect, norms governing how things are always done. They form the civic culture in the community.

These relationships and norms are reinforced by overt action of those who benefit from them, but they are also maintained through memory and tradition, reputation and family history. People know one another's families across generations, their good deeds and bad, power and vulnerability, successes and failures. Boom and bust cycles in the economy, acts of resistance and accommodation, are recorded not only in official historical records but also in peoples' decisions about work, family, or migration. The structure of daily life that takes shape over time is taken for granted. Because new ideas and new resources rarely penetrate this environment that the powerful have deliberately kept closed off—worlds apart—from the larger society, people form their cultural tool kit in the context of the relationships and norms they know. Their immediate social context shapes who they become and how they see their options, both as individuals and as a community. When people in Blackwell or Dahlia question the patterns of inequality, they are likely to face retribution from those in power, but they also are distrusted by those who have accepted life as it is.

While the poor in Appalachia and the Delta are trapped in dead-end, part-time jobs and ignored in disorganized schools, vulnerable to the internal politics and personal whims of managers, the haves live comfortably in a "rural suburbia." In Dahlia they send their children to the private school, in Blackwell to the independent public school in the county seat. With their neighbors, they support school and church programs that benefit their own families. They know one another, look out for each other's children, and devote themselves above all to their families and churches. In many ways their lives include all the good things we look for in small-community life—familiarity, neighborliness, safety, an unhurried pace. In fact, within their own social class, their everyday lives and relationships have much in common with the good relations everyone talks about in Gray Mountain.

But in Blackwell and Dahlia, professionals, small-business owners, government workers, and salespeople who have middle-class incomes or occupations hold themselves apart from the disadvantaged. They consciously put themselves in a group with the very wealthy, whom they emulate and often envy, and distance themselves from the poor, whom they deride as lazy and deviant. They disapprove of how the poor behave and do not view them as productive members of their community. They see them seek out charity, both public and private, rather than take a job mowing lawns or bagging groceries. They see young people in these families drop out of school, have children out of wedlock, abuse alcohol or drugs, get in trouble with the law—self-destructive behavior that confirms their notion that the poor have thrown opportunity away rather than been denied it. They do not want their children to associate with poor kids, and they deliberately maintain a two-class system.

When middle-income families ally themselves with the rich and powerful and safeguard their privileges and control, there is no group that holds local politicians or private employers accountable for good, fair government or just labor practices. There is no group investing time and money to build strong public institutions like schools, recreation facilities and programs, or libraries. Potential middle-class families look out for their own interests, and they do so through separate institutions and activities. They accept the corruption and patronage, watch out for their own family's well-being, and do not challenge the status quo. Consequently, their alliance with the elite and deliberate segregation affect not just the poor but the nature of the whole community.

The resulting distrust and greed that people perceive in public and private life prevent cooperation. Participation and open politics are discouraged, sometimes in subtle ways, other times through deliberate punishment of the activists and their family members. Investment in public, collective community goods is neglected or consciously eschewed. The poor are scorned and stigmatized, blamed for the failure of the public schools that supposedly serve them, and vulnerable to the politicians and powerful families who control scarce jobs. They do not have the economic independence and political clout necessary to change the public schools and other public programs that can make up for what their families lack. They have never had the experience of participating in an open, honest system—for this too is missing from their tool kit. When communities are rigidly divided by class, as in Blackwell, or by race and class, as in Dahlia, upward mobility is blocked and community change is thwarted.

These class and racial divisions, the atmosphere of distrust, and patterns of corruption emerged from the historical organization of local economies and from relationships evolving over time. In the early days of Appalachia's coal economy and the Delta's plantation economy, operators and bossmen maintained tight control over workers—not just in the workplace but in every dimension of social and political life. Community organizations of workers were discouraged or actively repressed. There were company and plantation stores where workers became indebted. Education was given little support and meager resources. And corrupt politics, arbitrary law enforcement, and complete control were firmly established. Those who challenged the system were punished. Although these actions went against the laws and American ideology that guaranteed democratic rules and equal opportunity, no outside force effectively intervened.

Poor people learned that the way to get along was to accept the way things were, to do what was expected of them, to not speak out or make waves. The combination of ignorance and fear of repercussions made the poor prey to and, often, participants in a corrupt system. Those who did not accept the status quo found themselves ostracized or openly encouraged to leave, forced to choose "exit" over "voice," to use development scholar Albert O. Hirschman's terms for migration and political activism.[13] In most cases those who gained an education had to leave to find decent work and to experience the freedom and independence to which they had come to feel entitled. The inequality and political grip of the powerful in Blackwell and Dahlia remained entrenched.

In contrast, Gray Mountain has benefited from trust, widespread participation, and steady, ongoing community investment. Again, different social relations and patterns were established early. Industry leaders lived in town next to the workers and sent their children to the same schools. They invested in education and culture for adults as well as children—in part because they saw it as good for business and in part because it fit their sense of community responsibility—and thus established civic norms of philanthropy and volunteerism. Diverse ethnic groups brought and maintained rich cultural traditions and active social organizations, run by and for workers. These organizations supplied real, material help like access to credit and health care. Just as important, they established habits of widespread participation. Steady work in a stable industry, combined with community-wide commitment to education, laid the foundation of a broad, independent, blue-collar middle class. This middle class, together with the civic responsibility demonstrated by the mill owners' investments and the workers' participation in community organizations, created a rich civic culture.

Thus we see greater equality and participation from the early days of the mill town through to the present. People today say they live in a community where differences are small and unimportant. Local business leaders feel a sense of responsibility to the community, and in their businesses and their community work they value trust and the lack of guile. The five women who work together to establish programs in Gray Mountain have a sense of belonging that comes with their collaboration with one another and their investment in the broader community. Mill workers and carpenters are involved in community organizations, helping to rebuild the hockey arena or put up a new playground, holding the school board accountable and ensuring strong programs that serve everyone's children. Trust, participation, and public investment emerged here in the late 1800s and have been sustained by a large middle class that is committed to the community as a whole.

When Gwen Boggs, the fast-food worker raising children in Blackwell, and Caroline Gage, the sewing factory worker raising children in Dahlia, matured and recognized that they had "messed up," as they would put it, and wanted to make a better life for their children, they faced formidable obstacles. They still looked and talked differently from those in the mainstream, and they had no social connections to employers in places where connections are everything. After all, they had grown up in an isolated hollow and on a remote plantation where life had been hard, in small, crowded, substandard houses. When they went to school, teachers and students reminded them that they were from poor families, that their daddies and mamas did not succeed. School was chaotic and even dangerous, and little learning went on. Neither was encouraged to finish school.

Gwen, Caroline, and others like them never acquired the cultural tool kit and social contacts that would permit them to walk the bridge to the world of steady workers and stable families. They were left behind. Even now, when they want more for their children, they do not feel they have the experience and contacts they would need to improve their children's schools. What is more, the civic culture discourages such activism. If they raise questions about the school's failures, there may be repercussions and they might lose what little they have. Opportunities in Blackwell and Dahlia are controlled by the haves for the haves.

Deborah Shannon, the young dropout who had a child out of wedlock in Gray Mountain, did get a second chance. She came from a troubled family, her father was an alcoholic, her mother relied on welfare for many years, and hard family times got her down. She "ran wild" and dropped out, just as Gwen Boggs and Caroline Gage had. Her behavior is not different, but the social context in her community is. She has friends in the middle class because Gray Mountain is open and inclusive. Her school, which is used by the middle class, provided real education while she was there. Thus she developed a cultural tool kit that expanded rather than restricted her choices as an adult. Here the poor are fewer in number and they are not treated as different and inferior. Instead of family reputation and political affiliation, merit is more likely to guide the distribution of opportunities. She can realize her goals and strive for her dreams.

We know from seeing a few people in Blackwell and Dahlia escape poverty that generous individuals can inspire and prod poor children so they get out from under the disadvantages of their background. Joanne and John Martin benefited from farsighted teachers, Diana Smith's stepmother was a real inspiration to her, Clare Green's grandparents pushed him far. These mentors played the same role that teachers and coaches played for Jeff Berk and Dan Tourneau, who overcame poor backgrounds in Gray Mountain—they were kind, forward-looking people who could see potential beyond someone's family background. Today the Martins and a handful of others in Blackwell and Diana Smith, Coach Wilson, and a few others in Dahlia carry out this role.

But in Gray Mountain the actions of these inspirational teachers and coaches are the norm, the way things are done, not the exception. Trust, wide participation and cooperation, and community-wide investment make up the civic culture. And that civic culture, as we have seen, germinated and grew in a community where the middle class made up the majority. The "class interests" of these middle-class families were best served by trust, inclusiveness, and investment in the public sector. Generous individuals' actions matter, and can help a few escape, but the patterns of action and relationships over time that make up the larger community context dominate social life. The constellation of social classes—their relative sizes, how they relate, and how they see their interests best served—determines the community culture in which opportunities are allocated. In Blackwell and Dahlia, the rigid two-class structure, and the self-serving, corrupt politics it engendered, played a crucial role in restricting Gwen's and Caroline's options, while in Gray Mountain the large middle class and its civic culture expanded Deborah's.

EQUALITY, DEMOCRACY, AND SOCIAL CHANGE

Those who study the structural underpinnings of social change consistently find a relationship between greater equality, democracy, and economic development. In a review of development studies, Peter Evans and John Stephens found that nations where property is predominantly in small landholdings rather than large, concentrated estates are more likely to develop a democratic political system when they industrialize. Where democracy is stronger and there is a large, active middle class, the opportunities and benefits associated with development are more widely distributed. Similarly, studies of the industrial revolution in western Europe by Barrington Moore, Jr., and Daniel Chirot show that democracy flourished early in places where there was a strong capitalist middle class whose well-educated members protected their own personal liberties and opportunities. They also found that when it included a large middle class, society was more likely to have open political institutions. In contrast, when the middle class was small, as in many peripheral societies with high inequality or, as Chirot points out, in the American South, political and social institutions tended to be closed and exclusive. Participation was limited to those at the top.[14]

Walter Goldschmidt's classic study comparing California agricultural communities in the 1940s showed that the standard of living was higher in places where ownership and control were more widely distributed. C. Wright Mills and his colleagues showed that civic welfare was greater in American communities dominated by small business and wide ownership. Greater equality in the economy brought greater participation in the political sphere, which in turn contributed to accountability and a better standard of living community-wide. The conclusions drawn from these studies echo the political philosophy of Aristotle, Thomas Jefferson, and Alexis de Tocqueville about how equality contributes to democracy and progress.[15]

More recently, political scientist Robert Putnam examined democracy and civic culture in Italy. In *Making Democracy Work* Putnam compared how well government worked in northern and southern Italy just as a new regional system was being implemented there in the 1970s and 1980s. He found that both democracy and economic development thrived in the north, where social relations had been "horizontal," as he put it, for hundreds of years. Communities in northern Italy have had numerous associations and clubs, recreational as well as political, and he argues that widespread participation in these groups—choral groups is one he often refers to—instilled social trust and habits of cooperation that spill over into the rest of community life, creating the conditions for good government and for economic prosperity.[16]

In contrast, communities in southern Italy have always been characterized by what he calls "vertical" relationships—patronage and personalistic allocation of opportunities, and a concentration of power among landowners who maintain rigid control over peasants. Here there was not widespread participation in small groups, and, as Banfield had argued many years earlier, people looked out only for their own families, not for other community members.[17]

More "horizontal" relations, of course, are possible when there is a more equitable class structure in which power and wealth are not concentrated; "vertical" relations characterize places with high inequality. In southern Italy, the economic and political systems were driven by patronage (where a powerful few give out favors and opportunities to those whom they select), and clientelism (where those at the bottom owe allegiance to those at the top). Gray Mountain clearly resembles Putnam's northern Italy case, whereas Blackwell and Dahlia follow the patterns he found in southern Italy. Putnam found the roots of these differences back as far as the 1100s, concluding that "social patterns plainly traceable from early medieval Italy to today turn out to be decisive in explaining why, on the verge of the twenty-first century, some communities are better able than others to manage collective life and sustain effective institutions."[18]

The southern towns, dominated by large landholders in a feudal system, had a small, powerless middle class of administrators, while the northern towns developed a communal republicanism that included a system of covenants and contracts. In the north, people were citizens rather than servants, and they formed groups such as guilds and associations. Civic commitment and civic engagement were practiced in these groups and in governing, and the ensuing predictable "civil order" gave merchants the confidence they needed to invest and trade. The northern communities thrived. He concludes, "communities did not become civic because they were rich. The historical record strongly suggests precisely the opposite. They became rich because they were civic."[19]

The implication seems to be that the habits and norms of a good civic society in Italy have their roots in medieval times. Indeed, one local reformer in southern Italy called Putnam's conclusions "counsel for despair," since they imply that "the fate of the reform was sealed centuries ago."[20] Putnam believes the lesson is that social context matters: "Where the regional soil is fertile, the regions draw sustenance from regional traditions, but where the soil is poor, the new institutions are stunted." The new structure of regional governments did not bring the southern communities in line with the north because they first need to build "a more civic community," something that, he concludes, must happen through "local transformation of local structures rather than reliance upon national initiatives."[21] As a political scientist interested in how to "make democracy work," Putnam is struck by the powerful impact that long-standing cultural patterns have on contemporary institutions. But by focusing on the importance of these civic norms rather than their foundation in the class structure, he mistakenly concludes that the key that will unlock change lies in the local community. The evidence from Blackwell and Dahlia suggests that, on the contrary, changes at the local level often require outside intervention to break the lock on social affairs held by the haves.

The rich civic culture that makes northern Italy prosperous and Gray Mountain a place where the poor have a better chance of escaping poverty is not just a historical happenstance or an inevitable, natural outcome based on traditions that were inherently more cooperative. The civic norms emerged from a certain political economy and the social relations that economy generated. When a few families wield great power over economic and political life, as they do in Blackwell, Dahlia, and southern Italy, they have the power to maintain the social arrangements and community norms that benefit them. Putnam is right that a new form of government cannot immediately change the effects of class relations developed over centuries. But it is also true that local efforts, even when people have the courage to undertake them, can be stopped, compromised, or commandeered by powerful elites in these places. Local efforts alone have not brought about change. Places like Blackwell and Dahlia, or southern Italy, need a significant outside intervention to provide the fulcrum that can unseat the long-standing social relations and civic norms that block change and perpetuate poverty.

POLICIES TO ENCOURAGE MOBILITY AND BUILD CIVIC CULTURE

In the early 1960s, when President Johnson's Commission on Rural Poverty wrote its report, *The People Left Behind*, and when Gwen Boggs and

Caroline Gage were little children, social conditions were appalling in rural America.[22] Nearly a third of all rural Americans (75 percent in Dahlia and 50 percent in Blackwell) lived in poverty. Houses were substandard, access to health care was rare, and education for the poor was minimal. Caroline Gage recalls that their little two-room house was *hot in the summer and cold in the winter*. Gwen Boggs and Randy Perkins remember having to live on beans and potatoes month after month. Joanne and John Martin talk of children who had never seen a doctor. Black leaders describe being pulled out of school to work in the fields while white children rode by in the school bus. Everyone recalls one-room schoolhouses with neither heat nor trained teachers as common for the children of poor Appalachian mountaineers and Delta sharecroppers.

In many ways, things have improved a great deal in these poor rural communities. Rural poverty is down to 16 percent, in part because so many were forced out by mechanization and left in the 1960s for industrial jobs in growing urban areas. Today, Gwen's trailer and Caroline's house have electricity and indoor plumbing. School, such as it is, is available to all black children in Dahlia year round. These improvements were largely the result of federally funded public investments in infrastructure, housing, and water through the Department of Agriculture's Farmers Home Administration, for example, and federal civil rights laws guaranteeing blacks an equal education.

But as we enter the twenty-first century, nearly nine million Americans live in poverty in rural areas, one third in communities with persistently high poverty rates such as Blackwell and Dahlia—places still left behind.[23] The poor who live in these communities, like their inner-city counterparts, do not participate in the American promise, and their diminished life chances and lack of economic productivity represent the most significant failure of domestic policy in the United States over the past thirty-five years. Alleviating poverty is not a high priority for today's policymakers. Rather we focus our attention on ways to end welfare dependency and move people into the workforce, with surprisingly little discussion about the need to widen opportunities so that those born into poor families can someday leave poverty behind.

National studies show that inequality is growing in America. The Center on Budget and Policy Priorities, a national research organization that analyzes social trends and policy, reports that the incomes of the richest fifth of American families increased by 30 percent between the late 1970s and mid-1990s, while the incomes of the poorest fifth of families with children declined by 21 percent. International trade, global labor markets, a declining manufacturing sector, and technological changes have brought about a growing gap between the upper-middle-class professionals who have high-skilled, high-paying jobs—America's haves—and the working poor in the lower class who make up the have-nots.[24]

Leading scholars and policymakers warn that growing inequality may threaten the whole American social fabric.[25] The stories we have heard in these rural communities give us a firsthand picture of the perils of inequality and the way it can undermine the public sector on which the poor must rely to improve their life chances. Life in Gray Mountain shows the benefits of greater equality, where a large middle class is committed to common public goods, while the social context in Blackwell and Dahlia illustrates the way inequality erodes even basic democracy and undermines equal opportunity. These stories help us better understand the social context and the dynamics of poverty in rural areas, and we can appreciate the conditions that nourish a rich civic culture.

Can we use what we have learned to break the cycle of dependency and vulnerability in these chronically poor areas? Are there policies that can counteract the trends toward greater inequality and an effectively class-segregated society? Are there policies that would affect the seemingly intractable poverty we see in Blackwell and Dahlia?

Scholars and policy analysts William Julius Wilson, Theda Skocpol, Sheldon Danziger and Peter Gottschalk, Rebecca Blank, Robert Reich, and Mickey Kaus have argued for investment in broad, universal social provisions that support families and provide public work as a strategy for dealing with poverty. Wilson, Danziger and Gottschalk, and Kaus stress the need for a new public works program, along the lines of the Works Progress Administration of the New Deal, to ensure that employment is available. Skocpol and Blank place special emphasis on the need for programs that put a floor under all families to protect them from unemployment and health problems and facilitate their education and training. Kaus, following political theorist Michael Walzer, describes his vision as "civic liberalism"—investment in the public sector to counter trends toward inequality in a market-driven, postindustrial economy shaped by global corporations. He argues for public investment in the "egalitarian public sphere of life," describing this as "a public, community sphere—where money doesn't 'talk,' where the principles of the marketplace (i.e., rich beats poor) are replaced by the principle of equality of citizenship. . . . Instead of worrying about distributing and redistributing income, [civic liberalism] worries about rebuilding, preserving, and strengthening community institutions in which income is irrelevant, about preventing their corruption by the forces of the market."[26]

These scholars call for a stronger, more comprehensive federal role to make equal opportunity a reality for all Americans. They fear that growing social inequality and increased segregation by class and race are undermining the nation's civic culture. Each recognizes that recommending increased federal investment in public goods is not "practical," given current trends toward devolution of social programs to the states and policymakers' interest in privatization and market-driven solutions for social problems. Nonetheless, they call for broad, universal policies to bridge class and race divides and to ensure political support in the long run. Wilson, for example, says it is crucial that these opportunities be "aimed at broad segments of the U.S. population, not just inner-city workers, in order to provide the needed solid political base of support." Skocpol, in making her case for a new "family security program," also argues that "universal" provisions are essential to garner broad-based political support from cross-class coalitions to fund the programs: "The history of the modern social security system demonstrates that Americans will accept taxes that they perceive as contributions toward public programs in which there is a direct stake for themselves, their families, and their friends, not just for 'the poor.'"[27]

Investment in public goods especially benefits those with fewer resources. A stronger, more comprehensive public sphere that provided work and family support would help the poor in Blackwell and Dahlia. Of course, it is in Gwen Boggs's family's best interests to have public health insurance, while it does not matter as much to Donna and Jim Campton, who have steady jobs with good benefits. A public works project would greatly benefit John Cooper in Dahlia and Virgil Bratcher in Blackwell, both of whom are desperate for steady work and economic independence. It matters little to Sharon and Edward Carter, and might even mean they would have to pay higher wages at their new fast-food restaurant. Public investment, or its absence, is part of what determines the social arrangements—our rules for who gets what and how. Families in the upper class often see their interests best served by a minimal public sector and as much local control as possible, while those in the lower class want the social arrangements that govern the allocation of resources to include more public goods. When middle-class families make up the majority, as they do in Gray Mountain, they see investment in the public sector being in their families' best interests, and poor families benefit because they too participate in the institutions the middle class builds for its own families.

We have seen how the people in Gray Mountain put resources into public schools and public parks and public hockey rinks. A place where inequality is not great and civic norms are inclusive, like Gray Mountain, is more likely to make local decisions to invest in a public sector that is open to everyone regardless of social class. But national resources and, perhaps more important, greater federal oversight are needed to build the public sphere in places where wealth and power are distributed unequally. Since those who control the resources in Blackwell and Dahlia are well connected to powerful politicians at the state level, they are likely to prevail when changes in the social arrangements are proposed at the local or state level. We saw that Dahlia's former superintendent, Jack Peabody, was praised for keeping costs down, and white school administrators frequently bypassed opportunities to bring in federal programs to benefit the disadvantaged because they might increase costs or entail federal oversight. In Blackwell we saw many public programs effectively commandeered by local politicians and made part of the patronage system because there is little accountability.

Federal programs like food stamps, Medicaid, and Head Start have been crucial sources of support for the rural poor. Children in the families we met in Blackwell and Dahlia would be even worse off without the assistance they receive from federal programs. The fact that these programs include federal oversight means they are generally less vulnerable to manipulation by the local elite who might try to use them as rewards or punishment. Recall that Creed Parker could not prevent the man he fired from receiving food stamps, and federal projects are required to have a diverse board of directors, so Diana and Charles Smith and Coach Wilson have a voice and hear about opportunities for the poor that are available to communities like theirs. Federal programs and federal rules can equalize opportunity and, with rigorous oversight, are less likely to be captured by the local and state elites who benefit from the status quo. As unpopular as the ideas are in an era of downsizing government, a public works jobs program and a universal family support program that provides a floor below which families cannot fall would be an enormous help to the poor we have met, most of whom work and struggle to patch together a livelihood in an economy with scarce jobs and low wages and no benefits.

But fundamental changes in American social arrangements seem far down the road. As Skocpol and her colleagues and Jill Quadagno have shown in their historical analyses of social policy, America's commitment to government decentralization and local control, combined with fierce competition among regional economies that is reinforced by powerful politicians, as well as long-standing ambivalence toward racial integration, have prevented such changes time and time again.[28] Public investment in broad family support and widespread work opportunities would certainly bring America closer to meeting its promise to all citizens. It would make the nation's social arrangements more closely resemble those in Gray Mountain, assuring greater equality of opportunity through the public sphere. But history as well as contemporary trends suggest that such a change will likely be a long time coming.

There is, however, one straightforward policy that would immediately help the poor in both rural and urban America: creating good public schools. A decent education, like that available in the nation's suburbs, would immediately expand the poor's cultural tool kit in significant ways. Education is always the first step for those who have moved from poverty and disadvantage in the lower class to stability and opportunity in the middle class. Joanne and John Martin left their poor farm and mountain backgrounds behind when they finished high school and went on to college. Diana Smith and Coach Wilson escaped the devastating poverty of their plantation childhoods when they finished school and went on to college. Everyone who has "made it" in Blackwell and Dahlia finished school, and everyone who finished school and went to college has left poverty behind. Education is, just as the American Dream has always implied, an avenue for upward mobility for individuals. But most schools in America's poor communities do not offer that opportunity.

One thing that makes establishing good schools a viable policy idea, even as we enter the twenty-first century, is that doing so does not require a complete turnabout in American social welfare policy. And the idea that every American child is entitled to a good public education is a well-established part of American ideology. Local control over education is, of course, also a strongly held tenet, and it is clear that creating good schools to serve poor children would require challenging local control, at least as it works in poor places like Blackwell and Dahlia. Our allegiance to the principle of local control in these places, as in the inner-city schools described by Jonathan Kozol, Alex Kotlowitz, William Julius Wilson, and others, protects bad practices and absolves us all of responsibility to provide equal opportunity for all American children.[29] The system cries out for change.

The public schools used by the have-nots in Blackwell and Dahlia are chaotic and ineffective because a bad form of local control goes unchallenged. No one holds accountable administrators and teachers who fail to do their jobs, and there is little support for principals and teachers who try to improve the schools. Petty patronage politics dominate decision making, and school jobs are rewards for the loyal lieutenants who form the base of the pyramid of political power in the community. Everyone acknowledges the schools' failure, even the elite and other haves who blame the parents and "elected" school boards for these districts. Of course, everyone agrees that these school board seats can be won only with the acquiescence, if not the active support, of these same elite families.

Education is not only the key to individual mobility in these communities. It is also the necessary catalyst for political change. Coal operators and plantation bosses deliberately restricted access to education in the late 1800s and early 1900s because they recognized its potentially disruptive impact. Even now some plantation bossmen are said to resist efforts of literacy workers to reach their employees. Local politicians like Judge Bobby Lee King in Blackwell and Charles Smith and Michael Long in Dahlia say their communities need economic independence before there will be political independence and true democracy. They recall the economic sanctions leveled against those who sought change, and they see day to day the way economic dependency translates into political dependency. They need a critical mass of people acting independently, and they believe that independence must have its roots in jobs that are not controlled by the elite. They know that in the past those who were educated left. Out-migration has always been, and continues to be, a component of maintaining the status quo. Indeed, the elites promote out-migration when they blackball troublemakers and resist diversification or job growth.

But those who are educated and do stay or return to their home communities—the Martins, the Smiths, Coach Wilson—actively participate in political life and community institutions as critical, public-minded citizens. Those who work for change in Blackwell and Dahlia, like community leaders across the nation involved in economic development efforts, see that economic diversity is the foundation of a vital and independent middle class. A community with a vibrant middle class is a developed community, as Robert Putnam found, in which the civic norms include trust, and businesspeople can invest and grow with confidence. But while history has shown this analysis to be right, it has also shown how hard it is to create jobs and new development, especially in remote places where workers lack skills and education. Homegrown businesses, while important and good, are fragile, and companies that can be attracted to these communities, even when the elite is open to new jobs, are generally footloose and show little commitment to community development. Thus poverty and underdevelopment seem intractable and the status quo firmly entrenched.

Still, people's ability to think and vote more independently holds promise for transforming the current structure. Critical thinking facilitates their ability to find better ways to make a living and create new social institutions. Effective schools would create these critical thinkers, who then would either find ways to improve themselves and their communities or leave for opportunities elsewhere. But in either case they would escape poverty in greater numbers. Young people who graduate from high school with a real education are unlikely to depend on welfare, far more likely to achieve mobility. There is no mystery here. Study after study shows that educated people are not chronically poor.

When schools are merely patronage delivery systems or targets of discriminatory neglect, it takes special intervention by a mentor to get a child an education. If federal funding—and, more important, federal accountability—replaced the local control that has permitted these schools to run amok, and made a meaningful educational experience available to poor children, many more would achieve the American Dream. And these individuals, like the tiny emerging middle class in Dahlia, would contribute to breaking down the walls that seal off these communities from the rest of the world. More community groups and organizations would have educated participants, as in Gray Mountain, instilling new habits of democratic participation, establishing new civic norms of engagement.

Creating good schools in these communities that are worlds apart from mainstream, suburban America requires replacing local control and local funding of education with national standards and equitable funding. When the economy is healthy and participation in political life is widespread, as in Gray Mountain, local control can release initiative, leadership, and energy in the community. But in the feudal kingdoms of Blackwell and Dahlia, these principles sustain the two-class society that perpetuates poverty. Changing the quality of schools in places like Blackwell and Dahlia will, of course, require local participants and commitment—people who want to see change and will work for it. But another thing we have seen in Blackwell and Dahlia is that these potential reformers are already there, working quietly in some cases, despairing about the prospects for change in others. A national program to ensure good public schools, accountable and challenging, would unleash the energy of existing change agents as well as would-be activists. Just as the new goals and procedures of the Family Support Act transformed the way the same people acted in the social welfare programs in Blackwell, a vigorous, well-designed national education intervention could change the old ways of running schools. It could be a vehicle for local community leaders to gain more power and unleash their energy and creativity. We know how to make good schools, and we know what they look like. We need the will to make them available to America's poor children.

The path out of poverty is remarkably similar across all three communities described here. Poor people who achieve mobility have been purposefully guided toward graduating from high school and often college, even though that achievement is a huge leap from the everyday context in which they formed their cultural tool kits. Some were prodded and inspired by a mother or father, others by an aunt, grandmother, teacher, nun, coach—anyone who took a personal interest and showed them options beyond their immediate surroundings. Others had the opportunity to see life outside their community, by visiting relatives in another city, for example, or joining the military. But when we take into account all that we have seen about poverty and culture and politics in Blackwell, Dahlia, and Gray Mountain, there is one factor that stands out. In every case, a good education is the key that unlocks and expands the cultural tool kits of the have-nots, and thus gives them the potential to bring about lasting social change in their persistently poor communities. With good public schools available to everyone, the have-nots would no longer be isolated in worlds apart from the haves, and poor communities like Blackwell and Dahlia would no longer be worlds apart from the rest of America.

POLICY FOR POOR PEOPLE IN POOR PLACES

Fifteen years ago I concluded that the oppressive civic culture and corrupt community politics that had emerged from the political economy in Blackwell and Dahlia were so entrenched that only an outside intervention could bring about change. I argued for a federal effort to make public schools work in these poor communities where the haves looked out only for the institutions serving their own families. Reflecting on my recent visits, I still believe federally supported human capital investment is the best strategy to help poor people in poor places. In fact, parental-support programs for children to age three and quality early childhood education have been shown to be especially effective in building a foundation that enables poor children to do better and escape poverty.

But human capital investment occurs through institutions embedded in a community. Investing in poor people, especially poor children, is important but not sufficient. As we have seen, when local institutions in poor communities are broken, the kind of local community organizing that African Americans have used in Dahlia to hold them accountable is critical as well. Poverty persists when members of an elite group control politics to benefit their own interests, and change is possible only when the politics change. The designers of the War on Poverty recognized that organizing was critical to achieving voice for the poor and thus real change, and poverty warriors since have continued to incorporate it to a greater or lesser extent depending on the context in which they work. Poor communities need outside investment in their children, and they need simultaneous local action to, as Putnam put it in his study of politics and change in Italy, "build a more civic community" to ensure that the investment can be effective.

Blackwell has had neither outside intervention nor signs of new organizing, and has been in decline, steadily losing jobs and population, especially coal jobs and younger people. Poverty and dependency remain high. Prescription drug abuse is pervasive. The same handful of families controls the businesses, the jobs, and the land. Corrupt, patronage-driven politics has been diluted over the years, but the old ways are still intact enough for the coal operators to prevent economic development and the good-old-boy school leadership to obstruct educational progress that might threaten their hegemony. For fifteen years Johnny Bledsoe worked for Blackwell and its surrounding coal counties in the state legislature, trying to improve education and to mitigate the effects of strip mining. But even as his school reform efforts began to bear fruit statewide, Blackwell coal operators and school board members used their power over scarce jobs to defeat him.

The region's coal industry will contract further—it is the end of an era. As Benny Corbett said, *coal's over* for Blackwell. Jobs in natural resources number only a quarter of what they were in the 1980s. While the community college and its programs provide opportunity for some, there is little evidence that local politics will change or new businesses or jobs will emerge in this remote, isolated, environmentally damaged region. People focus on their families and find ways to stay in Blackwell to be near them and, in many cases, to help them cope.

Dahlia experienced a big change in the 1990s when the casinos brought thousands of jobs to the area. People who were prepared—had some threshold level of education—seized the opportunity. The poverty rate was cut in half. Although casinos with their low-paying jobs are not considered a desirable engine of economic development, in a place as poor and desperate as Dahlia they have brought a form of economic and political progress. Millions in revenue pour into the county every year, permitting lavish investment in public infrastructure and new public jobs. College-educated black professionals could return home to Dahlia after school and find decent work. The black middle class grew to include not only the teachers, preachers, and juke joint or funeral home owners of earlier times, but now also casino and public-sector workers and retired return migrants.

Community organizing has been going on quietly for many years, but the "outside intervention" of the casinos gave the organizers' efforts new power. In 2012 African American political aspirants and their black middle-class supporters reached out to voters, especially young voters, and, buoyed by turnout for the Obama candidacy, took over county government. They were reaping years of patient mentoring by other black politicians in the state and tireless youth organizing by dedicated black leaders working in the poor black neighborhoods. Leaders in the black community, both the so-called radicals and those from the more traditional "good name" families, have long recognized that getting out from under and getting ahead were about organizing to gain political power. If they can bring expenses under control, the newly elected black school superintendent and the all-black county board of supervisors may be able to capitalize on the casino economy to improve public schools and neighborhoods for black families.

Like Blackwell, Gray Mountain has gone through a profound economic transition, losing thousands of decent manufacturing jobs. But without the burden of a large poor population, and with its community-minded civic culture intact, Gray Mountain has navigated a transition to a new economy that looks like many rural places in the twenty-first century—prisons, green energy projects, recreation facilities. The schools continue to prepare young people for work, some in the region, many elsewhere, and they are trying to wrap in the new low-income families who moved to the community for lower-cost housing, accommodating their needs and showing them the Gray Mountain way. People worked deliberately to retain what they value in their community—sports, outdoor activities, good schools, and a cooperative community spirit. While those in Blackwell say family holds them to the mountains, those in Gray Mountain say community holds them to the place.

Twenty years ago both Blackwell and Dahlia were mired in persistently high poverty. The chaotic and ineffective schools attended by the have-nots served only as political spoils. Poor families were held captive by the legacy of control and underinvestment that characterized the political economy of the coal industry and plantation agriculture in the nineteenth century. Coal operators and plantation bossmen had deliberately kept miners and field workers uneducated and vulnerable. They wanted cheap and compliant labor, fearing unions in coal country and civil rights organizing in the Delta.

This history of exploitation and vulnerability created the two-class society we encountered in the 1990s, the haves and have-nots, who were worlds apart. There was corruption and patronage, an entrenched patron-client social system, a broken civil sphere. The haves looked out for their own families, and sent their children to separate schools that did not face the challenge of educating large numbers of poor children.

In contrast, middle-income blue-collar families were the majority in Gray Mountain, and there were not deep divisions or institutions segregated by class. People trusted one another, participated in community organizations, and invested in the public sphere and a wide range of nonprofit organizations. Mill owners and community leaders valued education. The relatively small poor population benefited from good public schools attended by middle-income and less-well-off families alike.

The three-way comparison twenty years later has proved instructive. Blackwell is isolated and dependent on a dying coal industry. There are no local organizing efforts to challenge the old politics. The families who run things are still mostly looking after their own interests; others have left or hunkered down to take care of their families. Gray Mountain, enduring a less severe but similar economic shock, used its strong civic capital and community institutions to respond with pragmatic resilience. It was contentious at times, but most now agree that the community is pulling together.

Dahlia, with its new jobs and new politics, may be on its way to overcoming more than a century of poverty. Although the planters still control the same economic assets in their farms and land, they no longer control all the jobs and they no longer control local government. The new black leadership is more community-minded, more like the leadership in Gray Mountain. The question is whether these leaders can tackle the excessive spending of casino revenue over recent years and then use the resources they do have to bring about real change in their community and its institutions.

Poverty analysts, policymakers, and politicians have long cast the debate about why poverty persists in terms of culture versus structure, or human agency versus larger economic and social forces beyond the control of individuals. Conservatives emphasized personal responsibility and attributed poverty to bad decisions and bad behavior. Progressives would stress the barriers poor people face, from racism and sexism to the distribution of opportunity for education and work and the growing prevalence of low-wage jobs.

William Julius Wilson's work in the 1980s challenged this dichotomy, and inspired the research underlying *Worlds Apart*. In his study of poverty in Chicago, Wilson found that structural factors like job availability or the presence of a middle class affected culture, or how the poor behaved. Without jobs, without the examples and the institutional investments of a middle class, the poor experienced social isolation and turned to gangs or drugs, had children young and out of wedlock, and dropped out of school, making bad choices that further cut them off from participation in the mainstream. The have-nots in Blackwell and Dahlia were socially isolated as well, made to understand that they were from the "bad families" from whom little was expected. Like their urban counterparts, their isolation, the often unstable, stressful family situations they experienced, and the failed schools they attended deprived them of the cultural learning necessary to succeed in school and work. In Blackwell and Dahlia we met poor people, young and grown, who were rough, illiterate, living isolated in the hollows or out on a plantation. They scrabbled and scratched to make ends meet, and they were looked down upon by those who had education and steady jobs.

Nobel economist Amartya Sen says the poor are people who are deprived of basic "capabilities."[30] These include the capacity to have good health, to be literate, and other capabilities critical to "leading long, healthy and creative lives," as Mahbub ul-Haq, the development scholar who created the Human Development Index, put it. Sen argues that the aim of development is to build those capabilities. Using the word "deprived" acknowledges the structural and institutional, indeed the political, origins of poverty. People from poor families did not choose to be poorly educated or unhealthy. They may make bad choices, dropping out of school, having children too young, getting involved in substance abuse. But as Wilson showed, those bad decisions are connected to their community's conditions and its failed institutions. We have seen black leaders in Dahlia use the word "deprived" to describe how they were treated by whites. *We were locked out of everything, and also deprived educationally. On an education level we were deprived.*

Law and ethics professor Martha Nussbaum emphasizes the important role institutions play in building capability. She argues that we should think about what people can do and be, what they are capable of, and that supporting those capabilities requires "affirmative material and institutional support, not simply (as the neo-liberals would have it) a failure to impede."[31] She asks, "How can they flourish?" If children from families with few resources are to achieve the American Dream through hard work, they need more than a good attitude. They need adequate material and cultural resources to participate in the mainstream. Sociologist Peter Townsend defined poverty as "the lack of adequate resources to permit participation in the activities, customs and diets commonly approved by society," noting that "as resources diminish, there occurs a sudden withdrawal from participation."

Nussbaum and her colleagues remind us that a free-market approach to poverty alleviation does not create the capacity for participation. The poor need institutions that build their cultural tool kit, their capacity to learn and be healthy, to be literate, to acquire skills—work skills and also "life skills." We saw this in Dahlia when the new job opportunities at the casinos came and many workers were unprepared to take advantage of them. They needed to be literate, to know what holding a steady job entailed. *They need support to maintain those jobs.* We saw it when a fine recreation center and extensive youth programs were made available but a whole group of poor children in Dahlia were unable to take advantage of them. *You have to go get them.*

In our visits to Blackwell and Dahlia in 2013 we heard a lot about "mindsets." Some used the word to describe what they saw as the poor's lack of ambition, apathy, or even laziness, acceptance of their own dependency—a street-level explanation of the old culture-of-poverty idea. But local leaders see the connection between the apparent apathy of the poor, their acceptance of their place in the community, and their reluctance to be politically active.

In both Blackwell and Dahlia, they also used mindsets to explain people's failure to challenge the powerful elite, especially in the voting booth. One education leader in Blackwell put it this way: *It's a mindset. It's a mindset. It's folks who've been outta work for years who will still get that signal from the operators, you know, that's what you have to do. You have to go this way*. In Dahlia some black leaders linked the acceptance of one's lot in life to the acceptance of the status quo in economic and political leadership. *So I would say the influence of the white community on our people [persists]. We're trying to change that mindset. That will be the only thing that holds us back from growth, [people who are] scared of change*.

Development scholar Albert Hirschman captured the political roots of development and change in his incisive observation that people in struggling places have three choices: exit, loyalty, or voice. For many years the have-nots and the potential change agents in Blackwell and Dahlia chose either exit, leaving for places where they could find opportunity, or loyalty, accepting their lot and the politics of the place. We saw Johnny Bledsoe and others pushed out of office by the Blackwell families that run things and by those whom they favor with positions and contracts. In Dahlia, with the combination of economic independence and strategic political organizing, new black leaders are exercising their voices for change and the elites no longer have the power to punish them. The challenges are enormous, with poverty still at nearly 30 percent, the schools way behind, and casino revenues shrinking. To paraphrase Karl Marx and C. Wright Mills, "Men and women make their own lives but not under circumstances of their own choosing." People in Gray Mountain, Blackwell, and Dahlia are making decisions about school, about family, about work, and about their communities, and the circumstances, economic and political, are important and consequential.

When I wrote *Worlds Apart* in the 1990s there was alarm about growing inequality in the United States. Scholars pointed out that the widely shared prosperity of the 1950s and 1960s had ended in the early 1970s and workers at the bottom were being left behind. The 1980s and 1990s were a time when a restructured, more global economy meant fewer blue-collar jobs in America, with devastating consequences for workers with only a high school education or less, wherever they lived. At the same time, political attitudes in the country were becoming more conservative, supporting a "free-er" market and moving to minimize regulation and shrink public investment, and tolerating more inequality in wages. The social contract forged in the 1930s and extended in the late 1960s and early 1970s was coming undone.[32]

Today, concern and debate about poverty and inequality continue. But over the past fifteen years we have gathered more evidence about what policies are effective. We know that programs to help low-income parents parent better in the first three years can improve the architecture of poor children's brains, giving them both cognitive and social skills to navigate the mainstream. We know that quality early childhood education can prepare a poor child for school in fundamental ways and change his or her life trajectory.[33] We know decent, supportive schools with high expectations can give poor children the opportunity to get ahead. We know mentoring expands young people's tool kits and aspirations so they can live better lives and contribute to society.[34] We know that support for parents—access to mental health services, parenting guidance, workforce support, additional income—make it possible for poor adults to find some stability, stability that pays off for their children.[35] There is ample evidence that, for families with low-wage workers, the earned-income tax credit and SNAP provide critical stability that children need to learn and develop their potential.[36] We know these institutional supports can build children's and families' capacity to escape poverty. A 2013 Harvard working paper shows that progressive policies expand opportunities for upward mobility.[37] We know that the cost of these programs is made up in the savings we achieve when people are productive and not poor or in trouble.

But we also know from recent work on concentrated urban poverty that builds on Wilson's work in Chicago, and from what we have seen in Blackwell, Dahlia, and Gray Mountain, that place matters. Community context matters. Sociologists Robert Sampson and Patrick Sharkey have documented the cumulative effect of growing up in a disadvantaged community with failed institutions across generations. As Sharkey puts it: "If a child is raised by a parent who grew up in a similarly disadvantaged neighborhood—a parent who was taught in similarly deficient learning environments, who witnessed the same violence, who also had few employment opportunities—it is reasonable to think that the effects of the environment would be amplified, reinforced by the consistency of disadvantage as experienced over generations of a family."[38] Or, as Sampson put it, "legacies of neighborhood inequality are pervasive."[39] Douglas Massey's recent review of their books concludes that they link inheritance of poverty to inheritance of place. He finds the future discouraging, absent "a big intervention."

When I completed the first edition of *Worlds Apart* and went to work at the Ford Foundation as director of community and resource development I was looking for policies that addressed the social isolation of the poor. We looked closely at programs to revitalize public housing by integrating poor families with middle-class families, and our program at the foundation explored and invested in some of these efforts. We watched the federally sponsored research evaluating the Moving to Opportunity program, which relocated poor families to better neighborhoods, to see if they did better when they left their poor neighborhoods. As Sampson, Sharkey, Massey, and now Wilson in his update to *The Truly Disadvantaged* have observed, these programs' design, implementation, and evaluation presented many challenges and complicated results.[40] They were not a silver bullet for poor people in poor places.

But it is interesting that these urban scholars now look hopefully, as I do, to programs that invest in children and families in place, in their communities, from birth or even pre-birth through secondary and post-secondary education—programs like Promise Neighborhoods, which provides grants from the U.S. Department of Education for local initiatives that offer cradle-through-college-career programs for poor children, modeled after the Harlem Children's Zone, which has showed real increases in academic outcomes. Sampson concludes, "Linking investments in early child development with community context is thus an idea whose time has come."[41]

In the 1960s and 1970s we rightly worried about "blaming victims" of poverty, and that was extended to concern about "imposing middle-class values on the poor." There may be those who will criticize home visiting to help low-income parents better understand how to enhance early childhood development or early childhood education programs as interfering in poor families' lives and child rearing, or imposing middle-class values. But neuroscience and behavioral science show that very young children need language and engaged relationships. Stressed parents in poor communities often struggle to provide the stability they need. Research demonstrates that you can get powerful results if you intervene early. We should be giving poor children a more even starting place—with home visiting for fragile, isolated families and access to universal quality early childhood education.

This would be a big investment in better life chances for our "lost" poor children, and our future workforce. We know we would need the Michael Longs and Johnny Bledsoes to be organizing at the community level, changing mindsets and strengthening local institutions. But the whole nation would be more prosperous, and true to its promise of the American Dream, if we were to make a long-term commitment to policies that build poor children's capacity so they can seize opportunity and flourish. We might begin to break the cycle of intergenerational poverty, and break the link between inheritance of poverty and inheritance of place.

Appendix

Table 1. Social and Economic Indicators for Blackwell, Dahlia, and Gray Mountain

	BLACKWELL			
	1980	1990	2000	2010
Population	36,300	31,800	29,200	26,900
Change		–12%	–8%	–8%
Born in state where now residing*	83%	85%	85%	85%
Families	9,900	9,000	8,500	7,600
Female-headed households	1,300	1,500	1,500	1,400
Share of all family households	13%	17%	18%	18%
Grandparent caretaking*	–	–	300	600
Share of all family households	–	–	4%	8%
Births to teens (portion of all births)	27%	27%	–	–
Out of wedlock (portion of all teen births)	22%	37%	–	–
Education level (among those age 25 and over)*				
High school dropouts	16%	20%	19%	15%
High school graduates	38%	47%	59%	70%
College graduates	6%	6%	8%	11%
Employment rate (among those age 16 and over)*				
Men	54%	52%	41%	49%
Women	24%	24%	32%	34%
Disconnected youth (age 16–19 and not in school or working)*	–	–	–	14%
Working-age men with work disability (age 16–64)	22%	22%	24%	–
Employment by family*				
Families with no workers	26%	29%	33%	29%
Families with one worker	47%	41%	36%	40%
Families with two or more workers	28%	30%	32%	31%
Average median family income (in 2012 dollars)*	41,200	32,000	32,300	39,500
Income per capita (in 2012 dollars)*	15,000	13,000	15,700	17,200
Families in poverty*	23%	29%	27%	25%
Families with incomes less than 50% of U.S. median*	39%	53%	52%	48%

Note: A single asterisk indicates that data for 2010 were drawn from the American Community Survey (ACS), 2006–2010. A dash represents no data available for that year. Data for Blackwell and Gray Mountain are averaged from actual study county and a neighboring county; for Dahlia, sum of study county and neighboring county (with the exception of raw income figures, which are averaged data). Real numbers are rounded to nearest hundred. U.S. median family income in 1980 was $21,053, 50% cutoff used is $9,999; U.S. median in 1990 was $35,300, 50% cutoff is $19,999; U.S. median in 2000 was $50,046, 50% cutoff is $24,999; U.S. median in 2010 was $62,982, 50% cutoff is $34,999 (given data constraints).

DAHLIA				GRAY MOUNTAIN			
1980	1990	2000	2010	1980	1990	2000	2010
22,300	18,700	19,300	19,000	31,500	35,100	38,400	40,400
	–16%	3%	–2%		11%	9%	5%
88%	85%	83%	80%	56%	54%	50%	48%
5,100	4,400	4,700	4,600	8,700	9,700	10,700	11,200
1,100	1,300	1,800	1,800	900	1,100	1,300	1,500
22%	30%	38%	39%	10%	11%	12%	13%
–	–	500	400	–	–	100	200
–	–	11%	9%	–	–	1%	2%
29%	35%	25%	26%	17%	15%	8%	9%
82%	92%	94%	99%	42%	65%	80%	87%
17%	25%	24%	18%	15%	14%	11%	8%
34%	46%	58%	68%	68%	77%	83%	88%
8%	9%	10%	13%	15%	17%	20%	24%
57%	52%	57%	56%	65%	66%	65%	63%
31%	38%	46%	47%	41%	53%	56%	52%
–	–	–	32%	–	–	–	6%
14%	15%	20%	–	12%	11%	16%	–
17%	22%	16%	19%	16%	14%	16%	17%
38%	31%	39%	37%	31%	27%	27%	29%
44%	47%	45%	44%	53%	59%	57%	54%
28,400	25,600	33,900	33,500	50,700	56,100	58,400	59,400
11,200	11,300	15,200	15,200	19,600	22,800	26,100	27,100
38%	42%	28%	28%	14%	17%	6%	7%
53%	62%	49%	55%	24%	26%	21%	25%

Sources: U.S. Census, 1980, 1990, 2000, 2010; ACS, 2006–2010; Division of Vital Records Administration, New Hampshire Department of State; Mississippi State Department of Health; West Virginia Health Statistics Center; U.S. DHHS, CDC, National Center for Health Statistics

Table 2. Social and Economic Indicators for Central Appalachia, the Mississippi Delta, Northern New England, and the United States

	CENTRAL APPALACHIA				MISSISSIPPI	
	1980	1990	2000	2010	1980	1990
Population	1.35 mil.	1.26 mil.	1.3 mil.	1.31 mil.	509,384	490,221
Children	32%	27%	24%	22%	36%	32%
Working-age	53%	57%	60%	60%	48%	52%
Elderly	11%	13%	13%	14%	12%	13%
Family households	366,261	355,462	369,030	358,419	122,004	122,592
Households with children	59%	54%	49%	46%	62%	60%
Households with children, female-headed**	6%	8%	9%	9%	12%	16%
Births to teens (portion of all births)	23%	22%	15%	15%	28%	26%
Out of wedlock (portion of all teen births)	31%	51%	63%	80%	75%	85%
Education level (among those 25 and older)*						
High school graduates	41%	51%	62%	72%	47%	58%
College graduates	7%	8%	10%	12%	11%	13%
Employment rate (among those 16 and older)*						
Men	56%	53%	51%	49%	60%	60%
Women	29%	34%	40%	41%	38%	44%
Employment by industry*						
Natural-resource based	22%	14%	7%	8%	11%	9%
Construction	7%	7%	8%	7%	7%	6%
Manufacturing	14%	14%	14%	11%	20%	20%
Transportation, communication, public utilities	7%	7%	6%	5%	6%	6%
Services and trade	43%	51%	55%	59%	46%	51%
Finance, insurance, real estate	3%	4%	4%	4%	3%	3%
Public administration, information	4%	4%	7%	7%	5%	5%
Average median household income (in 2012 dollars)*	$33,324	$28,367	$31,438	$30,634	$31,346	$29,560
Share of labor force self-employed*	8%	8%	7%	6%	7%	7%
Social program use						
Adults receiving Supplemental Security Income	–	7%	10%	11%	–	9%
Adults receiving Social Security	28%	28%	30%	33%	27%	26%
Injury-related mortality (portion of deaths among those under 65)	23%	23%	22%	25%	21%	24%
Poverty rate*	24%	29%	25%	24%	33%	34%

Note: mil. = million. A single asterisk indicates that data for 2010 were drawn from the American Community Survey (ACS), 2006–2010; two asterisks indicate that data for 2010 were drawn from the ACS, 2005–2009. Data availability issues resulted in data on births to teens and out-of-wedlock births to teens being drawn from a reduced number of counties for Central Appalachia (all decades) and northern New England (2000 and 2010).

DELTA		NORTHERN NEW ENGLAND				UNITED STATES			
2000	2010	1980	1990	2000	2010	1980	1990	2000	2010
537,869	554,754	293,137	307,204	303,060	311,107	226.5 mil.	248.7 mil.	281.4 mil.	308.7 mil.
30%	27%	30%	26%	23%	20%	28%	26%	26%	24%
56%	58%	54%	57%	58%	59%	57%	59%	59%	60%
11%	12%	13%	14%	16%	18%	11%	13%	12%	13%
136,668	141,167	77,911	83,806	83,815	85,237	58.9 mil.	64.5 mil.	71.8 mil.	77.5 mil.
58%	54%	55%	51%	46%	40%	54%	52%	52%	50%
18%	18%	7%	8%	8%	9%	8%	9%	10%	11%
22%	18%	17%	15%	8%	9%	15%	13%	12%	9%
91%	96%	42%	65%	80%	87%	48%	67%	79%	88%
68%	76%	65%	75%	81%	86%	66%	75%	80%	85%
15%	17%	11%	14%	16%	19%	16%	20%	24%	28%
57%	55%	64%	66%	63%	59%	74%	70%	67%	65%
48%	50%	43%	51%	53%	52%	49%	53%	54%	55%
5%	3%	5%	4%	4%	4%	4%	4%	2%	2%
7%	7%	6%	8%	8%	9%	6%	6%	7%	7%
17%	12%	32%	23%	17%	12%	22%	18%	14%	11%
7%	8%	5%	5%	5%	4%	7%	7%	5%	5%
53%	59%	44%	52%	57%	61%	49%	54%	57%	61%
4%	4%	3%	4%	4%	4%	6%	7%	7%	7%
7%	6%	5%	4%	6%	6%	5%	5%	8%	7%
$35,504	$31,236	$40,767	$45,019	$44,552	$41,853	$53,259	$55,651	$57,873	$54,661
6%	5%	9%	10%	11%	10%	6%	7%	6%	6%
9%	8%	–	1%	2%	2%	–	3%	3%	3%
24%	26%	22%	21%	23%	26%	21%	21%	21%	22%
21%	19%	16%	17%	21%	17%	20%	19%	18%	20%
25%	25%	14%	13%	13%	14%	12%	13%	12%	14%

Sources: U.S. Census, 1980, 1990, 2000, 2010; ACS, 2005–2009, 2006–2010; Division of Vital Records Administration, New Hampshire Department of State; Mississippi State Department of Health; West Virginia Health Statistics Center; U.S. DHHS, CDC, National Center for Health Statistics

Table 2, Explanatory Notes

Jessica A. Carson

POPULATION TRENDS

The population of the United States grew by more than 35 percent between 1980 and 2010, and even with periods of slow growth in the mid-1980s, the population increased each year.[1] This is in contrast with the trend in two of the three rural regions explored here: Central Appalachia and the Mississippi Delta. In Central Appalachia, the population declined by 3 percent over the thirty-year period, including a larger decline in the region's population between 1980 and 1990, and some slow subsequent recovery between 1990 and 2010. Altogether, the region has about 40,000 fewer residents than in 1980. The Mississippi Delta also experienced some population shrinkage between 1980 and 1990 (by 4 percent), but unlike Central Appalachia, the population has rebounded since, with the 2010 population about 45,000 residents, or 9 percent, higher than its 1980 levels. Finally, more closely mirroring national trends, population has grown at a fairly steady pace in northern New England, with the exception of a 1 percent decline between 1990 and 2000. Still, while the United States grew by 35 percent, northern New England had only a 6 percent increase in population over the course of thirty years.

In all three regions, children made up a smaller portion of the population in 2010 than in earlier decades (roughly 20 to 25 percent of all residents), declining by 25–35 percent in each place since 1980. These drops were largely offset by an increase in the proportion of the population that is of working age, and to a lesser degree, in the proportion that is elderly. In northern New England just one in five residents was under eighteen, and 18 percent of the population was over sixty-five. Related to these shifts is the decline in the proportion of family households containing children, down by 22 percent in Central Appalachia, 13 percent in the Mississippi Delta, and 27 percent in northern New England over those thirty years. In contrast, the United States saw just a 14 percent decline in children's proportion of the population and a 7 percent drop in the proportion of family households with children.

These population changes may be linked to economic conditions at the regional and national levels. Research shows that the recession of 2007–2009 contributed to a slowing in fertility, driving down population increases normally resultant from births.[2] Regionally, declines in the availability of well-paying jobs or other opportunities may have shaped migration patterns. Declining proportions of families with children and rising shares of elderly people suggest that regional community leaders may benefit from considering the implications of an aging population, including an increased need for services amid a diminishing tax base.[3]

EDUCATION AND EMPLOYMENT

Nationwide high school graduation rates rose by about 10 percentage points between 1980 and 1990, and 5 percentage points each decade thereafter. More than 85 percent of Americans age twenty-five and older had a high school diploma in 2010, compared with 66 percent in 1980. Similar to the national trend, in northern New England, 86 percent of adults had graduated high school by 2010. In Central Appalachia and the Mississippi Delta, however, high school graduation rates still lagged by about 10 percentage points in 2010. Though graduation rates in both places have been rising by nearly 10 percentage points per decade, the percentage of graduates in these two regions looks similar to the national rate of more than twenty years ago.

The proportion of those twenty-five and older with a four-year college degree increased steadily in each region between 1980 and 2010. By 2010, nearly one in five northern New England residents had a college degree (19 percent), and those in the Mississippi Delta did not lag far behind (17 percent). Although the proportion of Central Appalachians with degrees rose each decade, just 12 percent had completed college in 2010. Despite these gains, all regions still trailed considerably behind the national rate of college graduation, which stood at 28 percent in 2010.

The workforce has seen some major shifts as well. The proportion of men sixteen and older who were employed shrank across the nation, from 74 percent in 1980 to 65 percent in 2010. This 12 percent decline is close to that seen in Central Appalachia (13 percent), and slightly higher than that among men in the Mississippi Delta or northern New England (8 percent decline in each). During the same period, women's employment rose sharply: nationwide, the 12 percent decrease in men's employment was matched by an identical increase in women's employment. However, women's employment rose 21 percent in northern New England, 32 percent in the Mississippi Delta, and 41 percent in Central Appalachia between 1980 and 2010.

The proportion of the national labor force working in natural resource–based and manufacturing industries shrank between 1980 and 2010, each down 50 percent. In 1980, 22 percent of the Central Appalachian workforce was employed in natural resource–based jobs (including coal extraction). By 2010, just 8 percent of the labor force remained in the industry, a decline of 64 percent in thirty years. As these jobs disappeared and service and trade jobs emerged in their stead, Central Appalachia witnessed an 8 percent decline in median household income, settling at $30,634 by 2010. While the Mississippi Delta and northern New England also saw declines in manufacturing and natural resource–based jobs, median household income declined less than 1 percent in the Delta and increased about 3 percent in northern New England between 1980 and 2010. It is worth noting that in all three sites, median household income was substantially lower than the national median ($54,661 in 2010).

Given the context of industry changes, it is possible that the decline in men's employment rates may be related to concurrent job loss in traditionally male-dominated industries.[4] For example, men who have experience in coal mining or factory work may have been unprepared to transition to another type of job when work in their industry began to disappear. For the jobs that do still exist in these industries, it is possible that they are difficult to obtain or provide low wages and few benefits, which can reduce men's incentive to work. The impetus to work may be further quelled if other sources of income are available, such as a working wife or girlfriend, disability checks, "under the table" jobs, or profitable illegal activities. Given the increases in women's labor force participation, it is entirely possible that the first of these options is increasingly prevalent.

ECONOMIC AND SOCIAL INDICATORS

Of course, changes in the availability of jobs and participation in the workforce have implications for a variety of additional indicators. Economic indicators like poverty and social program receipt, and social indicators like single parenthood and teenage childbearing, do not evolve in a vacuum; rather, they emerge from the complex economic, social, and political conditions in a given region. Nationally, poverty rates and receipt of Social Security and Supplemental Security Income (SSI, or "disability") remained fairly constant between 1980 and 2010.[5] Poverty hovered between 12 and 14 percent, about one in five people received Social Security, and about 3 percent received SSI. Rates in northern New England roughly mirrored the national trends on all counts during this period. In Central Appalachia, however, about one in four residents were living in poverty, in both 1980 and 2010. Poverty rates spiked to 29 percent in 1990, corresponding with a decrease in median household income at the time. By 2010, one in ten Central Appalachian residents claimed a disability check, and one in three received Social Security payments, after years of steadily rising rates. In contrast, poverty in the Mississippi Delta was even more extreme than in Appalachia early in this period: one in three Delta residents was poor in 1980 and 1990. Then, amid rapid increases in median household income between 1990 and 2000 (up about 20 percent across the decade), poverty rates dropped to 25 percent by the year 2000. Whereas Central Appalachia has seen fairly substantial increases in Social Security and disability receipt in the thirty-year period, the Delta has seen some small declines over time.

The nation has seen a steady decline in the proportion of all births to teenage mothers, from 15 percent in 1980 to 9 percent in 2010. Of teenage mothers in 2010, nearly 90 percent were unmarried at the time of giving birth, compared with just 48 percent of new teen mothers in 1980. The nation also saw a slight increase in the proportion of family households headed by a single mother between 1980 and 2010, up to about one in ten by 2010. Northern New England exhibited rates in teen births and single motherhood that were similar or slightly lower than the national averages across the whole period. Similar patterns of change have also occurred across the other two regions, albeit with substantial variation in the actual rates. For example, in Central Appalachia, 23 percent of 1980 births were to teenage mothers, though more than two thirds of them were to *married* teen mothers. By 2010, teen births were down to 15 percent (a 35 percent decline), and 80 percent were to *unmarried* teens. Households headed by single mothers also increased in this region, though they rested at 9 percent in 2010, lower than the national level. In the Mississippi Delta, teen births declined by 36 percent between 1980 and 2010, and almost all were to unmarried mothers (96 percent in 2010). Households headed by single mothers there increased at a pace similar to Appalachia, though by 2010 the proportion of single-mother homes was twice as high in the Delta as in Appalachia.

Across all three regions, there are some welcome indicators of positive change during this period. Poverty has declined. Increases in disability and Social Security payments across the board are generally unsurprising, given the rising proportions of older people in these regions, and the fact that those with retirement or disability checks are able to still eke out a living in areas where work is hard to find. And while the general decline in teenage childbearing is a positive shift, the increasing proportion of single-mother households may have some implications for social well-being, as research consistently shows that female-headed households with children have much higher poverty rates than other household types.

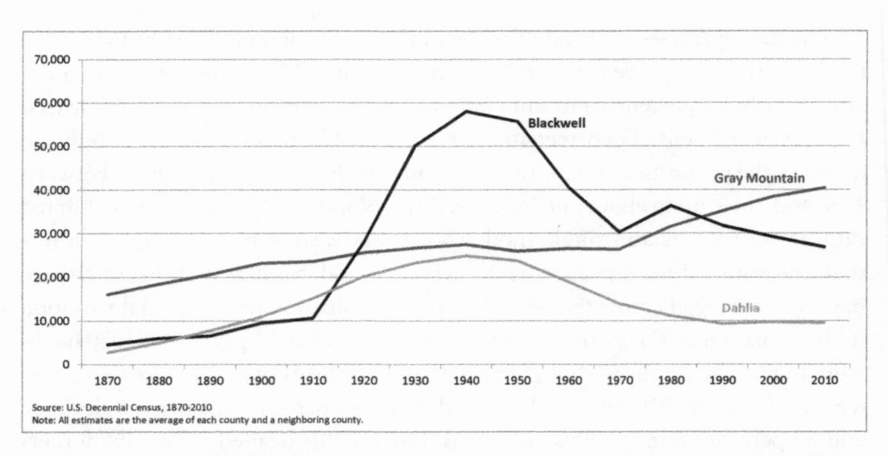

Figure 1. Population of Blackwell, Dahlia, and Gray Mountain, 1870–2010

In the context of a weak national economy and the demands of World Wars I and II, the promise of steady work in coal produced a sharp rise in Blackwell's population, which began to decline only as mechanization set in around the middle of the twentieth century.

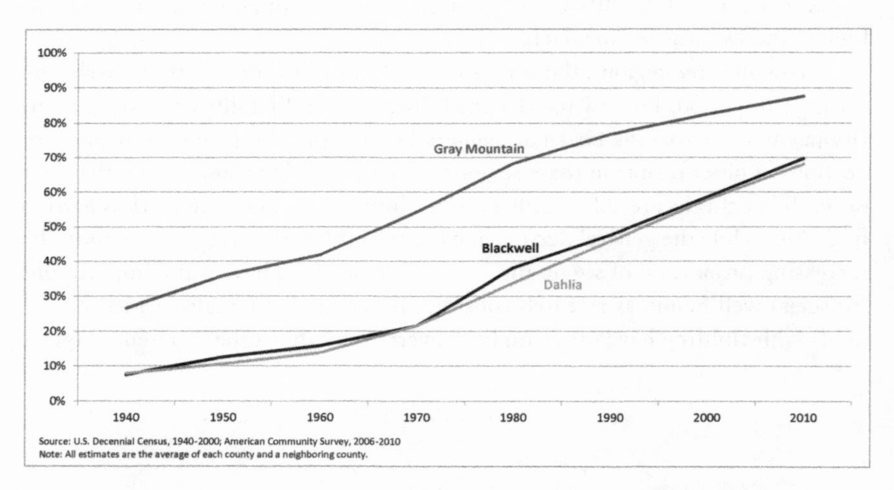

Figure 2. Adults (25+) with a High School Degree or More, 1940–2010

Despite steady increases in educational attainment since the 1940s, Blackwell and Dahlia still lag far behind Gray Mountain in the proportion of adults who hold at least a high school diploma.

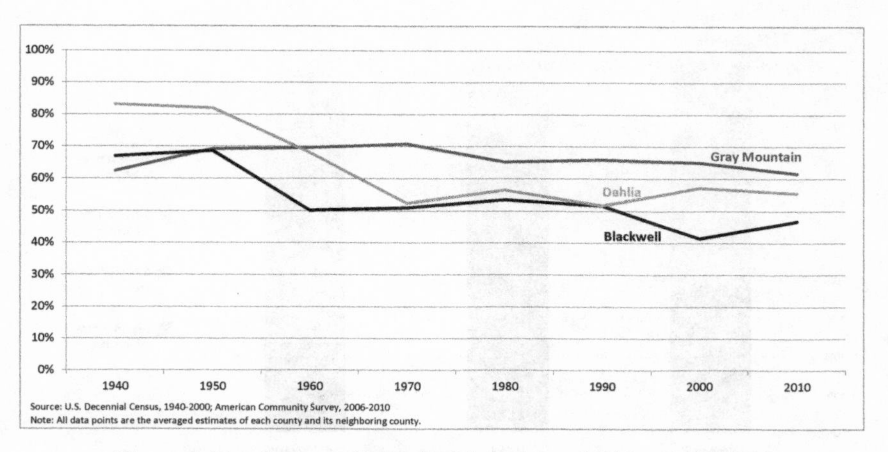

Figure 3. Employment Rates for Males 16 and Older, 1940–2010

In Dahlia and Blackwell, employment rates among men over sixteen declined precipitously after World War II, settling at around 50 percent in 2010.

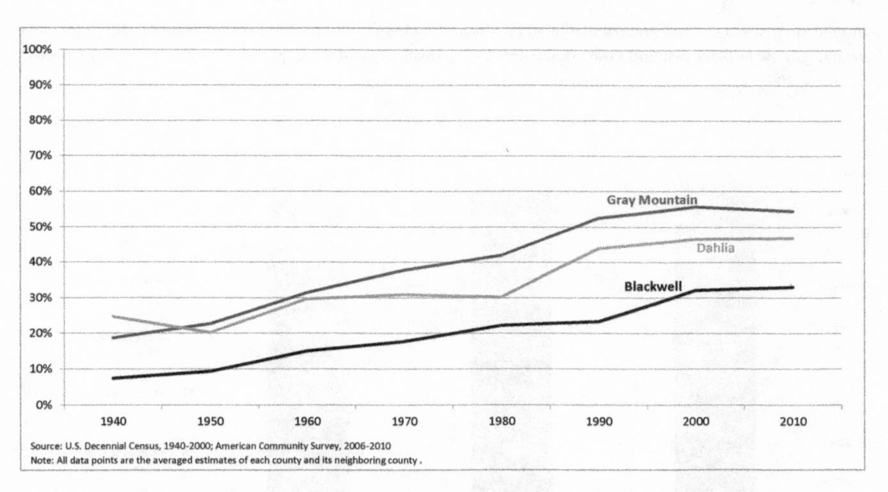

Figure 4. Employment Rates for Women 16 and Older, 1940–2010

All three sites saw increases in women's employment over time, with rates leveling off around the turn of the century.

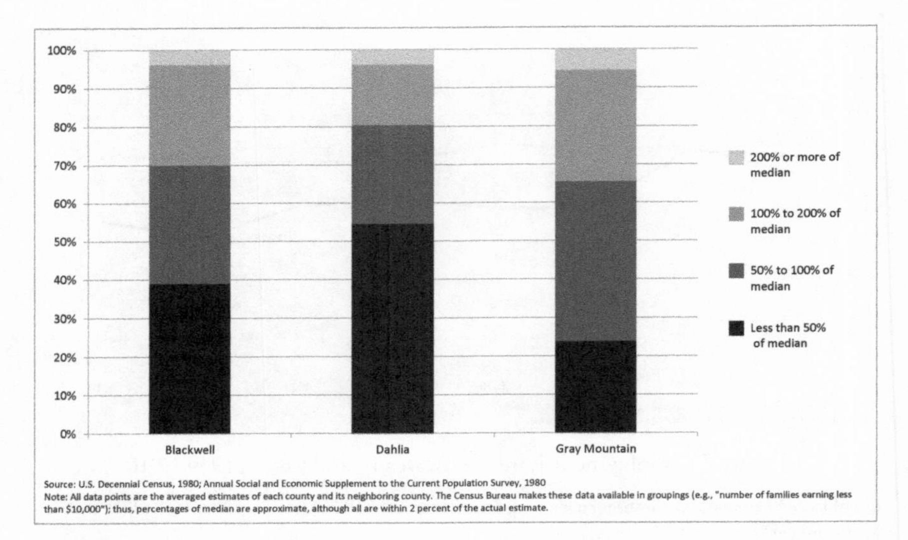
100%
90%
80%
70%
60%
50%
40%
30%
20%
10%
0%
Blackwell
Dahlia
Gray Mountain
200% or more of median
100% to 200% of median
50% to 100% of median
Less than 50% of median
Source: U.S. Decennial Census, 1980; Annual Social and Economic Supplement to the Current Population Survey, 1980
Note: All data points are the averaged estimates of each county and its neighboring county. The Census Bureau makes these data available in groupings (e.g., "number of families earning less than $10,000"); thus, percentages of median are approximate, although all are within 2 percent of the actual estimate.

Figure 5a. Family Income as an Approximate Percentage of U.S. Median, 1980

In 1980, there was a clear overrepresentation of low-income families in Dahlia, with greater shares of the middle two income groups in Blackwell and Gray Mountain. A very small share of the population in all three places reported income at 200 percent of the U.S. median or higher.

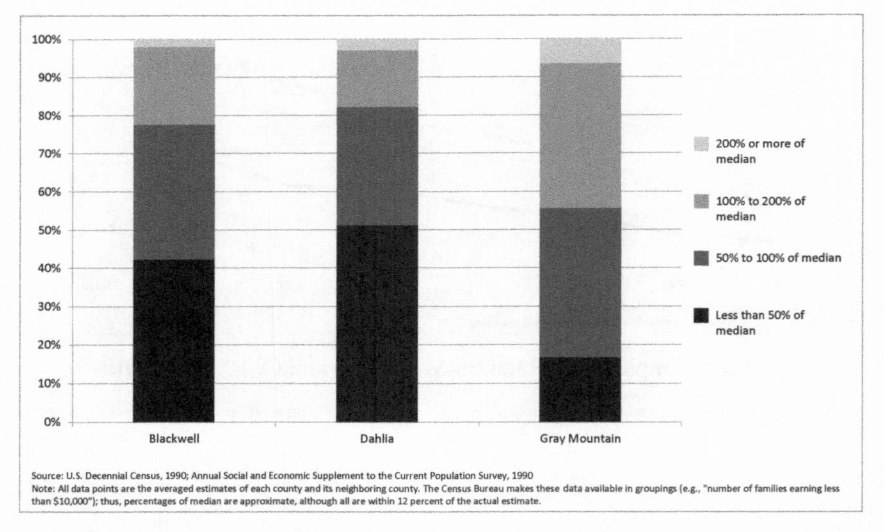
100%
90%
80%
70%
60%
50%
40%
30%
20%
10%
0%
Blackwell
Dahlia
Gray Mountain
200% or more of median
100% to 200% of median
50% to 100% of median
Less than 50% of median
Source: U.S. Decennial Census, 1990; Annual Social and Economic Supplement to the Current Population Survey, 1990
Note: All data points are the averaged estimates of each county and its neighboring county. The Census Bureau makes these data available in groupings (e.g., "number of families earning less than $10,000"); thus, percentages of median are approximate, although all are within 12 percent of the actual estimate.

Figure 5b. Family Income as an Approximate Percentage of U.S. Median, 1990

By 1990, many more Gray Mountain families were reporting incomes in the middle two categories, while Dahlia's and Blackwell's high poverty still skewed family income downward.

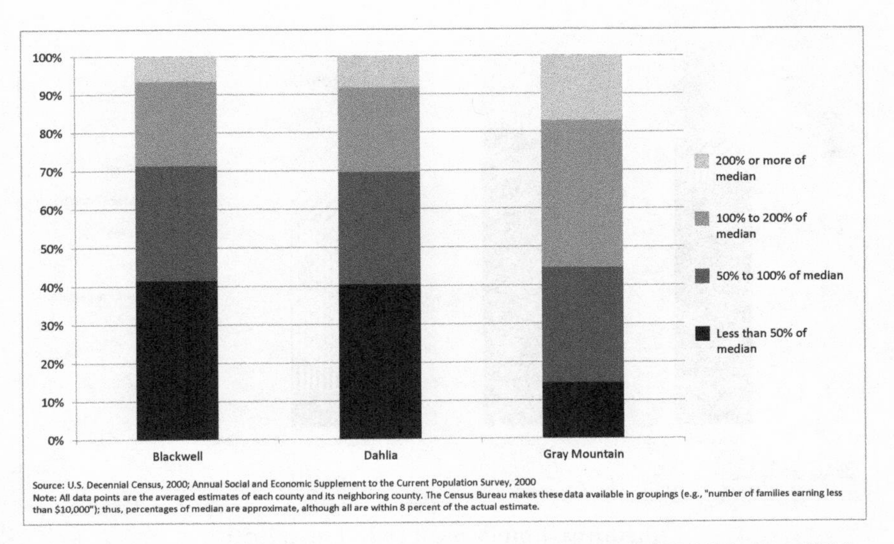
100%
90%
80%
70%
60%
50%
40%
30%
20%
10%
0%
Blackwell
Dahlia
Gray Mountain
200% or more of median
100% to 200% of median
50% to 100% of median
Less than 50% of median
Source: U.S. Decennial Census, 2000; Annual Social and Economic Supplement to the Current Population Survey, 2000
Note: All data points are the averaged estimates of each county and its neighboring county. The Census Bureau makes these data available in groupings (e.g., "number of families earning less than $10,000"); thus, percentages of median are approximate, although all are within 8 percent of the actual estimate.

Figure 5c. Family Income as an Approximate Percentage of U.S. Median, 2000

Similarities between Dahlia's and Blackwell's family income distribution continued, though more families reported incomes in the highest group than at either of the previous points.

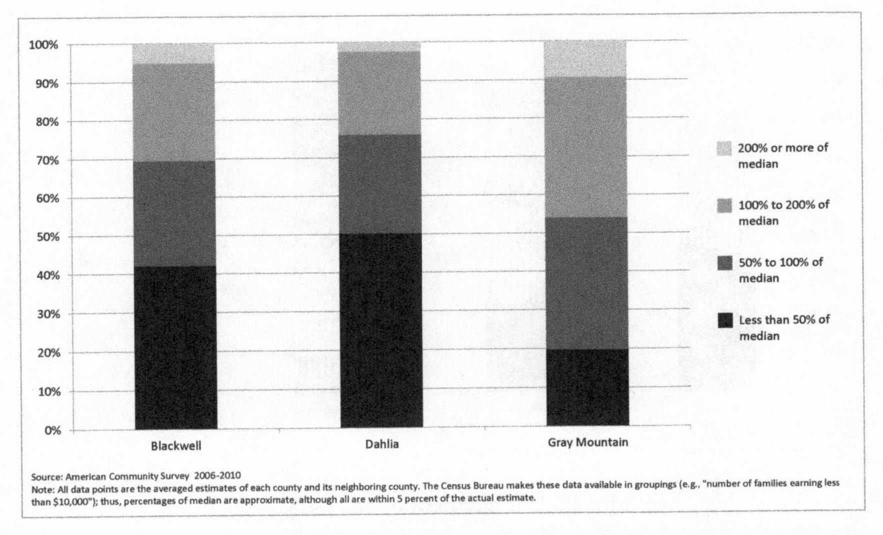
100%
90%
80%
70%
60%
50%
40%
30%
20%
10%
0%
Blackwell
Dahlia
Gray Mountain
200% or more of median
100% to 200% of median
50% to 100% of median
Less than 50% of median
Source: American Community Survey 2006-2010
Note: All data points are the averaged estimates of each county and its neighboring county. The Census Bureau makes these data available in groupings (e.g., "number of families earning less than $10,000"); thus, percentages of median are approximate, although all are within 5 percent of the actual estimate.

Figure 5d. Family Income as an Approximate Percentage of U.S. Median, 2006–2010

Low-earning Dahlia families increased in prevalence by this period, while Gray Mountain remained home to a large and solid share of middle-income families, and Blackwell retained its distribution from the previous decade.

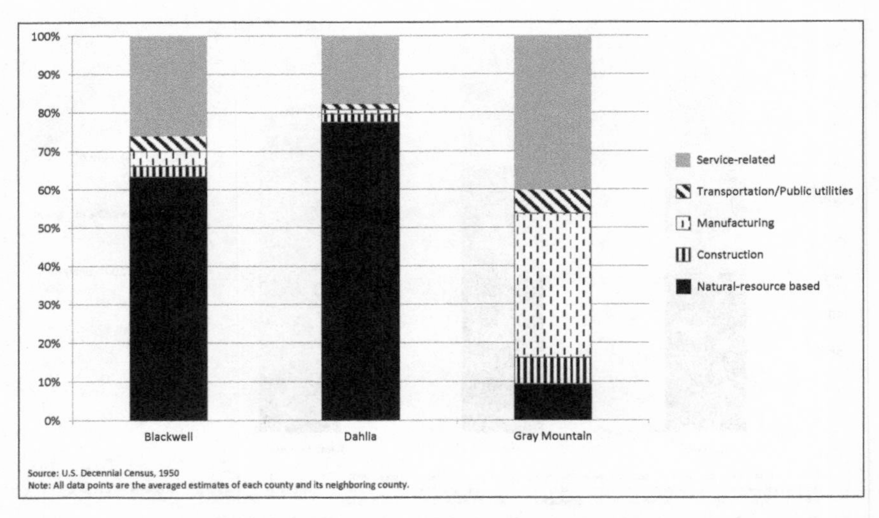

Figure 6a. Employment by Industry, 1950

At the middle of the twentieth century, Blackwell's and Dahlia's labor markets were dominated by natural resource–based jobs, while Gray Mountain had a more diverse economy, with roughly a third of its jobs in service-related and manufacturing industries.

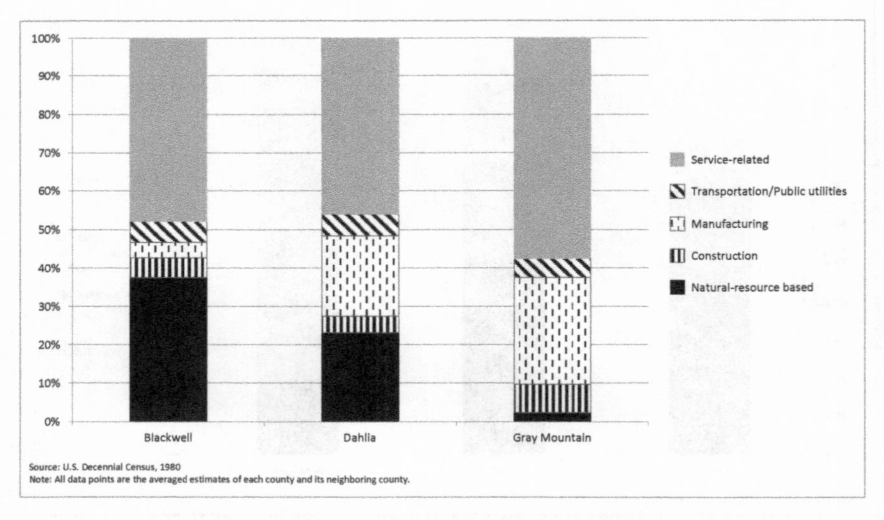

Figure 6b. Employment by Industry, 1980

By 1980, the share of jobs in service-related industries had risen considerably in all three places. While employment in manufacturing rose in Dahlia, both these and natural-resource jobs had begun to dwindle in Blackwell and Gray Mountain.

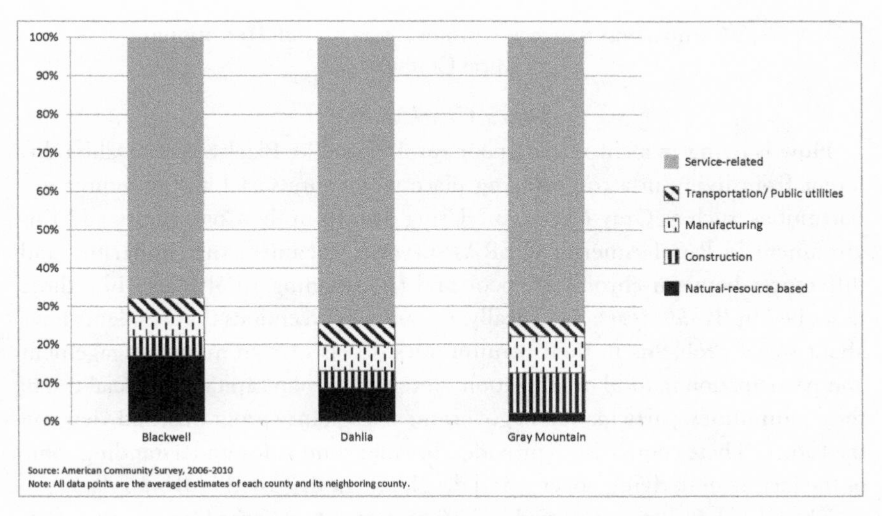

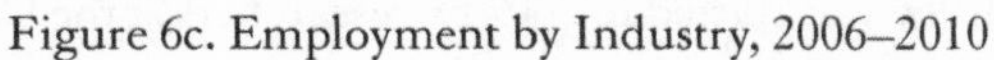
Figure 6c. Employment by Industry, 2006–2010

By 2010, service-related work represented three quarters of the jobs in Dahlia and Gray Mountain, and two thirds of those in Blackwell; concurrently, natural resource–based work had plummeted to fewer than one in ten jobs in Dahlia and fewer than one in five in Blackwell.

A Comparison Between Chronically Poor and Transitioning Rural Counties

Jessica Ulrich-Schad

How is living in a chronically poor rural place like Blackwell or Dahlia different from living in a transitioning place with more social and economic opportunities, such as Gray Mountain? Using data from the Community and Environment in Rural America (CERA) survey, I document the similarities and differences between chronically poor and transitioning rural places like those described in *Worlds Apart.* Specifically, I examine perceptions that residents have about social problems in their communities, levels of community engagement and participation in local organizations, levels of human capital and social ties to the communities, participation in government assistance programs, and views on the future. These comparisons provide a broader context for understanding some of the factors underlying poverty and development discussed in *Worlds Apart*.

The CERA survey was started in 2007 by researchers at the Carsey Institute at the University of New Hampshire to study rural Americans' perceptions about the socioeconomic, cultural, demographic, and environmental changes affecting their lives and communities. Nearly 19,000 Americans from a wide variety of rural places across the United States, including forty-three counties in fourteen states, have now taken part in the CERA survey via telephone. The three rural places profiled by Duncan are among the counties surveyed by the CERA project.

Early analyses of the CERA survey highlighted the social and economic diversity of rural America, which led to the development of a new rural typology. From these data, researchers identified four distinct types of rural places: amenity-rich, declining resource-dependent, chronically poor, and transitioning (or amenity/decline).[6] Amenity-rich rural places are characterized by their abundant natural amenities and are often growing in population as they attract tourists, retirees, and outdoor enthusiasts. Residents of amenity-rich rural places, such as Bozeman, Montana, Aspen, Colorado, and Lake Placid, New York, generally have relatively high levels of education, income, and employment. Declining resource-dependent counties are those that have relied on resource-extractive industries like forestry or agriculture that are now less central to their economies. Many of these counties, often concentrated in the Great Plains, are experiencing stagnant economic conditions and population decline.

Chronically poor rural places like Blackwell and Dahlia are those that have not prospered, even during periods of sustained economic growth in the nation overall, and poverty has plagued them for generations. Many persistently poor counties are concentrated in the Mississippi Delta, the Alabama "Black Belt," Appalachia, Native American lands, and *colonias* along the border with Mexico.

Decades of resource depletion and underinvestment in education, infrastructure, and civic institutions have left these places with high poverty and unemployment, and poor education and health systems. About 5,400 residents of twelve chronically poor rural counties in five different states have participated in the CERA survey at least once since 2007.

Gray Mountain represents a "transitioning" rural place, where economic and social growth is limited, but conditions are better than those in chronically poor places. The traditional resource-based economies of these places are in decline; however, they have begun to capture the potential for amenity-based growth as tourists, retirees, and second home owners increasingly arrive to enjoy the natural amenities. Nonetheless, many young adults are leaving these places to seek educational or employment opportunities elsewhere, resulting in an aging population. These transitioning rural places tend to have relatively high employment and education levels and often a strong civic culture. Since 2007, nearly 10,000 rural residents from twenty-two transitioning counties in seven states have taken part in the CERA survey.

PERCEPTIONS OF COMMUNITY-LEVEL SOCIAL PROBLEMS

As Duncan shows, the daily challenges that residents of Blackwell and Dahlia confront are generally much greater than those in Gray Mountain. Reflective of this, the CERA survey data show that residents of chronically poor and transitioning rural areas have somewhat different perceptions about the problems their communities are currently facing (Figure 7).[7] While residents of both types

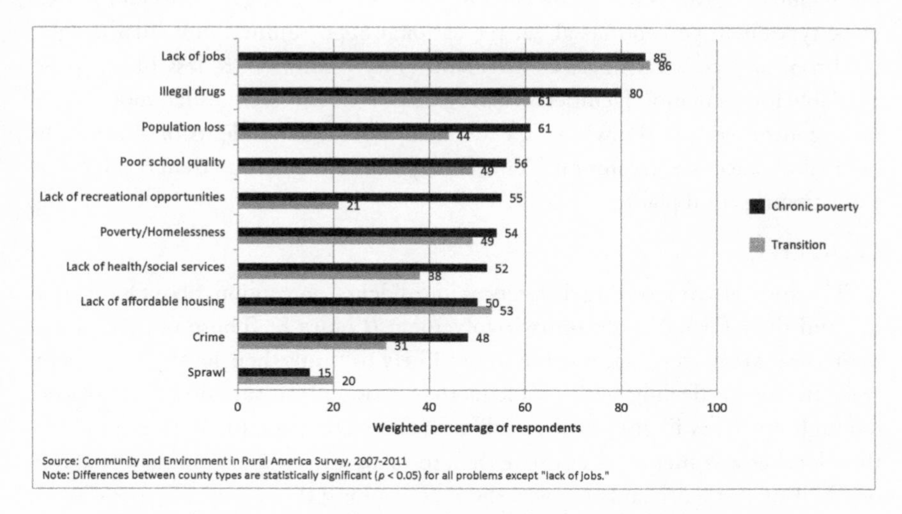

Figure 7. Percentage of Respondents Who Say Their Community Is Facing Particular Social Problems, by County Type

of places are equally concerned about the lack of employment opportunities, significant differences between the two place types exist on other issues. Residents of chronically poor rural places are significantly more concerned about drugs, population loss, school quality, the lack of recreational opportunities, poverty and homelessness, the lack of health and social services, and crime. On the other hand, residents of transitioning counties are significantly more concerned about the lack of affordable housing and sprawl.

Residents in both types of communities are most concerned about the lack of employment opportunities. As Duncan describes in the update, Blackwell residents are concerned about the decline in coal and related jobs, Dahlia residents worry about the ups and downs of casino employment and revenue, and Gray Mountain is still reeling from the closure of paper mills and two local manufacturing plants that provided relatively steady employment. These findings mirror concerns about job opportunities in all rural place types: 87 percent of all respondents in the CERA survey worry about the lack of employment opportunities in their community today.

Drugs are also a major concern, with 80 percent of those in chronically poor rural areas and 61 percent of those in transitioning places saying that they thought the manufacturing or sales of illegal drugs was an important issue facing their community today. Residents of Blackwell frequently talked about the prescription drug epidemic that has devastated families throughout their community. Issues like sprawl, on the other hand, are of the least concern in these rural communities. As both types of rural places are growing relatively slowly, or even losing population, this is not an unusual finding. The largest gap between the two place types is in perceptions about recreational opportunities. Not surprisingly, in chronically poor counties, where community resources are less likely to be available for recreation facilities and programs, residents were much more likely to be concerned. On the whole, CERA data show that residents of chronically poor rural places see greater problems facing their communities than residents of transitioning rural places.

CIVIC LIFE

There are also interesting differences in residents' perceptions about local civic life and their formal community involvement (Figure 8). Those in chronically poor rural areas were significantly more likely to think their local government was effective in dealing with problems than those in transitioning rural places. Though residents in chronically poor counties were more likely to report that their local government was effective than those in transition counties, only about one half of residents said this was the case. Among the chronically poor areas surveyed, however, there is significant variation that helps to explain this surprising finding. In Blackwell, for instance, belief in the effectiveness of the local

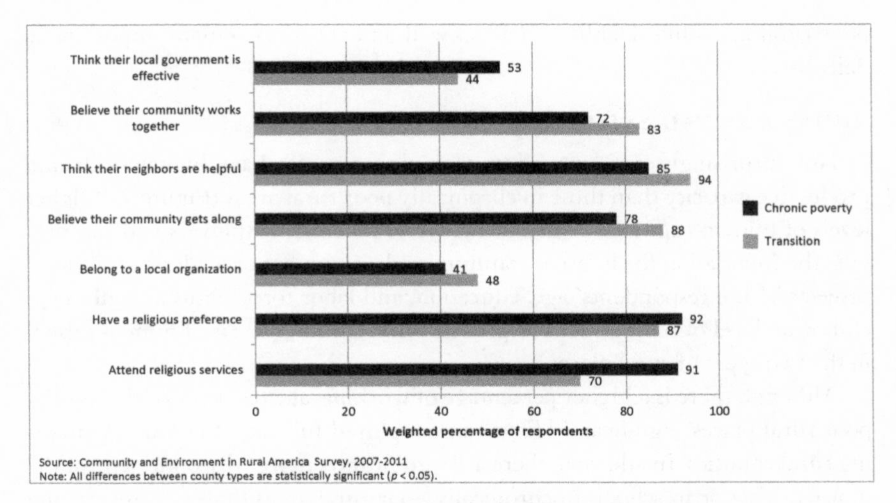

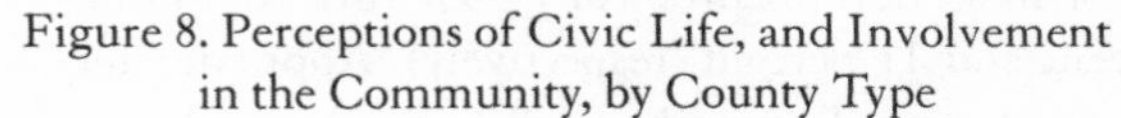
Figure 8. Perceptions of Civic Life, and Involvement in the Community, by County Type

government is much lower than in Dahlia, compatible with Duncan's description of general distrust of local government and a history of corruption in Blackwell. Perceptions also vary considerably within counties. In Dahlia, for example, perceptions of local government's effectiveness diverge between blacks and whites: 83 and 59 percent, respectively, feel that their local government is effective at solving problems. Despite past corruption in Dahlia politics, perhaps the higher levels of trust among black residents reflect the fact that the black majority has over time become more adequately represented in local leadership positions.

Residents of transitioning rural places were significantly more likely to believe that people in their communities work together when problems arise, that neighbors help and trust one another, and that community members generally get along. In addition, a greater percentage of residents of transitioning rural places belong to or play a role in a local organization that has regular meetings, such as a business group, a civic, service, or fraternal organization, or the local government. On the other hand, residents of chronically poor rural areas tend to be more religious and involved in regular church activities than those in transitioning rural areas. Nearly one half of the residents of chronic poverty counties attend church weekly and 85 percent consider themselves religious, compared with 26 and 73 percent of residents of transitioning rural areas.

In general, these findings align with Duncan's description of the strong civic culture and social institutions in a transitioning rural place, Gray Mountain. In places like Blackwell and Dahlia, trust is diluted in clashes over scarce resources. There does, however, continue to be strong religious commitment in chronically poor rural areas like Dahlia and Blackwell and churches remain important in daily life.

HUMAN CAPITAL AND SOCIAL TIES

Not surprisingly, residents of transitioning counties have higher skills and productive capacity than those in chronically poor rural areas (Figure 9). Higher levels of human capital are often attractive to potential employers and can provide the foundation for internal community development or leadership for local projects.[8] I use respondents' age, education, and labor force status as well as the education level of their parents as proxies for examining levels of human capital in the two types of rural places.[9]

Although there is a higher percentage of working-age residents of chronically poor rural places, significantly fewer are employed full-time than in transitioning rural counties. In addition, there are significantly more "disconnected youth" (not working or in school) in chronically poor rural areas than in transitioning areas (19 percent and 11 percent, respectively). Approximately 14.3 percent of youths eighteen to twenty-four in the CERA sample are disconnected, similar to national proportions.[10] Such disconnection from mainstream society can be costly to these young people, their communities, and the country as a whole.

Education levels are also higher in transitioning rural counties. More residents of transitioning rural areas have college degrees and they are significantly more likely to come from families where either their mother or father was also a college graduate.[11] The educational lag in chronically poor rural places runs deep:

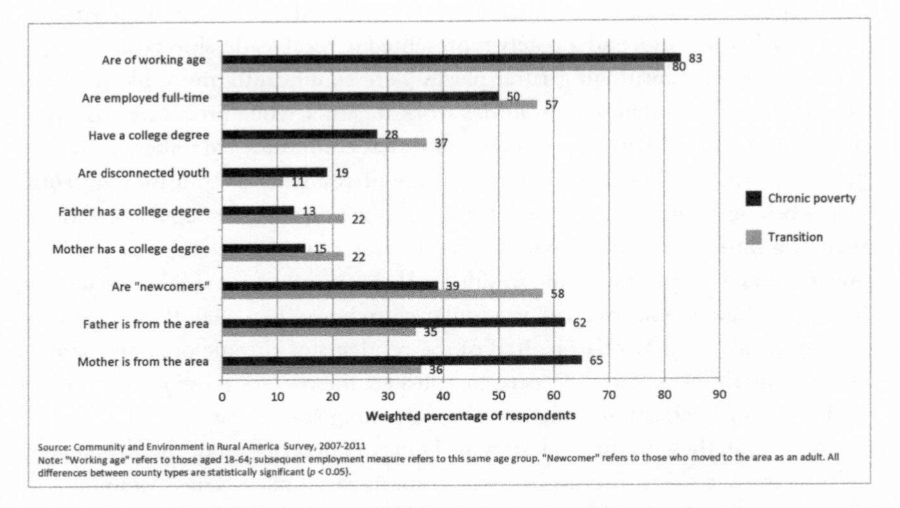

Figure 9. Measures of Human Capital, and Respondents' Ties to the Area, by County Type

almost a third of our respondents report that their fathers completed only the eighth grade or less. And in these poor places, as we see in *Worlds Apart,* schools underperform. Figure 7 also shows that a higher percentage of respondents from chronically poor rural areas are concerned about school quality than in transitioning rural places.

In terms of multigenerational ties to the area, chronically poor places have more people who are lifetime residents and whose parents who grew up in the area. As Duncan discusses in her update, these family connections are an important aspect of what keeps people in Blackwell and Dahlia. Although there might not be the same economic opportunities as elsewhere, there are strong social ties that keep many residents of high-poverty areas from leaving, or at least make staying a more desirable option. Families can also be important sources of economic and social support during tough times. Further illustrating these strong social ties, more respondents from chronically poor rural areas than from transitioning areas said that family was a very important reason to stay in their community (65 and 56 percent, respectively).

USE OF GOVERNMENT PROGRAMS

Again, not surprisingly, a higher percentage of residents in chronically poor rural places have yearly incomes less than $20,000, use the Supplemental Nutrition Assistance Program (SNAP; formerly food stamps), and receive Supplemental Security Income (SSI) or disability payments (Figure 10). There is also a slightly higher percentage of residents who used the Temporary Assistance for

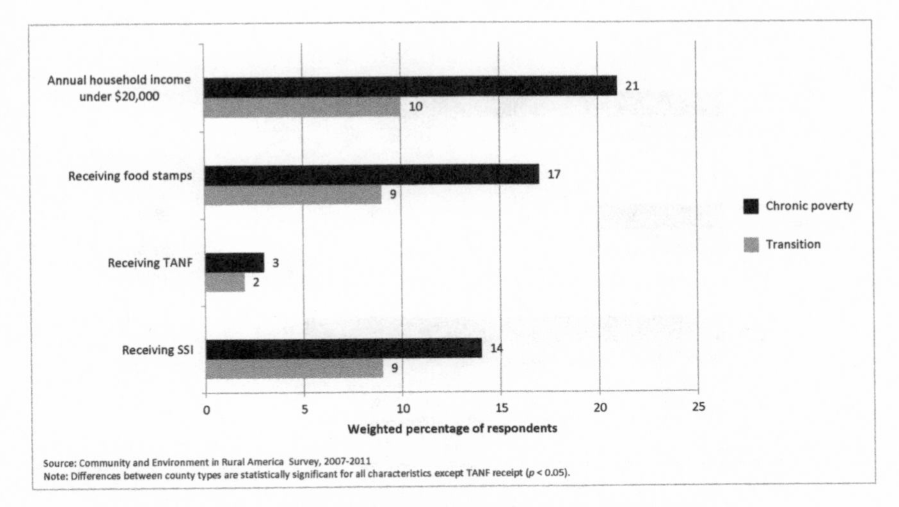

Figure 10. Economic Characteristics of Respondents and Use of the Social Safety Net, by County Type

Needy Families (TANF) program in the past year, although the difference is not significant in the CERA data. These findings are consistent with the data in Table 1 in the Appendix and the difficult economic circumstances described by those interviewed by Duncan and her colleagues in Blackwell and Dahlia.

VIEWS ABOUT THE FUTURE

Finally, residents of transitioning rural counties are generally more optimistic about the future of their community (Figure 11). For instance, a higher percentage of transitioning county residents think their community will be the same or better in ten years compared with those in chronically poor rural places. About the same percentage of residents from both places would advise teenagers to stay; however, when asked about their own plans for the future, residents of transitioning counties were more likely to plan to remain in their community for the next five years.

Although the majority of residents in both places plan to stay in their current community in the future and are relatively optimistic about what the future holds, a sizable percentage would advise teenagers to leave. This finding is congruent with research that documents the exodus of young adults from rural America and the role that adults play in encouraging teen outmigration.[12] Many leave because of the lack of employment and higher education opportunities. A disproportionate number of young adults from rural areas also leave to serve in the military, and at the time of the survey nearly three out of every four rural residents knew someone serving in either Iraq or Afghanistan.[13]

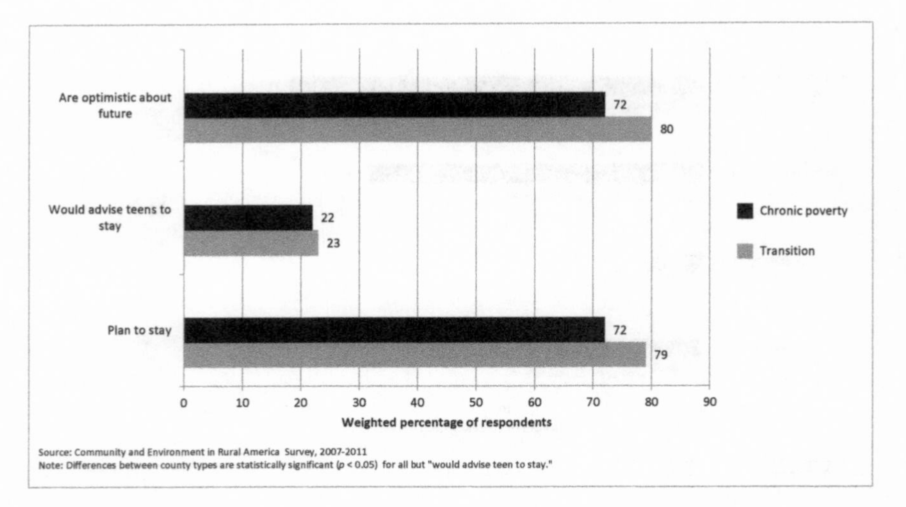

Figure 11. Respondents' Views About the Future of Their Communities, by County Type

Like *Worlds Apart,* the CERA data paint a picture of how living in a chronically poor rural place like Blackwell or Dahlia differs from daily life in a transitioning place such as Gray Mountain. Residents of chronically poor rural places are very concerned about the lack of employment opportunities, but also about social problems—drugs in particular. About half of the population thinks the local government is effective in solving issues. Levels of human capital are generally lower in these types of counties: fewer are employed and college educated, there are more disconnected youth, and residents' parents have lower education levels. Social ties also run deep, many people are lifetime residents and have parents who also grew up in the area, and religious involvement tends to be high. Family tends to be a very important factor in decisions to stay as well. Not surprisingly, the CERA survey data also show that there are many low-income families in chronically poor areas and use of government programs like TANF, SSI, and SNAP is relatively high. Although many residents think young adults should leave for opportunities elsewhere, the majority see their communities remaining the same or becoming better places to live over the next ten years.

In transitioning rural counties, residents are also worried about jobs and other social problems, but to a lesser degree than in chronically poor counties. These residents tend to see their local governments as less effective, but they have particularly strong civic culture and institutions. In transitioning places, residents tend to have high levels of human capital as measured by relatively high employment, more college graduates, fewer disconnected youth, and higher parental education levels. As retirees move in and young people leave for jobs or college, these counties are increasingly composed of more newcomers and fewer multigenerational families. Family is still an important reason to stay, but to a lesser degree than in chronic poverty counties. Incomes tend to be higher in transitioning rural counties, and receipt of government assistance is relatively low. A high percentage of residents plan to stay in these types of counties, and few see their communities as being worse places to live in the future. Many, however, are still worried about the opportunities for young adults.

Overall, these findings provide a comparative story of how place matters in the opportunities and challenges that rural Americans face. Daily life in a chronically poor rural place, shaped by broader social and economic circumstances, is much different than in a transitioning one. The social problems tend to be perceived as more severe, the civic culture less strong, the human capital not as high, and government program dependency much higher. The majority of people from both place types are optimistic about the future, however, and plan to stay even as they would advise the younger residents to leave for outside opportunities. Perhaps the strong social ties in chronically poor rural areas and the rich civic culture in transitioning ones help individuals and communities overcome tough times.

Notes

Chapter 1: Blackwell

1. All statistics are an average of the study county and a neighboring county to ensure that the identity of the study site is disguised.

2. Ronald Eller, *Miners, Millhands, and Mountaineers* (Knoxville: University of Tennessee Press, 1982), xv–xxvi and chapter 1; James Brown, *Beech Creek: A Study of a Kentucky Mountain Neighborhood* (Berea, Ky.: Berea College Press, 1988); John C. Campbell, *The Southern Highlander and His Homeland* (New York: Russell Sage, 1921); Kai Erikson, *Everything in Its Path* (New York: Simon and Schuster, 1976); Henry David Shapiro, *Appalachia on Our Minds: The Southern Mountains and Mountaineers in American Consciousness* (Chapel Hill: University of North Carolina Press, 1978).

3. Curtis Seltzer, *Fire in the Hole: Miners and Managers in the American Coal Industry* (Lexington: University Press of Kentucky, 1985); John Alexander Williams, *West Virginia: A History* (New York: Norton, 1976); John Hevener, *Which Side Are You On?* (Urbana: University of Illinois Press, 1978); Eller, *Miners, Millhands, and Mountaineers*, 57.

4. Eller, *Miners, Millhands, and Mountaineers*, 64.

5. Ibid., xxi.

6. Ibid., xx, 65–84; Kathleen Blee and Dwight Billings, "Reconstructing Daily Life in the Past: An Hermeneutical Approach to Ethnographic Data," *Sociological Quarterly* 27 (1986): 443–462. The U.S. Census shows less than one percent foreign born in Blackwell from 1880–1910; in 1920, 4 percent were foreign born, and then the figure drops to one percent for the next five decades.

7. Seltzer, *Fire in the Hole*, 9, 20; Eller, *Miners, Millhands, and Mountaineers*, 234, 235.

8. Seltzer, *Fire in the Hole*, 17, 18, 20; Eller, *Miners, Millhands, and Mountaineers*, 194.

9. Eller, *Miners, Millhands, and Mountaineers*, 194, 212–213.

10. Ibid., 187, 212–213.

11. Ibid., 194.

12. Ibid., 198. See Seltzer, *Fire in the Hole*, 19–21.

13. Quoted on p. 78 in Lee Balliett, "A Pleasing tho Dreadful Sight: Social and Economic Impacts of Coal Production in the Eastern Coalfields," a report to the Office of Technology Assessment, U.S. Congress (1978).

14. Hevener, *Which Side Are You On?*

15. F. Raymond Daniell, "Behind the Conflict in 'Bloody Harlan,'" *New York Times Magazine*, June 26, 1938.

16. Eller, *Miners, Millhands, and Mountaineers*, 206–215.

17. Seltzer, *Fire in the Hole*, chapter 5.

18. Harry Caudill, *Night Comes to the Cumberlands* (Boston: Little, Brown, 1963); Peter Schrag, "School and Politics," in *Appalachia in the Sixties: Decade of Reawakening*, ed. David Walls and John Stephenson (Lexington: University Press of Kentucky, 1972), 219–224; Robert Coles, *Migrants, Sharecroppers, Mountaineers* (Boston: Little, Brown, 1967), 283.

19. Coles, *Migrants, Sharecroppers, Mountaineers*, 292.

20. Similar to the Peace Corps, Vista was a program in which volunteers worked in poor communities in the United States.

21. These numbers are for only Blackwell, not the average of Blackwell and its neighboring county, as in the Appendix, because conditions in the counties have diverged somewhat.

22. *New York Times* journalist Barry Meier's account of Oxycontin abuse in Appalachia, *Pain Killer: A "Wonder" Drug's Trail of Addiction and Death* (Rodale, 2003).

Chapter 2: Dahlia

1. The Department of Agriculture's Farmers Home Administration (now the Farm Service Agency) has been the agency that works on rural housing projects, making low-interest mortgages or subsidized rental units available to low-income rural residents.

2. The U.S. Census statistics that I report for the Delta combine Dahlia's and a neighboring county's social and economic indicators in order to disguise the identity of Dahlia. Poverty, inequality, lack of education, and segregation are slightly greater in Dahlia alone.

3. Statistics are from the Web site of the Environmental Working Group, an environmental and agricultural watchdog organization in Washington, D.C.: www.ewg.org.

4. James C. Cobb, *The Most Southern Place on Earth: The Mississippi Delta and the Roots of Regional Identity* (New York: Oxford University Press, 1992), 28.

5. Ibid., 91, 92.

6. Sidney Baldwin, *Poverty and Politics: The Rise and Decline of the Farm Security Administration* (Chapel Hill: University of North Carolina Press, 1968), 25. Others include Arthur F. Raper and Ira de A. Reid, *Sharecroppers All* (Chapel Hill: University of North Carolina Press, 1941); Paul Mertz, *New Deal Policy and Southern Rural Poverty* (Baton Rouge: Louisiana State University Press, 1978).

7. Jay R. Mandle, *The Roots of Black Poverty* (Durham, N.C.: Duke University Press, 1978), 20.

8. John Dollard, *Caste and Class in a Southern Town*, 3d ed. (Garden City, N.Y.: Doubleday, 1957); Hortense Powdermaker, *After Freedom: A Cultural Study in the Deep South* (Madison: University of Wisconsin Press, 1993; originally published New York: Atheneum, 1939).

9. Cobb, *The Most Southern Place on Earth*, 207.

10. Ibid., chapter 11. See also Appendix, Figure 6.

11. William Julius Wilson, *When Work Disappears: The World of the New Urban Poor* (New York: Knopf, 1996); Elijah Anderson, *Streetwise: Race, Class, and Change in an Urban Community* (Chicago: University of Chicago Press, 1990).

12. Ibid., 209.

13. Carol Stack, *Call to Home: African Americans Reclaim the South* (New York: Basic Books, 1996).

14. These numbers are for only Dahlia, not Dahlia and its neighboring county as in the Appendix, because conditions are now unique in Dahlia itself, thanks to the casinos.

Chapter 3: Gray Mountain

1. Page H. Jones, *Evolution of a Valley: The Androscoggin Story* (Canaan, N.H.: Phoenix Publishing, 1975).

2. Richard W. Judd, "Reshaping Maine's Landscape: Rural Culture, Tourism, and Conservation, 1890–1929," *Journal of Forest History*, October 1988.

3. G. Merrill, *History of Coos County* (1888; reprint, Somersworth, N.H.: New Hampshire Publishing Company, 1972).

4. Charles E. Clark, *Maine: A History* (Hanover, N.H.: University Press of New England, 1990; originally published New York: Norton, 1977), chapter 6.

5. Robert Pike, *Tall Trees, Tough Men* (New York: Norton, 1967); William R. Brown, *Our Forest Heritage: A History of Forestry and Recreation in New Hampshire* (Concord, N.H.: New Hampshire Historical Society, 1958).

6. Clark, *Maine*, chapter 8.

7. Ibid., 137.

8. For example, Jones, *Evolution of a Valley*, 110; Clark, *Maine*, 137.

9. Dona Brown, *Inventing New England: Regional Tourism in the Nineteenth Century* (Washington, D.C.: Smithsonian Institution Press, 1995), chapter 5.

10. Judd, "Reshaping Maine's Landscape."

11. Clark, *Maine*; Brown, *Our Forest Heritage*; David Dobbs and Richard Ober, *The Northern Forest* (White River Junction, Vt.: Chelsea Green, 1996).

12. Margaret Walsh, "Mothers' Helpers: The Resources of Female-Headed Households in a Working-Class Community" (Ph.D. dissertation, University of New Hampshire, 1997).

13. Chris R. Colocousis, "The Biophysical Dimension of Community Economic Addiction: Examining the Emergence of Biomass Energy in a Northern Forest Community," *Society and Natural Resources* (2013): 1–14.

Chapter 4: Social Change and Social Policy

1. For reviews of urban and rural poverty research, see William Julius Wilson and Robert Aponte, "Urban Poverty," *Annual Review of Sociology* 11 (1985): 231–258; and Ann R. Tickamyer and Cynthia M. Duncan, "Poverty and Opportunity Structure in Rural America," *Annual Review of Sociology* 16 (1990): 67–86. Good historical accounts include James T. Patterson, *America's Struggle Against Poverty* (Cambridge: Harvard University Press, 1986); Robert H. Bremner, *From the Depths: The Discovery of Poverty in the United States* (New York: New York University Press, 1972); and Michael B. Katz, *The Undeserving Poor: From the War on Poverty to the War on Welfare* (New York: Pantheon, 1989).

2. William Julius Wilson, *The Truly Disadvantaged: The Inner City, the Underclass, and Public Policy* (Chicago: University of Chicago Press, 1987); William Julius Wilson, *When Work Disappears: The World of the New Urban Poor* (New York: Knopf, 1996); Jeanne Brooks-Gunn, Greg J. Duncan, and J. Lawrence Aber, eds., *Neighborhood Poverty*, 2 volumes (New York: Russell Sage Foundation, 1997).

3. Development economists Gunnar Myrdal and Albert Hirschman have pointed to the uneven spatial outcomes in a capitalist system, for example, in Gunnar Myrdal, *Economic Theory and Underdeveloped Regions* (New York: Harper Torchbooks, 1957); Albert O. Hirschman, *Essays on Trespassing: Economics to Politics and Beyond* (Cambridge: Cambridge University Press, 1981). Also see Katz, *The Undeserving Poor*; Frank Levy, *Dollars and Dreams: The Changing American Income Distribution* (New York: Russell Sage Foundation, 1987); Bennett Harrison and Barry Bluestone, *The Great U-Turn: Corporate Restructuring and the Polarizing of America* (New York: Basic Books, 1988).

On racism, see Gunnar Myrdal, *An American Dilemma: The Negro Problem and American Democracy* (New York: Harper and Brothers, 1944); St. Clair Drake and Horace R. Clayton, *Black Metropolis* (New York: Harcourt, Brace, 1945); Kenneth B. Clark, *Dark Ghetto: Dilemmas of Social Power* (New York: Harper and Row, 1965).

4. Douglas S. Massey and Nancy A. Denton, *American Apartheid: Segregation and the Making of the Underclass* (Cambridge: Harvard University Press, 1993); Wilson, *When Work Disappears*.

5. Oscar Lewis, "The Culture of Poverty," *Scientific American* 215 (1966): 19–25; Katz, *The Undeserving Poor*, 16–23.

6. Edward C. Banfield, *The Moral Basis of a Backward Society* (Glencoe, Ill.: Free Press, 1958); Edward C. Banfield, *The Unheavenly City Revisited* (Boston: Little, Brown, 1974); Lawrence M. Mead, *The New Politics of Poverty: The Nonworking Poor in America* (New York: Basic Books, 1992).

7. Ann Swidler, "Culture in Action: Symbols and Strategies," *American Sociological Review* 51 (1986): 273–286. See also Paul DiMaggio, "Social Stratification, Life-Style, and Social Cognition," in *Social Stratification: Class, Race, and Gender in Sociological Perspective*, ed. David B. Grusky (Boulder, Colo.: Westview Press, 1994), 458–465; and Pierre Bourdieu, *Reproduction in Education, Society, and Culture* (Beverly Hills, Calif.: Sage Publications, 1977).

8. See Terry Williams and William Kornblum, *Growing Up Poor* (Lexington, Mass.: Lexington Books, 1985); Brooks-Gunn, Duncan, and Aber, *Neighborhood Poverty*; Susan E. Mayer and Christopher Jencks, "Growing Up in Poor Neighborhoods: How Much Does It

Matter?" *Science* 243 (1989): 1441–1445; William Julius Wilson, ed., *The Ghetto Underclass: Social Science Perspectives* (Newbury Park, Calif.: Sage Publications, 1989).

9. Wilson, *The Truly Disadvantaged*; Wilson, *When Work Disappears*.

10. William Julius Wilson, "Research and the Truly Disadvantaged," in *The Urban Underclass*, ed. Christopher Jencks and Paul E. Peterson (Washington, D.C.: Brookings Institution, 1991), 463.

11. E. P. Thompson, *The Making of the English Working Class* (New York: Vintage, 1966; originally published London: Victor Gollancz, 1963), 9.

12. This is not to say that the class structure and relations between races are unrelated to forces and structures outside the community, only that we can see them in microcosm.

13. Albert O. Hirschman, *Exit, Voice, and Loyalty: Responses to Decline in Firms, Organizations, and States* (Cambridge: Harvard University Press, 1972).

14. Peter B. Evans and John D. Stephens, "Development and the World Economy," in *Handbook of Sociology*, ed. Neil Smelser (Newbury Park, Calif.: Sage, 1988), 739–773; Daniel Chirot, *Social Change in the Modern Era* (New York: Harcourt Brace Jovanovich, 1986), 127–128; Barrington Moore, Jr., *Social Origins of Dictatorship and Democracy* (Boston: Beacon, 1966).

15. Walter Goldschmidt, *As You Sow: Three Studies in the Social Consequences of Agribusiness* (Glencoe, 111.: Free Press, 1978; originally published New York: Harcourt, Brace, 1947); C. Wright Mills and Melville J. Ulmer, "Small Business and Civic Welfare," in *The Structure of Community Power*, ed. Michael Aiken and Paul E. Mott (New York: Random House, 1970), 124–154.

16. Robert D. Putnam, *Making Democracy Work: Civic Traditions in Modern Italy* (Princeton, N.J.: Princeton University Press, 1993); Robert D. Putnam, "The Prosperous Community: Social Capital and Public *Life," American Prospect* 13 (1993): 35–42.

17. Banfield, *Moral Basis of a Backward Society*.

18. Putnam, *Making Democracy Work*, 121.

19. Putnam, "The Prosperous Community," 37.

20. Putnam, *Making Democracy Work*, 183.

21. Ibid., 182, 185.

22. President's National Advisory Commission on Rural Poverty, *The People Left Behind* (Washington, D.C.: Government Printing Office, 1967).

23. Economic Research Service, U.S. Department of Agriculture, http://www.econ.ag.gov.

24. Center on Budget and Policy Priorities, http://www.cbpp.org; Isaac Shapiro and Robert Greenstein, *Trends in the Distribution of After-Tax Income: An Analysis of Congressional Budget Office Data* (Washington, D.C.: Center on Budget and Policy Priorities, 1997). Also, Sheldon Danziger and Peter Gottschalk, *America Unequal* (New York: Russell Sage Foundation, 1995); Rebecca M. Blank, *It Takes a Nation: A New Agenda for Fighting Poverty* (New York: Russell Sage Foundation, 1997).

25. Wilson, *When Work Disappears*; Mickey Kaus, *The End of Equality* (New York: Basic Books, 1992); Michael J. Sandel, *Democracy's Discontent: America in Search of a Public Philosophy* (Cambridge, Mass.: Belknap, 1996); Michael Walzer, *Spheres of Justice: A Defense of Pluralism and Equality* (New York: Basic Books, 1984); Robert Reich, *The Work of Nations:*

Preparing Ourselves for Twenty-first-Century Capitalism (New York: Knopf, 1991); Massey and Denton, *American Apartheid*.

26. Kaus, *End of Equality*, 20.

27. Wilson, *When Work Disappears*, 235; Theda Skocpol, "Targeting Within Universalism: Politically Viable Policies to Combat Poverty in the United States," in *The Urban Underclass*, ed. Christopher Jencks and Paul E. Peterson (Washington, D.C.: Brookings Institution, 1991), 432.

28. Margaret Weir, Ann S. Orloff, and Theda Skocpol, eds., *The Politics of Social Policy in the United States* (Princeton, N.J.: Princeton University Press, 1988); Jill Quadagno, *The Color of Welfare: How Racism Undermined the War on Poverty* (New York: Oxford University Press, 1994).

29. Jonathan Kozol, *Savage Inequalities: Children in America's Schools* (New York: Crown, 1991); Alex Kotlowitz, *There Are No Children Here: The Story of Two Boys Growing Up in the Other America* (New York: Doubleday, 1991); Deborah Meier, *The Power of Their Ideas: Lessons for America from a Small School in Harlem* (Boston: Beacon, 1995); James P. Comer, "Education for Community," in *Common Decency: Domestic Policies After Reagan*, ed. Alvin Schorr (New Haven, Conn.: Yale University Press, 1986), 186–209.

30. Amartya Sen, "Conceptualizing and Measuring Poverty," in *Poverty and Inequality*, ed. David B. Grusky and Ravi Kanbur (Stanford: Stanford University Press, 2006), 30–46.

31. Martha C. Nussbaum, "Poverty and Human Functioning: Capabilities as Fundamental Entitlements," in *Poverty and Inequality*, ed. David B. Grusky and Ravi Kanbur (Stanford: Stanford University Press, 2006), 47–75.

32. Frank Levy and Peter Temin, "Inequality and Institutions in Twentieth-Century America," MIT Industrial Performance Center Working Paper, 2007; Joseph E. Stiglitz, *The Price of Inequality: How Today's Divided Society Endangers Our Future* (New York: W. W. Norton, 2012); George Packer, *The Unwinding: An Inner History of the New America* (New York: Farrar, Straus and Giroux, 2013).

33. Greg J. Duncan and Katherine Magnuson, "The Nature and Impact of Early Achievement Skills, Attention Skills, and Behavior Problems," in *Whither Opportunity? Rising Inequality, Schools, and Children's Life Chances*, ed. Greg J. Duncan and Richard J. Murnane (New York: Russell Sage Foundation, 2011), 47–69; Sharon Lerner, "Pre-K on the Range," *American Prospect*, December 4, 2012.

34. Robert Ivry and Fred Doolittle, "Improving the Economic and Life Outcomes of At-Risk Youth," MDRC Working Paper, 2003.

35. Greg J. Duncan, Aletha C. Huston, Thomas S. Weisner, *Higher Ground: New Hope for the Working Poor and Their Children* (New York: Russell Sage Foundation, 2006), and various evaluation reports at MDRC, www.mdrc.org (formerly the Manpower Demonstration Research Corporation).

36. Center on Budget and Policy Priorities: www.cbpp.org/cms/index.cfm?fa=view&id=4022 and www.cbpp.org/cms/index.cfm?fa=view&id=3793.

37. Raj Chetty, Nathaniel Hendren, Patrick Kline, and Emmanuel Saez, "The Economic Impacts of Tax Expenditures: Evidence from Spatial Variation Across the U.S.," *Research Computing*. Harvard University Faculty of Arts and Sciences, 2013, http://obs.rc.fas.harvard.edu/chetty/tax_expenditure_soi_whitepaper.pdf.

38. Patrick Sharkey, *Stuck in Place: Urban Neighborhoods and the End of Progress Toward Racial Equality* (Chicago: University of Chicago Press, 2013), Kindle Locations, 231–238.

39. Robert J. Sampson, *Great American City: Chicago and the Enduring Neighborhood Effect* (Chicago: University of Chicago Press, 2012), 363.

40. William Julius Wilson, *The Truly Disadvantaged: The Inner City, the Underclass, and Public Policy*. 2nd ed. (Chicago: University of Chicago Press, 2012). See also Xavier De Souza Briggs, Susan J. Popkin, and John Goering, *Moving to Opportunity: The Story of an American Experiment to Fight Ghetto Poverty* (New York: Oxford University Press, 2010).

41. Sampson, *Great American City*, 424.

Appendix

1. World Bank Group, Washington, D.C., "Population Growth (Annual %) Data," http://data.worldbank.org/indicator/SP.POP.GROW?page=6 (retrieved April 22, 2013).

2. See, for example, Kenneth M. Johnson, "Deaths Exceed Births in Record Number of U.S. Counties," Fact Sheet no. 25 (Durham, N.H.: Carsey Institute, 2013).

3. Kenneth M. Johnson, "Rural Demographic Change in the New Century: Slower Growth, Increased Diversity," Issue Brief no. 44 (Durham, N.H.: Carsey Institute, 2012).

4. See, for example, Larry DeBoer and Michael Seeborg, "The Female-Male Unemployment Differential: Effects of Changes in Industry Employment," U.S. Bureau of Labor Statistics, *Monthly Labor Review* (November 1984): 8–15; Barbara H. Wootton, "Gender Differences in Occupational Employment," U.S. Bureau of Labor Statistics, *Monthly Labor Review: Occupational Employment* (April 1997): 15–24; and "Labor Force Characteristics by Race and Ethnicity, 2010," U.S. Bureau of Labor Statistics, Report 1032, 2011.

5. Data on SSI were not available for 1980, but to preserve the linguistic flow of this section, I discuss trends from "1980 to 2010."

6. Lawrence C. Hamilton, Leslie R. Hamilton, Cynthia M. Duncan, and Chris R. Colocousis, *Place Matters: Challenges and Opportunities in Four Rural Americas*, Reports on Rural America, vol. 1, no. 4 (Durham, N.H.: Carsey Institute, 2008).

7. All percentages using CERA data are calculated using weights based on census age, race, and sex estimates for each county. Missing values are taken into account when calculating percentages.

8. Cornelia Butler Flora and Jan L. Flora, *Rural Communities: Legacy and Change* (Boulder: Westview, 2008).

9. Richelle Winkler, Cheng Cheng, and Shaun Golding, "Boom or Bust? Population Dynamics in Natural-Resource Dependent Counties," in *International Handbook of Rural Demography*, ed. Laszlo J. Kulcsar and Katherine J. Curtis (Dordrecht, The Netherlands: Springer, 2012), 349–367.

10. Sarah Burd-Sharps and Kristen Lewis, "One in Seven: Ranking Youth Disconnection in the 25 Largest Metro Areas" (PDF report), *Measure of America, A Project of the Social Science Research Council*, 2012.

11. Jessica D. Ulrich, "Education in Chronically Poor Rural Areas Lags Across Generations," Issue Brief no. 24 (Durham, N.H.: Carsey Institute, 2011).

12. Kenneth M. Johnson, Richelle Winkler, and Luke T. Rogers, "Age and Lifestyle Patterns Driving U.S. Migration Shifts," Issue Brief no. 24 (Durham, N.H.: Carsey Institute, 2013). See also Patrick J. Carr and Maria J. Kefalas, *Hollowing Out the Middle: The Rural Brain Drain and What It Means for America* (Boston: Beacon, 2010).

13. William O'Hare and Bill Bishop, "U.S. Soldiers Account for a Disproportionately High Share of Casualties in Iraq and Afghanistan," Fact Sheet no. 3. (Durham, N.H.: Carsey Institute, 2006).

Acknowledgments for the 1999 Edition

I am grateful to the people with whom I talked in the course of this study. Their candor, perceptive reflections, and goodwill are the heart of the book. I am also indebted to those who guided us in Blackwell, Dahlia, and Gray Mountain. Colleagues and students have contributed generously, and in some ways this is a book coauthored by many people. Margaret Walsh worked with me for several years, providing thoughtful analysis. Gemma Beckley shared her practical, intelligent understanding of the Delta and conducted many interviews there. Stephen Sweet, Nita Lamborghini, and Julie Ardery gathered insightful data in Appalachia and Gray Mountain. Heather Crocker and Esther Pank skillfully assembled the census data. Jody Grimes provided excellent archival assistance. The Institute for Policy and Social Science Research at the University of New Hampshire provided crucial support, including expert assistance from Jennifer Bakke, Angele Cook, Cindy Corriveau, and Dennis Meadows.

Ann Tickamyer advised me wisely throughout, and her comments, with those of Bonnie Thornton Dill, Bill Falk, Carol Lamm, Michael Donnelly, Cliff Brown, Jess Gilbert, Larry Busch, Ian Duncan, Larry Hamilton, Kathleen McCartney, and Sally Ward, improved my argument. I am especially grateful to Priscilla Salant, Alice Shabecoff, and Leslie Hamilton for their engaged, thoughtful editing on more than one draft.

This long project was made possible by support from the Ford Foundation. Susan Berresford, Susan Sechler, Norm Collins, Betsy Campbell, and Walt Coward combine confidence in rigorous analysis with a deep faith in the power of ordinary people to make their communities good places to live. I also received support from the U.S. Department of Agriculture, through a subcontract from Pennsylvania State University, to conduct a second round of interviews in the Delta and northern New England. Of course, the conclusions drawn here are my responsibility alone and do not reflect policies of the Ford Foundation, the USDA, or Pennsylvania State University.

John Harney believed in this book from the beginning. John Covell, senior editor at Yale University Press, expressed early support and, with manuscript editor Phillip King, guided the book through its last stages. Mark Nord of the Department of Agriculture drew the fine maps. Larry and Leslie Hamilton, Kathleen McCartney and Bill Hagen, Lucy Salyer, Laurie Frye, Julie Leavenworth, Don and Sue Leavenworth, Ian Duncan, and Graham Duncan all encouraged me throughout the project.

I dedicate *Worlds Apart* to Bill Duncan. His remarkable intellect, high standards, and unfaltering moral sense always guide me, and our great love is everything to me.

Index